THE ANOINTED COMMUNITY

The Holy Spirit in the Johannine Tradition

GARY M. BURGE

WILLIAM B. EERDMANS PUBLISHING COMPANY
GRAND RAPIDS, MICHIGAN

Library of Congress Cataloging-in-Publication Data:

Burge, Gary M., 1952–
  The anointed community.

  Bibliography: p. 225
  Includes indexes.
  1. Bible. N.T. John—Theology. 2. Bible. N.T.
Epistles of John—Theology. 3. Holy Spirit—Biblical
teaching. I. Title.
BS2601.B87 1986   231'.3   86-29226

ISBN 0-8028-0193-5

To Carol, without whom . . .
"T.G., G.!"

Table of Contents

FOREWORD   ix
PREFACE   xi
ABBREVIATIONS   xiii
INTRODUCTION   xvi

Part I
THE PARACLETE AND PNEUMATOLOGY

1 A PROSPECTUS ON JOHANNINE PNEUMATOLOGY   3
  A. The Paraclete Problem   6
  B. Finding a Background for the Paraclete   10
    1. Proto-Gnostic Antecedents   10
    2. Hellenistic Antecedents   12
    3. Old Testament and Jewish Antecedents   13
      a. The Advocate before Qumran   13
      b. The Advocate after Qumran   16
      c. A Forerunner/Perfecter Motif   23
      d. The *Gattung Abschiedsrede*   25
      e. The Development of an Old Testament Theme   28
    4. Conclusion   30
  C. The Paraclete in Johannine Reflection   31
    1. Persecution Sayings   31
    2. Christology and Eschatology   32
      a. An Eschatological Continuum   33
      b. Pentecost Becomes Parousia   35
    3. Witness and Revelation   36
    4. Prophets and Prophecy   38
    5. Conclusion   41

D. Pneuma in the Johannine Literature   41

E. Prospectus   44

Part II
THE HOLY SPIRIT IN JOHN

2 SPIRIT AND CHRISTOLOGY   49

A. The Baptism of Jesus: John 1:29-34   50

   1. The Synoptic Gospels   50

   2. The Fourth Gospel   51

     a. The Significance for the Baptist   52

     b. The Significance for Jesus   53

       (1) The Synoptic Gospels   53

       (2) The Use of Μένειν: 1:32, 33   54

       (3) The Descending Dove: 1:32, 33   56

     c. Psalm 2 or Isaiah 42? The Pronouncement   59

   3. Conclusion   61

B. Jesus in the Power of the Spirit   62

   1. The Synoptic Gospels   62

     a. Works of Power   63

       (1) Exorcisms and Satan   64

       (2) Miracles   65

     b. Words of Authority   67

       (1) Jesus as Prophet   68

       (2) Jesus as the Eschatological Prophet   68

     c. Conclusion   71

   2. The Fourth Gospel   71

     a. Preliminary Remarks   71

     b. Works of Power   73

       (1) Exorcisms and Satan   73

       (2) Miracles   74

         (a) Sign (Σημεῖον)   78

         (b) Work (Ἔργον)   79

         (c) Glory (Δόξα)   80

     c. The Spirit and Johannine Christology   81

       (1) Jesus, a Man Anointed   81

         (a) John 3:34   81

         (b) John 6:27, Σφραγίζειν   84

         (c) John 1:51   86

       (2) Spirit Christology   87

         (a) John 7:37-39   88

         (b) John 19:34   93

         (c) 1 John 5:6-8   95

         (d) John 4:7-15   96

     d. Words of Authority   101

       (1) Spirit and Word   101

       (2) Spirit as the Word   102

       (3) John 6:63   104

       (4) The Johannine Prophet Christology   107

         (a) Jesus as Prophet   107

         (b) Jesus as the Eschatological Prophet   108

   3. Conclusion   110

EXCURSUS: VIRGIN BIRTH OR PREEXISTENT LOGOS? THE SPIRIT AND JESUS' ORIGINS   111

3 SPIRIT AND ESCHATOLOGY: JOHN 20:22   114
  A. The Problem   114
    1. Eschatology   114
    2. John 20:22   116
  B. Interpreting John 20:22   117
    1. John 20:22 as Symbol   117
    2. John 20:22: A Pre-Pentecost Anointing   119
      a. An Ordination Gift   119
      b. The Power of Life   120
      c. The Embryonic Paraclete   122
    3. A Johannine Pentecost   123
  C. The Johannine Expectation/Interpretation   131
    1. The Unified Events of the Hour   132
      a. Glorification   132
      b. John 19:30, 34   133
      c. The Ascension and John 20:17ff.   136
    2. The Unity of Christ and Spirit   137
      a. The Johannine Expectation   137
      b. Parallels: Christ and the Paraclete   140
      c. The Personalization of the Paraclete   142
      d. The Problem of the Parousia   143
  D. Conclusion   147

4 THE SPIRIT AND THE SACRAMENTS   150
  A. The Traditional Problem of the Sacraments in John   151
    1. Sacramentalism   152
    2. Non-Sacramentalism   154
    3. Critical/Corrective   156
  B. Sacramental Interest in John 3 and 6   157
  C. John 3: Spirit and Rebirth   158
    1. Baptismal Interest in John 3   159
      a. Textual Considerations   160
      b. The Background and Meaning of Ὕδωρ   161
        (1) A Symbolic Interpretation   161
        (2) Ὕδωρ and Ritual Purification   162
      c. Ὕδωρ and John's Baptism   163
        (1) John 3:22-30   163
        (2) John 4:1-3   164
    2. The Meaning and Significance of Rebirth   165
      a. The Relation between Ὕδωρ and Πνεῦμα in Rebirth   166
        (1) John 3:3   167
        (2) John 3:6-8   168
      b. The Objective Basis of Rebirth: The Cross and Faith   169
    3. Spirit and Identity in 1 John   171
      a. 1 John 3:24; 4:13   173
      b. Χρῖσμα in 1 John 2:20, 27   174
      c. Σπέρμα in 1 John 3:9   175
      d. Revelation 3:19-22   176
    4. Conclusion   177

D. John 6: Spirit and Eucharist   178
   1. A Eucharistic Allusion in John 6:1-15, 35-50?   178
   2. The "Eucharistic Section," John 6:51/52-58   181
     a. Eucharistic Realism   181
     b. Authenticity and Coherence   183
     c. John 6:60-63 and the Antecedent of Σάρξ   185
   3. John's Theology of the Eucharist   186
     a. The Nature of the Corrective   186
     b. *Praesentia Realis* and the Spirit   188
   4. Does John 15:1-17 Refer to the Eucharist?   189
E. Worship in Spirit and Truth: John 4:20-24   190
   1. The Criteria of True Worship   191
     a. God Is Spirit   192
     b. Worship in Spirit   192
     c. Worship in Truth   193
   2. Samaria, Stephen, and John   195
     a. The Temple and Samaria   196
     b. The Johannine Expression   197

5 SPIRIT, MISSION, AND ANAMNESIS   198
A. Spirit and Mission: John 20:21   199
   1. Jesus: God's Apostle   200
   2. Agency and Apostolic Mission   201
     a. The Disciples   202
     b. The Paraclete   203
B. Trial and Revelation   204
   1. The Origin of the Paraclete Sayings: John 15:18–16:4a   205
   2. The Paraclete as Advocate: John 16:8-11   208
   3. The Paraclete as Witness   210
     a. Anamnesis: John 14:25-26   211
     b. The Johannine Hermeneutic: John 16:12-15   214
   4. Prophecy and Heterodoxy   217
     a. The Johannine Adjustment   219
     b. Early Catholicism?   220
C. Conclusion   221

EPILOGUE   223
BIBLIOGRAPHY   225
INDEXES   255

Foreword

In recent years there has been a revival of interest in the biblical doctrine of the Holy Spirit. This has been due to the contemporary experience of the presence and power of the spirit in the life of believers and the church which is associated with the Pentecostal and charismatic movements. Any serious theologian would agree that while Christian experience may direct our attention to areas of Christian doctrine that we may otherwise neglect, our doctrine must ultimately be developed under the supreme authority of the divine revelation in Holy Scripture. Thus, while God may lead us to recognize his activity through what happens in our Christian experience, it is his Word given in Scripture which enables us to understand his activity and to give it its pure theological expression. It is not surprising, then, that theologians have been directing renewed attention to the biblical doctrine of the Spirit, and finding there both indications of how the church should expect to experience the Spirit in its life today and also warnings against the dangers of a false understanding of the work of the Spirit.

Until now, as Dr. Burge comments, interest has centered on the writings of Luke and of Paul. These are the areas of Scripture with which the charismatic movement has felt the strongest sense of identity. But there is another important area of Scripture, the Johannine writings, which has not received comparable attention from biblical scholars in the English-speaking world, and yet John has a profound understanding of the Spirit and his work expressed in terms of a close relationship to Jesus himself. Here, then, is an area of biblical revelation which must stand alongside the writings of Luke and of Paul and which must be taken fully into account in framing a New Testament understanding of the Spirit.

Dr. Burge offers here a detailed and profound study of the place of the

Spirit in the Johannine Gospel and Epistles which will fill the gap that has hitherto existed. His book is based on the doctoral thesis which he completed in the University of Aberdeen. In my judgment a thesis is not meant to sit gathering dust on the shelves of a university library. If it has merit, it deserves to be published and read by other scholars. If it has something to say to the church today, it needs to be presented in a readable form so that it can enjoy a broad circulation. The scholarly world is grateful to publishers who are prepared to present theses to a wider public.

I am sure that many readers will be grateful to Dr. Burge for this study and to William B. Eerdmans Publishing Company for publishing it so attractively, and I am glad to be associated with this venture by giving my warm commendation to this piece of careful scholarship. May it not only serve the cause of Christian scholarship but also encourage the revival of concern in the church today that it should know increasingly in its daily experience the powerful work of the Spirit, the "other Paraclete," whose function is to glorify Jesus.

I. HOWARD MARSHALL
ABERDEEN, SCOTLAND

Preface

My interest in this study came initially from questions arising within my own experience. What is the place of the Holy Spirit within normative Christian experience? What model, if any, does the New Testament provide?

Answers to these questions generally lean in one of two directions. On the one hand, some urge that the Spirit is an immediate power—a personal presence powerfully engaging the Christian. For them enthusiasm, spontaneity, inspiration, and worship are the immediate expressions of the Spirit. On the other hand, some stress what might be called a "horizontal" or human dimension to the Spirit. Here the Spirit of God is evidenced in right belief and the moral and ethical leadership of the church within the world. Christian experience may even be doctrinaire and sedate.

The experience of the church has shown that both expressions are necessary and one without the other will lead to imbalance. Enthusiasm needs the balance of painstaking doctrinal reflection and serious church order, while more sober forms of Christianity need the dynamic life brought about only through the vitality of the Spirit.

Most discussions of New Testament pneumatology focus on the writings of Luke and Paul. This is readily explainable by the clear emphasis of each on the lively activity of the Spirit in the early days of the church and the ultimate development of charismatic Pauline communities. If Luke witnesses to the spontaneity and enthusiasm of the early church, Paul describes the need for order and control in the Spirit (esp. before the Corinthian enthusiasts).

But what of the Johannine community? No community was more concerned with doctrine. No community was more rigid in its ethical demands. Yet in the midst of this community there persisted a passionate interest in the Spirit. It is my belief that the Johannine community's experience of the Spirit offers us an important and necessary balance. Here there was spiritual vitality and sober reflection. There was genuine spiritual fervor. But as 1 John shows us, this community experienced a "charismatic/pneumatic crisis" not dissimilar to many modern ones.

* * *

It only remains to render thanks to the many people who contributed in a variety of ways to the present work: to Dr. Kenneth E. Bailey of Jerusalem, who modeled a scholarly enthusiasm and excellence which I would like to emulate; to the late Prof. George E. Ladd, who taught careful, clear-headed exegesis; to Prof. Everett Harrison, that most gracious gentleman and scholar, who urged the futility of knowing theology without knowing God; and finally to Prof. Ralph P. Martin, whose outstanding lectures in New Testament inspired my interest and led me to pursue post-graduate study.

I am indeed grateful to Mr. Jon Pott of Eerdmans Publishing Company who, together with his editorial associate, Mr. Gary Lee, accepted the manuscript and brought it to its final form. Without the gentlemanly prodding and warm friendship of Mr. LeRoy King, however, many a deadline would have passed unmet. I must also extend thanks to Miss Angela Tymon and to Miss Betty Ann Pruner of King College for their assistance with the indexes.

The bulk of this research was completed during my doctoral studies at King's College, Aberdeen University. In Scotland I worked under the tutelage of many outstanding scholars. I wish to render special thanks to Prof. Robin Barbour for his careful reading of the manuscript and ready advice, and to Prof. James B. Torrance for giving me a deep appreciation for Scottish history and theology. I must also express warm thanks to Prof. James D. G. Dunn of Durham, England, whose accurate and constructive criticism consistently proved invaluable. Above all, no postgraduate could hope to have a better supervisor than Prof. I. Howard Marshall. His steady hand kept at least one ship off the rocks on many occasions. I am thankful to have worked with a biblical scholar whose expertise and personal Christian devotion I have long respected and admired.

Gary M. Burge
November, 1986

Abbreviations

The conventional sigla are used for abbreviations for biblical books, the Apocrypha, the Pseudepigrapha, Rabbinic writings, and the Dead Sea Scrolls.

AB	The Anchor Bible
AER	*The American Ecclesiastical Review*
ATR	*The Anglican Theological Review*
AV	Authorized (King James) Version
BAG	Bauer, W., *A Greek-English Lexicon of the New Testament and Other Early Christian Literature*, 2nd ed. fully revised by F. W. Gingrich and F. W. Danker (Chicago: University Press, 1979)
BDF	Blass, F., Debrunner, A., Funk, R. W., *A Greek Grammar of the New Testament* (Chicago: University Press, 1957)
Bib	*Biblica*
BibLeb	*Bibel und Leben*
BiTod	*The Bible Today*
BJRL	*Bulletin of the John Ryland's Library*
BK	*Bibel und Kirche*
BLit	*Bibel und Liturgie*
BSac	*Bibliotheca Sacra*
BTB	*Biblical Theology Bulletin*
BVC	*Bible et vie chrétienne*
BZ	*Biblische Zeitschrift*
CBQ	*Catholic Biblical Quarterly*
Chmn	*Churchman*
CJT	*Canadian Journal of Theology*
CQ	*Church Quarterly*
CrozQ	*Crozer Quarterly*
CTM	*Concordia Theological Monthly*
DThom	*Divus Thomas*

ET	English translation
ETL	*Ephemerides theologicae lovanienses*
EvQ	*The Evangelical Quarterly*
EvT	*Evangelische Theologie*
Exp	*Expositor*
ExpTim	*The Expository Times*
GeistLeb	*Geist und Leben*
HeyJ	*The Heythrop Journal*
HTR	*Harvard Theological Review*
IBS	*Irish Biblical Studies*
ICC	International Critical Commentary
IDB	*Interpreter's Dictionary of the Bible*, 4 vols., ed. G. A. Buttrick et al. (New York: Abingdon, 1962)
IDBS	*IDB Supplementary Volume*, ed. K. Crim et al. (1976)
Int	*Interpretation*
ITQ	*Irish Theological Quarterly*
JB	Jerusalem Bible
JBL	*Journal of Biblical Literature*
JETS	*Journal of the Evangelical Theological Society*
JSNT	*Journal for the Study of the New Testament*
JSNTSup	*JSNT* Supplement Series
JSOR	*Journal of the Society of Oriental Research*
JSS	*Journal of Semitic Studies*
JTS	*Journal of Theological Studies*
LSJ	Liddell, H. G., and Scott, R., *A Greek-English Lexicon*, 7th ed. (Oxford: Clarendon, 1883)
LXX	Septuagint
ms(s).	manuscript(s)
MT	Masoretic Text
MTZ	*Münchener theologische Zeitschrift*
NASB	New American Standard Bible
NEB	New English Bible
NICNT	New International Commentary on the New Testament
NIDNTT	*New International Dictionary of New Testament Theology*, 3 vols., tr. C. Brown et al., ed. C. Brown (Exeter: Paternoster; Grand Rapids: Zondervan, 1975-78)
NIV	New International Version
NovT	*Novum Testamentum*
NovTSup	*NovT* Supplements
NRT	*La nouvelle revue théologique*
NT	New Testament
NTA	*New Testament Abstracts*
NThS	*Nieuwe Theologische Studien* (Groningen)
NTS	*New Testament Studies*
OT	Old Testament
par.	parallel(s)
RB	*Revue biblique*
RestQ	*Restoration Quarterly*
RevExp	*Review and Expositor*
RevQ	*Revue de Qumran*
RevScRel	*Revue des sciences religieuses*

RevThom *Revue thomiste*
RGG   *Die Religion in Geschichte und Gegenwart*, 7 vols., ed. K. Galling (Tübingen: Mohr, 1957-65)
RHPR   *Revue d'histoire et de philosophie religieuses*
RHR   *Revue de l'histoire des religions*
RSPT   *Revue des sciences philosophiques et théologiques*
RSR   *Recherches de science religieuse*
RSV   Revised Standard Version
RTR   *Reformed Theological Review*
SacPag   *Sacra Pagina*
SBFLA   *Studii biblici franciscani liber annuus*
SBT   Studies in Biblical Theology
ScEc   *Sciences ecclesiastiques*
SCR   *Studies in Comparative Religion*
SE   *Studia Evangelica*
SJT   *Scottish Journal of Theology*
ST   *Studia Theologica* (Oslo)
Str-B   Strack, H. L., and Billerbeck, P., *Kommentar zum Neuen Testament aus Talmud und Midrasch* (München: Beck, 1956)
SWJT   *Southwestern Journal of Theology* (Ft. Worth, Tx)
TDNT   *Theological Dictionary of the New Testament*, 9 vols., ed. G. Kittel and G. Friedrich, tr. and ed. G. Bromiley (Grand Rapids: Eerdmans, 1964-76)
Tg.   Targum
Theol   *Theology*
TheolRev *Theological Review* (Melbourne)
TLZ   *Theologische Literaturzeitung*
TRu   *Theologische Rundschau*
TS   *Theological Studies*
TThQ   *Tübinger Theologische Quartalschrift*
TToday   *Theology Today*
TTZ   *Trierer theologische Zeitschrift*
TU   *Texte und Untersuchungen*
TynBul   *Tyndale Bulletin*
TZ   *Theologische Zeitschrift*
UBS   *The Greek New Testament*, 3rd ed., ed. K. Aland et al. (London/New York: United Bible Societies, 1975, 1983)
VD   *Verbum domini*
ZKG   *Zeitschrift für Kirchengeschichte*
ZNW   *Zeitschrift für die neutestamentliche Wissenschaft*
ZTK   *Zeitschrift für Theologie und Kirche*

Introduction

Despite the absence of the term ἐκκλησία in the Fourth Gospel, it is clear that the Gospel's communal images (e.g., the shepherd and flock, the vine and branches), the prayer for unity in chap. 17, and especially the undertone of the Farewell Discourses point to the assumption that after the death of Jesus the disciples were to constitute a continuing community.[1] Alan Culpepper has pointed to these factors as well as to the role of the Beloved Disciple in John and the presence of distinctive historical traditions and concluded that there was a Johannine community in the first century which shared the essential characteristics of other ancient schools in Hellenism, Qumran, and contemporary Judaism.[2]

Our aim will be to examine one feature of this community's belief and experience, namely, the role of the Spirit in its view both of Christ and of Christian experience. We will urge that the Johannine community was a charismatic (or pneumatic) community in that the anointing of each member was an important distinctive of community life. This meant that the experience of Christ was paradigmatic: he was the Spirit-anointed man whose model was to be emulated. He was the source of the Spirit for the Church. And his Spirit was the Spirit that sustained the Church in power. *Therefore the foremost feature of Johannine pneumatology was its christocentric basis.*

The study falls into two major sections. The first (chap. 1) is devoted to recent research on Johannine pneumatology and uncovers the enduring interest of this field: John's enigmatic title for the Spirit, the Paraclete. After looking

---

1. D. M. Smith, "Johannine Christianity: Some Reflections on its Character and Delineation," *NTS* 21 (1974-75) 222-23.

2. A. Culpepper, *The Johannine School* (Missoula: Scholars Press, 1974).

at the traditional interpretation of Pneuma in John, we will then offer a comprehensive, systematic study applying the emphasis on Johannine pneumatology to the major categories of Johannine theology.

The second major section (chaps. 2–5) discusses the formal pneumatology of the Johannine literature. It is clear that the anointing of Jesus formed the precedent later enjoyed by the community. Therefore we shall initially look at John's christology (chap. 2) to see how the Spirit played a role in the period of Christ's earthly ministry.

John's silence about Jesus' water baptism is not inadvertent but joins his stress elsewhere on the notion of Christ as the supremely anointed Lord. In Johannine christology the Spirit is fully integrated into the person of Christ—so much so that the Synoptic portrait is substantially refashioned. In this regard the anointing of Jesus is a continuing motif in the Gospel, but remains second to John's concept of the Spirit indwelling and residing in the Messiah as a part of his life. This is metaphorically described as living water which only Jesus can distribute and which ultimately becomes available through the cross. Thus the Spirit and Jesus are closely linked before the Farewell Discourses in that the Spirit is viewed as an integral part of Jesus' life and being and is finally released through his death.

The implied union of Spirit and Christ is made explicit in Johannine eschatology (chap. 3). The Fourth Evangelist stresses the present reality of Christ in Spirit in contrast to the traditional focal point of the parousia. This emphasis is achieved not only by aligning the gift of the Spirit with the hour of glorification and Jesus' resurrection, but in the parallel expectation running throughout the discourse that when believers encounter the Paraclete, they will effectively encounter Jesus. Again, the Spirit is Jesus' life which is released in death (19:30, 34; cf. 7:39), and when Jesus gains resurrection life, this life is passed on to his followers in the insufflation of 20:22. Therefore the unity of Christ and Spirit is seen with particular clarity in the glorification when through the Spirit Jesus will be with his disciples in a new way.

In the Johannine community Spirit-experience was thus Jesus-experience. But how was this experience realized within the community? The final two chapters will examine how the Spirit must have been perceived within this community. In chapter 4 John's corrective view of baptism and the Lord's Supper will be related to his message about the experiential Spirit. The mark of discipleship in this community was not baptism as much as it was spiritual birth (3:5ff.), and this dynamic anointing was characteristic of ongoing community life (as seen esp. in 1 John).

Similarly, the eucharist was not an empty tradition but a meeting place wherein the believer could encounter the living Christ in Spirit (6:52ff.). This is the definition of true worship: it is the believer's expression of faith in the light of the work of the cross when joined with the adoration of God in Christ who is encountered powerfully in the Spirit. In concert with traditional expressions of worship, the Johannine expression was based on the objective criteria of the cross and faith. But its distinctive element was subjective: it reflected a vitality and enthusiasm that could only be attributed to the Spirit. Johannine worship was pneumatic worship.

Thus as Jesus was anointed, so too the believer must be anointed with the Spirit of Jesus. But likewise, as Jesus was persecuted, his followers would be tested with parallel persecutions (chap. 5). The trial motif which runs through the Fourth Gospel was to be indicative for the Beloved Disciple and his community. They were to be agents as Jesus was an agent of God (17:18; 20:21). Similarly, they found in the Spirit Paraclete the power to sustain their witness before the world (15:26ff.) and to engage in an offensive posture before Christ's opponents (16:7ff.). But again, Jesus himself was the central point of the Paraclete's witness. The Paraclete recalled the tradition of what Jesus taught, provided words for the present crisis, and revealed the future. Above all, the Paraclete exegeted Christ to the world. He revealed Jesus in truth, conviction, and power through the compelling witness of the church.

It is also clear, however, that the view of revelation embraced in the Paraclete sayings provided difficulties. 1 John shows the community being torn by a division that may have stemmed in the first instance from the pneumatic or ecstatic nature of the community itself. What controls were available within a fellowship in which prophecy flourished? Despite the theological adjustment evident in this Epistle, it is clear that the community continued to be a pneumatic community challenging the conventional expression of Christian experience and identity.

CHAPTER ONE

A PROSPECTUS ON JOHANNINE PNEUMATOLOGY

New Testament scholarship has generally affirmed the conclusions of E. F. Scott given early in this century regarding the unimportance of the Spirit in Johannine theology: "Indeed, the more closely we examine the Johannine doctrine of the Spirit, the more we are compelled to acknowledge that there is no real place for it in the theology as a whole."[1] But a more recent, exhaustive study on Johannine pneumatology has concluded just the opposite. Felix Porsch (*Pneuma und Wort*, 1974) has emphasized the intimate connection between Jesus and the Spirit in John's Gospel. He notes that especially in John "the work of the Spirit" informs the Gospel's descriptions of the person and work of Jesus. Although this is true of all NT writings, Porsch adds that "Only in the Fourth Gospel is this fact clearly made the subject of reflection. For this reason John's 'teaching' about the Spirit is virtually a 'hermeneutical key' to the understanding of this 'pneumatic' Gospel."[2] Although we might hesitate to label John's teaching on the Spirit a "hermeneutical key" to his Gospel, Porsch has effectively pointed out the significance of this theme.

---

1. *The Fourth Gospel: Its Purpose and Theology* (Edinburgh: T. & T. Clark, 1906) 347, 320. Scott contended that John made a confusing synthesis of his own doctrine of a completely realized eschatology and Paul's doctrine of the Spirit, thus making his pneumatology only obscure the main intention of his Gospel. See further below, pp. 33-38; cf. also idem, *The Spirit in the New Testament* (London: Hodder and Stoughton, 1923) 206-207; and I. G. Simpson, "The Holy Spirit in the Fourth Gospel," *Exp* 4 (1925) 293.

2. F. Porsch, *Pneuma und Wort: Ein exegetischer Beitrag zur Pneumatologie des Johannesevangeliums* (Frankfurt: J. Knecht, 1974) 406. G. Bornkamm understands the Paraclete sayings to be "a type of hermeneutical key for understanding Johannine christology." See his "Der Paraklet im Johannesevangelium," in *Festschrift für Rudolph Bultmann* (Stuttgart: Kohlhammer, 1949) 12-35; completely updated in *Geschichte und Glaube, Gesammelte Aufsätze*, Erster Teil, Band III (München: Kaiser, 1968) 68-89; all citations are from this 1968 edition.

One aspect of Johannine teaching about the subject has dominated recent discussion. This is the Paraclete, a topic on which U. B. Müller (1974) has contributed striking new suggestions. I. de la Potterie's two-volume work, *La Verité dans Saint Jean* (1977), devotes an important section to the Johannine themes of the Spirit Paraclete, revelation, and the truth. M. E. Boring (1978) has had similar interests. He wonders if the term παράκλητος was a functional title of the Johannine community's own prophets. And lastly, against all critical trends, J. Kremer (1978) has sought to anchor John's Paraclete/Spirit of Truth passages in the Synoptic tradition.

This list of the most recent studies uncovers what appears to be a consistent trend. The question of the Johannine Paraclete has regularly dominated the discussion of Johannine pneumatology. Few recent scholars (except Porsch) have attempted to understand John's unified message about the Spirit. Do the Pneuma and Paraclete passages have a unified theme, or are the Paraclete passages to be studied in isolation? How does John contribute to the NT message about the Spirit? At what stage in the development of early Christian pneumatology does John stand? Finally, how can we relate Johannine pneumatology to recent research concerning the community of the Beloved Disciple?

Aside from short studies, two recent monographs which attempt this broader goal stand out. G. Johnston's book, *The Spirit-Paraclete in the Gospel of John* (1970), begins with a discussion of the Spirit in the OT and ends with a critical evaluation of Johannine spirituality. One would therefore expect all aspects of John's pneumatology to be discussed. But Johnston's primary interest is in the background of the Fourth Evangelist's use of παράκλητος, where he does offer unique contributions (see below). His treatment of πνεῦμα in John 1–12 (as well as chaps. 19 and 20) is far from adequate. According to Johnston, the Johannine Spirit is simply an impersonal power which equips Christian leaders for unique tasks (prophets, teachers, martyrs, etc.).[3] These leaders can be called "Paracletes" because they are the vehicles through which the Spirit Paraclete shows its power.[4] Therefore the Pneuma passages give us evidence of the power available for ministry, and the Paraclete passages detail the specific duties which Christian leaders may be equipped to do.[5]

The second recent monograph on Johannine pneumatology is Felix Porsch's *Pneuma und Wort* (1974). Although we will look at Porsch's contribution in detail below, a condensed overview might be of use here. Porsch studies all the Spirit passages in detail. He notes the vital connection between the role

---

3. Johnston, *The Spirit-Paraclete in the Gospel of John* (Cambridge: University Press, 1970) 16, 22, 32, 81, 99, 127ff.

4. Johnston, ibid., pp. 16, 126.

5. Barnabas Lindars represents most reviewers of Johnston's work when he notes with disappointment how the monograph focuses on "speculative theories" and generally lacks "concentration" (*Theol* 74 [1971] 37-38); see also R. E. Brown, *CBQ* 33 (1971) 268-70; C. K. Barrett, *CQ* 3 (1971) 329; I. H. Marshall, *Chmn* 84 (1970) 292; S. Smalley, *EvQ* 43 (1970) 119; G. B. Caird, *JTS* 22 (1971) 576-77; W. A. Meeks, *JBL* 90 (1971) 240-43; E. Malatesta, *Bib* 54 (1973) 539; R. S. Barbour, *ExpTim* 82 (1971) 152.

of the Paraclete and its teaching and recalling functions.[6] Bringing to memory the words of Jesus is one of the Paraclete's primary responsibilities (John 14:26). But Porsch also brings to our attention an equally important relation between the words of Jesus and the Pneuma passages. When Jesus offers his words, he in fact is offering "the Spirit and life" (John 6:63).[7] A careful study of John 3:34 suggests that when the Spirit is given "without measure" (v. 34b), John takes this to mean the "word of God" spoken by Jesus (v. 34a). Porsch provides a kind of existentialist interpretation and concludes: "In his word, which is God's word, Jesus gives the Spirit. That is, the Spirit communicates itself to believers in Jesus' word. A 'word event' [Wortgeschehen] is therefore according to John a 'spiritual/pneumatic' event."[8]

Although Johnston's study is helpfully balanced by Porsch's serious concentration on the Pneuma passages, the majority of scholars have generally reflected Johnston's emphases. For example, R. Schnackenburg (1977) is convinced that a study of the Spirit in the Johannine literature will uncover how that early Christian community understood Christian revelation, prophecy, and the role of the Christian prophet. But his study of how the Johannine community understood this experience focuses primarily on the Paraclete passages.[9] One cannot avoid wondering if the emphasis on revelation in the Paraclete texts may have influenced Porsch's discovery of revelatory motifs throughout the Pneuma sayings.

The constant interest that the Paraclete arouses stems from three sources. First, the passages themselves are limited to three chapters in the Farewell Discourses. Why are they confined thus and not integrated into the whole of the Gospel? Do they reflect a non-Johannine theological bias? Early form-critical studies by J. Wellhausen and H. Windisch (recently revived by J. Becker) sought to isolate these passages and demonstrate a primitive Paraclete source.[10] The Paraclete sayings, they affirmed, stemmed from a non-original, extra-Johannine source. Today, many scholars still hold these conclusions to be sound. Second, interest has also centered on the foreign nature of these Paraclete sayings in any Jesus tradition. Could Jesus have announced the Spirit in these terms? Or more basically, was the Paraclete an independent salvific figure later confused with the Holy Spirit (so Bultmann, Betz)? Finally,

---

6. Porsch, ibid., 257ff., 299ff.

7. Ibid., 192ff.

8. Ibid., 211; see the reviews by R. E. Brown, *TS* 37 (1976) 684-85; Y. Congar, *RSPT* 59 (1975) 475-77; L. Sabourin, *BTB* 6 (1976) 94-95; X. Léon-Dufour, *RSR* 64 (1976) 451-53; J. Schlosser, *RevScRel* 52 (1978) 41-43.

9. R. Schnackenburg, "Die johanneische Gemeinde und ihre Geisterfahrung," in *Die Kirche des Anfangs. Festschrift für Heinz Schürmann zum 65. Geburtstag*, ed. R. Schnackenburg, J. Ernst, and J. Wanke (Leipzig: St. Benno, 1977) 277-306.

10. J. Wellhausen, *Das Evangelium Johannes* (Berlin: G. Reimer, 1908); H. Windisch, *The Spirit-Paraclete in the Fourth Gospel*, tr. J. W. Cox (Philadelphia: Fortress, 1968) 1-26; J. Becker, "Die Abschiedsreden Jesu im Johannesevangelium," *ZNW* 61 (1971) 215-46. O. Betz, *Der Paraklet* (Leiden: Brill, 1963) 5-11, helpfully outlines the early form-critical research on the Paraclete. At one point the quest for the origin of the Paraclete sayings became so extreme that H. Delafossa, *La Quatrième Evangile* (Paris: 1925), suggested that they were the composition of Marcion used by the heretic to establish his own prophetic authority!

the etymology of παράκλητος and its Johannine meaning has proved to be a baffling problem. Do we look to proto-Gnostic sources (Bauer, Bultmann) or Jewish antecedents (Mowinckel, Behm)? Do we follow up the Paraclete's association with the Spirit of Truth and uncover hints of Qumran's influence (Betz, Johnston), or can sufficient background be found in Orthodox Judaism (Bornkamm, Müller)?

These three concerns have kept the Paraclete in the spotlight. This focus may certainly be justified if, as recent study has suggested, the Paraclete sayings are genuine to the Johannine tradition.[11] In this case, these sayings may provide an excellent window through which we may view John's world. Not only will they uncover John's unique interest in the Spirit, but they will also clarify a host of complementary themes as well. But we cannot confine ourselves to this approach. In discussing the research attempted thus far on Johannine pneumatology, we would therefore do well first to introduce the Paraclete problem and review major contributions. We can then discuss various approches to understanding John's overall concept of Spirit and finally look at further avenues of study. Thus this introductory survey will provide a starting point for our effort to outline Johannine pneumatology generally and to give serious attention to the Pneuma texts in the Gospel.

A. THE PARACLETE PROBLEM

In the NT παράκλητος is peculiar to the Johannine literature. It occurs four times in the Gospel of John (14:16, 26; 15:26; 16:7) and once in 1 John (2:1). As a verbal adjective παράκλητος has a passive sense (cf. παρακεκλημένος), referring to one who has been summoned. As a noun, its meaning was often narrowed to one who was called into court as an assistant, helper, or advocate.[12] It is in this sense that we can best interpret 1 John 2:1, "but if anyone does sin, we have a 'Paraclete' with the Father, Jesus Christ the righteous." Here Jesus is viewed as the believer's advocate before God in heaven (cf. Heb. 7:25; 9:24).

The Gospel of John refers to the coming Spirit as "another Paraclete" (14:16). It thereby implies that Jesus is the former Paraclete and thus parallels the same notion in 1 John.[13] It is here, however, that the use of the title

---

11. F. Mussner, "Die johanneische Parákletsprüche und die apostolische Tradition," *BZ* (1961) 56-70; also Porsch, *Pneuma*, passim. See the unusually clear outline of the subject in R. E. Brown, "The Last Discourse, General Remarks," in *The Gospel According to John*, 2 vols., AB (New York: Doubleday, 1966, 1970) 2: 581-604. [Hereafter, major commentaries will be indicated by the author's name and *John* (or *Johannesevangelium*).]

12. Behm cites various helpful references, *TDNT* 5: 801; see LSJ, 1313: "παράκλητος, *called to one's aid*, in a court of justice: as Subst., *legal assistant, advocate.*" In contrast, BAG, 618, cautions that "the technical mng. 'lawyer', 'attorney' is rare. In the few places where the word is found in pre-Christian and extra-Christian lit., it has for the most part a more general mng.: *one who appears in another's behalf, mediator, intercessor, helper.* The pass. idea of παρακεκλῆσθαι retreated into the background, and the active idea of παρακαλεῖν took its place."

13. W. Michaelis, "Zur Herkunft des johanneischen Paraklet-Titels," *Coniectanea Neotestamentica 11*, Fridrichsen Festschrift (Uppsala: 1947) 147-62, has argued that 14:16 did not refer to

becomes inconsistent. The setting of 1 John 2:1 is clearly forensic: Jesus stands as defense counsel before a heavenly court. But this forensic metaphor is not strictly maintained. John 16:7-11 presents the Paraclete as a divine accuser of the world. In addition, the Paraclete is a revealer (14:25-26) who will instruct and assist the disciples after Jesus' departure (14:15ff.). Therefore John's usage departs from the standard understanding of the Greek term. John has given a special forensic title to a figure which barely fits the customary pattern. The Paraclete is described very much like a helper or even a counselor.[14]

This is the essence of the Paraclete problem.[15] The title and the tasks ascribed to the Paraclete seem to be out of step. Παράκλητος is a passive term which has been given an active sense in John. It would be of help to discover what Hebrew or Aramaic word John had in mind. But exhaustive research into this field has consistently proved unfruitful. Παράκλητος does not appear in the LXX or in Josephus.[16] In his concise *TDNT* article, Behm cites various compounds from these sources, but none supplies the sought-after key.[17] More recently, Betz has studied various terms used at Qumran to describe persons in roles like those of the Paraclete.[18] Unfortunately, none of his suggestions has received any scholarly confirmation. The question is even more complicated when we see that Rabbinic writing adopted παράκλητος as a common loan-word (פרקליט). But the common Rabbinic meaning was generally "advocate" or "defender" (related to סניגור), describing an advocate before God.[19]

Jesus as a Paraclete. "Αλλος (as in *another* Paraclete) can be taken pleonastically to mean "another who is indeed a Paraclete (or: an Other, namely, the Paraclete)," 152-53; see BDF, § 306.4, 5; on the other hand, Behm, *TDNT* 5: 800n.1, has effectively challenged this view, as do Schnackenburg, *John* 3: 74-75; Morris, *John*, 648n.42; cf. E. A. Abbott, *A Johannine Grammar* (London: A. & C. Black, 1906) § 2793.

14. F. Delitzsch was aware of this difference in meaning when he translated his Hebrew New Testament (1877). He employed מליץ in the Epistle and פרקליט in the Gospel. Cf. Brown, "The Paraclete," 116n.1. It is interesting to note that all of the Latin versions translated παράκλητος with *advocatus* in 1 John 2:1. Although many of the Old Latin versions used *advocatus* in the Paraclete passages of the Gospel, some used the transliteration *paracletus* or *paraclitus* (as does the Vulgate). The Syriac, Ethiopic, and other versions employ this Greek loanword as well.

15. Behm provides a very detailed introduction to this problem in *TDNT* 5: 800-814. R. E. Brown, "The Paraclete in the Fourth Gospel," *NTS* 13 (1966-67) 113-32, offers a less detailed but refreshingly concise outline. Note also idem, *John*, 2: 1135-44, Appendix V, as well as "The Paraclete in Light of Modern Research," *SE* 4 (1968) 158-65; Porsch, *Pneuma*, 305-24; and I. de la Potterie, *La Verité dans St. Jean* (Rome: Biblical Institute Press, 1977) 1: 330-41. For bibliography, see O. Betz, *Der Paraklet*; Porsch, *Pneuma*; and more recently, J. Kremer, "Jesu Verheissung des Geistes. Zur Verankerung der Aussage von Jn. 16:13 im Leben Jesu," in *Die Kirche des Anfangs. Festschrift für Heinz Schürmann zum 65. Geburtstag*, ed. R. Schnackenburg, J. Ernst, and J. Wanke (Leipzig: St. Benno, 1977) 247-76.

16. Aquila and Theodotion used παράκλητος once to translate מנחם in Job 16:2 ("miserable comforters [παράκλητοι] are you all"), but Behm notes this to be "unusual Jewish usage" (*TDNT* 5: 801). This is an incidental occurrence and does not reflect the Johannine title. Behm further remarks that "the Johannine Paraclete bears no relation to the later Jewish messianic title מנחם, comforter" (*TDNT* 5: 804n.32); cf. Str-B, 1: 66.

17. *TDNT* 5: 800-814.

18. *Der Paraklet*, 137-38; these include מליץ (interpreter); מורה (teacher); משכיל (one with insight, *einsichtiger*); מוכיח (corrector); מנחם (comforter).

19. See Mish. *Abot* 4: 11; Behm, *TDNT* 5: 802; Str-B, 2:560-62.

Since the linguistic background cannot help us, we are forced to analyze the Greek term alone. Raymond Brown has helpfully outlined four possibilities for translating and understanding παράκλητος: two contribute to a forensic understanding and two are nonforensic.[20]

First, παράκλητος may simply be a passive form of παρακαλεῖν. In this case, the Spirit becomes "one called alongside to help" and a defense attorney. This conforms well with other NT examples of the Spirit appearing in the defense of Christians on trial (Matt. 10:20; Acts 6:10). From John 15:26-27 and 16:8-9 the Paraclete clearly has a forensic function. As we have already noted, however, his role is that of an accuser of the world and his witness seems to defend Jesus rather than the disciples. To maintain this forensic understanding we have to say that the Gospel has shifted the meaning of παράκλητος. If we consistently translate it "advocate" in these passages, we will fail to appreciate the Paraclete's roles as revealer and teacher.

Second, if we take παράκλητος in its active sense, we arrive at the definition "one who intercedes, entreats, or appeals to." Rather than a defender in persecution (as above), the Paraclete may be a spokesman or mediator. Although we may understand the heavenly Jesus of 1 John 2:1 in this way, the Gospel depicts the Paraclete as dwelling within the disciples on earth. He does not speak *for* them as much as he speaks *through* them (John 15:26-27). On the other hand, the Paraclete may be a type of spokesman for Jesus: "He will speak only what he hears . . . for he will take what is mine and declare it to you" (John 16:13-14). Again, this restricted definition of the term fails to incorporate the Paraclete's teaching and revealing roles.

Bauer, Bultmann, and others have suggested the title "helper" for the Paraclete.[21] They argue that this expresses the active sense of παρακαλεῖν and yet includes a broader understanding of his aid. "Because the intercessor and mediator is in effect a helper, παράκλητος can sometimes simply be translated 'helper,' all the more because παρακαλεῖν can have the sense: 'to ask for help.'"[22] As Brown points out, the real attraction of this suggestion is its vagueness. But nothing in John 14–16 immediately leads us to think of the Paraclete as a mere helper. This understanding is also not helpful in dealing with the Paraclete's role as a witness who "convicts the world of sin" (16:8). This hypothesis is further weakened because it is completely bound up with a proto-Mandean source theory for the Gospel (see below).

Third, the active force of παρακαλεῖν is also reflected by the traditional rendering "Comforter" or "Consoler" in Wycliffe and the AV (possibly echoed in Luther's *Tröster*)[23]. In addition, J. G. Davies has found support for this sense

---

20. Brown, "The Paraclete," 116-19; also, idem, *John* 2: 1136-37.

21. W. Bauer, *Johannesevangelium*, 177-78, 182-83; R. Bultmann, *John*, 566-67. In a later section we shall examine the *religionsgeschichtliche* parallels they have offered in support.

22. Bultmann, *John*, 569; on 569n.5 Bultmann cites linguistic evidence from classical and Jewish wisdom sources.

23. Note Behm's detailed defense of Luther's use of *Trost* and the etymological history of the term, *TDNT* 5: 804n.31.

in the LXX use of παρακαλεῖν.[24] It is significant, however, that John never uses the verb παρακαλεῖν, though in the context of the Paraclete passages the role of consolation does seem to appear. John presents the Paraclete as meeting the disciples' needs in a time of sorrow: "I will not leave you desolate, I will come to you" (14:18). "Because I have said these things to you, sorrow has filled your hearts" (16:6). Therefore, "comfort" illuminates one aspect of the Paraclete but hardly will suffice as a comprehensive title.

Finally, various scholars have suggested a dependence on the early Christian concept of παράκλησις. Paul tells the Thessalonians, for example, that Timothy was sent to them "to establish and exhort [παρακαλέσει]" them in their faith (1 Thess. 3:2). Acts 9:31 describes the early church "walking in the fear of the Lord and in the παράκλησις of the Holy Spirit." C. K. Barrett wonders if John has condensed in his title the essence of early Spirit-led apostolic paraclesis. According to Barrett, prophetic Christian preaching "was exhortation and could therefore properly be described by words of the παρακαλεῖν group."[25] After demonstrating this from the NT, he shows how the functions of the Paraclete highlight the specific tasks of Christian preachers. To be sure, the Paraclete announces its witness to Jesus through the voice of Christian proclamation (15:26-27). 1 John 4:13-14 sharpens this interdependence concerning the Spirit: "He has given us of his own Spirit, and we . . . can testify."

This brief summary of possible translations for John's unique title demonstrates the problem well. The variety of traits given to the Paraclete defy any attempt to give him a comprehensive title. For example, Windisch finds in the role of the Paraclete the convergence of three themes: a witness that vindicates and judges; a helper and aid; a counselor and teacher.[26] Thus the great multiplicity of activities in the Paraclete's role suggests that John has applied a term common in his world to a particular Christian figure (the Holy Spirit). In order to preserve the uniqueness of this title and not obliterate the manifold functions of the Johannine Spirit, perhaps no translation should be adopted. Jerome

---

24. "The Primary Meaning of Parakletos," *JTS* 4 (1953) 35-38; also A. Richardson, *An Introduction to the Theology of the New Testament* (New York: Harper & Row, 1958) 114-15. Cf. Hoskyns and Davey, *John*, 468-69. Bernard, *John*, 2: 497, notes that Origen (*De Princ.* 2.7.4), Cyril of Jerusalem (*Cat.* 16.20), and Gregory of Nyssa (*C. Eunom.* 11.14) favored the idea of consolation in the Paraclete.

25. C. K. Barrett, "The Holy Spirit in the Fourth Gospel," *JTS* 1 (1950) 1-15 (his emphasis); F. Mussner has developed this point further in "Die johanneischen Parakletsprüche," 56-70. Mussner also discusses the relation of the Spirit, apostolic teaching, and "continuing revelation" according to John. See further his *The Historical Jesus in the Gospel of St. John* (ET: London: Burns and Oates, 1967) 59-67. See also B. S. Brown, "The Paraclete Sayings," *TheolRev* 3 (1966) 1-10; A. Lemonnyer, "L'Esprit-Saint Paraclet," *RSPT* 16 (1927) 293-307; and E. D. Stockton, "The Holy Spirit in the Writings of St. John" [A Thesis of the Theological Faculty of Sydney] (Manly, 1960), 20-33, have developed the relation between the Spirit and NT paraclesis. See the examples of Rom. 12:8; Heb. 13:22; Acts 13:15; 2:40. Cf. J. T. Forestell, *The Word of the Cross* (Rome: Biblical Institute Press, 1974) 134-39; Schmitz-Stählin, *TDNT* 5: 773-99; and G. Haufe, "Form und Funktion des Pneuma-Motivs in der frühchristlichen Paränese," *TU* 103 (1968) 75-80.

26. Windisch, "The Spirit Paraclete," 18.

faced this same quandary when he worked on the Latin Vulgate. Rather than choose *advocatus* or *consolator,* he simply and wisely employed the transliteration *paracletus* throughout the Farewell Discourses.

B. FINDING A BACKGROUND FOR THE PARACLETE

Mowinckel once despaired of the linguistic attempt to trace the Paraclete. "The problem of the Paraclete is . . . not lexicographical, it is a problem of the history of religion."[27] Throughout this century scholars have attempted to discover the background of the Fourth Gospel and likewise of its Paraclete. They have asked whether John's picture of the Spirit Paraclete is the result of religious reflection in John's community. Rather than trace the roots of this ambiguous word, they have sought parallels in contemporary first-century religions.

1. PROTO-GNOSTIC ANTECEDENTS

In his 1933 commentary on John, W. Bauer developed the hypothesis that the Fourth Gospel was the result of "a world of syncretism," notably seen in the syncretistic Gnostic religion of the Mandeans.[28] In particular, Bauer noted how the role of the Johannine Paraclete had immediate parallels in the vast Mandean pantheon of "helpers." These spiritual helpers were sent from the upper world of light into the earthly realms to bring instruction, encouragement, and guidance to righteous individuals. In the Ginza, one such figure says, "I was their helper . . . whosoever shines and is clear, to him will I be a helper, a helper and support from the place of darkness to the place of light." In essence, Bauer argued, the Paraclete is simply another form of the same idea. He is a heavenly being sent to aid and tutor all struggling believers. He is a revealer, sustainer, mediator, and guide just as the Mandean helper is. Furthermore, the Paraclete lives in a world of explicit dualism just like its Mandean counterpart.[29]

Bauer's contemporary Rudolf Bultmann became this theory's most eloquent and powerful expositor. In an influential article in 1925, Bultmann

---

27. S. Mowinckel, "Die Vorstellung des Spätjudentums vom heiligen Geist als Fürsprecher und der johanneische Paraklet," *ZNW* 32 (1933) 118n.75, cited in Behm, *TDNT* 5: 806n.45.

28. Bauer, *Johannesevangelium,* 3. On the complicated issue of the Gnostic and Mandean antecedents to John, as well as the early discussions of Lidzbarski, Reitzenstein, Bousset, and Bultmann, see the following: C. H. Dodd, *The Interpretation of the Fourth Gospel* (Cambridge: University Press, 1953) 97-130; E. Haenchen, "Aus der Literatur zum Johannesevangelium 1929-1956," *TR* 23 (1955) 313-26; Brown, *John,* 1:lii-lix; Schnackenburg, *John,* 1:135-52; S. Smalley, *John: Evangelist and Interpreter* (Exeter: Paternoster, 1978; Nashville: Nelson, 1984) 41-59.

29. Bauer, *Johannesevangelium,* 179-80; Windisch, "The Spirit Paraclete," 26. The quest for Paraclete parallels found its most creative expression in J. Grill, *Untersuchungen über die Entstehung des vierten Evangeliums,* 2 vols. (Tübingen: Mohr-Siebeck, 1902, 1923). Grill felt that the Paraclete stemmed from the cosmic dualism and conflict in Persian religion. There the Spirit of Zarathustra fights the powers of darkness at the aid of the disciples of truth (pp. 327-37). Like most scholars, Windisch dismisses the suggestion with a footnote ("The Spirit Paraclete," 26n.81).

sought to demonstrate twenty-eight basic parallels between John and the Gnostic milieu.[30] He concluded that behind the Fourth Gospel there stood a well-known and influential redeemer myth which was carefully combined with the Synoptic tradition in the writing of this Gospel.[31] He further maintained that the origin of the Paraclete figure was to be found in the supreme Mandean helper bearing the title *Yawar* (meaning "helper"). Citing numerous references about Yawar from Mandean liturgies and the Ginzas, Bultmann summarized: "that he [Yawar] establishes dwellings for the righteous, that he institutes baptism; he is the Revealer, who has gentle and sincere discourses; he receives from the divinity the title 'our word,' 'word of life'; because of his name the believers separate themselves; for his sake they are persecuted."[32]

Although the Mandean helper image does indeed parallel many of the Paraclete's characteristics, the Mandean theory as a whole faces formidable difficulties.

First, in Bultmann's 1949 *Festschrift*, G. Bornkamm pointed out that the Mandean system includes a variety of helpers and a variety of descriptions for them. Yawar does not parallel the Paraclete because the latter has no contemporary associates. Jesus is followed by the Spirit of Truth who alone will meet the disciples' needs.[33] Hence, while the Mandean system would recognize many simultaneous revelers, it has no parallel to the tandem relationship shared by Jesus and the Paraclete.

Second, the Mandean helper figures also do not have any forensic traits. They bring spiritual exhortation, encouragement, and special revelation, but they do not convict and confront the world as the Paraclete does.

---

30. R. Bultmann, "Die Bedeutung der neuerschlossenen mandäischen und manichäischen Quellen für das Verständnis des Johannesevangeliums," *ZNW* 24 (1925) 100-146; also, idem, *Theology of the New Testament*, 2 vols., tr. K. Grobel (London: SCM; New York: Scribner's, 1952, 1955) 1: 164-83; 2: 1-92; cf. E. Peterson, "Urchristentum und Mandäismus," *ZNW* 27 (1928) 55-98.

31. Bultmann, "Die Bedeutung," 103-104, 144-45. Schnackenburg, *John*, 1: 543-57, provides a concise excursus on the Gnostic redeemer myth. According to Bultmann, John found this myth in the third of his three sources for his Gospel: (1) the miracles source; (2) the Passion/Easter source; (3) the Gnostic/dualistic sayings source. Although his commentary has no introduction, these views are outlined in *RGG* 3: 841-43.

32. *John*, 571; Bultmann cites Liturgy 195 in which the Mandaic messenger exhorts the believers: "Endure the world's persecutions / With genuine, believing hearts. / Revere me in uprightness / That I may present myself to be to you a helper, / A helper and a sustainer." On p. 570n.4 Bultmann notes how in these texts the soul's lament is regularly followed by the coming of a helper (cf. Ginza 328, 27-28). In his comment on John 12: 20-33 he applies these parallels to Jesus' lament. Bultmann also points to parallels in the Gnostic Odes of Solomon. But as Behm has demonstrated, "the thought of divine help is on a different level here . . . it can hardly be compared with the concept of the Paraclete in John" (*TDNT* 5: 808).

33. Bornkamm, "Der Paraklet" (1949 ed.), 12-35. Bultmann responded in 1957 in his commentary on John: "the doubts raised by Bornkamm . . . do not seem decisive to me" (*John*, 571). In his updating of the 1949 article Bornkamm repeated that this theory is "vulnerable, because the Mandean texts make use of varying names for the different Helper-images. Above all, the large number (which is basically unlimited) and the repetition of the Gnostic redeemers therefore provide no authentic analogy for the Paraclete, because the Johannine texts speak only about *two* characters. They refer exclusively to one another and are strictly dissimilar with regard to the time of their work and their functions in spite of all the parallel sayings" (1968 ed., p. 70).

Third, Brown argues that because of the great number of Mandean revealers, Yawar cannot be necessarily singled out as an equivalent title for the Paraclete. Even if it were, παράκλητος does not primarily mean "helper" in Greek. If this were John's intention, βοηθός should have been chosen.[34]

Finally, various scholars have pointed to the work of the Mandean specialist E. S. Drower.[35] She has concluded that Yawar does not refer to a "helper" at all. Rather, it is a Semitic participle meaning "the carrier of heavenly light." This definition fits the Mandean cosmic, dualistic setting well and definitely estranges this mythological figure from any relationship with the Johannine Paraclete. We are therefore left with only a general kinship between the two figures. There are conceptual parallels, but the extreme differences rule out any literary dependence. When we add to this evidence the strong possibility that Mandaism might be a post-Christian development (as C. H. Dodd contends),[36] its use as a source for John becomes highly speculative.

Bultmann and others who have championed the Gnostic source hypothesis have felt the weight of these difficulties. In particular H. Becker expressed confidence that Gnostic sources provided the most useful background for the Paraclete. Agreeing with Bultmann, Becker saw genuine parallels between the Paraclete and Gnostic helper/revealer figures. Nevertheless, he wisely dissented from adducing any parallels between the Yawar and the Paraclete.[37] In a subsequent edition of his commentary on John, Bultmann incorporated and adopted Becker's reservations by quoting him: "We do not maintain that we have proved parallels to John 14:16, but only that we have outlined a body of opinion analogous to that which has produced the mythologoumenon of the ἄλλος παράκλητος."[38]

2. HELLENISTIC ANTECEDENTS

We have already noted that Dodd dismissed the notion of a Mandean background to John. In the same volume he challenged the supporters of any Gnostic source theory to produce a Gnostic text which positively antedates the

---

34. Brown, "The Paraclete," 119; cf. W. Michaelis, "Zur Herkunft," 150-62 on the doubtful possibilities of finding a successful translation of παράκλητος in the Mandean literature and the Odes of Solomon. Michaelis further objected that a persuasive theory of the Paraclete's origins had to locate a title linked to a matching concept which firmly paralleled the Johannine Paraclete (pp. 150ff.). Similarly compare O. Betz, Der Paraklet, 28-29.

35. Betz, Der Paraklet, 29-30; Brown, "The Paraclete," 120n.1, cites E. S. Drower, The Secret Adam (Oxford, 1960) 62-63; and idem, The Canonical Prayer Book of the Mandaeans, 252-53.

36. Dodd, Interpretation, 115-30. Dodd concludes, "It seems that we must conclude that the Mandaean literature has not that direct and outstanding importance for the study of the Fourth Gospel which has been attributed to it by Lidzbarski, Reitzenstein and Bultmann, since it is hazardous, in the presence of obvious and pervasive Christian influence, to use any part of it as direct evidence for a pre-Christian cult or mythology" (p. 130).

37. Die Reden des Johannesevangeliums und der Stil der gnostischen Offenbarungsrede, in FRLANT (Göttingen: Vandenhoeck & Ruprecht, 1956) 123; on the Mandean helper figure see pp. 98-102.

38. Becker, ibid.; Bultmann, John, 571-72. Note Bultmann's reservations in Theology of the New Testament, 2: 88n.2.

NT. "Gnosticism," Dodd affirmed, "has in part the same roots as Johannine Christianity," but cannot be used as a source for it.[39] Any such attempts he labeled "speculative."

Dodd's research pointed him to the "higher religion of Hellenism": the Hermetic literature. Philo—whose unique faith presupposed this religion—also stood out as a clear indicator of John's background. Dodd suggested that John is "sympathetically in touch with Hellenistic Judaism as represented by Philo. Like Philo himself, he is in contact with the higher pagan thought of the time, as represented to us by the Hermetic literature." Therefore Dodd felt that John had simply coined a "Philonic term" when he applied the name "Paraclete" to Christ.[40]

The further application of this term to the Holy Spirit was an easy next step. Johannine eschatology made a "bold reinterpretation of the 'return' of Christ by appealing to the guidance of the Spirit in the church."[41] Where John has set this term in a nonforensic situation (e.g., 14:25) he has simply applied it to the familiar traditions of early Christian pneumatology evident throughout the rest of the Gospel.[42]

3. OLD TESTAMENT AND JEWISH ANTECEDENTS

Modern scholarship has all but abandoned the attempt to find a Gnostic or Hellenistic background for the Paraclete. But dissent from this method has not been only recent. In 1933 S. Mowinckel felt that the concept could be traced in the OT and Jewish concept of intercessors. This, he argued, was the proper hermeneutical approach to the problem since Christianity stemmed from these sources. If the Paraclete problem could not be solved within the NT alone, its OT and Jewish antecedents should first be given a thorough and complete study.[43]

a. The Advocate before Qumran

Although the word παράκλητος does not appear in the Greek OT, it does enjoy a conceptual familiarity with the OT idea of religious intercessory advocates. In Gen. 18:23-33, for example, Abraham intercedes for the righteous of Sodom and Gomorrah. In Exod. 32:11-14 Moses makes a moving intercession for the

---

39. *Interpretation*, 98, 133.

40. Ibid.; note chaps. 2–3, pp. 10-73, esp. 72. Objections against Dodd's use of the Corpus Hermeticum have been raised by G. D. Kilpatrick, "The Religious Background of the Fourth Gospel," in *Studies in the Fourth Gospel*, ed. F. L. Cross (London: Mowbray, 1957) 38-39.

41. Dodd, *Interpretation*, 415; Dodd developed this theme more fully in *The Apostolic Preaching and Its Developments*, 2nd ed. (London: Hodder and Stoughton, 1963) 57-78; cf. idem, *Historical Tradition in the Fourth Gospel* (Cambridge: University Press, 1963), where Dodd shows how the promises of a trial-like persecution (and spiritual aid) in the Synoptic tradition provided the setting for this unique forensic title (pp. 407-13).

42. In contrast, E. F. Scott, *The Fourth Gospel*, 331, has rejected any suggestion that Philo and John share any common understanding of πνεῦμα; cf. Dodd, *Interpretation*, 219-22.

43. Mowinckel, "Die Vorstellung," 98.

Israelites in the wilderness (cf. Exod. 33:12-17 and Num. 14:13-19). Samuel (1 Sam. 7:8-9) and prophets such as Amos (Amos 7:2, 5-6) and Jeremiah (Jer. 14:7-9, 19-22) can also be noted as characteristic OT advocates for Israel. Thus through the intercession of righteous individuals Israel's problems and needs could be brought before God. In addition, however, the OT advocate could play an important role on behalf of God. In Zech. 3:1-10 we find angelic intercessors conveying the will of God to human beings. Hence the OT advocate could become a guide and witness. But further, such intercessors could also become accusers. They could encourage God's judgment on Israel's sin (Num. 16:15-16; Jer. 18:20-23).[44]

Mowinckel was the first to point NT research on the Paraclete in this direction. In 1940 Mowinckel's contribution was given full attention in the exhaustive dissertation of Nils Johansson.[45] In the NT Jesus is the Christian's sole heavenly intercessor (Rom. 8:34; Heb. 7:25; cf. Matt. 10:32 par. Luke 12:8). Moreover, in 1 John 2:1 he is called a Paraclete. The further use of this term for the Spirit (as the advocate who also accuses, teaches, and leads) may simply represent the natural development of an OT intercessory figure. Therefore, Jesus and the Spirit could fit into the developing Jewish schema of divine intercessors.

Mowinckel and Johansson emhasized the growth of these concepts after the OT in the vast literature of the intertestamental period. In this era Jewish faith upheld a firm conviction that the pious would have supernatural, heavenly helpers, including the righteous dead (1 En. 39:5; 2 En. 83:10) and especially angels (1 En. 47:2). In the apocalypses, angels were said to unveil or announce (ἀναγγελλεῖν) to the believer the whole truth (cf. Dan. [Gk. Theod.] 2:4, 7, 9; etc.). In John 16:13-14 the verb ἀναγγελλεῖν is used of the Paraclete who "will announce . . . the things to come."[46] In particular, this period singled out the angel Michael as the supreme heavenly advocate (T. Naph. 9:2; 1 En. 9:4; Dan. 10:13). This whole spectrum of intercessors could appear for the defense of the faithful—or in the role of their accuser. They could teach and counsel in order to strengthen the disheartened Jews.[47]

The writings of the Rabbis affirmed this trend completely. Sacrifices, good works, a personalized Torah, and any expression of religious zeal stood by the believer as his heavenly advocate. It is here that the loanword פרקליט and its frequent synonym סניגור were used to describe any heavenly defender of the righteous. For example, Rabbi Eliezer ben Jacob is quoted as saying, "He that performs one precept gets for himself one advocate, but he that commits

---

44. Behm, *TDNT* 5: 809-10, gives many examples; see also the detailed discussion of N. Johansson, *Parakletoi. Vorstellung von Fürsprechrern für die Menschen vor Gott in der alttestamentlichen Religion, im Spätjudentum, und Urchristentum* (Lund: Gleerup, 1940) 3-62.

45. Johansson, ibid. Criticisms of Mowinckel's work can be found in D. E. Holwerda, *The Holy Spirit and Eschatology in the Gospel of John* (Kampen: Kok, 1959) 32-35; Betz, *Der Paraklet*, 14-15; Johnston, *The Spirit-Paraclete*, 96-99; U. B. Müller, "Die Parakletenvorstellung im Johannesevangelium," *ZTK* 71 (1974) 32; Porsch, *Pneuma*, 310-11.

46. Brown, "The Paraclete," 121n.2, cites I. de la Potterie, "Le Paraclet," in *La Vie selon L'Esprit* (Paris: Cerf, 1965) 95-96, where Potterie has developed this association.

47. Behm, *TDNT* 5: 810, cites various references; see Johansson, *Parakletoi*, 65-66.

one transgression gets for himself one accuser. Repentance and good works are as a shield against retribution" (Mish. *Abot* 4:11).

More important still, a plethora of defending angels was maintained; and again, Michael was considered the chief סניגור of Israel.[48] With the increasing personalization of heavenly advocates (angels, etc.) Mowinckel and Johansson were not surprised to uncover the development of the Spirit as a heavenly advocate. Of very few relevant passages, Behm cites Rabbi Acha's comment on Prov. 24:28 as typical: "The Holy Spirit conducted the defense [סניגוריא] on both sides" (Lev. Rab. 6:1). Here the Holy Spirit as mediator plays the dual function of pleading before God for grace to Israel and of reminding Israel of its responsibilities before God.[49]

According to Mowinckel, the Babylonian-Persian "guardian spirits" *(Schutzgeister)* were the original source of such spirit intercessors in Judaism. T. Jud. 20 especially intrigued him: "Two Spirits haunt man: the Spirit of Truth . . . and the Spirit of Deceit. The Spirit of Truth testifies to all things and accuses all."[50] In addition, he pointed to the מליץ figure of Job. When a man had sinned and fallen sick he looked for "an angel, a mediator [מליץ; Targum: פרקליטא], one of the thousand" who could redeem his soul from death and declare to him what was right (Job 33:21-28; cf. 16:19-22).[51] Mowinckel wondered if John had built from this late Jewish conception his own unique Paraclete intercessor.

As we mentioned, Johansson attempted to develop further Mowinckel's thesis. He combed the OT and little-used intertestamental literature looking for advocate images (his *Fürsprecherkomplex*). In many ways, as O. Betz has shown, Johansson overworked his thesis and thereby weakened it.[52] In every instance where advocacy, instruction, or dedication occurred, Johansson was quick to highlight them as useful parallels. For example, he discussed the Servant Songs of Isaiah in detail, but Betz shows how they can refer to a personal advocate figure only with difficulty.[53] Betz even used the very Targums basic to Johansson's work to show that the Rabbis viewed the Servant to be the Messiah himself!

Johansson's thorough attention to the apocryphal and pseudepigraphical

---

48. See examples in Str-B, 2: 560; Johannson, *Parakletoi*, 145-57; and Behm, *TDNT* 5: 810-11.

49. Behm, *TDNT* 5: 811; Str-B, 2: 138, 562; Johansson, *Parakletoi*, 157-58; C. K. Barrett, "The Holy Spirit in the Fourth Gospel," 11-12, reminds us of the late date of this text (A.D. 320) and that this is almost the only Rabbinic passage of useful parallel. He concludes, "This is not impressive when an explanation is sought of John's use of the Greek word παράκλητος."

50. Mowinckel, "Die Vorstellung," 98-109; again, Barrett's criticisms are decisive: "It seems clear that the Spirit of Truth [in T. Jud. 20] is not the Spirit of God, but the good *yetzer*; the Spirit of Deceit is the bad *yetzer* which incites man to sin." See "The Holy Spirit in the Fourth Gospel," 12; cf. idem, *John*, 463.

51. Mowinckel, "Die Vorstellung," 109-18; in *The Spirit-Paraclete*, 100-102, G. Johnston studies מליץ in Job carefully, and praises Mowinckel: "The identification of *melits* as the most likely Hebrew prototype for παράκλητος seems to be the greatest contribution made by any scholar in the pre-Qumran period" (p. 99).

52. Betz, *Der Paraklet*, 15-22; Betz comments: "It appears to me to be an unfortunate methodological misuse of a correct observation" (p. 16).

53. Johansson, *Parakletoi*, 49-62.

literature has often been noted favorably. Again, however, Betz has complained that many of Johansson's images were exceedingly inaccurate. Spiritual "leader images" do not reflect a developed Jewish *Fürsprecherkomplex*. According to Betz, again and again this is the false track Johansson follows. This applies particularly to Johansson's creative use of the Son of Man image in the Enoch literature.[54]

It must be affirmed that Johansson's overstating his case has not discredited it completely (despite the severity of Betz's criticism). Johansson did effectively point out in detail the development of advocate images in the intertestamental period. The מליץ image of Job and its Targumic importance was helpfully drawn out. Further, Behm for one is persuaded that a more moderate connection between these early intercessory forms and the Johannine Paraclete is safely in order. He is persuaded that this vast and complex spectrum of Jewish advocates undoubtedly contributed to John's thought. The early use of פרקליט in this spectrum and the "heaping up" of conceptual themes convinces him "that there is a historico-religious connection between the concept of advocacy in the OT and Jewish world and the concept of παράκλητος in the New Testament."[55]

b. The Advocate after Qumran

We have already noted the development of angelic advocates in the OT and Judaism. In the late intertestamental period, however, a closely related theme developed. From preexilic times, Israel understood that Yahweh was surrounded by an angelic host (often "sons of God" or demoted pagan gods) aiding him in his endeavors (1 Kgs. 22:19; Ps. 82; Isa. 6). This Council of Yahweh could intervene directly on earth. Thus in Josh. 5:13-14 Israel's leader is met by the armed "commander of the army of the Lord"— an angelic warrior aiding in the conquest of Jericho.[56]

With the elaborate growth of late Jewish angelology, this specialized role of angels became increasingly important. Especially with the introduction of dualism, evil and good were viewed as having their own celestial supporters. Therefore personalized angels came to play key roles. Thus in Job 1 we find the person of Satan opposing the "sons of God." Furthermore, in Dan. 10 the angel Michael ("one of the chief princes") champions Israel's cause before his Persian counterpart (cf. Dan. 12:1; Jub. 1:29; T. Levi 5:6; Rev. 12:7).

At Qumran this dualistic conflict was developed in full. In particular 1QS 3:18-19 describes all people as being led by either the forces of light or the forces of darkness. The good spirit is variously described as "the Spirit of Truth" (3:19), "the Prince of Lights" (3:20), "his [God's] Angel of Truth" (3:24), and

---

54. Ibid., 96-119.

55. Behm, *TDNT* 5: 812; a consistent attempt to understand the Paraclete in forensic terms is found in D. E. Holwerda, *The Holy Spirit and Eschatology in the Gospel of John*, and A. E. Harvey, *Jesus on Trial* (London: SPCK, 1976) 103-22.

56. B. W. Anderson, "Hosts, Host of Heaven," *IDB* 2: 654-56; H. W. Robinson, "The Council of Yahweh," *JTS* 45 (1944) 151-57.

"the Holy Spirit" (4:21; 8:16). In opposition, the evil spirit is termed "the Spirit of Perversion" (3:19), "the Angel of Darkness" (3:21), and "the Angel of Destruction" (4:12; CD 2:6). The angel Michael again played a significant role for the Qumran sectarians. In the War Scroll, Michael leads the forces of light against Belial, the leader of darkness (1QM 17:6-8 and 1QM 13:10).[57]

Of particular interest for Johannine studies is the expression *Spirit of Truth*.[58] John placed the Paraclete in apposition to this title three times in his Gospel (14:17; 15:26; 16:13), and the only pre-Christian parallels are found at Qumran and in T. Jud. 20:1-5. These parallels have led many scholars to ask if Qumran's personalized dualism offers the best prototype of John's Paraclete image.

Otto Betz's monograph, *Der Paraklet* (1963), was the first to make thorough use of Qumran in a study of the Spirit Paraclete.[59] Betz was intrigued with Qumran's unique mythological dualism. According to Betz, it appears that the function of advocacy for and defense of the pious played a vital role in the sectarians' understanding of the cosmos. The Qumranians envisaged a vicious battle taking place in heaven between the forces of good and evil. Betz summarizes: "The Qumran sect . . . shows how vital for them is the Spokesman who contends for the embattled saints before the throne of God. A great drama is going on in the universe: between God and man stand the puissant [*grossen*] powers, Light and Darkness, embodied in a host of good and murdering spirits, and led by two angelic princes, Michael and Belial. Spokesmanship is [thus] tied to this dualism."[60]

This same conflict appears on the earth, yet the "mythological component is further diminished."[61] Rather than personal beings in conflict (Michael versus Belial), the Spirit of Truth and the Spirit of Error control people's lives and powerfully continue the battle. It is in this sense that the Manual of Discipline can be understood: "And he [God] allotted unto man two spirits . . . they are the spirits of Truth and Error. Dominion over all the sons of righteous-

---

57. Betz has given much attention to the figure of Michael in Qumran; see *Der Paraklet*, 66-69, 149-58.

58. On the relationship of John to Qumran, see esp. Brown, "The Qumran Scrolls and the Johannine Gospel and Epistles," *CBQ* 17 (1955) 403-19, 559-74; H. M. Teeple, "Qumran and the Origin of the Fourth Gospel," *NovT* 4 (1960) 6-25; L. Morris, "The Dead Sea Scrolls and St. John's Gospel," in *Studies in the Fourth Gospel* (Grand Rapids: Eerdmans, 1969) 321-58; J. H. Charlesworth, ed., *John and Qumran* (London: Chapman, 1972); R. E. Breck has made the Spirit of Truth the subject of a dissertation: "The Spirit of Truth. A Study of the Background and Development of Johannine Pneumatology," Rüprecht-Karl Universität, Heidelberg, 1971.

59. Critical appraisals of Betz's work can be found in the reviews of K. Schubert, *BLit* 37 (1963) 67; and R. Schnackenburg, *BZ* 9 (1965) 138-40. Note G. Johnston, *Spirit-Paraclete*, 102-19; A. R. C. Leaney, "The Johannine Paraclete and the Qumran Scrolls," in *John and Qumran*, ed. J. H. Charlesworth (London: Chapman, 1972) 38-61; idem, "The Historical Background and Theological Meaning of the Paraclete," *Duke Divinity School Review* 37 (1972) 146-59; H. M. Dion, "L'origin du titre 'Paraclet' à propos d'un livre récent," *ScEc* 17 (1965) 143-49; and most recently, U. B. Müller, "Die Parakletenvorstellung," 32-35.

60. Betz, *Der Paraklet*, 113-14, as translated by G. Johnston, *Spirit-Paraclete*, 105; concerning this cosmic conflict, see esp. 1QM 1:10-11; 14:15-16; 1QH 7:28; 10:8.

61. Betz, ibid., 114.

ness is in the hand of the Prince of Light . . . all dominion over the sons of error is in the hand of the Angel of Darkness" (1QS 3:18-20).

Betz's most significant contribution appears in his comparison of John's Paraclete with Qumran's dualism. We can summarize Betz's own conclusions as follows.[62]

(1) Betz believes that John was fully acquainted with Jewish apocalypticism and the literature of Qumran. The Greek loanword παράκλητος was known to John through its use for advocates throughout Judaism. The Johannine cosmology was therefore heavily indebted to Qumran's strict dualism: there were personal figures in heavenly conflict and impersonal forces in conflict on earth. Both of these spheres (the personal and the impersonal) were incorporated by John.

(a) The Michael myth contributed directly to the formation of the Paraclete figure. Taking his clues from the Christ/Michael relationship in Rev. 19:11–20:10 (cf. Rev. 12), Betz asked if this is the disguised Jesus/Paraclete relationship of the Fourth Gospel. In Revelation we find this figure's personal name (Michael; note that παράκλητος is absent), while in John we learn his functional title (the Paraclete; "Michael" does not appear). Furthermore, at Qumran Michael is sometimes called the Spirit/Angel of Truth (e.g., 1QS 3:24), which is also the more complete name John gives to the Paraclete.[63]

(b) John likewise understood that a parallel conflict existed on the earth. Here the Spirit of Truth (or Holy Spirit) defends and supports the faithful as a power. Here indeed is the evil that Jesus encountered on earth (John 3:19-20; 7:7; 8:44). Likewise, this is the power behind "the ruler of this world" (John 12:31; 14:30; 16:11; cf. 1 John 5:19).

(2) Betz contends that the bringing together of Qumran's Jewish mythology with his own christology was John's unique genius. John could speak of a heavenly conflict being waged during Jesus' lifetime. Yet the final victory of Christ resulted in Satan's expulsion from heaven (John 12:31; cf. Luke 10:18; Rev. 12:9), where he had formerly been fought by the angelic Paraclete Michael!

(a) At the ascension, Christ went to heaven where he took up the role of advocate (the heavenly Paraclete, 1 John 2:1). In exchange, he sent Michael (cf. John 16:7), the second Paraclete, to join forces with the Spirit of Truth in fighting the powers of darkness. Figure 1 shows a schematization of this exchange.

Betz sums up thus: "Christ, the first Paraclete, travels to heaven, where until then Michael was. Christ works in heaven as an advocate for the community; he covers its sins (1 John 2:1, cf. Rom. 8:34) and confirms their petitions (John 14:13f.; 15:16; 16:23f.). Michael, the great Paraclete, is sent to earth as 'the Spirit of Truth.' Here he testifies to God's truth, he leads the disciples, and protects them against the power of evil."[64]

---

62. See Betz, ibid., 117-214, and his conclusions, 206-12. Cf. the notes by Johnston on this section of *Der Paraklet* in his *Spirit-Paraclete*, 108-13.

63. Betz, *Der Paraklet*, esp. 149-59; "Michael is simply the Paraclete and the myth which is worked out in the Apocalypse forms the background for the Johannine Paraclete" (p. 154).

64. Ibid., 155; on p. 155n.2 Betz suggests that early Christian theology was sensitively

FIGURE 1. BETZ'S THEORY OF THE IDENTITY OF THE PARACLETE

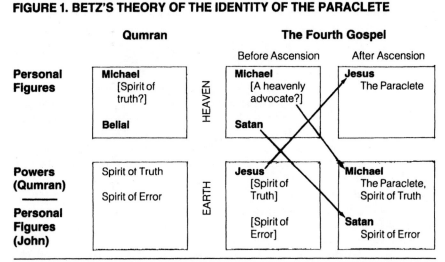

(b) Therefore, Betz explains, we can find in the Johannine Paraclete both personal and impersonal traits. John's combination of the Michael image with the Spirit of Truth on earth has formed this unique hybrid. Hence John has attempted to present the message of Christ and remain faithful to his own Jewish heritage. Yet he has reframed the Qumran cosmology by adapting it to the all-important work of Christ.

We have discussed Betz's contributions at length because of the very important nature of his subject matter (Qumran) and his exhaustive marshalling of evidence. To be sure, his treatments of dualism, advocacy, and intercession are generally excellent. He notes in detail how the sectarians of Qumran developed the then-current Jewish trend toward angelic advocates. But Betz's theory about the origin of the Johannine Paraclete has received serious criticisms.

First, Betz assumes a direct line of influence between John and Qumran which has not at all been proven. Indeed, John contains no citations or near citations of the Qumran literature. As Raymond Brown has concluded, if there is any influence, it is only indirect. G. Quispel has rightly identified that this lack of direct influence might even jeopardize Betz's starting point.[65]

---

aware of comparing the Michael tradition with the message of Christ. He cites Heb. 1:4; Gal. 1:8; Col. 2:18; Phil. 2:10; and 1 Tim. 3:16 as possible evidences. Other extrabiblical sources suggest that Michael was a contender with Christ as his equal. See Hermas Sim. 9.6.1; 12.7; and the Gospel of the Hebrews. Cf. J. Daniélou, *The Theology of Jewish Christianity*, tr. J. A. Baker (London: Darton, Longman, and Todd, 1964) 145-46, 185-87, 190-91.

65. R. E. Brown, "The Paraclete," 126; Brown concludes elsewhere that "there remains a tremendous chasm between Qumran thought and Christianity." Although there are similarities between John and Qumran, "the resemblances do *not* seem to indicate *immediate* relationship, as if St. John were himself a sectarian or were personally familiar with the QL" ("The Qumran Scrolls," 571). See G. Quispel, "Qumran, John and Jewish Christianity," in *John and Qumran*, 148.

Second, with Bornkamm, U. B. Müller has pointed out that "if advocacy were in fact a central idea in the Paraclete concept, it must also apply to the other Paraclete, 'the Spirit of Truth,' not only the glorified Christ."[66] The other Paraclete should play some advocate role beyond that in his former, heavenly function (as Michael). In Betz's schema, only the heavenly Christ is truly a *Fürsprecher*.

Third, Betz is particularly pleased with Qumran's Michael myth as a background for the Paraclete because it solves the riddle of why the Johannine Paraclete exhibits so many personal traits. The person behind this image is Michael. But many scholars have shown that personal attributes were given to the Spirit in pre-Johannine thought (e.g., Rom. 8:16; 1 Cor. 12:11). Furthermore, angelic traits do not appear in the Paraclete. Brown remarks, "there is not the slightest evidence in John's picture of the Paraclete that these remote angelic origins have remained influential."[67]

Fourth, Betz also contends that at Qumran the angel Michael and the Spirit of Truth were separate entities. In his Gospel, John conflated the two in order to form the Spirit Paraclete. This is directly the origin of the Paraclete's personal/impersonal composition. On closer examination, however, Brown and Johnston wonder if the conflation is not rather a Qumran phenomenon.[68] Qumran's Spirit of Truth, for example, is very ambiguous. It appears to be synonymous with Michael and the Prince of Lights in 1QM, but in 1QS it clearly has a psychological sense of spiritual forces in people's hearts. Brown stresses that "holy spirit," "angelic spirit," and "spirit of truth" had already come together in pre-Christian Judaism. For example, in the similar book of Jubilees (1:20-24) Moses prays that God will give the people an upright spirit to defeat Belial. Instead of an angel (as Betz expects at Qumran) God sends a *holy spirit*. Therefore, a "Holy Spirit" as well as an angelic "Spirit of Truth" could confront Belial.

Finally, Betz's use of the book of Revelation to uncover the Michael/Paraclete association is highly speculative. Johnston does his best to demonstrate that Revelation could not possibly belong to the Johannine school in the first place.[69] But more importantly, the "Michael" of Rev. 12:7 acts as Christ's aid in the consummation of the age, while in John the Paraclete is an intermediate figure (between Pentecost and the parousia) with no such apocalyptic role. The Paraclete is patterned much more after Christ. Any suggestion that the Paraclete image was shaped by the angel Michael would require far more substantial proof.[70]

---

66. U. B. Müller, "Die Parakletenvorstellung," 32; cf. Bornkamm, "Der Paraklet," 71; Quispel, op. cit., 147; J. Blank, *Krisis: Untersuchungen zur johanneischen Christologie und Eschatologie* (Freiburg: Herder, 1964) 324.

67. Brown, "The Paraclete," 126; Betz does concede this to be a weakness of his argument (*Der Paraklet*, 155-56); Schnackenburg (*John*, 1:134; 3:145-46) as well as Porsch (*Pneuma*, 314) are critical on this point; see also F. M. Cross, *The Ancient Library of Qumran* (London: Duckworth, 1958) 156-62, esp. 159-60.

68. Brown, "The Paraclete," 124-26; Johnston, *Spirit-Paraclete*, 109-10, 115-16; cf. Leaney, "The Johannine Paraclete," 43-44.

69. Johnston, *Spirit-Paraclete*, 110, 116-18.

70. That the Qumran texts may be pressed to serve surprising interests may be seen in a

The work of George Johnston directly follows a discussion of Qumran and Otto Betz.[71] In his 1970 monograph, Johnston focused much of his energy on analyzing Betz's book. More importantly, Johnston believed that Betz had hinted at the correct *Sitz im Leben* of the Paraclete sayings but had failed to interpret the evidence correctly.

In Johnston's estimate, John was fully aware of the rapidly developing angelology of the first century. The key link between Qumran and John is the Spirit of Truth, a title locking the two into the same milieu. Further, John knew that the angelic figure Michael was being identified with the Spirit of Truth. This identification was "a product of the religious imagination and to some extent a relic of ancient polytheism in Israel."[72] But Johnston thinks it inconceivable that John would cloak this angelic figure in his Paraclete (contra Betz). This would be to encourage the growing Jewish myth. Instead, John's intentions are polemical: "We suggest that the identification of the angel Michael with the true Spirit of God is pre-Johannine and that it had become a menace to the orthodox faith in Jesus as the Christ. . . . Hints that certain sectarian groups within the church were toying with the ideas and worship of angelic mediators are given in Gal. 1:8; 3:19; Col. 2:18; and Heb. 1:4f. By making skillful use of terminology that was current in such groups, John turned the tables on his opponents and safeguarded the primacy of Jesus."[73]

Therefore John's use of the terms *Paraclete* and *Spirit of Truth* is polemical and aimed at combating a Michael heresy. But Johnston goes further. His second thesis is that John does not intend the Paraclete to be a person, but rather "an active divine power."[74] In order to complete his rebuttal against any

---

recent article by A. Shafaat of Saudi Arabia, "Geber of the Qumran Scrolls and the Spirit-Paraclete of the Gospel of John," *NTS* 27 (1981) 163-69. Shafaat points to 1QH 3:8 and 1QS 3 and 4. The latter texts have commonly been employed to trace Qumran's pneumatology, but 1QH 3:8-9 is clearly messianic (cf. Isa. 9:5-6). His conclusion is exceedingly speculative: "The Johannine tradition about the Paraclete is ultimately dependent on a Qumran tradition about Geber [man] which did not use the word 'Geber' but only the titles 'Counsellor' and 'Spirit of Truth' and which, because of the latter title, was applied by Christians to the coming of the Holy Spirit on the day of Pentecost" (p. 266). The attempt to tie the original Paraclete to the expectation of a coming "Man" is suggestive of popular Islamic apologetics.

71. A preview of Johnston's research was given in an article by the same title in *Perspective* 9 (1968) 29-38; Johnston's study of Qumran's pneumatology appeared in "Spirit and Holy Spirit in the Qumran Literature," in *New Testament Sidelights: Essays in Honor of A. C. Purdy*, ed. H. K. McArthur (Hartford: Hartford Seminary Foundation, 1960) 27-42.

72. Johnston, *Spirit-Paraclete*, 120.

73. Ibid., 122.

74. Ibid., 119; Johnston goes out of his way to deny that the Spirit Paraclete is a person: "Objection must first be made to the assumption without further ado that in John 'paraclete' is the title of a person and that it is proper to speak about 'The Paraclete.' The present book intends to challenge this assumption which is widespread" (p. 81; cf. pp. 84, 87, 126). Yet at other times Johnston gives the opposite impression when the spirit is said to be "personal" (p. 79) and "the Spirit of Christ" (p. 121). Elsewhere (p. 85) John 20:22 is used (dubiously) to suggest that if "personal references" are employed to demonstrate personality, "we should have to identify this Successor (the Paraclete) with Christ's own breath!" A. R. C. Leaney gives more compelling reasons for a Hebrew understanding of an impersonal Spirit in the Paraclete, "The Historical Background/Paraclete," 146ff.

angelic persons contending with Christ, John has shown that God's Spirit (sent after the resurrection) is only a divine, dynamic force empowering Christian ministry. Certain functionaries in the community (prophets, preachers, teachers, etc.) possess this Spirit, are "to be identified as agents of the divine Spirit," and "fulfill precisely those functions that are ascribed in the Farewell Discourse to the Spirit itself."[75]

On the whole, Johnston's contribution has received very critical treatment.[76] Aside from severe criticisms about its difficult structure, logic, and style, various problems immediately confront the reader.

First, Johnston assumes that early Christian thought saw itself threatened by the Michael myth. He even maintains that the angelic Spirit of Truth which Qumran aligned with Michael "had been domesticated in the synagogues and sects of Judaism long before the Fourth Gospel had been written."[77] Sadly, no proof for this view is given. Should not undisputed polemical evidence be extant in the NT literature? Michael appears only twice, in Jude 9 and Rev. 12:7. The text from Jude is irrelevant to the issue and Rev. 12 has a debated application.

Second, we have already noted Johnston's stress on the Spirit Paraclete as a power rather than as a person. In particular, he has charged "R. E. Brown and the British school" with having missed the mark on this important point.[78] What these scholars want to say, however, is that the Spirit Paraclete is personal—he has personality. Even Johnston occasionally uses this language.[79] Does claiming personhood for the Paraclete make him an angelic figure like Michael? Amazingly, this appears to be Johnston's fear. He even rejects the possibility of seeing the "person" of Christ behind the Paraclete.[80] But for G. B. Caird this refusal opens up the problem of Johannine eschatology. If the Paraclete cannot reflect the alter ego of Jesus, there is a problem (as Caird sees it) in understanding the reinterpreted parousia in John.[81]

Finally, Johnston sees in the tasks of the Paraclete a unique description of the apostolic church. "The Spirit Paraclete is the Spirit of God . . . an active divine power that becomes embodied in certain outstanding leaders within the catholic church."[82] The specific traits of the Paraclete therefore point forward to prophets, pastors, and church leaders in the Johannine church. At one point, Johnston affirms that even John the Evangelist could rightly be

---

75. Johnston, *Spirit-Paraclete*, 126; cf. 16, 127-48.

76. See esp. the critical review by R. E. Brown, *CBQ* 33 (1971) 268-69; cf. the other reviews cited above, p. 4n.5.

77. Johnston, *Spirit-Paraclete*, 120-21; Brown, "The Paraclete," 126; and Müller, "Die Parakletenvorstellung," 34, wonder if we should seek the origin of the Christian use of "Spirit of Truth" in early christology rather than Qumran. That is, Jesus is the Truth, the true Spirit points to Jesus, therefore he is the Spirit of Truth.

78. Johnston, *The Spirit-Paraclete*, 92-96, 123-25; Johnston completely misreads Brown on this point: nowhere does Brown suggest that the Paraclete is another "mediator of salvation"—i.e., Christ's successor (p. 95).

79. Johnston, ibid., 79.

80. Ibid., 94-95.

81. G. B. Caird, *JTS* 22 (1971) 576-77.

82. Johnston, op. cit., 119.

honored with the title "Paraclete of the Christians."[83] One of his concluding chapters develops who these people are.[84] We might ask if the roles of the Paraclete point backward instead. That is to say, these traits link the Paraclete with Jesus primarily and inform the nature of the apostolic church only incidentally. The impressive parallels between Jesus and the Paraclete in the Fourth Gospel receive only marginal attention by Johnston.[85] For this reason, he can easily dismiss a christological understanding of the Paraclete's presence (against Brown, Barrett) and turn to the life of the church.

c. A Forerunner/Perfecter Motif

A completely different approach to the Paraclete problem has been suggested by G. Bornkamm. He has seen in the Jesus/Paraclete relation a Jewish successor motif. "Jesus appears here . . . as a type of forerunner—one who prepares the way. The Paraclete, however, comes as a perfecter who brings fulfillment."[86]

From the OT Bornkamm and others have noted a pattern in which a significant leader dies and leaves another to take his place, complete his work, and interpret his message. This can be said, for example, of Moses and Joshua as well as Elijah and Elisha. Furthermore, the Spirit even played a role in these successions: Joshua is said to have the "spirit of wisdom" through the laying on of Moses' hands (Deut. 34:9). The confirmation of Elisha's new authority was in his having "a double share" of Elijah's spirit (2 Kgs. 2:9-15). Bornkamm points to further parallels in late Judaism such as the messianic prophet-like-Moses expectation (Deut. 18:5) and Qumran's Teacher of Righteousness, who was a type of forerunner of the "Teacher" in the last days (CD 6:11).[87]

All these examples constituted a pattern for the early traditions about the successor relationships between John the Baptist and Jesus as well as Jesus and the Paraclete. But Bornkamm notes how this forerunner motif in the Baptist tradition was made secondary in John's Gospel. In Matthew, the arrest of the Baptist marks the beginning of Jesus' ministry (Matt. 4:12), and both men share identical announcements inaugurating their ministries (Matt. 3:2; 4:17). But John has apparently changed this relation. For him (as Bornkamm argues), the Baptist is "not precisely the forerunner of the Messiah, but rather the witness to Jesus."[88] The Baptist enjoys a simultaneous ministry with Jesus

---

83. Ibid., 126.

84. Ibid., 127-48.

85. Ibid., 93-94.

86. "Der Paraklet im Johannes-Evangelium," in *Geschichte und Blaube, Gesammelte Aufsätze*, Erster Teil, Band III (München: Kaiser, 1968) 71.

87. Ibid., 71-76; Bornkamm also suggests that John 4:25 reveals John's awareness of the Samaritan messianic expectation: a returning, end-time prophet and teacher following the Moses typology of Deut. 18:15, 18; see p. 80. Cf. E. D. Freed, "Samaritan Influence in the Gospel of John," *CBQ* 30 (1968) 580-87; J. MacDonald, *The Theology of the Samaritans* (London: SCM, 1964) 362-63; and O. Cullmann, *The Johannine Circle*, tr. J. Bowden (London: SCM; Philadelphia: Westminster, 1976) 39-56.

88. Bornkamm, "Der Paraklet," 76; see further R. E. Brown, *John*, 1:153-55; Schnackenburg,

(John 3:25-26; 4:1; cf. 5:33-34): he is the rejoicing friend of the bridegroom (3:29). Nevertheless, significant hints of a forerunner motif prevail. A careful comparison of the Baptist discourse in John 3:25-26 with the Paraclete passages shows that the announcement of the coming Christ by the Baptist closely parallels Jesus' later prediction of the Paraclete.[89]

These noteworthy parallels between Jesus and the Paraclete lead Bornkamm to a second striking suggestion. This motif was taken over by a christology which recognized a dual manner of existence in the Redeemer. First, "he comes as one who suffers and dies—but then he appears in a new form as one who judges and perfects all things." Therefore, for John, the Paraclete is none other than the glorified Christ. He is the same redeemer, now returned.[90] Furthermore, the origin of this now glorified perfecter is to be found in the Son of Man expectation of late Judaism. In the apocalyptic literature of this period Bornkamm demonstrates five basic parallels between the Son of Man and the Paraclete (world judgment, the Spirit, preexistence, etc.).[91]

Bornkamm's work has been praised from many quarters for its clear presentation of the parallels between Jesus and the Paraclete. But at the same time many have found his major thesis unacceptable.

Bultmann and a host of others have criticized the forerunner/perfecter categories themselves.[92] Can the Paraclete be termed a "perfecter"? Despite the parallels, Jesus' work is not preparatory but decisive. The Paraclete is sent by Jesus (15:26; 16:7; 14:16; etc.) and offers what Jesus has (16:14) and what Jesus has said (14:26). Clearly, the Paraclete is a subordinate figure.

In the same way Jesus is hardly a forerunner. He does not prepare for the work of God through another. All that is left, therefore, is a structural analogy between Jesus and the Paraclete and the forerunner hypothesis. Nothing substantial remains.[93]

Betz complains that the suffering/death motif is basic to Johannine christology. Yet in the forerunner models cited by Bornkamm (Moses, Elijah, etc.), none exhibits a parallel experience.[94]

John, 1:27-28, 410-18; and esp. W. Wink, John the Baptist in the Gospel Tradition (Cambridge: University Press, 1968) 87-106, esp. 105-106.

89. Bornkamm, "Der Paraklet," 76-79. He also notes significant parallels between 8:21-29 and the Paraclete promises, esp. verbal parallels in 8:26 and 16:12.

90. Ibid., 84, 88.

91. Ibid., 81-85. This theme was developed particularly in his earlier 1949 essay. Bornkamm's use of the apocalyptic Son of Man was accepted and fully developed by S. Schulz, "Der Paraklet Thematradition," in his Untersuchungen zur Menschensohn-Christologie im Johannesevangelium (Göttingen: Vandenhoeck & Ruprecht, 1957) 142-58; see also his commentary, Johannes, 189-90; for criticisms of Schulz, see Müller, "Die Parakletenvorstellung," 38; Betz, Der Paraklet, 12; Schnackenburg, John, 3: 145; and R. Kysar, The Fourth Evangelist and His Gospel (Minneapolis: Augsburg, 1975) 130-31.

92. Bultmann, John, 567n.2; Porsch, Pneuma, 316-17; Betz, Der Paraklet, 34-35; Müller, "Die Parakletenvorstellung," 37. Müller concludes: "The Paraclete carries further what Jesus had done in his earthly existence. The Paraclete does not exactly become the perfecter of Jesus. For this reason I believe Bornkamm's thesis is weak."

93. Schnackenburg, John, 3:145; Müller, "Die Parakletenvorstellung," 37.

94. Betz, Der Paraklet, 33-34.

Bornkamm's use of late Jewish Son of Man imagery is likewise problematic. The presence of the Spirit in the Son of Man may be only commonplace evidence of his messianic traits (e.g., 1 En. 49:3; 62:2). On the other hand, this is the raison d'être of the Paraclete. It is also true that the Son of Man and the Paraclete are both judges. But the Paraclete's judgment is that of God—or the Messiah. Nothing necessarily links it directly to the Jewish Son of Man.[95] Finally, it is unclear whether late Judaism brought together the image of a suffering servant with the glorified Son of Man. This no doubt is the assumed but unproved premise of Bornkamm.[96]

d. The *Gattung Abschiedsrede*

The major study of U. B. Müller contends that although Betz, Bornkamm, and others have shown useful parallels between the Paraclete and various Jewish antecedents, they have failed to consider form criticism.[97] That is, concepts rarely enter a religious literature without bringing with them their own literary form. Therefore, if these forms can be detected, the *religionsgeschichtlich* analogies for the Paraclete may be more confidently secured.

Müller believes that he has found such a parallel form in the Jewish farewell discourses (*Abschiedsreden*). But first he must establish the precise limits of Jesus' farewell in John. Accepting the conclusions of J. Becker,[98] Müller maintains that John 13:31–14:31 is the original core of Jesus' farewell discourse while chaps. 15 and 16 are later editorial expansions. In this discourse, five essential elements roughly characterize this Jewish form in John: (1) the announcement of Jesus departure, 13:31-33; (2) comfort in view of this departure, 14:1-3; (3) promise as a basis for this comfort, 14:12-26; (4) exhortation, 14:1-11; and (5) the pronouncement of peace, 14:27a. All this material is focused on the promise of the Spirit to come.[99]

Müller's assembly of evidence from Jewish farewell discourses is the heart of his unique essay.[100] Jewish leaders and literary figures overcame the problem of their departure or death in many ways. They could minister to those left behind through revealing and speaking of the future, as each of the

---

95. Müller, "Die Parakletenvorstellung," 38.

96. Porsch, *Pneuma*, 316; Betz, *Der Paraklet*, 34; see the discussion by H. H. Rowley, "The Suffering Servant and the Davidic Messiah," in *The Servant of the Lord* (London: Lutterworth, 1952) 61-88; and esp. J. Jeremias, *TDNT* 5: 677-700; F. Hahn concludes, "In the Son of Man idea proper to late Judaism there is lacking, so far as we can see, any clear proof of the assimilation of elements from the suffering servant," *The Titles of Jesus in Christology* (London: Lutterworth, 1969) 19.

97. U. B. Müller, "Die Parakletenvorstellung im Johannesevangelium," *ZTK* 71 (1974) 31-78.

98. J. Becker, "Die Abschiedsreden Jesu im Johannesevangelium," *ZNW* 61 (1970) 215-46; cf. Müller, "Die Parakletenvorstellung," 40-43, 65-75.

99. Müller, ibid., 40-43; Müller further shows that John's label of "Spirit of Truth" is in harmony with the understanding of the Spirit in the NT (cf. Gal. 4; Revelation passim) and John's understanding of revelation and the legitimacy of his own Gospel (see John 2:22; 6:63; 3:11; 20:31), pp. 43-52.

100. Ibid., 52-65.

patriarchs was understood to have done (e.g., Testaments of the Twelve Patriarchs). Indirect parallels can be found here with the Paraclete. He is Jesus' provision for the disciples' future.

Also, the departing one could exhort his followers to be obedient to the law. For example, Jub. 36 records one such plea for obedience (vv. 3, 5; cf. 1 En. 91:3ff.). Although Jesus does parallel this aspect with a final call to obey his commands (14:15, 23), his provision of someone to aid in this obedience (the Paraclete) has no Jewish counterpart.

Of particular interest is the dying saint who gives writings to his followers. Jacob is reported to have given such to his son Levi (Jub. 45:16) as was the dying Moses (As. Mos. 10:11). 4 Ezra 14 depicts the curious departure of Ezra. In order to continue his threefold role of exhorting, comforting, and teaching, Ezra prays that God will send the Holy Spirit (vv. 19-22). God answers his prayer, the Holy Spirit fills his heart, and he dictates ninety-four books of wisdom and understanding (v. 46). According to Müller, there are strong parallels here with the Spirit of Truth. The same form of ministry (*Ermahnung*, exhortation) is promised in the Paraclete (from παρακαλεῖν, "to exhort"). Furthermore, the Gospel of John itself may parallel this Jewish model. This is how the "anonymous author" legitimized his writing—just as did the authors of Jewish pseudepigraphical works. "Through the writing up of the Gospel it appears that the disciples were able to recall what Jesus had said—and this according to the mission of the Paraclete (14:26). Through the formation of the Gospel therefore the continued working of Jesus' word has been assured. The same also appears to be the case in the books which Ezra had dictated, for the books continue Ezra's activity."[101]

Finally, Müller notes the successors who leave behind Spirit-filled representatives. With Bornkamm he notes Elisha and particularly Joshua, both of whom possessed a unique spiritual charisma (Num. 27:18; Deut. 34:9). The Assumption of Moses gives a full account of Joshua's succession (As. Mos. 10–11). Joshua's lament concerning wisdom (11:4-15) is answered variously: while Moses is in heaven interceding for the people's sins (12:6), Joshua will take up his predecessor's prophetic and priestly roles. Moses is termed "the sacred spirit" (11:16), and the power which he had is now understood as being passed on to Joshua, just as it had been passed on to Moses' elders (As. Mos. 11:15-16; Num. 11:17, 25). For Müller, the Johannine parallels are significant. The Spirit Paraclete carries on the functions of Jesus in his absence. Just as the Spirit rested on both Moses and Jesus, so too their representatives are known as Spirit-bearers (*Geistträger*).

Müller is ultimately persuaded that four aspects of these Jewish farewell discourses can usefully inform our understanding of John 13:31–14:31.[102] First, the departure of the loved one is announced and the lament of his followers is

---

101. Ibid., 55; Müller finds a further example in 2 Bar. 77, where Baruch's letter exhorts, comforts, and instructs as well (pp. 55-57). He suggests that 2 Peter may be from this same literary genre as it recalls the church to the apostle's teaching. Cf. 2 Pet. 1:15: "And I will see to it that after my departure you may be able at any time to recall these things."

102. Ibid., 60-65.

answered with promises of comfort and hope. Often a certain *Grösse* is expected (another person, Ezra's 94 books, etc.).

Second, instructive revelation continues. The Holy Spirit which directed the writing of 94 books is likewise present in the Spirit of Truth who will recall all that Jesus had taught. If this revelation comes through a specific person, he is endowed with the Spirit. For John, these people may be the disciples or even the Evangelist himself.

Third, in the language of the Farewell Discourses we find the repeating themes of exhortation, comfort, and instruction. These clearly echo the work of the Johannine Spirit of Truth and suggest that παράκλητος originated in the early understanding of Christian paraclesis. That is, John expected Spirit-directed preaching to recall the words of Jesus and thereby bring Jesus' exhortation, comfort, and instruction.

Fourth, the Spirit functioned to legitimize the authority of a person or writing. To be sure, John's Gospel takes pains to affirm that its Jesus tradition has the stamp of the Spirit (14:26; 16:13; cf. 1 John 3:24-25). The Gospel account is speckled with assurances that the Evangelist has "recalled" (via the Spirit) correct events and interpretations (2:22; 3:11; 12:48; 21:24).

On the whole, Müller's approach has much to commend it. The function of the context has been given needed emphasis and rightly paralleled with similar texts in Jewish sources. Above all, even if the meaning of the title παράκλητος remains problematic (as Müller admits), such sayings about an exhorting, teaching Spirit have been shown to have a legitimate place in the Jewish farewell discourse. The Paraclete sayings at any rate belong to just this setting.

With Schnackenburg, however, we wonder if Müller has allowed for John's full "Christianizing" of his message.[103] That is, in order to fit the farewell discourse model, Müller must reject chaps. 15 and 16. He gives various reasons for this rejection. For example, a later redactor felt that John had not developed the Spirit's relation to the world. While in chap. 14 the world cannot know the Paraclete, in chap. 15 there is conflict, and chap. 16 introduces the theme of judgment. According to Müller, this development reflects a "reapocalypticizing" *(Reapokalyptisierung)* of the gospel firmly rooted in similar Jewish traditions. The judgment formula of John 16:8 in this example stems from 1 En. 1:9 (cf. 4 Ezra 12:32; 13:37; 2 Bar. 40).[104] Furthermore, John 14 declares that the Paraclete will recall what Jesus has said. But the later redactor has expanded this material. New revelation of what Jesus has yet to say is promised in 16:12-13.

Although many of Müller's suggestions are convincing and helpful, it is possible that he has pushed his thesis too far. All aspects of Jesus' farewell that fail to fit his paradigm are secondary. But must Jesus' farewell be entirely Jewish? Is there no room for Christian distinctives? It should not surprise us that the Paraclete will judge the world. Jesus already claimed to be just such a judge (John 5:22, 30; 8:16; 12:31). Also, continuing revelation was a basic aspect

---

103. R. Schnackenburg, *John*, 3: 147-50.
104. Müller, "Die Parakletenvorstellung," 69-70.

of the earliest church's experience of the Spirit (Luke 24:45-46; 1 Cor. 2:13; Eph. 1:17-18).[105] Therefore it likewise need not stem from Jewish apocalyptic sources. Against Müller, John 15 and 16 may be that which makes Jesus' farewell discourse fully his own and in harmony with the earliest understanding of the Spirit.

e. The Development of an Old Testament Theme

A less common but certainly no less important approach to the Paraclete problem is provided by those who see a unique OT theological motif standing behind παράκλητος.

Alan Richardson notes how παρακαλεῖν carries a "marked eschatological sense" in Isaiah's anticipations of the future (Isa. 66:13 LXX).[106] Isaiah's concluding chapter depicts the coming of the Lord with stormwinds and fire (66:15-16)—both paralleling the Christian Pentecost of Acts 2. In the same way, Simeon of Luke 2:25 is expecting the παράκλησις of Israel. He is looking for Isaiah's longed-for messianic comfort (cf. Isa. 40:1; 51:12; etc.). Thus it is clear that what Isaiah had predicted, the early Christian community knew it had received in Christ and the Spirit (Matt. 5:4; cf. Luke 4:17-21; 2 Cor. 1:7; Rev. 7:17; 21:4). From this consistent early use of παρακαλεῖν, Richardson wonders if John has found in his Paraclete the fulfillment and personal experience of Isaiah's comfort.

J. G. Davies has given substantial linguistic support for translating παράκλητος with "comforter."[107] His starting point is a "contextual study" of the Paraclete. He has identified the critical word groups surrounding παράκλητος in John and located similar contexts in the LXX which use παρακαλεῖν. His conclusions show that נחם is usually the Hebrew equivalent and that a high concentration of such passages are to be found in Isaiah (esp. Isa. 66:10-19—66:14 is possibly cited in John 16:22). Therefore Davies concludes it is highly likely that John was familiar with the Isaiah passages of eschatological comfort and incorporated these word-groups into his Farewell Discourses.[108]

For Bruce Vawter, both the Paraclete and John's Son of Man christology point to Ezekiel's influence on the Fourth Evangelist.[109] Vawter does not wish

---

105. See J. D. G. Dunn, *Jesus and the Spirit* (London: SCM; Philadelphia: Westminster, 1975) 212-48.

106. A. Richardson, *An Introduction to the Theology of the New Testament* (New York: Harper & Row, 1958) 114-16; cf. idem, *Christian Apologetics* (London: SCM, 1947) 211-20.

107. J. G. Davies, "The Primary Meaning of Παράκλητος," *JTS* 4 (1953) 35-38; see also G. Reim, *Studien zum alttestamentlichen Hintergrund des Johannesevangeliums* (Cambridge: University Press, 1974) 162-83; and F. W. Young, "A Study of the Relation of Isaiah to the Fourth Gospel," *ZNW* 46 (1955) 215-33.

108. Leaney, "The Johannine Paraclete," 42, suggests that Nicodemus in John 3 was searching for the נחם of Israel. C. K. Barrett, "The Holy Spirit in the Fourth Gospel," 9, notes that in the fragment of the Acts of John in Ox. Pap. 850:10, "Jesus is called the Paraclete, evidently meaning 'comforter.'" See idem, *John*, 462, on "messianic consolation" and the Paraclete.

109. B. Vawter, "Ezekiel and John," *CBQ* 26 (1964) 450-58; cf. idem, "Johannine Theology," in *The Jerome Biblical Commentary*, ed. R. E. Brown, J. A. Fitzmyer, and R. E. Murphy (London: Chapman, 1968) 2: 836-37.

to imply any verbal connection between the two, but rather that there has been a marked conceptual influence. The prophetic role of the Paraclete as one who witnesses, convicts, and proclaims is well known. It is striking, however, that this image is combined with priestly mediatorial tasks which parallel Ezekiel's prophetic/priestly functions.[110] Ezekiel was a classical prophet, yet he saw his life as bearing the suffering of his people (Ezek. 12:6-7; 21:11-12). Israel's sins were laid on him (4:4-8) and he interceded on their behalf (9:8; 11:13). This dual role, argues Vawter, helped to form John's figure of the Paraclete.

Research has regularly affirmed the central place of personified OT Wisdom in much of the Fourth Gospel. John's Logos christology is generally pointed out as direct evidence that John not only knew but "quoted words and phrases" from OT and apocryphal wisdom sources.[111] As early as 1917, J. R. Harris argued that almost everything declared about the Logos in John's prologue had been affirmed elsewhere in Jewish sapiential literature for Wisdom.[112]

These same conclusions have been recently applied to the Paraclete. M. E. Isaacs has studied the related use of σοφία, λόγος, and πνεῦμα in late Judaism.[113] She claims that the figure of Wisdom in Hellenistic Judaism supplied John with his pattern for the Paraclete. In both traditions, Wisdom and Spirit are personified and sent from God (Wis. 7:7; John 14:26). Wisdom dwells with God's chosen people (Sir. 24:12; John 14:17) and brings the gift of understanding (Sir. 24:26-27; John 14:26). Wisdom reveals the future (Sir. 24:33; John 16:13) and is rejected by humanity (1 En. 42:2; John 14:17). R. E. Brown even notes that John 15:26-27 may parallel Matt. 10:19-20 in that the Spirit is promised in a persecution setting. It is curious, however, that in the parallel Synoptic passage of Luke 21:14-15, wisdom (not personified) is promised.[114] So compelling are these parallels that H. Riesenfeld has concluded, "It is probable that the sapiential texts describing Wisdom in her peculiar comforting functions have given rise to the idea as well as to the name Paraclete."[115]

---

110. Cullmann argues that this priestly concept as seen esp. in Hebrews provided the impetus for John's concept of the Paraclete, *The Christology of the New Testament*, tr. S. C. Guthrie and C. A. M. Hall (London: SCM; Philadelphia: Westminster, 1959) 106-7.

111. E. M. Sidebottom, *The Christ of the Fourth Gospel* (London: SPCK, 1961) 203, 201n.2; see also B. DePinto, "Word and Wisdom in St. John," *SCR* 19 (1967) 20-27; Cullmann, *Christology*, 256-57; Brown, *John*, 1:cxxii; Morris, *John*, 115-26.

112. J. R. Harris, *The Origin of the Prologue to St. John's Gospel* (Cambridge: University Press, 1917) 43.

113. M. E. Isaacs, *The Concept of Spirit*, Heythrop Monographs 1 (London: 1976) 135-37; F. Nötscher believes that at Qumran the Holy Spirit is likewise "the Spirit of Wisdom"; see "Geist und Geister in den Texten von Qumran," in *Mélanges Bibliques rédigés en l'honneur de André Robert* (Paris: Bloud et Gay, 1957) 305-15.

114. C. K. Barrett, *The Holy Spirit in the Synoptic Tradition* (London: SPCK, 1966) 131-32, is convinced that the promise of Wisdom in Luke 21:14 "preserves the oldest form of the logion." The other Synoptic persecution promises of the Spirit (Mark 13:11; Matt. 10:19-20; Luke 12:11-12) are "due to church interpretation and application." He believes that the Holy Spirit "was what the church later experienced, not what it had been led to expect."

115. H. Riesenfeld, "A Probable Background to the Johannine Paraclete," in *Ex Orbe Religionum: Studia Geo. Widengren*, ed. C. J. Bleeker et al. (Leiden: Brill, 1972) 272-73; Riesenfeld

4. Conclusion

From our survey it appears that the attempts of Bauer and Bultmann to find an antecedent to the Paraclete in proto-Gnostic revealer figures should be considered unfruitful. The parallels stemming from the OT and intertestamental Judaism are far too persuasive. In particular, the extensive work of Mowinckel and Johansson cannot be dismissed lightly. Serious attention must at all times be given to the fact that John has chosen a particular title for the Spirit, ὁ παράκλητος, and this title received specific attention in the intertestamental concern about advocacy. Scholars are right in their objection that not all of the functions of the Paraclete fit this background. But this discrepancy can be explained in terms of development. In the course of our study we hope to show how the Fourth Evangelist has elevated the forensic metaphor to a literary motif both for his pneumatology and for his presentation of Christ. Moreover, it is just this metaphor that inspired the Johannine interest in revelation. The Spirit Paraclete was a Jewish idea that had undergone thorough Johannine development.

Betz and Johnston helpfully bring to our attention the importance of Qumran and its dualism. To be sure, reflections of the Johannine Paraclete can be seen here (although there is insufficient evidence for dependence). But while late Jewish angelology certainly employed the notion of advocacy, it is incorrect to apply this heavenly drama (and its constituent characters, e.g., Michael) to John. Both Qumran and John have specialized in their own unique ways the juridical metaphor which they inherited from Judaism. Qumran may have found its principal advocate in Michael, but John has independently found his advocate first in Christ and then in the Spirit. *The personal metaphors surrounding the Johannine Spirit Paraclete therefore stem from Christ, not from a model of an intercessory angel.*

Finally, it has become increasingly clear that the Johannine presentation of the Paraclete is extremely nuanced. In particular, as we hope to explain below, the Fourth Evangelist's christology and eschatology have been primary contributors in this presentation. Bornkamm's mention of OT succesor motifs is helpful only if we accept the proviso that John does not adopt the idea that this Spirit is a "perfecter." Here Müller's contribution is a certain step forward in that the genre of the Farewell Discourses has been identified and aligned with numerous relevant models. Contra Bornkamm, Müller shows that the spotlight must remain on Jesus and his departure. The center point is Christ. The Paraclete is Jesus' provision for the disciples while he is away, and this provision involves not only the continuation of his presence but the advance of his work—- particularly the work of revelation. Again, the work never belongs to the Paraclete. It is christocentric throughout.

Our conclusion regarding the backgrounds of the Paraclete suggests that a well-formulated Jewish idea had landed in the extremely fertile theological

---

made a presentation of this thesis in August, 1971, at a seminar of the Society for New Testament Studies in Noordwijkerhout, Holland. The Notes and report of the seminar's director, I. de la Potterie, appear in *NTS* 18 (1971-72) 448-51.

soil of the Johannine community. In fact, many scholars, while not denying the importance of these backgrounds, would stress that the events in earliest Christianity were of primary importance in John's thought. This perception is accurate. The Fourth Evangelist's reconstruction of this traditional Jewish image was so elaborate that only the vestiges of the traditional model may be extant.

C. THE PARACLETE IN JOHANNINE REFLECTION

1. PERSECUTION SAYINGS

For R. E. Brown, John 15:18–16:4a "may be the key to how the figure of the Paraclete came to play such an important role in the Johannine discourse." Elsewhere he remarks, "Although this traditional material has been shaped into Johannine thought patterns, no other long section of Johannine discourse resembles a section of synoptic discourse so closely as does John 15:18–16:4a."[116] For example, in 15:18 Jesus warns of the world's hatred (Matt. 10:22; 24:19 par.) and in v. 20 he speaks of coming persecutions (cf. Matt. 10:23; Luke 21:12). Verse 21 gives the reason: "All this they will do to you on my account" (cf. Matt. 10:22; Mark 13:13). But despite this persecution, the Paraclete will be present (John 15:26; cf. Matt. 10:20; Mark 13:11). Indeed, Jesus has given these teachings to keep the disciples' faith "from being shaken" (John 16:1; Matt. 24:10) because they will be cast out of the synagogues (John 16:2; Matt. 10:17 par.) and even killed (Matt. 24:9; Luke 21:16). For Brown, these parallels are conclusive. "It is precisely this mention of the Spirit in the context of facing the persecution of the world that may have been the principal catalyst for the development of John's understanding of the Paraclete."[117]

This thesis has received its most comprehensive presentation in an important study by J. Kremer.[118] Kremer does not feel compelled to demonstrate the authenticity of the Paraclete sayings from the Synoptic sources. In fact, his final conclusion is that these Johannine discourses probably do not represent the *ipsissima verba Jesu*. But they are legitimate promises of Jesus securely rooted in the earliest Synoptic traditions. For him, the question of strict authenticity is neither a vital nor a useful quest. Instead, he asks, "What major concepts can be credibly anchored in Jesus' historical ministry?"

Kremer begins his essay with hermeneutical reflections about the skepticism of modern critical scholarship. For example, we maintain the reliability of Jesus' persecution warnings but reject his discourses about the Spirit. It is true that the early church's experience of the Spirit was primary—and that this experience sparked avid reflection of Jesus' teachings. But does this necessarily

---

116. Brown, *John*, 2: 699, 685; also R. H. Strachan, *The Fourth Gospel. Its Significance and Environment*, 3rd ed. (London: SCM, 1941) 285-89; C. H. Dodd, *Historical Tradition*, 407-13; D. Hill, *Greek Words and Hebrew Meanings* (Cambridge: University Press, 1967) 292.

117. Brown, *John*, 2: 699; cf. A. E. Harvey, *Jesus on Trial*, 107ff.

118. J. Kremer, "Jesu Verheissung des Geistes. Zur Verankerung der Aussage von Joh 16:13 im Leben Jesu," in *Die Kirche des Anfangs*, 247-76; see the discussion of Porsch, *Pneuma*, 268-69, 320-22.

invalidate the possibility that Jesus spoke of the Spirit? Does this historical sequence mean that Jesus' Spirit sayings must be church creations justifying the early experience? For Kremer, the answer is no. He feels that modern presuppositions may be as biased as those regularly attributed to the ancients.[119]

A good case in point are the Johannine Paraclete sayings. Kremer focuses on John 16:12-13, and works to anchor it securely into the life of Jesus.

First, John 16:12 suggests that Jesus had more to teach the disciples, but their doubting and fearful condition prohibited Jesus from giving them this teaching. Therefore Jesus affirms that a later situation will change the present situation. Jesus has hope. Has he come to grips with his death and found the disciples unable to bear it? Are these "the things that are to come" (16:13)? It is natural to expect that Jesus would make some provision for his followers. He has experienced persecution and will promise aid for the same severe treatment to come. Therefore, according to Kremer, Jesus' logical provision of the Paraclete is exactly what we should expect.

Second, it comes as no surprise then to find parallels in the Synoptic tradition. After the significance of Jesus' death was comprehended, persecution continued. Therefore Jesus' persecution promises were elevated in importance. Kremer carefully examines the traditions of Spirit promises in the Synoptics. Consistent parallels with John suggest to him that the Paraclete sayings are "the Johannine rendering of the earliest church tradition."[120]

Finally, Kremer discusses the context of Jesus' preaching about the kingdom. In the Jewish world of his time, how could Jesus talk about the coming reign of God without mentioning the coming Spirit? Jewish expectation would demand mention of the Spirit. Furthermore, how do we explain the fact that the early church saw this expectation to be fulfilled (cf. Joel 2:28-29; Acts 2:17)? They had the Spirit and were equipped with the power of the kingdom. Therefore, Kremer concludes, these sayings must be firmly rooted in Jesus' own words.[121]

2. CHRISTOLOGY AND ESCHATOLOGY

In his brief discussion of current trends on Johannine theology, C. K. Barrett notes how the interpretation of John must be fundamentally christological.[122] The figure of Jesus is foremost in the Fourth Evangelist's thought. But another problem plagued John's generation: namely, eschatology. Elsewhere Barrett writes that "the earliest task of Christian apologists was to explain the novel

---

119. Kremer, ibid., 247-52; 261-62.

120. Ibid., 265.

121. See M. deJonge, "Jewish Expectations about 'Messiah' According to the Fourth Gospel," *NTS* 19 (1973) 246-70.

122. Barrett, *John*, 97. Porsch, *Pneuma*, 405-406, concludes that John links christology and pneumatology in a way different from any other NT writing. Cf. W. Schmithals, "Geisterfahrung als Christuserfahrung," in *Erfahrung und Theologie des heiligen Geist*, ed. C. Heitmann and H. Mühlen, (Hamburg: Agentur des Rauen Hauses; München: Kösel, 1974) 101-17, esp. 114-15; cf. R. E. Brown, "The Kerygma of the Gospel According to St. John," *Int* 21 (1967) 387-92.

position of a messianic community whose Messiah had lived in obscurity, died, and been taken up to heaven, but who had not appeared in power and glory. The explanation given, and prompted by the unprecedented gift of God to the church, was in terms of the Holy Spirit."[123] According to Barrett, the Fourth Gospel is a thorough attempt by an early Evangelist to solve this problem using the Spirit. Yet here christology "spills over" into eschatology. In John the Spirit Paraclete had adopted personal features similar to the person of Jesus. If Jesus has come forth from the Father (6:57) so will the Paraclete (15:26). As Jesus was sent (3:17) so is the Paraclete (16:7). If the Paraclete is the Spirit of Truth, Jesus is the Truth (14:6). If the Paraclete is the Holy Spirit, Jesus is the Holy One of God (6:69). As the world cannot receive the Paraclete (14:17), so too evil persons do not accept Jesus (5:43; 12:48). "As *another Paraclete*, the Paraclete is, as it were, another Jesus."[124] In what way, we might ask, has John developed his image of the Paraclete from the image of Christ found in the Gospel of John? Is the Paraclete in fact Jesus returned?

In his study on salvation in John, T. Müller has noted the important link between the person of Christ and the Spirit.[125] There are, he contends, three possible approaches to relating the Spirit and Christ. First, the Spirit may be posited as another, separate entity who replaces Jesus at his death. His link with Jesus is secondary while his autonomous origins are generally highlighted. Here no doubt the work of Betz and Bultmann are to be found. In contrast, however, such scholars as E. F. Scott and I. Simpson once believed that this view is just the mistaken notion that John is wishing to correct.[126] Second, the Spirit may be seen as a separate person working closely and intimately with the living, glorified Christ. Third, the Spirit may be identical with the glorified Christ. As we discuss christology and eschatology, it is the last two categories which shall hold our interest. How does John's Christ-like Paraclete relate to Jesus in the problem of early eschatology?

a. An Eschatological Continuum

Barrett and Brown understand John to have linked the Paraclete closely with Jesus. That is to say, he is "the presence of Jesus when Jesus is absent."[127] Barrett concludes, "the Spirit's work is to bear witness to Christ [and] to make operative what Christ had already effected. The Spirit is thus the eschatologi-

123. Barrett, "The Holy Spirit in the Fourth Gospel," 1; cf. idem, *The Holy Spirit and the Gospel Tradition*, 122-62; Barrett discusses his conclusions with his critics (esp. Beasley-Murray and Kümmel) in "Important Hypotheses Reconsidered: The Holy Spirit and the Gospel Tradition," *ExpTim* 67 (1955-56) 142-45.

124. Brown, "The Paraclete," 128; for parallels between Jesus and the Paraclete, see Brown, *John*, 2: 1140-41; Porsch, *Pneuma*, 239, 322-24; Bornkamm, "Der Paraklet," 79-81; and A. L. Mansure, "The Relation of the Paraclete to the Spiritual Presence of Jesus in the Fourth Gospel" (unpub. diss., Boston, 1950). We will discuss this subject at length in chapter 3 below.

125. T. Müller, *Das Heilsgeschehen im Johannesevangelium* (Zurich: Gotthelf-Verlag, 1961) 80-81.

126. E. F. Scott, *The Fourth Gospel*, 320-21; and I. G. Simpson, "The Holy Spirit in the Fourth Gospel," *Exp* 4 (1925) 292-99.

127. Brown, *John*, 2: 1139.

cal continuum in which the work of Christ, initiated in his ministry and awaiting its termination at his return, is wrought out."[128] Therefore John's futurist eschatology is maintained by making the Spirit an interim figure present in lieu of Jesus until the consummation of the age. He is the alter ego of Jesus but not Jesus himself.

We have already noted that Brown sees Jesus' persecution promises as the catalyst behind John's Paraclete. But he feels that the Jesus-Paraclete connection was the dominant theme nurtured in John's community. Two problems in John's *Sitz im Leben* brought about this reflection.[129] First, there was the confusion caused by the death of the apostolic eyewitnesses. Formerly the community had a visible link between itself and Jesus. But now this security had been severed. Undoubtedly, the impact of the death of the Beloved Disciple (the eyewitness par excellence, 19:35; 21:24) was of critical concern. But here the Paraclete fulfills a vital role. Only through the post-resurrection gift of the Spirit did the apostles understand what they had seen (2:22; 12:16), and now this very Spirit dwelt with all Christians (14:17). In one sense the Gospel itself was a Spirit/Paraclete-inspired work which tangibly linked the Johannine community with the historical Jesus.

The second problem was the delay of the parousia. No doubt a few had expected Jesus' return within the lifetime of some of his companions (Mark 13:30; Matt. 10:23). This group certainly included the Beloved Disciple (21:23). The deaths of these eyewitnesses, the delay, and a growing skepticism (cf. 2 Pet. 3:3-10; Jude 18) produced great anguish. But the Paraclete brought a profound answer. John did not lose hope in the parousia but emphasized that in a way Christ had come back already. "The Christian need not live with his eyes constantly straining toward the heavens from which the Son of Man is to come; for as the Paraclete, Jesus is present within all believers."[130]

Barrett accepts that it was this eschatological tension that caused John to wrestle "afresh with the problem which had confronted the primitive church when it looked for the Lord and received the Spirit."[131] He would, however, add a third *Sitz im Leben*. How does the Paraclete continue and complete the work of Christ? John's answer is the church. This also may "be described as the eschatological *continuum* in which the purposes of God are being worked out."[132] Barrett continues that it is for this reason that we should understand

---

128. Barrett, *John*, 90; these views are shared by J. D. G. Dunn, *Jesus and the Spirit*, 351, 356; R. P. Martin, *New Testament Foundations*, 2 vols. (Grand Rapids: Eerdmans, 1975, 1978) 1: 276, 286; and W. R. Hutton, "The Johannine Doctrine of the Holy Spirit," *CrozQ* 24 (1947) 334-44.

129. Brown, *John*, 2:1142-43; Barrett, "The Holy Spirit," 1ff.

130. Brown, *John*, 2: 1143 and 1: lxxviii; cf. Barrett, *John*, 139-40; and R. Kysar, *John: The Maverick Gospel* (Atlanta: John Knox, 1976) 84ff. Against the significance of the delay of the parousia for John, see S. Smalley, *John, Evangelist and Interpreter*, 130-32; and idem, "The Delay of the Parousia," *JBL* 83 (1964) 41-54; cf. R. J. Bauckham, "The Delay of the Parousia," *TynBul* 31 (1980) 3-36.

131. Barrett, "The Holy Spirit in the Fourth Gospel," 3; cf. idem, "The Place of Eschatology in the Fourth Gospel," *ExpTim* 59 (1947-48) 302-305.

132. Barrett, *John*, 90. The importance of the church in John's understanding of the Spirit is also emphasized by S. Smalley, *John, Evangelist and Interpreter*, 227-35; cf. W. B. Hunt, "John's Doctrine of the Spirit," *SWJT* 8 (1965) 45-65.

the meaning of παράκλητος through the NT usage of παρακαλεῖν and παρά-κλησις. The church's prophetic Christian preaching was the repository of the ministering activities of the Spirit Paraclete.

The idea that the eschatological presence of Christ in the Paraclete manifests itself in the ministry of the church has received particular attention from G. Johnston and J. L. Martyn. We have already seen how Johnston wishes to affirm that the Paraclete "becomes visible in a very real way in those 'representatives' or 'Paracletes' who are the Christian prophets, remembrancers, teachers, and martyrs of the Johannine church."[133] Martyn believes that the Paraclete descriptions parallel not only Christ but also the call of the Christian witness.[134] This then is the presence of Christ through the Paraclete. If Christ and the Paraclete have been sent into the world, so has the Christian witness (17:15). The world did not know Jesus or the Paraclete—for this reason it will not "know" the Christian (1 John 3:1). The world hated them, so too it will hate the witness (John 15:18). The Paraclete works to duplicate and recall the works and words of Jesus, just as the Christian is promised that "he who believes in me will also do the works that I do" (14:12). Martyn sums up: "The paradox presented by Jesus' promise that his work on earth will be continued because he is going to the Father is 'solved' by his return in the person of the Paraclete. It is, therefore, precisely the Paraclete who creates *the two-level drama*. . . . In order for the Paraclete to create [this] two-level drama, he must look not only like Jesus, but also like the Christian witness who is Jesus' 'double' in that drama."[135]

b. Pentecost Becomes Parousia

In their understanding of Johannine eschatology, Barrett and Brown would say that John has replaced the realized eschatology of the Synoptic Gospels with his own specialized doctrine of the Paraclete. In contrast, other scholars believe that John's Paraclete replaced futurist eschatology as well. C. H. Dodd once remarked that "in the Fourth Gospel the crudely eschatological elements in the kerygma are quite refined away."[136] E. F. Scott feels that John "has grasped the underlying truth of the parousia while discarding the inadequate form, and is able to conceive of Christ as already come and inwardly present to his people."[137] According to Scott, John wrestled with the first-century's eschatologi-

---

133. *Spirit-Paraclete*, 16, 126, 127-28.

134. J. L. Martyn, *History and Theology in the Fourth Gospel*, 2nd ed. (New York: Harper & Row, 1979) 143-51.

135. Ibid., 148.

136. C. H. Dodd, *Apostolic Preaching*, 65; cf. J. A.T Robinson, *Jesus and His Coming* (London: SCM, 1957) 160-85; G. B. Stevens, *The Theology of the New Testament* (Edinburgh: T. & T. Clark, 1918) 215-16.

137. *The Fourth Gospel*, 348; E. K. Lee holds this view as well: "The evangelist wishes us to understand that Christ's promise had been fulfilled in a manner quite different from the expectation of the early disciples. He deliberately interprets the Second Coming as a spiritual and invisible coming by the Holy Spirit into the hearts of believers" (*The Religious Thought of St. John* [London: SPCK, 1950] 210); cf. H. Schlier, "Zum Begriff des Geistes nach dem Johannesevangelium," in

cal crisis and found in the Paraclete an answer corresponding to Paul's mystical union with Christ (Χριστός ἐν ὑμῖν, Col. 1:27; cf. John 14:17). The most important expositor of this thesis has undoubtedly been R. Bultmann. We noted earlier how Bultmann suggested that the origin of the Paraclete was to be found in the Mandean figure of Yawar. He added, however, that John's doctrine of the Spirit represented a profound reworking of early eschatology. "For John, Easter, Pentecost, and the Parousia are not three separate events, but one and the same. Consequently, the terminology appropriate to Easter again and again mingles with that appropriate to the parousia. And into the midst of these the promise of the Spirit is thrust. But the one event that is meant by all these is not an external occurrence, but an inner one: the victory which Jesus wins when faith arises in man."[138]

Therefore the presence of the Spirit becomes the presence of Christ—and the possibility of differentiating the two is lost when the idea of a later parousia is fully jettisoned. For Bultmann, then, the believer can have a complete eschatological existence because in the Spirit, Christ and the eschaton have already come to him. But is the sphere of the Spirit's life only in faith and in the heart? Bultmann would point to the church as well and in particular to proclamation. "The Paraclete marks no new stage of development in the history of dogma. Nor is he an 'inner light' or anything of that sort. He is Jesus himself who will come to his own in the Paraclete. The promise of the Paraclete is nothing other than the promise that the *revelation* will be continued in the community's proclamation of the word. The 'witness' of the Paraclete is the authorized witness-bearing of the community."[139]

3. WITNESS AND REVELATION

In concert with Bultmann's emphasis on revelation, some scholars have argued that the Paraclete is John's vehicle for assuring his readers that either Jesus' own words were not forgotten (ὑπομιμνήσκειν, 14:26) or that new prophetic revelation will continue (ἀναγγέλλειν τὰ ἐρχόμενα, 16:13). B. Olsson sees in John 14:25 two stages in the revelatory work of Christ. Jesus spoke plainly to the disciples and yet there will still be a need for "all things" to

---

Besinnung auf das Neue Testment, Exegetische Aufsätze und Vortrage II (Freiburg: Herder, 1964) 264-71. Schlier comments (p. 268): "The return of Jesus is his coming in his glory through his glorious revealed spirit. If this is so, then that which is mentioned in the Gospel about the second coming of Jesus can and must also be referred to the Spirit in which he comes. Jesus will come to the disciples in the Spirit (John 14:3, 18, 23, 28)."

138. Bultmann, *Theology*, 2: 57; 1: 153-64; cf. R. Kysar, "The Eschatology of the Fourth Gospel. A Correction of Bultmann's Redactional Hypothesis," *Perspective* 13 (1972) 23-33; the chief aim of D. E. Holwerda's study, *The Holy Spirit and Eschatology in the Gospel of John: A Critique of R. Bultmann's Present Eschatology*, is to disprove Bultmann's demythologization of consistent eschatology through a study of the Fourth Gospel. Holwerda's often difficult exegetical "proofs" have received unfavorable acceptance. So P. W. Meyer: "The total argument of the book I find to be entirely unconvincing" (*JBL* 79 [1960] 179-81); see also the review by F. F. Bruce, *EvQ* 32 (1960) 172.

139. R. Bultmann, "The Eschatology of the Gospel of John," in *Faith and Understanding I*, tr. L. P. Smith, ed. R. W. Funk (London: SCM, 1969) 178.

be taught again by the Paraclete (14:26). "The Paraclete will realize all Jesus' sayings to the disciples, he will interpret them in their situation and thus give rise to new insights and experiences."[140] Texts such as John 2:22 and 12:16 suggest that Jesus tradition has not only been recalled but recalled correctly, through the work of the Spirit (cf. μιμνήσκομαι, 2:22; 12:16; ὑπομιμνήσκειν, 14:26; cf. Luke 24:44-45, τότε διήνοιξεν αὐτῶν τὸν νοῦν τοῦ συνιέναι τὰς γραφάς). According to two lengthy studies by A. Kothgasser, the Spirit has become the authority and motive for John's own Gospel. John's message is therefore a "thoroughgoing recollection by the Spirit; a new insight, understanding, and experience of the entire reality of Christ." Hence John writes the history of Jesus "not κατὰ σάρκα, but rather κατὰ πνεῦμα, and so his Gospel becomes the spiritual Gospel."[141]

Felix Porsch and I. de la Potterie are the most recent spokesmen in this concern for Johannine revelation. For them, both the Paraclete and Christ must be first understood within John's literary technique of a "trial motif" (Prozessmotivs). De la Potterie comments: "The Sitz im Leben of these five [Paraclete] passages is that of the great theological trial between Jesus and the world. In the Paraclete promises [John] does not envisage anything more than this ambiguous reality of the 'world' which is hostile to Jesus."[142]

Porsch feels that this motif is a formal development from the Synoptic conflict sayings. Jesus' encounter with the world (further identified as the Jews) is described as a judicial debate. The world is on trial before God because (ironically) Jesus is on trial before the Jews. Witnesses enter, testify, and disappear. But it is the testimony of the Son which is crucial. His testimony is revelation: "For this I have come into the world, to bear witness to the truth" (18:37). His testimony cannot be checked or verified. Porsch remarks: "Jesus testifies basically always to himself, of his divine origins, or of his mission, his sonship, and his unity with the Father. He is the same as the revelation which he brings so that in him the revelation and the revealer are one."[143]

De la Potterie and Porsch are convinced that the Paraclete stems from this dual origin of judicial conflict and revelation. "Only in this particular context does the hatred of the world allow us to understand effectively the five

---

140. B. Olsson, *Structure and Meaning in the Fourth Gospel* (Lund: Gleerup, 1974) 269; also see I. de la Potterie, "Le Paraclet," in *La Vie Selon l'Esprit. Condition du Chrétien*, ed. I. de la Potterie and S. Lyonnet (Paris: Cerf, 1965) 85-105; H. Schlier, "Zum Begriff des Geistes," 267, 271-72; O. Cullmann, *The Johannine Circle*, 18-19; J. E. Yates, "The Spirit as Producer of the Gospel History," in *The Spirit and the Kingdom* (London: SPCK, 1963) 215-31.

141. See A. M. Kothgasser, "Die Lehr-, Erinnerungs-, Bezeugungs-, und Einführungsfunktion des johanneischen Geist-Paraklet gegenüber der Christus-Offenbarung," *Salesianum* 33 (1971) 593; see also idem, 34 (1972) 2-51. Kothgasser stresses that the Paraclete reveals nothing new but simply supplies new understanding of what Jesus has already said and done; see esp. 33: 590-98 and 34: 29-34.

142. I. de la Potterie, *La Verité dans Saint Jean*, chap. 5, "Le Paraclet, L'Esprit de la Vérité," citation, p. 468; see also pp. 336-39 and 396-99; cf. Porsch, *Pneuma*, 222-27. On this theme generally, see T. Preiss, *Life in Christ* (London: SCM, 1954) 9-31; O. Betz, *Der Paraklet*, 120-26; A. E. Harvey, *Jesus on Trial: A Study of the Fourth Gospel*, 107-108; and A. A. Trites, *The New Testament Concept of Witness* (Cambridge: University Press, 1977) 78-128, esp. 113-24.

143. F. Porsch, *Pneuma*, 225-26.

promises [of the Paraclete] with their synthesis of traits which are sometimes judicial and forensic, sometimes kerygmatic and doctrinal."[144] In this forensic setting Jesus could be termed a Paraclete. But now the disciples share in these conflicts and their Aid (the Spirit) can rightly be termed a Paraclete as well. This discrepancy between the forensic title and revelatory functions of the Paraclete's testimony to believers becomes revelation precisely because it recalls the truth (the revelation) which Jesus himself spoke (16:12-13). Thus it comes as no surprise to find the Paraclete called the Spirit of Truth. That is, he "is the Spirit which always leads us more deeply into the truth of Jesus." Hence the Paraclete can never function autonomously from the person of Christ. Porsch concludes: "Behind the presentation of the Fourth Gospel stands simply the experience of the church. The Spirit had introduced it to the revelation of Jesus and this Spirit was even the 'Spirit of Jesus' (cf. 2 Cor. 3:17; 1 Cor. 12:3) whose work entirely referred to the person and work of Jesus. Consequently he appeared as the one who continues the revelation of Jesus. Or better still, he is the one who realizes Jesus' revelation."[145]

4. PROPHETS AND PROPHECY

Interest in the Paraclete from the vantage point of revelation has taken a unique turn in those scholars who ask if the Paraclete is actually a disguised prophetic figure in John's community. As we have seen, Johnston understands specific church functionaries to be behind the Paraclete. F. Mussner has advanced the hypothesis that the Paraclete was promised only to the Twelve, who alone "incarnated" his activity.[146] A. Kragerud and others have submitted that the Beloved Disciple himself was the Paraclete who served as a model charismatic figure.[147]

In a provocative article M. E. Boring has suggested that John molded both the figure of Jesus and that of the Paraclete from "traits taken from the Christian prophets of his own church."[148] Concerning the Johannine Jesus, Boring notes how the title of Prophet is reserved almost exclusively for him. Jesus' miracles (signs) are subordinate to his message in John and point to the early prophetic activity of declaration accompanied by charismatic phenomena. In John, Jesus performs no exorcisms—because (supposedly) such never occurred among Christian prophets. But Jesus is an ecstatic much like the prophets: he experiences "hyper-excitement" (2:17), he neglects to eat (4:32), and his preaching is termed a "cry" (κράζειν, 7:28, 37; 12:44).[149] He

---

144. I. de la Potterie, *La Verité dans Saint Jean*, 468; Porsch, op. cit., 322-24.

145. Porsch, *Pneuma*, 323-24; Porsch uncovers revelatory language for the Paraclete esp. in the use of διδάσκειν and ὑπομμνήσκειν, 257-67; on John 14:26 see esp. pp. 265-66.

146. F. Mussner, "Die johanneisch Parakletsprüche," 67-69.

147. A. Kragerud, *Der Lieblingsjunger im Johannesevangelium. Ein Exegetischer Versuch* (Oslo: Universitätverlag, 1959); H. Sasse, "Der Paraklet im Johannesevangelium," *ZNW* 24 (1925) 260-77; Schlier, "Zum Begriff des Geistes," 269-70.

148. M. E. Boring, "The Influence of Christian Prophecy on the Johannine Portrayal of the Paraclete and Jesus," *NTS* 25 (1978) 113-23; citation, 120; cf. E. Schweizer, *TDNT* 6: 443-44.

149. These suggestions are vulnerable at every point. If anything, ecstatic activity is a theme

provokes hostility with the world (4:44), he is charged with being mad (7:20), and he is persecuted for "leading the people astray" (7:12, 47). Boring argues that all these stem from the activities and experiences of early prophetism.

Boring's discussion of Jesus is instructive for us because of the close connection between Jesus and the Paraclete. These parallels between the two serve to assure the reader that such prophetic activity is legitimately to continue into his own day. Boring gathers eleven correspondences between early prophets and the Paraclete from which we can only note a sampling. (1) In early Christian circles, to speak of the presence of the Holy Spirit was tantamount to claiming the "rebirth of prophecy."[150] (2) The verbs describing the work of the Paraclete all relate to speech functions (λαλεῖν, ἀναγγέλλειν, διδάσκειν, μαρτυρεῖν, even παρακαλεῖν) and suggest a "pneumatic Christian speech charisma." (3) Most compelling is the Johannine "revelatory chain-of-command": Father/Jesus/Paraclete/Community/World (John 14:16; 15:26). In the Apocalypse of the Johannine community (Rev. 1:1-2) a parallel chain emerges with two noteworthy exceptions: Father/Jesus/*Angel*/*Prophet*/Community/World. "The Paraclete seems to combine the roles of the revelatory angel and the Christian prophet."[151] (4) Both the close dependence of the Paraclete on the words of Jesus (recalling, etc.) and the absence of any of its own intrinsic authority (16:13b) underscore the prophet's responsibility only to transmit what has been given to him.

Without doubt, Boring has read the evidence correctly. General parallels between the Paraclete and early prophetism do exist. Nevertheless, some of his conclusions are unfounded. The portraits of Jesus and the Paraclete need not have been formed from the early prophetic office. Indeed, any prophet wishing to legitimize his role might conform himself to the pattern of Jesus or to the predictions of Jesus. Furthermore, if the Paraclete promises are authentic, their realization in early church figures should hardly be used as evidence demonstrating the talents of John's literary hand. The Paraclete may have created the prophetic office, but the later office did not necessarily formulate the earlier promise. Finally, Boring fails to deal with the concern about false prophets in the Johannine community (1 John 4:1). Could prophetism have been discredited in John's circle of believers? Why are there no positive remarks about the role of the prophet in the Johannine literature?

Central to this discussion about prophecy is the tacit assumption of Boring and others that the Paraclete promises "should not be taken in a mystical sense to refer individually to every believer, particularly since the Paraclete is represented as distinct from the disciples in general. . . . This would seem to portray a function within the community performed by an identifiable group endowed with the Spirit in a particular manner and exercis-

---

John has not emphasized in his christology. John 2:17 and 4:32 hardly qualify as supporting evidence. See Barrett, "The Holy Spirit in the Fourth Gospel," 3-4; and E. Schweizer, *TDNT* 6: 438, esp. 438n.714.

150. M. E. Boring, "The Influence of Christian Prophecy," 113; cf. J. Jeremias, *New Testament Theology*, 75; Dunn, *Jesus and the Spirit*, 82-83.

151. Boring, ibid., 115; see the chart of verbal parallels, p. 116.

ing its gifts on behalf of and for the benefit of the community as a whole, but not a gift possessed indiscriminately by all its members."[152]

If this is so, John must mean two different things when he speaks of the Spirit as πνεῦμα and as the Paraclete. The former can clearly be received by all believers (1:33; 3:5; 7:39; 1 John 3:24; 4:13). But this distinction is by no means proven. In an article on the opponents in 1 John, R. E. Brown has discussed the authority crisis in the late Johannine community which may have arisen from pneumatology: "The failure of the author to crush his opponents by authority (such as the appeal to the teaching of bishops in the Pastorals, 1 Tim. 1:3; Titus 1:9) may reflect a situation bound by the Johannine tradition (known to his opponents) wherein the Spirit/Paraclete is the teacher and the Spirit is possessed by each follower of Jesus. The most he can do is to seek a criterion for discerning the Spirit of God (1 John 4:1-6)."[153]

Rudolf Schnackenburg has stated that the unique unifying factor within the Johannine community was the universal experience of the Spirit. Commenting on the Paraclete passages, he concludes that "we must understand the promised assistance of the Spirit also as a promise for the entire community."[154] In this regard, 1 John 2:27 is very instructive: "But the anointing [χρῖσμα] which you received from him abides in you; as his anointing teaches you about everything, and is true, and is no lie, just as it has taught you, abide in him." This important connection between the reception of the χρῖσμα (the Spirit in Schnackenburg's judgment) and teaching is significant. This is not so much a polemic against false teachers as an attempt to reinforce the notion that every Christian already has the truth (1 John 2:21).[155] Hence the Paraclete (the Spirit of Truth) applies to all and forms no special class of "Spirit bearers" (Geistträger).[156] All teachers need to be checked by the inner witness of the Spirit (1 John 4:1).

This amazing Johannine individualism directly affects the ecclesiology of John. Leadership was very decentralized, even charismatic. Although contemporary writings (e.g., Did. 11:3, 7; 13:1-4) held favorable views toward prophets, the Johannine literature refers only negatively to "false prophets" as if they were a suspect class. Schnackenburg concludes, "Evidently 'prophecy' is not the way in which the [Johannine community] experienced the work of the Spirit."[157] In other words, if John's church saw a connection between prophecy

---

152. Ibid., 114; cf. R. Schnackenburg, "Die johanneische Gemeinde und ihre Geisterfahrung," 302n.46.

153. R. E. Brown, "The Relationship to the Fourth Gospel Shared by the Author of First John and by His Opponents," in *Text and Interpretation: Studies in the New Testament Presented to Matthew Black*, ed. E. Best and R. McL. Wilson (Cambridge: University Press, 1979) 68; see also idem, "The Kerygma of the Gospel According to John," 387-400, esp. 391-92; for a similar expression of the radical decentralization of the Johannine church, see E. Käsemann, *The Testament of Jesus According to John 17*, tr. G. Krodel (Philadelphia: Fortress, 1968) 30-32.

154. R. Schnackenburg, "Die johanneische Gemeinde und ihre Geisterfahrung," 297; cf. 291ff.

155. Ibid., 283-87.

156. Ibid., 294-98, "Träger des Geistes," § 5.

157. R. Schnackenburg, "Die johanneische Gemeinde und ihre Geisterfahrung," 302-303;

and the Paraclete, all believers would in some sense be "prophets" because all shared the Spirit equally.

5. CONCLUSION

If we are correct in our judgment that the most important feature of the Paraclete is how the Evangelist has adapted this traditional image into his own context, then two foci emerge around which this adaptation must be seen. First, the almost universal emphasis on christology and eschatology is certainly justified. The parallels between Christ and Paraclete are well known and serve as an important datum confirming this emphasis. Moreover, the Johannine stress on realized eschatology must be applied to this result. How did the returning Christ figure into the Fourth Evangelist's eschatological perspective, and how does this relate to his pneumatology?

Second, next to christology/eschatology, John exhibits an acute awareness of the revelatory work of the Spirit—yet this must be seen through his own situation of trial and persecution. In this regard, Porsch, de la Potterie, and Kothgasser have helpfully emphasized the Johannine trial motif. When this motif is extended by John beyond the earthly life of Jesus and into the era of the church, then we may have located the exact forensic context which have rise to a juridical Spirit (the Paraclete) whose evidence before the world consisted in unique revelations. As Christ was on trial and revealed the Father, so too the disciples (and the Paraclete) were on trial, and in their witness they glorified and revealed Christ.

In practice, these two foci (christology/eschatology, revelation) really become one. The person of Christ and his work inform both the image of the Paraclete and all that he does. As Christ was to his disciples, so the Paraclete will be to them. Indeed, the Paraclete has no autonomy from Christ. The Paraclete is not entirely a replacement figure for Christ because Christ in effect is still present. It is *Christus Praesens* that speaks through the Paraclete and directs his revealing activity. When one encountered the Spirit Paraclete in the Johannine community, one encountered the risen Christ. *Therefore we can conclude that the single most important feature of the Johannine Paraclete is its christological concentration. Christ is the template within the Fourth Evangelist's thinking that has given shape and meaning to the Spirit in the Farewell Discourses.*

D. PNEUMA IN THE JOHANNINE LITERATURE

While extensive study has given attention to the Farewell Discourses and the Paraclete in John, one remarkable fact is the paucity of studies on πνεῦμα in the Fourth Gospel. In some respects George Johnston's monograph could be hailed as the Johannine counterpart to C. K. Barrett's careful work on the

---

see also idem, *John* 3: 150-54, Excursus 16, part 4: "The Significance of the Sayings about the Paraclete for the Johannine Community's Understanding of Itself and the Later Church."

Synoptic tradition.[158] But Johnston's reluctance to deal comprehensively with the Pneuma texts and his specialized focus on one remote theory for the Paraclete has forced most reviewers to judge his overall work as possessing a limited usefulness.

This lack of attention is especially surprising because, as W. F. Howard once remarked, "the Johannine teaching about the Spirit is one of the most distinctive features of the gospel."[159] One striking feature of the Fourth Gospel is the sheer volume of attention given to the Spirit. Πνεῦμα appears 24 times in John and 12 times in 1 John.[160] The occurrences of πνεῦμα in the Fourth Gospel are as follows:

τὸ πνεῦμα	11 times	1:32, 33; 3:6, 8a, 8b, 34; 6:63; 7:39
πνεῦμα	7 times	3:5, 6; 4:23, 24a, 24b; 6:63; 7:39
πνεῦμα ἅγιον	2 times	1:33; 20:22 (7:39? p⁶⁶)
τὸ πνεῦμα τὸ ἅγιον	1 time	14:26
τὸ πνεῦμα τῆς ἀληθείας	3 times	14:17; 15:26; 16:13

Among the Johannine Epistles, πνεῦμα appears only in 1 John, which omits any reference to τὸ πνεῦμα τὸ ἅγιον. The Spirit texts in this Epistle are as follows:

τὸ πνεῦμα	6 times	3:24; 4:1, 13; 5:6a, 6b, 8
πνεῦμα	3 times	4:1, 2, 3
τὸ πνεῦμα τοῦ θεοῦ	1 time	4:2
τὸ πνεῦμα τῆς ἀληθείας	1 time	4:6
τὸ πνεῦμα τῆς πλάνης	1 time	4:6

Among the various studies on these passages a few conclusions have found general scholarly consent. The early suggestion of Goguel—developed by A. Schweitzer and E. F. Scott—that John may have been dependent on Paul is best revised to say that both Paul and John reflect the primitive ecclesiology which elevated the Spirit as the primary endowment of the church.[161] On the other hand, Eduard Schweizer has sought to fit the Johannine πνεῦμα into the theological schema inherent within the Gospel. This effort has led him to suspect that John's dualism is the stage on which the πνεῦμα texts have been

---

158. C. K. Barrett, *The Holy Spirit and the Synoptic Tradition* (London: SPCK, 1966).

159. W. F. Howard, *Christianity According to St. John* (London: Duckworth, 1943) 71-72.

160. In comparison, πνεῦμα occurs in Matthew 19 times, in Mark 23 times, in Luke 36 times. But many of these refer to unclean spirits or demons, a usage which John nowhere attests. Outside of two references to personal emotion (11:33; 13:21) and a possible reference to "wind" (3:8a), all other references point to the divine Spirit either within Jesus or anticipated for believers. G. Ferraro has even argued that 13:21 refers to the Holy Spirit in Jesus, *"Pneuma* in Giov. 13,21," *Rivista Biblica* 28 (1980) 185-211, as cited in *NTA* 25/2 (1981) 140-41.

161. M. Goguel, *La notion johannique de l'Esprit et ses antécédents historiques* (Paris: 1902) as cited by Porsch, *Pneuma*, 6; cf. M. Goguel, "Paulinisme et Johannisme," *RHPR* 10 (1930) 504-26; and 11 (1931) 1-19, 129-56; E. F. Scott, *The Fourth Gospel*, 347-48. A. Schweitzer developed this point in detail in *The Mysticism of Paul the Apostle*, tr. W. Montgomery (London: A. & C. Black, 1953) 349-75; cf. H. S. Benjamin, "Pneuma in John and Paul: A Comparative Study of the Term with Particular Reference to the Holy Spirit," *BTB* 6 (1976) 27-48.

called to play.[162] But he explains that John does not defend substantial distinctions (as in Hellenistic dualism) where the spheres are in violent opposition. Rather, πνεῦμα denotes the reality of God that transcends the created order. Πνεῦμα, ἄνω, and θεός denote the sphere of God, while σάρξ, κάτω, διάβολος, and κόσμος denote the sphere of the world.

The most important recent contributor to this subject is again Felix Porsch in *Pneuma und Wort*. The preeminent value of his study is his detailed exegetical consideration of the πνεῦμα texts as well as of the Paraclete. But just as Porsch stressed the place of revelation in the Paraclete, so here he believes that revelation—the close connection between Spirit and word—is John's overarching message. In this respect, John 6:63 is a pivotal text for him. Equally important, he adopts the interpretation of 3:34 in which Jesus is the giver of the Spirit: this means that in the words of Jesus one can also encounter the divine Spirit. Porsch remarks: "From the fact that Jesus gives the Spirit (informally), it is established that he speaks God's words. Jesus' words are recognized as God's words in that they are joined with the gift of the Spirit. Hence *the giving of the Spirit and the speaking of the word of God* are not two different acts but are to be understood as a single event. Since Jesus speaks the words of God (or reveals, λαλεῖ) he also gives the Spirit at the same time."[163] It is in this sense that for him a "word event *[Wortgeschehen]* is therefore according to John a spiritual/pneumatic event *[pneumatisches Geschehen]*."[164]

The major strength of this interpretation is that Porsch has proposed a basic unifying theme connecting each text. But does every occurrence of πνεῦμα unveil John's supreme interest in revelation? Initially, Porsch's interpretation of 3:34 can be quickly challenged (as we shall show). Moreover, finding this emphasis in a major passage such as the Johannine "baptismal" account (1:29-34) is open to serious questions.[165] The pericope has clearly been modified by the Evangelist, and the event at the Jordan has been depicted as Jesus' revealing to both the Baptist and Israel. But, as we believe, the Johannine emphasis on πνεῦμα does not serve this agenda as much as it underscores the unique anointing of the Messiah. On the other hand, Porsch's insights on revelation must not be dismissed. The primacy of the word is central to Johannine pneumatology and must have been of some concern to the Fourth Evangelist and his community.

---

162. Schweizer, *TDNT* 6: 438-39; idem, "The Spirit of Power: The Uniformity and Diversity of the Concept of the Holy Spirit in the New Testament," *Int* 6 (1952) 259-78, esp. 275-76; cf. Brown, *John*, 1:cxv-cxvi; Bultmann, *Theology*, 1: 172-83; Dodd, *Interpretation*, 213-27. Betz compares John with the dualism of Qumran (*Der Paraklet*, 51-55, 117-21).

163. F. Porsch, *Pneuma*, 200, emphasis his. See also J. Pascher, "Der Glauben als Mitteilung des Pneumas nach Joh 6:61-65," *TThQ* 117 (1936) 301-21; cf. the conclusion of W. Thüsing that "the revelation of Jesus and the communication of the Spirit are identical" (*Die Erhöhung und Verherrlichung Jesu im Johannesevangelium* [Münster: Aschendorff, 1960] 153-54).

164. Porsch, *Pneuma*, 211.

165. Porsch remarks that "already with the analysis of the first Pneuma-passage . . . we can . . . establish an emphasis on the [Spirit's] function of revelation" (*Pneuma*, 211); cf. 20-51; we will examine this passage in chapter 2 below.

E. PROSPECTUS

The present study will attempt to approach Johannine pneumatology by investigating John's view of the Spirit in relation to some other major themes in his Gospel, namely, christology, eschatology, sacramentalism, and witness.

The Synoptics give us some indication that in the earthly life of Jesus the Spirit was at work within his ministry. How does the Fourth Evangelist address this question and what has become of the "pneumatic" motifs of the Synoptics? In addition, Johannine eschatology has always aroused a lively debate. How does the Evangelist integrate the Spirit into his realized eschatology? In both areas, christology and eschatology, we shall find that John urges a unique relation between Christ and Spirit. The christological features of the Paraclete are well known. But it can also be argued that 20:22 and John's general eschatological outlook assert this same unity. Moreover, this unity is anticipated prior to the Farewell Discourses in the presentation of Christ in this Gospel. Throughout the Gospel, the christological concentration of John's pneumatology will become evident.

One recent development in Johannine studies has been the view which holds that the Johannine writings were the product of a community. Cullmann, Käsemann, Schnackenburg, Brown, Martyn, Boismard, and Culpepper (among others) have urged that within the Fourth Gospel and the Johannine Epistles we can obtain glimpses of an early Christian community affirming its beliefs and describing its own experiences. As R. Schnackenburg emphasized in "Die johanneische Gemeinde und ihre Geisterfahrung" (1977), pneumatology played a vital role in this community's self-identity. This role is particularly evident when we view the sacraments in John. The immediacy of spiritual experience hallmarked Johannine Christianity in its view of both baptism and the eucharist. But equally, in its witness before and conflict with the world, the Johannine community experienced the direct presence of Christ in Spirit: aiding, revealing, directing. In both areas, sacraments and witness, christological concentration will again emerge. Sacramental worship should lead to an effective encounter of Christ in Spirit, and in witness it is the Paraclete, as the alter ego of Jesus, who glorifies Christ and conveys to the disciples a mission strictly patterned after Jesus.

One feature of this community was that it experienced development and, as Brown has so masterfully shown, this is seen if we view 1 John as reflecting a subsequent stage in the community's life.[166] Unfortunately, this is one aspect of Johannine pneumatology that Porsch gave limited attention. Does the crisis affecting the community of 1 John have one of its roots in the pneumtology of the Fourth Gospel? Does 1 John confirm the suggestion of John 3 that this community's self-identity was pneumatic in that each member was *anointed* and this was the mark of discipleship (in contrast to baptism)? Again, did the revelatory emphasis in the Farewell Discourses provide the tools that equipped the secessionists in their departure from Johannine orthodoxy?

---

166. R. E. Brown, *The Community of the Beloved Disciple* (London: Chapman; New York: Paulist, 1979); see my review, *JETS* 23 (1980) 167-68.

We shall urge that the Johannine community was a vital, pneumatic community, but that its pneumatology was entirely christocentric. The glorification of Christ was its central concern. In its experience, to receive the Spirit indicated that a believer was receiving Jesus (and all that was revealed about him). Indeed, the Spirit was made available through Jesus' glorification alone (7:39; 19:30, 34). This then may have inspired the projection that Spirit and Christ were uniquely bound up—even in the earthly ministry—and this explained their ultimate functional unity within the community's later experience.

THE HOLY SPIRIT IN JOHN

CHAPTER TWO

SPIRIT AND CHRISTOLOGY

Prior to the exaltation of Christ, the Spirit had been viewed primarily in its relation to God, as God's dynamic, mysterious power among human beings (esp. working in Christ). After Pentecost, this previously uncomplicated view entered a new complexity as the Spirit was defined primarily in its relation to Jesus. This relation is especially evident in Paul, who comfortably refers to "the Spirit of Christ," "the Spirit of God's Son," and "the Spirit of Jesus Christ" (Rom. 8:9; Gal. 4:6; Phil. 1:19; cf. Acts 16:7). 1 Cor. 15:45 directly associates the exalted Christ and the Spirit—"the last Adam [Christ] became a life-giving Spirit." In early Christian experience, therefore, the exalted Christ was seen in a dialectical role: to believers in their experience, he was found in the Spirit of Pentecost; but at the same time, the exalted Christ was separate and enthroned at God's right hand (Acts 2:33; 1 Cor. 15:24-28). J. D. G. Dunn has surveyed this evidence and concluded: "So in some sense that is not clear the life-giving Spirit and exalted Christ *merge* in Paul's thinking, the Spirit can now be thought of as the Spirit of Christ—that is, as that power of God which is to be recognized by the consciousness of oneness with Christ (and in Christ) which it engenders and by the impress of the character of Christ which it begins to bring about in the life of the believer."[1]

As Dunn also shows, Johannine theology made a marked advance in this direction. As we shall see in a subsequent chapter, in the religious experience of Johannine Christianity the Spirit was viewed entirely in terms of a personal encounter with Christ. It was Jesus living powerfully within the community and continuing his work among his followers.

---

1. J. D. G. Dunn, *Christology in the Making* (London: SCM; Philadelphia: Westminster, 1980) 149.

But while early Christian experience—and especially later Johannine reflection—drew this connection through experience, this experiential association between Spirit and Christ also sparked inquiries concerning the relation of Christ and Spirit before Christ's exaltation. What was the relation between the Spirit and Jesus during Jesus' earthly ministry? Did his mighty works and prophetic inspiration unveil the Spirit? Moving a step further back, what was the significance of Jesus' baptism and anointing in this relation? Matthew and Luke press the issue further still and point to an even earlier date: at Jesus' birth the Spirit was the key participant in the nature of Christ's conception.

Johannine theology also probed this connection between the Spirit and the earthly Christ. Of primary importance is John's explicit reminder that Jesus' death was the key (the only key) which could unlock the Spirit for the church (7:39; cf. 16:7). But John's probings go earlier as well. If the Spirit and Christ were ultimately to exhibit an inseparable functional unity, what then of Jesus before the cross? What has become of the traditional markers of pneumatic activity within Jesus' ministry? When did this functional union begin? Two remarkable features of the Fourth Gospel make this question particularly difficult. First, unlike Matthew and Luke, John does not begin to explicate this Christ/Spirit relation with the birth of Jesus. As we shall indicate in the Excursus below, John answers this same question in terms of a preexistent Logos which enters human history as the divine Spirit entered Mary of Nazareth. Second, when John does turn to the baptism tradition, he completely omits any mention of the water baptism itself and elevates only one emphasis: this event hallmarked the anointing of Christ and inaugurated the indwelling and union of the Spirit in Jesus. Despite his Logos proem, John cannot jettison the traditional foundation. It was the event of the Jordan that inaugurated Christ's ministry and empowered his work. Even for John, Jesus is consistently presented as related to the Spirit of God in a remarkable, unique fashion.

A. THE BAPTISM OF JESUS: JOHN 1:29-34

1. THE SYNOPTIC GOSPELS

Why Jesus was baptized by John the Baptist was one of the most pressing problems of first-century Christianity. Mark's Gospel leaves the issue almost untouched,[2] but Matthew faces the problem squarely. He alone stresses Jesus' intention to be baptized (τοῦ βαπτισθῆναι ὑπ' αὐτοῦ, 3:13)[3] and the distress of the Baptist (ὁ δὲ Ἰωάννης διεκώλυεν αὐτόν, 3:14). Later apocryphal works (e.g., the Gospel of the Hebrews) found relief from the paradox by stressing Jesus' own dismay in having to be baptized by John because he knew he was sinless. "Wherein have I sinned that I should go and be baptized by him?"[4] On

---

2. But see the comments of J. D. G. Dunn, *Baptism in the Holy Spirit*, 34-35.

3. One of Matthew's rare uses of the articular infinitive denoting purpose; see BDF, § 400 (5); Turner, *Syntax*, 141; τοῦ plus the infinitive occurs only 7 times in Matthew.

4. E. Hennecke, *New Testament Apocrypha*, 2 vols., tr. R. McL. Wilson et al. (London:

the other hand, G. Barth has aptly shown that this is not Matthew's solution. Matthew is concerned with salvation history and Jesus' fulfillment of "all righteousness" to achieve God's will.[5]

Another solution, however, is evident in the Synoptics. Matthew and Luke—and to a lesser extent Mark—exhibit a tendency to shift their emphasis away from the baptism to the anointing of Jesus by the Spirit.[6] Luke stresses, for example, that his chief interest is not in Jesus' water baptism but in the event of the Spirit (Luke 3:21-22). His difficult sentence structure alone (ἐγένετο, genitive absolute, plus four infinitives) subordinates Jesus' baptism to an aorist participle and thereby suggests that it preceded the heavenly theophany. In accordance with his emphasis elsewhere the descent of the Spirit is coincident with Jesus' praying—not with his baptism (cf. 11:2, 13; Acts 1:14; 2:1-4; 4:23ff.; 8:15; etc.). He implies that Jesus was baptized in a crowd (NEB: "during a general baptism of the people"); hence the water rite which Jesus shared with the masses is secondary and the Spirit's descent is not dependent upon it. We might even say that Jesus' water baptism was his preliminary participation in an event of the old aeon about to end. Jesus still stood on the threshold. But the pivot on which the dawning eschaton was about to turn would be the emergence of the Spirit. As Luke believes, this alone is what would hallmark the messianic age (Acts 2:17; Joel 2:28). In Acts 10:38 when Luke records Peter's résumé of the salvation-historical events in Jesus' life, the baptism with water is omitted entirely: "God anointed Jesus of Nazareth with the Holy Spirit and power."[7]

2. THE FOURTH GOSPEL

The Fourth Evangelist has completed this shift which the Synoptics had begun. Through the testimony of the Baptist, Jesus' experience of the Spirit is described but his baptism in water is not mentioned. If, with Cullmann, we see this as "the first commentary on the Synoptic account,"[8] John's silence is all the

---

Lutterworth; Philadelphia: Westminster, 1963, 1965) 1: 146-47, citing the Gospel of the Nazareans as taken from Jerome *Adv. Pelag.* 3.2.

5. G. Bornkamm, G. Barth, and H. J. Held, *Tradition and Interpretation in Matthew*, tr. P. Scott (London: SCM; Philadelphia: Westminster, 1963) 137-41; cf. O. Cullmann, *Baptism in the New Testament*, SBT 1/1, tr. J. K. S. Reid (London: SCM; Naperville: Allenson, 1950) 18-19.

6. I am chiefly indebted here to the insights of Dunn, *Baptism in the Holy Spirit*, 33-37; on Luke, cf. I. H. Marshall, *The Gospel of Luke*, New International Greek Testament Commentary (Exeter: Paternoster; Grand Rapids: Eerdmans, 1978) 150-57; Lampe, *Seal of the Spirit*, 42-45; E. Ellis, *The Gospel of Luke*, New Century Bible Commentary, rev. ed. (London: Oliphants, 1974; repr. Grand Rapids: Eerdmans, 1981) 91ff.; C. K. Barrett, *The Holy Spirit and the Synoptic Tradition*, 25-45; M. M. B. Turner, "Luke and the Spirit," unpub. diss., Cambridge University, 1980, 54-57.

7. Mark may achieve this shift by burying the baptism in three pericopae about the Spirit (1:4-8; 1:9-11; 1:12-13) and by preserving the strong antithetical contrast between Spirit and water baptism (1:8). Matthew may even suggest that Jesus left the water (ἀνέβη ἀπὸ τοῦ ὕδατος, 3:16) before the Spirit's descent.

8. O. Cullmann, *Baptism in the New Testament*, 20; cf. Barrett, *The Holy Spirit and the Gospel Tradition*, 34; on the comparison of Luke and John, see J. McPolin, "The Holy Spirit in Luke and John," *ITQ* 45 (1978) 124-25.

more impressive. He has certainly elided from the tradition all but what is of chief importance for his own purposes. For John, then, Jesus' anointing with the Spirit and the revelatory significance of this anointing for the Baptist are all that matter.

a. The Significance for the Baptist

For John the Baptist the event embodied a divine revelation. The Synoptics assume that the Baptist knew Jesus before his baptism (Matt. 3:13ff.; cf. Luke 1:41, 44). But John nowhere makes this clear. The entire Baptist narrative presupposes that Jesus has already been baptized and that the Baptist's account here is a *recollection*. Therefore Jesus' identity is unveiled to John only in the Jordan River: not through water baptism, but in the Spirit's descent. In the first instance, John has witnessed the Spirit's anointing (1:34), and he reaches the same conclusion given by the Synoptic pronouncement: "This is the Son/Chosen of God" (1:34; cf. 1:14, 18). But the Fourth Evangelist records an added feature. John himself was the recipient of his own private revelation which interpreted Jesus' Spirit baptism.

The Synoptic Gospels describe the divine pronouncement as φωνὴ ἐκ τῶν οὐρανῶν. According to Rabbinic understanding, when the prophetic voice had ceased in Israel, God spoke through heavenly echoes (בת קול).[9] In contrast, the Synoptics record God speaking directly to Jesus as at Sinai God spoke to Moses (Exod. 19:19). In John, this voice is absent. In 1:33 the Fourth Gospel shows the Baptist having received a direct prophetic experience. But as Betz has pointed out, the qualitative contrast between the *bath qol* and such prophecies was not a first-century phenomenon and should not be pursued.[10]

Thus John 1:33 does not refer to the Johannine version of the Synoptic pronouncement, but itself implies a supplementary revelation (ἐκεῖνος, emphatic, μοι εἶπεν). It is, as it were, Yahweh's prophetic hint at what would occur in the Jordan. "John was thus prepared for what happened at the baptism since God himself had given him the correct understanding of it."[11] The effect of this revelation is almost to overshadow Jesus' inauguration as the Christ.[12] But the intention here is important. John is not among the Rabbis and teachers of Israel. He is now a bona fide OT prophet with the proper credentials to be Jesus' supreme witness.[13]

Therefore the Fourth Evangelist's portrayal of John as witness is evident.

---

9. Str-B, 1: 125, 127; Barrett, *The Holy Spirit and the Gospel Tradition*, 39-45; O. Betz, *TDNT* 9: 288-90; E. Sjöberg, *TDNT* 6: 384-86.

10. O. Betz, ibid.

11. R. Schnackenburg, *John*, 1: 304; cf. Betz, ibid., 299; and Dodd, *Historical Tradition*, 260.

12. So Dodd, *Historical Tradition*, 260; cf. H. J. A. Bouman, "The Baptism of Christ with Special Reference to the Gift of the Spirit," *CTM* 28 (1957) 2, 7ff.

13. Τεθέαμαι in 1:32 does not necessarily imply that John had a vision. But Abbott (*Vocabulary*, § 604) and Brown (*John*, 1:502) think John's use is deeper than physical seeing (for which βλέπω should be used). Abbott would translate it "contemplate," and we might add "insight." Cf. G. Johnston, *Spirit-Paraclete*, 18.

His use of the baptism tradition to bring about a public witness may also be seen in an incipient stage in the pronouncement of Matt. 3:17 (οὗτός ἐστιν vs. Mark and Luke, συ εἶ). There also the revelation is given a wider audience.[14]

Further, in 1:33 the Spirit is noted to the Baptist as the sole signal of the Messiah's identity. The Spirit, as it were, is the revelatory key which will tell the Baptist when his expectation has been fulfilled. Only then will John be able to serve as a witness. "He on whom you see the Spirit descend and remain, this is he." Hence, we can see the interdependence of Spirit, witness, and revelation.

But even this theme is still secondary to the Fourth Evangelist. Of chief importance is the object of this Spirit-inspired revelation: the anointing of Jesus. Unlike any other Gospel writer, this Evangelist is concerned to stress the Spirit's empowering of Jesus.

b. The Significance for Jesus

We may grant with most scholars that John assumes his readers are generally acquainted with the Synoptic story. But that is a far cry from concluding that John then submerged the event in his own dogma of witness and left no meaning in the event for Jesus.[15] On the contrary, John defends a higher theology of Jesus' Spirit baptism than any other NT writer.

(1) The Synoptic Gospels

In harmony with the Synoptic Gospels, John records (however obliquely) the descent of the Spirit as a dove. No direct dependence is discernible.

John 1:32	τὸ πνεῦμα	καταβαῖνον ὡς περιστερὰν ἐξ οὐρανοῦ	ἐπ' αὐτόν
Matt. 3:16	πνεῦμα θεοῦ	καταβαῖνον ὡσεὶ περιστερὰν	ἐπ' αὐτόν
Mark 1:10	τὸ πνεῦμα	καταβαῖνον ὡς περιστερὰν	εἰς αὐτόν
Luke 3:22	τὸ πνεῦμα τὸ ἅγιον	καταβῆναι σωματικῷ εἴδει ὡς περιστερὰν	ἐπ' αὐτον

Although John has no parallel to the Synoptic account of the heavens being opened and of a voice from heaven, he is alone in his mention of the dove coming out of heaven. In the simple τὸ πνεῦμα John patterns Mark, yet Mark alone used εἰς in his final phrase. Further, Matthew alone mirrors John's word order. As Brown has argued, the eclecticism of similarities shows that John is recording traditional, though independent, sources.[16]

---

14. D. Hill, *The Gospel of Matthew*, New Century Bible Commentary (London: Oliphants, 1972; repr. Grand Rapids: Eerdmans, 1981) 97; Jeremias, *Theology*, 1: 53-55. This may also be the case in Luke's σωματικῷ εἴδει—so A. Richardson, *Theology*, 18.

15. So Bultmann, *John*, 94; M. Goguel, *Jean-Baptiste*, 160ff.; E. Schweizer, *TDNT* 6: 438. In 438n.717 Schweizer claims: "It might be said that for John Jesus was not baptized at all; at any rate, the baptism had no significance for Jesus himself."

16. Brown, *John*, 1:66; but see R. T. Fortna, *The Gospel of Signs* (Cambridge: University Press, 1970) 176-77; H. Greeven, *TDNT* 6: 68-69.

(2) The Use of Μένειν: John 1:32, 33

John's own creative thinking emerges in his description of the activity of the dove: πνεῦμα καταβαῖνον καὶ ἔμεινεν ἐπ' αὐτόν. John twice records the Spirit's remaining on Jesus (1:32, 33) and this is for him a significant inference. The permanence of Jesus' anointing is directly stressed in contrast to the transitoriness of every other previous prophetic inspiration in Israel's history.[17]

As has often been shown, μένειν is an important theological term for John.[18] Although the Fourth Gospel and the Johannine Epistles make up only about 12% of the NT, 58% of the occurrences of μένειν appear here. The general distribution is as follows:

Synoptics	John	Johannine Epistles	Revelation	Other	Total NT
12	40	27	1	38	118

Aside from common nontheological use (1:39; 4:40; 7:9; 10:40; etc.), μένειν underscores permanence in state of being or relationship. Thus in 12:34 the crowds affirm that the Christ remains forever, and by this affirmation the Evangelist indicates (apologetically) the eternal character of Jesus. Similarly, in 1 John 2:17 the believer who is obedient to the will of God shall remain forever. Μένειν thus denotes duration both of divine blessings (6:27) and of their opposite, divine disfavor (3:36; 12:46).

More important for John, however, is the phrase μένειν ἔν τινι, which always denotes "an inward, enduring personal communion."[19] This introduces the entire subject of John's theology of God's immanence. Μένειν ἐν depicts the mutual indwelling of Father and Son (14:10-11), and this in turn becomes the paradigm (cf. 15:10, comparative καθώς) of the believer's abiding in God (1 John 4:15), in Jesus (John 6:56; 15:6), and even in Jesus' word (8:31; cf. 5:38). Likewise μένειν ἐν is used to describe God's communing in the believer through the Spirit (1 John 3:24) as well as Jesus' mystical unity with each of his followers (John 15:4ff.). Significantly, this term describes the permanence of the Spirit of Truth as it abides within the Christian (14:17).

Although Barrett rightly cautions that "too much should not be built upon the word,"[20] it still is true that μένειν appears in the baptism pericope

---

17. E. Schweizer is one of the few to refer to μένειν negatively here. Still he says, "At most μένειν might indicate that there is still to be found here a relic of the Lucan attempt to make the endowment of the Spirit into a lasting one" (*TDNT* 6: 738n.717).

18. See Brown, *John*, Appendix 1, 1: 510-12; G. Pecorara, "De Verbo *manere* apud Johannem," *DThom* 40 (1937) 159-71; J. Heise, *Bleiben, Menein in den Johanneischen Schriften* (Tübingen: Mohr-Siebeck, 1967); F. Hauck, *TDNT* 4: 574-76; Abbott, *Vocabulary*, 195-96; R. Schnackenburg, "Johanneische Gemeinde und Geisterfahrung," 283-87; and E. Malatesta, *Interiority and Covenant. A Study of* εἶναι ἐν *and* μένειν ἐν *in the First Letter of St. John* (Rome: Pontifical Biblical Institute, 1978) (see bibliography, idem, p. 3n.7, 335-36 on μένειν).

19. BAG, 504.

20. C. K. Barrett, *John*, 178.

deliberately, and this passage coheres with the overall Johannine concept behind the term. John wants to stress that Jesus' anointing was no passing moment of inspiration. *The unity of Spirit and Son was as permanent and comprehensive as the unity between Father and Son (10:30).*[21] Heinrich Schlier comments: "With the stress on the 'remaining' of the Spirit, the Gospel probably refers to the relationship of the Spirit with Jesus—the subjection of the Spirit to Jesus not only during his earthly work, but rather precisely after his glorification."[22]

Complete endowment with the Spirit is, as it were, characteristic of what it means to be the Messiah. John 3:34 echoes this thought (if θεός is the subject of δίδωσι, as we believe). Till then, no one but Jesus had received a full measure of the Spirit that would remain, and by virtue of this endowment he was equipped to baptize in the Spirit. Hence this anointing made him more than a super-endowed prophet. He could now be the distributor of the Spirit.

Various sources for John's emphasis are certainly possible. The permanence of Jesus' divine anointing may echo the OT theme that God and the things of God characteristically endure forever. This is underscored especially in the LXX use of μένειν. For example, God remains forever (Dan. 6:26; cf. Ps. 9:7; 101:12) as do both his council (Isa. 14:24) and his wisdom (Wis. 7:27). In Isaiah his word of promise abides (40:8), especially when referring to his future work of new creation (66:22).

The idea that the Spirit of God will anoint the Isaianic Servant is well attested (Isa. 42:1; 48:16; 61:1). But further, in Isa. 11:2 the Spirit is said to rest upon him: καὶ ἀναπαύσεται ἐπ᾽ αὐτὸν πνεῦμα τοῦ θεοῦ (MT: ונחה עליו רוח יהוה). That the Spirit rests (using the related ἐπαναπαύειν) on God's prophets and servants appears elsewhere, for example, in the story of Eldad and Modecd (LXX, Num. 11:26-29). In 4(2) Kgs. 2:15 the LXX records that ἐπαναπέπαυται τὸ πνεῦμα Ἡλιοὺ ἐπὶ Ἐλισαιέ. Knowing John's predilection for μένειν, he may have adopted such themes into the mold of his idiom.[23] In 1 Pet. 4:14 ἀναπαύειν is used of the Spirit's resting on the Christian in what may be a direct allusion to the LXX of Isa. 11:2.

In addition, other sources from the intertestamental period show a marked interest in viewing the Spirit as having taken residence upon the great personages of the OT. The Rabbis believed that the Holy Spirit and the shekinah of God rested (שרי, שרה) upon particular individuals and prophets.[24] Mish. *Abot* 3:6 thus says, "When ten men sit together and occupy themselves with the Torah, the shekinah abides [שרויה] among them." Isa. 11:2 even became a proof text to affirm that the eschatological Spirit of wisdom and power would rest upon the Messiah (1 En. 49:3; 62:2; cf. T. Jud. 24:2). His permanent anointing was regularly reiterated (Ps. Sol. 17:37, 42; 18:7; cf. Sir.

---

21. A. Wurzinger, "Der Heilige Geist bei Johannes," *BLit* 36 (1962-63) 289-90.

22. "Zum Begriff des Geistes," 264; cf. Hauck, *TDNT* 6: 576; and Dunn, *Jesus and the Spirit*, 350.

23. See Johnston, *Spirit-Paraclete*, 19; C. K. Barrett, *The Holy Spirit and the Synoptic Tradition*, 41; G. Reim, *Studien zum Hintergrund*, 163, 220.

24. Barrett, *John*, 178; cf. Bauernfeind, *TDNT* 1: 350-51.

48:12, 24; Jub. 25:14; Zadokite Fragment 2:10). The Targum on Isa. 42:1-4 has God say, "I will cause my Holy Spirit to rest on him" (cf. Tg. Isa. 11:2). But as Sjöberg has argued, this messianic emphasis should also be seen in the context of a Rabbinic understanding that the great epoch of prophetic inspiration was over.[25]

The Testaments of the Twelve Patriarchs expresses a unique concern for the effects of the Spirit upon people (T. Jud. 20:1-5; 24:2; T. Sim. 4:4; T. Levi 18:11; T. Ben. 8:2; T. Reub. 2:1-2; etc.). Clearly, πνεῦμα can often mean psychological influences, but frequently it implies a divine Spirit resting on a person. The messianic hymn found in T. Levi 18 is particularly important. 18:6-7 describes the anointing of the new messianic priest thus: "The heavens shall be opened, and from the temple of glory shall come upon him sanctification, with the Father's voice as from Abraham to Isaac. And the glory of the Most High shall be uttered over him, and the spirit of understanding and sanctification *will rest upon him* [καταπαύσει ἐπ' αὐτόν] [in the water]."[26]

R. H. Charles rightly concluded that "in the water" was an early Christian interpolation, but he did not accept a complete Christian reediting of the Testaments.[27] M. Black is persuaded that "Abraham to Isaac" and ἁγίασμα in 18:6 reveal Maccabean martyrdom terminology which may secure these verses in a pre-Christian era.[28] At least the concepts written here were not unknown to pre-Christian writers. Thus this text may provide evidence for an early idea which was later developed into a vital Christian doctrine.

Specific parallels to the NT baptism tradition include the rending of the heavens, the divine pronouncement, and the Spirit's resting (καταπαύειν related to Isa. 11:2 LXX ἀναπαύειν with a perfective or definite force).[29] Therefore it seems clear that by the NT era the ideas of Spirit, Messiah, and "Spirit resting" all enjoyed a common background and messianic application. The Fourth Evangelist has used his favorite μένειν and applied these concepts to Jesus' own anointing.

(3) The Descending Dove: John 1:32, 33

Not only has John inherited a Jewish tradition, but we have seen that some form of the Synoptic tradition lies behind his work. Therefore we might ask if the baptismal dove tradition could have contributed to John's use of μένειν. No

---

25. Cf. the extensive Rabbinic citations of E. Sjöberg, *TDNT* 6: 384-85; also, Str-B, 1: 127: "Since the last prophets Haggai, Zechariah, and Malachi died, the Holy Spirit has ceased in Israel" (Tos. *Sota* 13:2).

26. R. H. Charles, *Apocrypha and Pseudepigrapha of the Old Testament*, 2 vols. (Oxford: Clarendon Press, 1913) 2: 314; for the Greek text a critical edition has been supplied by M. deJonge, *The Testaments of the Twelve Patriarchs* (Leiden: Brill, 1978).

27. "In the water" is omitted by one 11th-century Greek ms.; see deJonge, ibid., 49. Barrett agrees with Charles (*The Holy Spirit and the Gospel Tradition*, 44).

28. M. Black, "The Messiah in the Testament of Levi 18," *ExpTim* 60 (1948-1949) 321-22; and 61 (1949-50) 157-58; cf. G. R. Beasley-Murray, "The Two Messiahs in the Testaments of the Twelve Patriarchs," *JTS* 48 (1947) 1-12; Stauffer, *New Testament Theology*, 334ff., sees numerous direct parallels between the Johannine literature and the Testaments.

29. Moulton, *Grammar*, 2: 316; κατά gives the verb an intransitive function, BDF, § 309 (2); cf. § 318 (5).

scholarly consensus has been reached on the meaning of the dove,[30] but various suggestions have come from Johannine studies.

Early in this century, E. A. Abbott argued at length that the metaphor of the Spirit resting like a dove stemmed from an early verbal confusion between the similar Hebrew terms for "dove" (יונה) and "rest" (נוח, future ינוח). His only evidence consisted of early Christian apocryphal accounts that used a literal rendering of Isa. 11:1 (the "rod . . .") along with this Hebrew confusion to call up the story of Num. 17:1ff. These elements—a rod, a dove, divine selection, and Isa. 11:1—were then conflated to portray God's choice of Joseph as Mary's husband (see Protevangelium of James; Gospel Pseudo-Matthew). The Gospel of the Nativity of Mary even quotes Isa. 11:1 directly.[31] The chief problem with this theory is the lack of firm evidence for this specific Hebrew confusion (a lack Abbott admits). In the LXX "dove" is confused with "oppress" (ינה, Zeph. 3:1) and "Greece" (יון, Jer. 46:16) but never with "rest." Furthermore, the apocryphal conflation enters only the nativity accounts; it is not evidenced in the baptismal scene as we might hope.[32]

Noah associations have often been suggested for the baptismal dove.[33] Johnston feels that this association gave John the impetus for his baptismal account. "Our conclusion is that Gen. 8:8f. in combination with Isa. 11:1f. has provided the essential background." He believes that together these texts "sufficiently connect messiah, water, a heavenly descent and a dove resting." "As the dove found its resting place in the midst of the flood waters, so the Spirit of God found a resting place in Israel in the Man who stood in the midst of the water."[34]

Unfortunately, there is no evidence for this hopeful parallel either. True, early Christian art and the later Church Fathers (post-Tertullian) connected the two doves, and 1 Pet. 3:18-21 (the probable source of such art) may connect Noah's flood with Christian baptism. But nowhere is the link between the Jordan event and Noah specific. Keck's criticism is decisive: "Neither this subsequent correlation nor *ex post facto* Christian logic can account for the *origin* of the baptismal dove. That Noah's dove was related to the divine Spirit

---

30. We cannot directly discuss the complex interpretation of the dove. Keck's suggestion of an "adverbial metaphor" seems most promising, however. See L. E. Keck, "The Spirit and the Dove," *NTS* 17 (1970) 41-67 and references given there; cf. Str-B, 1: 125; H. Greeven, *TDNT* 6: 63-72; A. Feuillet, "Le Symbolisme de la Colombe dans les récits évangéliques du bapteme," *RSR* 46 (1958) 524-44.

31. E. A. Abbott, *From Letter to Spirit* (London: A. & C. Black, 1903) 106-35; also argued in M. A. Chevallier, *L'Esprit et le Messie* (Paris: Presses Universitaires, 1958) 60ff. Abbott does not argue for a "variant reading of Isa. 11:1f." (so Johnston, *Spirit-Paraclete*, 20); for a critique of Abbott and Chevallier, see Keck, "The Spirit and the Dove," 43-44, 44nn.1, 2.

32. Possible evidences may come from the fact that most accounts seem to either mention the dove (Synoptics, Ebionite Gospel, Justin Martyr, Celsus [in Origen], the Sibylline Oracles) or resting (Ephraem on the Diatessaron, Gospel of the Nazareans, Testament of the Twelve Patriarchs) but not both (only John and the Arabic Diatessaron). Minor variants in Mark 1:10 and Matt. 3:16 are harmonizations with John 1:33; see Abbott, *From Letter to Spirit*, 102-103.

33. See Keck, "The Spirit and the Dove," 48n.6; also, G. Lampe, *The Seal of the Spirit* (London: Longmans, 1951) 36; A. Richardson, *Theology*, 181; Johnston, *Spirit-Paraclete*, 20-21.

34. Johnston, *Spirit-Paraclete*, 20-21.

is nowhere said, nor should we be surprised, since that dove was among the birds *saved* in the ark, not a heavenly bird *sent* to it."[35]

No doubt we should interpret John's use of μένειν and the dove not in terms of literary dependence but in terms of theological development. Isa. 11:2 undoubtedly stands behind the baptismal tradition. John's use of this text (possibly T. Levi 18) and his discovery that the resting metaphor of Isa. 11 was compatible with the older dove tradition gave birth to his present text. In emphasizing the anointing of Jesus, John heightened the relation of the dove and the baptism.

Here John represents the first stage in a tradition which soon witnessed speedy extracanonical development. Early writers elaborated the intimacy between the Spirit and Christ at the baptism. Jeremias, for example, points to the Gospel of the Nazareans, which omits mention of the dove but depicts a restless Spirit searching in vain among the prophets for a resting place. "And when it came to pass when the Lord was come up out of the water, the whole fount of the Holy Spirit descended upon him and *rested [requievit]* on him and said to him: 'My Son, in all the prophets was I waiting for thee that thou shouldest come and I might *rest* in thee. For thou art my *rest;* thou art my first-begotten Son that reignest forever.'"[36]

The early Christian hymnbook, the Odes of Solomon, exhibits the same stress but with an important difference. Where the dove tradition was preserved, a unique, even intimate, relation between the dove and Christ was described. Ode 24 records: "The dove fluttered over the head of our Lord Messiah because he was her head. And she sang over him, and her voice was heard."[37]

Justin likewise records the dove tradition: "like a dove the holy spirit flew [ἐπιπτῆναι] upon him" (*Dial.* 88). That the dove fluttered (ἐπιπέτομαι) over Jesus became a common attempt to describe an affectionate familiarity between the two. Bernard notes that the Sibylline Oracles, Origen, and Tertullian (using *volare*) also refer to this thought, and this evidence suggests to him the remnant of an early extracanonical tradition with this theme.[38]

---

35. Keck, "The Spirit and the Dove," 49, italics mine.

36. Jerome, *Comm. Isa.* 11:2, in Hennecke, *Apocrypha*, 1:163-64; see Jeremias, *New Testament Theology*, 1: 50n.2, 52. The most extreme case of this attempted Spirit/Christ unity may be found in the Pistis Sophia. There the bed-fettered Spirit is met by a youthful Jesus: "And he [the Spirit] that was bound to the bed was set free, he embraced thee [Jesus], and kissed thee, and thou didst kiss him, and ye became one." See Hennecke, *Apocrypha*, 1: 257-58.

37. ET by J. H. Charlesworth, *The Odes of Solomon* (Oxford: Clarendon Press, 1973) 98; cf. the highly unusual Ode 19, which uses fertility metaphors to this end; on the Spirit and the Odes of Solomon, see Lampe, *Seal of the Spirit*, 111-14.

38. Bernard, *John*, 1:50. Stress on Jesus' Spirit anointing was given christological significance esp. within Gnostic circles (e.g., Cerinthus). The incarnation (John 1:14) was found here in the Jordan. Thus the Nag Hammadi tractate, *The Testimony of Truth* (ET: S. Giversen and B. A. Pearson, in J. M. Robinson, ed., *The Nag Hammadi Library* [San Francisco: Harper & Row, 1977] 407), reads: "And John bore witness to the [descent] of Jesus. For he is the one who saw the [power] which came down upon the Jordan river." See further R. H. Fuller, "Christmas, Epiphany, and the Johannine Prologue," in M. L'Engle and W. B. Green, eds., *Spirit and Light* (New York: Seabury, 1976) 63-73; and R. E. Brown, *Community of the Beloved Disciple*, 152-53. "Incarnationism" has

We conclude that John's stress on the anointing of Jesus developed out of Isa. 11 and adopted the earlier dove tradition. As John completed the shift in emphasis away from the water baptism to the Spirit, his use of the dove tradition to that end may have inspired later reflective writers to elaborate their Spirit christologies within the Jordan event.

c. Psalm 2 or Isaiah 42? The Pronouncement

All four Gospels agree that two events occurred here in the Jordan. First, Jesus experienced the Spirit, and second, a heavenly pronouncement identified him from key OT messianic texts. That such pronouncements were important in early thought is evidenced by parallel logia in the Synoptic transfiguration story (cf. John 12:28-30). The Fourth Evangelist, however, entertains no voice from the sky. Consistent with his stress on the Baptist elsewhere, John climaxes his baptismal account by placing the pronouncement on the Baptist's lips as a witness: "And I have seen and have born witness that οὗτός ἐστιν ὁ **υἱὸς/ἐκλεκτὸς** τοῦ θεοῦ"(1:34).

Set within this subject is the perplexing question of the original form of the pronouncement and the OT text(s) in the background. In their final form, the Synoptics clearly see messianic sonship and Ps. 2:7 behind the voice (esp. Luke 3:22 D). On the other hand, Jeremias has argued that a dual meaning for παῖς (LXX Isa. 42:1, ὁ παῖς μου, MT עבדי) gave rise to the Synoptic ὁ υἱός to appease more eager gentile Christian circles. In this case, the Synoptic pronouncements "are not mixed quotations from Ps. 2:7 and Isa. 42:1, but are originally only from the latter."[39] This thesis, though, has suffered heavy criticism. No doubt both texts came into play in early interpretation, and "a denial of the presence of ideas from either Ps. 2:7 or Isa. 42:1 is to be rejected."[40]

The Fourth Gospel enters this discussion because John 1:34 harbors an important variant which points away from Ps. 2. The majority of the external witnesses support ὁ υἱός (p[66] p[75] א[c] A B C K L P et al.). But ὁ ἐκλεκτός is found in the original hand of Sinaiticus, the Old Latin, the Old Syriac, and various Church Fathers (as well as apparent support from p[5], Oxyrhynchus Papyrus 208). Various scholars support the former reading because of the abundant manuscript evidence and the fact that "son" is a common Johannine term. But most modern exegetes argue for the latter.[41]

---

been argued for John 1:32 in E. C. Colwell and E. L. Titus, *The Gospel of the Spirit: A Study in the Fourth Gospel* (New York: Harper & Row, 1953) 107-41.

39. Jeremias, *TDNT* 5: 701ff.; idem, *Theology*, 1:53-55.

40. I. H. Marshall, "Son of God or Servant of Yahweh—A Reconsideration of Mark 1:11," *NTS* 15 (1968-69) 335; cf. M. D. Hooker, *Jesus and the Servant* (London: SPCK, 1959) 68-73; and R. H. Gundry, *The Use of the Old Testament in St. Matthew's Gospel* (Leiden: Brill, 1967) 29-32.

41. In support of the former reading are Braun, Bousset, Bultmann, Bernard, R. H. Lightfoot, Westcott, Dodd, Nestle, Gundry, Howton; cf. UBS rating "B." In support of the latter reading are Harnack, Jeremias, Lindars, Burkitt, Cullmann, Schnackenburg, Barrett, Reim, Sidebottom, T. W. Manson, Porsch, Zahn, Lagrange, de la Potterie, Boismard, Marsh, Morris, Tasker, Spitta, Loisy, Brown, NEB.

Ἐκλεκτός is clearly to be preferred here for a variety of reasons. (1) It does have manuscript support, and as Schnackenburg believes, the diversity of witnesses shows its existence in a very early tradition. The harmonizations ὁ ἐκλεκτὸς υἱός (syrᵖᵃˡᵐˢˢ copˢᵃ = Latin *electus filius* in itᵃ itᶠᶠ²ᶜ) and ὁ μονογενὴς υἱός (syrᵖᵃˡᵐˢ) demonstrate an early reading in various linguistic regions.

(2) But ἐκλεκτός is also the more difficult reading. It is easier to understand a scribe changing the unusual "chosen one" to "son" than vice versa. Ἐκλεκτός only occurs here and in Luke 23:35 as a christological title. But an analogous form in Luke 9:35 (ὁ ἐκλελεγμένος) suggests that such a thought may have been connected to early pronouncement traditions. Further, John 6:69 exhibits an editorial tendency in the Johannine tradition to insert "the Son of God" into some texts.[42] Added to this evidence is the early desire to harmonize the Gospel accounts.

(3) It is true that "elect of God" is a distinct title which is not attested in the OT or in the intertestamental literature. But this lack cannot be used to argue for its improbable use here in 1:34. Research at Qumran has uncovered its appearance there (1QpHab 10:13; 4QMess ar) with a possible messianic application.[43] Further, "elect of God" could have come from the commonly messianic "elect one." At any rate, in John 1:41 Andrew immediately makes the messianic application clear.

(4) Finally, although υἱός is an important Johannine term,[44] much the same can be said for ἐκλεκτός. Even through this word and related forms are infrequent in John (ἐκλέγομαι, 5 times), the thought that the Twelve (6:70; 13:18) and all disciples (15:16, 19) are chosen by Jesus (and the Father, 6:65) is underscored by John. But as G. Schrenk has shown, "the basic and determinative Father-Son relation underlies the whole."[45] Jesus elects his chosen ones by virtue of his being the Chosen One of God. The prior knowledge and calling of the Father underlies what it means to be either a disciple (6:65) or the Messiah (3:31; 6:46). And from this *election* both believer and Messiah share a similar mystic oneness: the believer is in Jesus as Jesus is in the Father (14:20; 17:21, 23). But if it is true that election means divine calling to a divine relationship, then sonship is not substantially different from election. Sonship in John means this

---

42. Cf. 9:35; compare a similar contrast in Matt. 27:40 ("Son of God") par. Luke 23:35 ("Chosen of God"); Jeremias's suggestion (*TDNT* 5: 689n.260) that the change to "Son" in John 1:34 came in the 4th century to battle Adoptionism is invalidated by the appearance of this word in p⁶⁶ and p⁷⁵.

43. So J. Starcky, "Un texte messianique araméen de la grotte 4 de Qumran," *Ecole des Langues orientales anciennes de l'Institut Catholque de Paris: Memorial du cinquantenaire 1914-1964* (Paris: Bloud et Gay, 1964) 51-66; idem, "Les quatres étapes du messianisme à Qumran," *RB* 70 (1963) 481-505. J. A. Fitzmyer reviews the work of Starcky but argues that Elect of God has no messianic application in 4QMess ar. See "The Aramaic 'Elect of God' Text from Qumran Cave 4," *CBQ* 27 (1965) 348-72.

44. See E. Schweizer, *TDNT* 8: 385-88; J. Howton, "Son of God in the Fourth Gospel," *NTS* 10 (1963-64) 227-34; Sidebottom, *The Christ of the Fourth Gospel*, 149-65; Smalley, *John, Evangelist and Interpreter*, 215-17.

45. *TDNT* 4: 172-73; cf. A. Richardson, *Theology*, 271-78; Kümmel, *Theology*, 270; A. Corell, *Consummatum Est*, 166-200.

very thing for both Jesus (1:14) and his followers (1:12; 1 John 3:1ff.).[46] There-fore it is all the more curious why John omitted υἱός from his received tradition.

The explanation may be found in John's exclusive emphasis on Isa. 42. If so, the consequences for the Evangelist are important. Jesus' baptism in John's eyes does not refer to the enthronement of a king or to adoption rites, as Ps. 2:7 might suggest. In fact, the Johannine prologue's emphasis on Jesus' eternal status may have been viewed as incompatible with this enthronement psalm. Rather, "it becomes clear that all the emphasis lies on the event of the com-munication of the Spirit."[47] John points to Isa. 42 alone in order to stress Jesus' anointing with the Spirit. Unlike the Synoptics, in John's Gospel Jesus' sonship has already been established in the introductory prologue. Now it only remains to stress his empowering.

This conclusion is further supported by John's interest in Isaiah else-where in this section. The Baptist's label of Jesus as the lamb of God (ὁ ἀμνὸς τοῦ θεοῦ, 1:29, 36) shows, in Cullmann's estimate, that the Isaianic Servant of Yahweh is clearly in the Fourth Evangelist's mind.[48] The connection between lamb and the Servant could easily have come from Isa. 53:7, where, as C. F. Burney argued, in Aramaic טליא דאלהא could mean both lamb and servant of God.[49] At any rate, the essential point is that texts and images from Isaiah's Servant passages have been determinative for John in 1:29-34. If so, John has identified Jesus as the Isaianic Servant from the outset and uniquely brought together Servant, sacrifice, and Spirit in his baptism account. At his own baptism Jesus thus experienced the messianic Spirit in order to fulfill the atoning suffering of the Servant of God in Isaiah. This Isaianic background is therefore a key reason for John's stress on the Spirit in these verses.[50]

3. CONCLUSION

We have found that the Fourth Evangelist has employed the baptismal tradi-tion in a unique way and refashioned it to stress the anointing and indwelling of the Spirit with Jesus. (a) In line with a theological tendency evidenced in the Synoptics, John has completed the refocusing from water baptism to Spirit baptism by omitting all reference to water. John may assume his readers

---

46. But in John υἱός is never applied to disciples. "Jesus is so uniquely God's Son from all eternity that he always without exception uses τέκνα for believers, and they alone, and never Jesus are said to be born of God" (E. Schweizer, TDNT 8: 390-91); cf. Oepke, TDNT 5: 653-54; W. F. Lofthouse, "Fatherhood and Sonship in the Fourth Gospel," ExpTim 43 (1931-32) 442ff.; W. Grundmann, "Zur Rede Jesu vom Vater im John," ZNW 52 (1961) 214-30; O. Michel (and I. H. Marshall), NIDNTT 3: 639-48.

47. Jeremias, Theology, 55; although he concludes this for the Synoptic account as well; cf. R. E. Brown, John, 1: 65-67.

48. Cullmann, Early Christian Worship, 63-66; idem, Baptism, 20-22.

49. C. F. Burney, The Aramaic Origin of the Fourth Gospel (Oxford: Clarendon Press, 1922) 107-108; cf. Cullmann, Early Christian Worship, 65.

50. Cullmann, Baptism, 21; A. Corell, Consummatum Est, 55-56.

already know the Synoptic story. In this case his account becomes a commentary highlighting his own contribution.

(b) Through the influence of Isa. 11 and an intertestamental tradition possibly seen in T. Levi 18, John adds that the Spirit remained on Jesus as a dove. Jesus could not be mistaken for an OT prophet enjoying mere transitory experiences of the Spirit. For John, Jesus' empowering was permanent, which confirmed that he was God's Chosen One.

(c) Finally, Isaiah has been further determinative for John in that his pronouncement account points exclusively to Isa. 42 and omits all reference to Ps. 2. For John this text stresses the Spirit more acutely and again underscores Jesus' anointed messianic status. Jesus is the Chosen One precisely because he possesses the messianic endowment. Through this possession he will be able to anoint in power those who believe.

B. JESUS IN THE POWER OF THE SPIRIT

We have seen that the Evangelists were concerned with both Jesus' origins and his anointing in the Spirit. But their concerns go further. How did the Spirit reveal its power in the career of the Messiah? The Synoptic answer (which we shall initially examine) moves in two directions. Jesus both exhibited works of power and spoke authoritative, prophetic words. John echoes these emphases but adds his own distinctive nuance. Pneumatology serves John's christology—the Spirit finds its primary relation to Christ—and the Spirit of power becomes the Spirit of revelation.

1. THE SYNOPTIC GOSPELS

Both Mark and Q record that the immediate result of Jesus' baptism was the temptation. Although various differences can be observed,[51] both accounts agree that Jesus was empowered and constrained to enter the wilderness by the Spirit. Mark depicts this influence in OT terms as if the Spirit were the compulsive power of God coming upon him (τὸ πνεῦμα αὐτὸν ἐκβάλλει). On the other hand, Luke makes Jesus "the subject of an action in the Holy Spirit."[52] He enters the wilderness full of the Spirit (πλήρης, Luke 4:1) and returns in its power (δύναμις, Luke 4:14). Luke shows that Jesus, as it were, is not so much a man in the Spirit as he is the Lord of the Spirit.

This introduction establishes the thought that Jesus, filled with the Spirit in the Jordan, now emerges fully empowered for testing by and conflict with Satan.[53] From the outset, therefore, Jesus is identified within the Spirit world.

---

51. C. K. Barrett, *Holy Spirit*, 46-53; H. Seesemann, *TDNT* 6: 33-36.

52. E. Schweizer, *TDNT* 6: 404-405; so too J. H. E. Hull, *The Holy Spirit in the Acts of the Apostles* (London: Lutterworth, 1967) 37; and M. E. Isaacs, *The Concept of Spirit: A Study of Pneuma in Hellenistic Judaism and its Bearing on the New Testament*, Heythrop Monographs 1 (London: Heythrop College, 1976) 121.

53. Luke's reference to the Jordan in 4:1 explicitly connects the baptism and temptation despite the intervening genealogy.

Hence the temptations Jesus experienced were by no means ordinary. They were strictly messianic. Jesus was to prove his messiahship by exhibiting his messianic power ("if you are the Son of God . . .," Matt. 4:3). He adamantly refuses, but still the point is made that messiahship and supernatural power are now united in him.[54]

Mark portrays this unity as he unfolds the story of Jesus' early ministry. It is significant that demons are the first to be aware of his complete identity (Mark 1:24). Jesus brandishes the authority of the Spirit and, as it were, spirit casts out spirit. Yet this term *authority* (ἐξουσία) is applied equally to Jesus' exorcism (1:27b) and to his teaching (1:22). It is striking that Jesus' authority over spirits is first uncovered in the synagogue. Spiritual power in word and work will comprehensively outline Jesus' messianic activities.

The use of Isa. 61:1 further describes Jesus' empowering by the Spirit. Luke also finds Jesus in a synagogue at the outset of his ministry—but here Jesus' self-ascription of messianic power is cited from Isa. 61:1, formally quoted in Luke 4:18ff. The historical credibility of this possible Lukan construction has often been discussed.[55] We can be sure, however, that two other allusions to Isa. 61 in Q (Luke 6:20 par. Matt. 5:3ff. and Luke 7:18-23 par. Matt. 11:2-6) firmly secure the self-ascription in this passage within the historical self-consciousness of Jesus. Thus its importance can hardly be overstated. Jesus saw himself as the anointed Servant fulfilling Isa. 61. Yet his power was to be seen not only in extraordinary healings and exorcisms, "but chiefly in his preaching [would] God's eschatological reign [be] visible and present."[56]

Therefore Jesus experienced the activity of the Spirit in his life in both works and words. This dual emphasis is even found in the apostolic commission of Mark 3:14-15. The presence of the Spirit would be the mainspring of Jesus' power and would express itself in works of power and words of authority.[57]

a. Works of Power

In the memory of the early church, Jesus' ability to demonstrate works of power was understood in close connection with his Spirit anointing (Acts 10:38). In Mark 11:27-33, when Jesus' authority is directly challenged, he seems to appeal to the event of his baptism as the ground of his authority. He had once passed on this ability to his followers (Mark 3:15; 6:7; cf. 9:14ff.), and for

---

54. See H. Riesenfeld, "The Messianic Character of the Temptation in the Wilderness," in *The Gospel Tradition* (Oxford: Blackwell, 1970) 75-94.

55. See the discussions and citations by Schürmann, *Lukasevangelium*, 1: 242; Dunn, *Jesus and the Spirit*, 53-62; Marshall, *Luke*, 177-84; R. T. France, *Jesus and the Old Testament* (London: Tyndale, 1971; repr. Grand Rapids: Baker, 1982) loc. cit. The parallel setting of this passage is clearly Mark 6:1-6 par. Matt. 13:53-58, where no mention is made concerning what Jesus taught at the synagogue "in his own country."

56. Dunn, *Jesus and the Spirit*, 60-61; cf. also, R. H. Fuller, *The Foundations of New Testament Christology* (New York: Scribner's, 1965) 128-29.

57. See Matt. 11:5-6; Luke 24:19. These two themes (works of power and words of authority) form a general outline for Jeremias, *Theology*, 76-121.

the era following his resurrection he had promised that such abilities would hallmark the power of the church (Mark 16:17-18; John 14:12).[58] For Jesus, this ability showed itself in two chief features, exorcisms and miracles.

(1) Exorcisms and Satan

According to J. D. G. Dunn, Jesus' ability to exorcise evil spirits is of paramount importance in uncovering Jesus' own consciousness of the Spirit. This, he affirms, "belongs to the base-rock historicity of the gospels."[59] Three points warrant attention. First, it is implicit in the record of the demonic recognition of Jesus that he is the bearer of the Spirit. He has come as their destroyer, and the awareness of his authority (ἐξουσία) is the basis on which they are expelled. If nothing else, the criticism that Jesus himself was possessed by Beelzebul admits that there was recognition here of supreme spiritual power (Mark 3:22ff.).

Second, Spirit and exorcism are explicitly aligned in the undoubtedly authentic Matt. 12:28 par. Luke 11:20. That Jesus casts out demons by the power of God is undisputed. But Matthew records "the Spirit of God" and Luke opts for "the finger of God." Luke's predisposition for "spirit sayings" has led most scholars to argue for the originality of Luke's version of Q here. But the case is hardly closed.[60] Traditional elements in Matthew include his use of "kingdom of God" (only 4 times in Matthew) in view of his preference for "kingdom of Heaven" (33 times).[61] Also, if a Moses typology has been determinative for Matthew, it seems unlikely that he would have passed over a clear allusion to Exod. 8:19 (LXX, 8:15) in Q. In addition, Spirit sayings are rare in Matthew. But this debate may be largely academic. Both "Spirit" and "finger" point to Jesus' awareness that the power of God was channeled through him— and this pointed to the presence of the kingdom.

Third, both Mark 3:28-29 and Q (Matt. 12:31-32 par. Luke 12:10) record Jesus' enigmatic statement that all sins shall be forgiven except blasphemy against the Holy Spirit. There are various difficulties in comparing the two texts to determine the original form of the Son of Man phrase.[62] Of chief

---

58. See G. W. H. Lampe, "Miracles in the Acts of the Apostles," in *Miracles*, ed. C. F. D. Moule (London: Mowbray, 1965) 165-78; cf. 205-18.

59. *Jesus and the Spirit*, 44; cf. Jeremias, *Theology*, 85-96.

60. For the originality of Luke's Q here see esp. T. W. Manson, *The Teaching of Jesus* (Cambridge: University Press, 1951) 82-83. Barrett, *The Holy Spirit and the Gospel Tradition*, 63, remarks, "The arguments in favour of Luke's δακτύλῳ θεοῦ seem better; and accordingly we must see one of the few references to the Spirit disappear from the earliest stratum of the gospel tradition." But cf. C. S. Rodd, "Spirit or Finger?" *ExpTim* 72 (1960-61) 157-58, who has urged that Luke has a greater tendency to add and delete Spirit passages from the Q tradition. R. G. Hamerton-Kelly, "A Note on Matt. 12:28 par. Luke 11:20," *NTS* 11 (1964-65) 167-69, opts for the priority of Matthew's version but sees both terms as synonymous and stemming from the OT (Ezek. 8:1ff.; 37:1ff.); more recently, see Dunn, *Jesus and the Spirit*, 44-49.

61. Matthew is well known for altering his source to "kingdom of heaven" (see 5:3; 8:11; 10:7; 11:11-12; 13:11, 31, 33, etc.). Only in 19:24 has he left "kingdom of God" unchanged. See Dunn, *Jesus and the Spirit*, 44-46.

62. See esp. Barrett, *The Holy Spirit and the Gospel Tradition*, 103-107; C. Colpe, *TDNT* 8: 442-43; see the exhaustive sources cites in Dunn, *Jesus and the Spirit*, 49-53, esp. 374n.44.

importance is the context which Mark has preserved (so too Matthew, although Luke possibly reflects Q). Jesus' work of exorcism must not be ascribed to the prince of demons. Jesus is acutely aware of the source of his power and warns that seemingly harmless criticisms of him and his work in fact are applied to the Spirit of God within him.

Together these passages highlight Jesus' well-known powers of exorcism. As C. K. Barrett's thorough study concludes, however, this fact should not be over-stressed. Barrett demonstrates the preoccupation of the ancient world with spirits and exorcism and shows that there is "hardly anything in the gospel exorcisms which cannot be paralleled in more or less contemporary pagan or Jewish literature (or both)."[63] The uniqueness of Jesus' exorcisms is found not in their form but in their christological context. To be a potent bearer of the Spirit in exorcism did not differentiate Jesus from other exorcists and magicians. Rather, his exorcisms were viewed as uniquely revealing who he was (through demon recognition), and his explanations further stressed that this power was the power of the kingdom of God unleashed in the world. Thus the Evangelists were not impressed with "pneumatic" people as such. Only the messianic significance that lay behind the exorcism was important. "Because Jesus was Messiah, 'pneumatic' details were bound to arise; but they were bound to arise, as it were, as by-products, of only secondary significance."[64]

(2) Miracles

In many ways, "exorcism" could be subsumed under the more general rubric of "miracles." We have retained the distinction, however, because exorcism is so directly relevant to our interest in pneumatology. Here, as it were, the Spirit embattles spirits. On the other hand, Jesus' healing miracles and nature miracles (δυνάμεις) are less obviously related to "spirit." Yet even here, Jesus' same authority is evident. He does not appear as a doctor who works with diseases but as one who commands disease. He does not make use of natural laws but overrules them.

In the Synoptics only Luke directly conjoins δύναμις and πνεῦμα. The might of the Baptist rests here (1:17), and in 1:35 the two terms are poetically paralleled in the angelic announcement to Mary. Jesus functions in the power of the Spirit (ἐν τῇ δυνάμει τοῦ πνεύματος, 4:14) and this same power is the promised gift of Pentecost (24:49). Thus, as Grundmann concludes, Luke views the mighty works of Jesus as directly related to the presence of the Spirit. "As the essence of God is power, so endowment with power is linked with the gift of His Spirit."[65]

Grundmann goes on to show that Luke correctly found a precedent for this alignment of Spirit and power in his own Jewish tradition (e.g., Mic. 3:8;

---

63. Barrett, *The Holy Spirit and the Gospel Tradition*, 57; cf. Grundmann, *TDNT* 2: 286-90, 302-303; cf. J. M. Hull, *Hellenistic Magic and the Synoptic Tradition* (London: SCM, 1974) 5-72.

64. Barrett, op. cit., 120; cf. E. Schweizer, *TDNT* 6: 402-404.

65. *TDNT* 2: 301; cf. A. Richardson, *The Miracle Stories of the Gospels* (London: SCM, 1941) 108-14.

Ps. Sol. 17:24, 42-43, 47; cf. Josephus *Ant.* 8.408).[66] This was also the understanding in earliest Christian circles. Miracles were a gift of the Spirit (1 Cor. 12:10, 28) which could authenticate someone as a person of the Spirit (2 Cor. 12:12; Gal. 3:5; cf. Heb. 2:4). And, it would be affirmed, the same could be said for Jesus (Acts 2:22; cf. 10:38).[67]

The notion of a special "substance" residing in the Messiah and breaking out with mighty effects is not unknown to the other Synoptic writers. In Mark 1:40-45 Jesus "touches" the leper and seems to transmit power. Especially relevant is the story of the woman with an issue of blood (Mark 5:30 par.). She touches Jesus' garment and he perceives "that power had gone forth from him." Luke records this story but elsewhere gives his own précis: "And all the crowd sought to touch him, for power [δύναμις] came forth from him and healed them all" (Luke 6:19; cf. Mark 3:10). This power seems to exude from Jesus, but no source is possible other than the Spirit of God resident within him.

But does this power present in Jesus become a basis from which the Evangelists argue for his messianic status? Is Jesus a divine man (θεῖος ἀνήρ) and therefore the Son? J. M. Hull has recently agreed with the earlier conclusion of Dibelius that Mark unknowingly portrayed his Christ as a wonder worker surrounded by magic.[68] On the other hand, it is significant how reticent the Gospel writers are to stress this fact. This reticence has also been argued for Mark[69] and indeed for all the Gospels when they are compared with the miracles of Hellenism, Hellenistic Judaism, and early Christian apocrypha (esp. the infancy narratives).

The sound caution of Barrett still seems valid. Miracles were secondary in christological importance because they could easily lead to the belief that Jesus was a common *thaumaturge*. Pneumatic miracle workers were common. But unique elements in the Synoptic tradition lift Jesus' pneumatic abilities outside the norm.

First, Jesus' miracles evoke repentance and faith (Matt. 11:20-21). It is remarkable that well over half of the occurrences of πιστεύειν (and related forms) in the Synoptics occur in the context of miracles. This usage has no Jewish or Hellenistic antecedent.[70] Yet the faith that Jesus calls forward is not mere belief in miracles nor confidence in his abilities as a wonder worker; "it includes an attitude to Jesus' person and his mission."[71] The miracles therefore are not meant to be objects of faith but pointers to faith in him.

---

66. Grundmann, *TDNT* 2: 299-300.

67. For further discussion see Dunn, *Jesus and the Spirit*, 70, 209-12; also, G. W. H. Lampe, "Miracles in Acts," in *Miracles*, 163-78.

68. J. M. Hull, *Hellenistic Magic*, 73-86; M. Dibelius, *From Tradition to Gospel*, tr. B. L. Woolf (New York: Scribner's, 1934) 80; cf. P. J. Achtemeier, "Gospel Miracle Tradition and the Divine Man," *Int* 26 (1972) 179-97.

69. M. E. Glasswell, "The Use of Miracles in the Markan Gospel," in *Miracles*, 151-62.

70. Jeremias, *Theology*, 162-64; H. Baltensweiler, "Wunder und Glaube in Neuen Testament," *TZ* 23 (1967) 241-56.

71. Jeremias, ibid., 163; so too, R. H. Fuller, *Interpreting the Miracles* (London: SCM, 1963) 11-15, 42-43; Glasswell, "Miracles in Mark," 159.

Second, Jesus' miracles point beyond themselves. The expression of power is not their aim. Through the faith they inspire, Jesus is revealed as the one in whom God is present. Therefore it is proper to call them "signs" (Acts 2:22; John, passim) even though Jesus denied any sign to the evil and faithless about him (Matt. 16:1-4).[72] Jesus refused a persuasive proof of his messiahship. Thus his signs were not compelling. His miracles were sometimes met with a lack of faith and understanding (Matt. 11:2-6). But to the faithful they were meant to reveal (almost parabolically) the advent of the kingdom.

* * *

To sum up, it is clear that the Synoptic Evangelists recognized that the Spirit in Jesus was evidenced through his exorcisms and mighty works. Yet the reverse was not the case. Exorcisms and miracles did not conclusively prove that Jesus bore the Spirit. They were portals through which the presence of the Spirit might be viewed. They pointed to who Jesus was and demanded a response from the viewer in the light of this revelation.

b. Words of Authority

It has often been shown that orthodox Judaism in Jesus' day had long understood that the Holy Spirit had been "quenched" in Israel.[73] Tos. *Sota* 13:2 typically affirms, "when . . . the latter prophets were dead, the Holy Spirit departed from Israel." Further, the primary evidence of the Spirit's withdrawal was the absence of prophecy. "The authority of the ancient prophet's writings had taken the place of the spoken prophetic word."[74] Therefore the equation was gradually formed that "to possess the Spirit of God was to be a prophet."[75] In the Targums, the OT phrases referring to the Holy Spirit were regularly paraphrased, "the (holy) spirit of prophecy."[76]

In line with this background it is significant that the Evangelists evaluated both John the Baptist and Jesus in prophetic categories. John is clearly a prophet (Mark 11:32; Matt. 11:9 par. Luke 7:26), but more importantly, he is viewed as an OT prophet bearing an eschatological ministry: he is the forerunner of the Messiah.[77] For Jesus, this prophetic status is even more important. If Spirit and prophecy are so related, the Spirit baptism which inaugurates Jesus' ministry should be viewed in prophetic terms.[78] To say Jesus is a prophet—or

---

72. Richardson, *Miracle Stories*, 44; Barrett, *The Holy Spirit and the Gospel Tradition*, 90; K. H. Rengstorf, *TDNT* 7: 231-39.

73. R. Meyer, *TDNT* 6: 812-28; E. Sjöberg, *TDNT* 6: 381-89; Jeremias, *Theology*, 80-82; Str-B, 1: 127-30.

74. Cullmann, *Christology*, 14. But see the recent contrary view of R. A. Horsley and J. S. Hanson, *Bandits, Prophets and Messiahs. Popular Movements at the Time of Jesus* (New York: Seabury, 1985) 135-89.

75. Jeremias, *Theology*, 78.

76. Str-B, 2: 127-34.

77. That John was considered in some circles to be the eschatological prophet heralding the Day of the Lord is carefully brought out by Cullmann, *Christology*, 23-30. The issue of the primacy of John is evidenced in the later disputes with John's followers (the predecessors of the Mandeans?) found in the Fourth Gospel and the Kerygmata Petrou.

78. I. de la Potterie, "L'onction du Christ, Etude de théologie biblique," *NRT* 8 (1958)

better, the eschatological prophet—is to say a fortiori that he bears the eschatological Spirit.

(1) Jesus as Prophet

That Jesus was popularly considered a prophet is well known. C. H. Dodd's early essay on this topic has yet to be surpassed.[79] For the most part the Synoptics present persons who either give Jesus this title (Mark 6:15; 8:28; Luke 7:16; etc.) or reveal this popular estimate by their refusal to give Jesus prophetic status (Luke 7:39 B*). David Hill points to Mark 14:65 in which incidental trial mockeries reveal the judicial judgment that Jesus is a false prophet.[80] On two occasions Jesus applies the term προφήτης to himself (Mark 6:4 par.; Luke 13:33). Although he does not adopt the formal title of a prophet per se, he nevertheless is numbering himself among those with a prophet's fate (rejection, persecution, martyrdom).[81] As Dodd has shown, his ministry carried all the characteristic features of a prophet.

(2) Jesus as the Eschatological Prophet

But more can and must be said about this topic. Jesus was more than a prophet. Friedrich shows how Mark 6:15 and 8:28 have been enhanced by the other two Synoptists (Luke 9:8 and Matt. 16:14 par. Luke 9:19, respectively) to lift Jesus out of the company of contemporary prophetism into that of the classical prophets.[82] He is a peer of Jeremiah and Elijah. Jesus' unprecedented authority in teaching hints at this correlation. He is called and authorized by God—not by a Rabbinic school. Thus he can display supernatural knowledge: reading both individual's thoughts (Mark 2:8; cf. Luke 7:39) and the future (Mark 11:2; 14:27ff.). Finally, his passion and death clearly bear the form of an OT prophet (Luke 13:33). But Jesus exceeds the OT model as well: "A greater than Jonah is here" (Matt. 12:41). Jesus was not just a prophet—but he fulfilled the prophecies. In him the prophetic spirit was active in an unparalleled way.

R. H. Fuller points to this uniqueness in his conclusion that "the eschatological prophet" was the working concept which guided Jesus in his

---

225-52; D. Hill, *New Testament Prophecy*, 49; F. Hahn, *Christology*, 382: "The story of the baptism has therefore its traditio-historical place first of all within the circuit of the eschatological prophet conception."

79. "Jesus as Teacher and Prophet," in *Mysterium Christi*, ed. Bell and Deissmann (London: Longmans, 1930) 53-66; see also V. Taylor, *The Names of Jesus* (London: MacMillan, 1953) 15-17; C. K. Barrett, *The Holy Spirit and the Gospel Tradition*, 94-95, who uses Dodd's outline; J. D. G. Dunn, *Jesus and the Spirit*, 82-84; G. Friedrich, *TDNT* 6: 841-48; H. Riesenfeld, "Jesus als Prophet," in *Spiritus et Veritas: Festschrift K. Kundsin* (San Francisco: A. Ernstons, 1953) 135-48; F. Hahn, *Christology*, 352-406; Cullmann, *Christology*, 30-38; F. Schnider, *Jesus der Prophet* (Freiburg: Vandenhoeck & Ruprecht, 1973); and D. Hill, *New Testament Prophecy*, 48-69.

80. Hill, *New Testament Prophecy*, 52; and Riesenfeld, "Jesus als Prophet," 135-36.

81. Friedrich, *TDNT* 6: 841; R. H. Fuller, *Christology*, 127.

82. Friedrich, ibid., 842; also Hill, *New Testament Prophecy*, 52-53; Schnider, *Jesus der Prophet*, 173-81; Friedrich goes on to see OT ecstatic traits in Jesus, 843-44. Criticisms of this view are rightly held by Oepke, *TDNT* 2: 456. Jesus is more properly a *Pneumatiker* (Oepke, Dunn) or a Charismatic (Hill) in that he exerts rather than experiences power and authority as his chief evidence of the Spirit.

earthly ministry.[83] To be sure, Jesus nowhere accepts this specific title for his own. But it is difficult to agree with Cullmann that the Synoptic evidence demonstrates that both the Evangelists and Jesus rejected the popular suggestion that Jesus was the expected prophet-like-Moses.[84] Indeed, "prophet" proved to be an inadequate and noncomprehensive christological category everywhere but in later Jewish Christianity. But still, Jesus' messiahship expresses features of the Jewish expectation which had fused together Moses and messianic expectations.[85]

The term προφήτης is applied to Jesus in various settings. In Mark 6:14 Herod identifies Jesus as John the Baptizer raised from the dead. Such rumors of a wonder worker being John *redivivus* were certain to be eschatological.[86] When Jesus makes his entry into Jerusalem (Matt. 21:11), the enthusiastic crowd labels him a prophet and ascribes messianic titles to him. When Jesus raises the widow's son in Nain, the crowd cries that a "great" prophet is here (Luke 7:16). This ascription is paralleled by "God has visited his people," which for Luke is clearly eschatological (Luke 1:68; cf. 19:44).

More importantly, Jesus' ministry contained aspects characteristic of the eschatological prophet-like-Moses. Jeremias points to the importance of Matt. 5:17 and Jesus' conflict sayings about the Torah.[87] Jesus claims a unique authority in that his teachings surpass the Torah. His word now supersedes that of Moses (Mark 10:1-12). Jesus' pneumatic authority is summed up in his characteristic phrase, "truly, I say to you" (ἀμήν, λέγω ὑμῖν).[88]

In addition to having a prophet's sense of mission (Matt. 10:40; 15:24), Jesus' frequent use of "I came" (ἦλθον) and "I was sent" (ἀπεστάλην) (Mark 2:17; 10:45; 9:37; Matt. 15:24) give his mission a sense of urgency. He is the final prophet. Following his triumphal entry, Jesus' authority is challenged by the scribes and priests (Mark 11:27-33). All three Evangelists follow this debate with the parable of the wicked husbandmen: Jesus is the final messenger. He is the son.

Most scholars point to the transfiguration episode as crucial. Here R. H. Fuller finds evidence for a prophet-like-Moses christology in the earliest Palestinian strata.[89] The narrative certainly makes use of a Moses typology (the

---

83. R. H. Fuller, *Christology*, 129-30; such a prophetic category Fuller finds to be central in the earliest strata of Palestinian Judaism.

84. Cullmann, *Christology*, 36-38; Friedrich rightly remarks, "The fact that Jesus never calls himself the eschatological prophet cannot be regarded as proof that he did not view himself as such" (*TDNT* 6: 848).

85. Jeremias finds early evidence for this fusion in the Rabbis, Qumran, and Josephus (*TDNT* 4: 859-61). Of course, Samaritan expectations made the Moses/Messiah identification explicit; so Jeremias, ibid., 862; cf. J. MacDonald, *The Theology of the Samaritans* (London: SCM, 1964) 362-71. A synthesis of various messianic expectations into a single prophetic figure is apparent at Qumran; so Jeremias, ibid., 4: 861; cf. R. Longenecker, *The Christology of Early Jewish Christianity*, SBT 2/17 (London: SCM; Naperville: Allenson, 1970) 34.

86. Friedrich, *TDNT* 6: 838-39; Schnider, *Jesus der Prophet*, 182-83.

87. *Theology*, 83-85.

88. C. K. Barrett, *The Holy Spirit and the Gospel Tradition*, 95; Manson, *Teaching*, 105ff. Hill, *New Testament Prophecy*, 64-66, discusses the recent challenges to Jeremias's contention that Jesus' use of ἀμήν is unprecedented.

89. *Christology*, 49, 172; see the excellent discussion of A. Richardson, *Theology*, 181-85.

mount, three friends, the vision, Jesus' face and clothes).[90] Luke even adds the feature that Elijah and Moses were talking to Jesus about his exodus (ἐξόδον, 9:31). We should no doubt accept that the heavenly command, "Listen to him" (Mark 9:7), parallels Deut. 18:15, "Him shall you heed." Jesus is now the new Moses, and, as Franz Schnider concludes, the presence of Elijah and Moses and this typological scene serve to legitimize the new, end-time prophet.[91]

Finally, Jesus has an unparalleled prophetic knowledge of God. He is not merely a mouthpiece of Yahweh. The transfiguration supports this theme by making him a peer of heavenly companions. In this connection T. W. Manson directs attention to the "Johannine" saying preserved in Q, Matt. 11:27 par. Luke 10:22.[92] Both its presence in Q and its extremely Semitic idiom urge that this is not a later "Hellenistic Revelation Saying."[93] Here only Jesus is able to reveal the definitive will of God. The context (11:25-26) says that the hidden things of God are selectively revealed. But here Jesus is found as the only one from whom nothing is hidden. He is the custodian of the mystery (τὸ μυστήριον) of the kingdom (Mark 4:11).

All these features point to the conclusion that eschatological prophecy was an important category not only for the Evangelists but also for Jesus. In particular, Jesus was readily identified as the prophet-like-Moses, who exceeded the OT forerunner in significant ways. It is a tribute to the Evangelists that they did not force this category on Jesus. No doubt the transfiguration was especially tempting in this regard. But even here the absence of important parallels to Moses shows the Evangelists' respect for history.

Parenthetically, one should note that prophet christology did not fare well in the development of NT thought. Cullmann explains that it was too narrow a concept to do justice to the entirety of early Christian faith.[94] He points out, however, that it did take root in Jewish Christianity, as can be seen in Matthew's literary attempt to make Jesus the new Moses (esp. the infancy, temptation, and Sermon on the Mount narratives). In the early chapters of Acts the analogy is explicit. Both Peter (3:22) and Stephen (7:37) cite the Deut. 18 promise and apply it directly to Jesus. Hebrews likewise puts the typology to good service.[95]

Two other uses of prophet christology deserve mention. Franz Schnider demonstrates that the Jewish-Christian Pseudo-Clementine literature (esp. the

---

90. Friedrich, *TDNT* 6: 846ff.; Jeremias, *TDNT* 4:867ff.; G. B. Caird, "The Transfiguration," *ExpTim* 67 (1955-56) 291-94; W. Liefeld, "Theological Motifs in the Transfiguration Narratives," in *New Dimensions in New Testament Study*, ed. R. Longenecker and M. Tenney (Grand Rapids: Zondervan, 1974) 162-79.

91. *Jesus als Prophet*, 101; cf. E. L. Allen, "Moses in the New Testament," *ExpTim* 67 (1955-56) 104-106; and C. Chavasse, "Jesus Christ and Moses," *Theol* 54 (1951) 244-50, 289-96.

92. T. W. Manson, *Teaching*, 109-12; cf. J. Jeremias, *The Central Message of the New Testament* (London: SCM; Philadelphia: Fortress, 1965) 22-27.

93. Bultmann, *History*, 166; against this view, see Manson, *Sayings*, 79ff.; and Jeremias, *Theology*, 57.

94. *Christology*, 49.

95. Most recently see M. R. D'Angelo, *Moses in the Letter to the Hebrews*, SBLDS 42 (Missoula: Scholar's Press, 1976).

Kerygmata Petrou) gave particular attention to this theme.[96] It was the only christological system to be built entirely on the concept of prophet. As we know, its life in the ongoing church was short. Elsewhere this thought found serious interest only in the Fourth Gospel (see further below).

c. Conclusion

We have seen the dual dimension in the Synoptic portrait of Jesus the *pneumatiker*. On the one hand, their pages appear as a spiritual battlefield where Jesus maneuvers among satanic adversaries. He commands demons, diseases, and nature with unprecedented authority. The Spirit is a part of his weaponry. Yet even these magnificent powers are secondary for the Evangelists. Jesus is not a mere exorcist or magician. His acts of power point beyond themselves to his person and message. They are chiefly christological powers: they unveil his messianic identity.

But bearing the Spirit means being a prophet. Therefore Jesus' pneumatic power can also be discovered in a second kind of authority: teaching and revealing. He is shown to supersede Moses because he is the prophet-like-Moses inaugurating the era of the Spirit. But the Synoptics point to more than the office Jesus holds. His prophetic authority also stems from his intimate knowledge of and relation to the Father. "And I will put my words in his mouth, and he shall speak to them all that I command him" (Deut. 18:18b). In some fashion, the intercourse between Father and Son authenticates the Son's revelation.

2. THE FOURTH GOSPEL

a. Preliminary Remarks

When we approach the Fourth Gospel with the same conceptual categories which we have used with the Synoptics, we are at once faced with difficulties. It appears, in the words of W. G. Kümmel, that the "conception of the earthly Jesus' endowment with the Spirit plays no essential role for John."[97] Two problems have been seen. First, H. Windisch observed a functional problem of Jesus and the Spirit. Jesus is not empowered and directed by the Spirit, but "sees" and "hears" his instructions directly from the Father. The numerous Johannine Spirit passages then stress a strict subordination of the Spirit to the Lord. Jesus can thus appear to baptize followers during his earthly ministry. He freely offers the Spirit and can authoritatively summon the Paraclete to earth after his glorification.[98]

Second, scholars who stress an exaltation christology in John often point to an ontological problem with regard to the Spirit. E. Schweizer discusses the Spirit in these terms and argues that John had to abandon the Synoptic idea of

---

96. *Jesus als Prophet*, 241ff.

97. Kümmel, *Theology*, 314.

98. See his second article, "Jesus und der Geist im Johannesevangelium," translated in *The Spirit Paraclete in the Fourth Gospel*, 27-38; see also M. E. Isaacs, *Concept of Spirit*, 121-22.

inspiration in order to downplay any distinction between God and Jesus. In Jesus, the Father himself is encountered and not any gift of the Father.[99]

These two issues, function and ontology (how Jesus works; who Jesus is) will become recurring themes in our discussion. But we must note at the outset that they are not separable. In Johannine christology Jesus functions uniquely because of his unique status (as preexistent Son and descended redeemer). And his Being is defined by what he does (revealing, mediating). Therefore these two concepts intermingle, and the Spirit is one of the threads which weaves them together.

In John two shifts from the Synoptics are evident when we look for Spirit passages relating to Jesus' earthly ministry. First, there is a difference in the nature of the Spirit with Jesus. The Spirit is not an alien force empowering the Messiah as, say, Markan christology would have it. Jesus does not seem to "have" the Spirit; instead, the Spirit is an attribute of his very life (much like Luke). Second, the effects of the Spirit are noteworthy. The miracles so common to the Synoptic picture have been severely reduced and redefined: now, they are "signs." John has limited the miraculous and elevated the revelatory nature of the miracle. Spirit, as it were, evokes epiphany in John.

To point out such differences from the Synoptics is not to say that we can isolate "the Spirit" in the Johannine Christ and point by point identify where John has moved on. Although (in our view) John did not have the Synoptics as we have them, he did know a general Synoptic (or better, primitive) christology. This explains one of the anomalies of this Gospel: why high and low christological concepts stand side by side. John seized on the earlier tradition and refashioned it as a whole. C. K. Barrett aptly comments: "The result of this is that any attempt to itemize [John's] theology and present it in neat compartments is bound to misrepresent it. Eschatology is bound up with christology, salvation with faith and knowledge, miracles with sacraments; and if any of these themes is isolated from the rest, indeed if any is discussed in isolation from the rest, distortion becomes inevitable."[100]

Johannine pneumatology must be treated in the same way. It has been refashioned by John in stark new categories. In particular, it has been swept up by him into his christology and given new shape. But we would be missing the mark if with some scholars we said John's Gospel is only christological and there is no longer a place for the Spirit. The Fourth Evangelist has also been faithful to the primitive tradition. Like his Synoptic peers, he has used pneumatology to explain christology. G. W. H. Lampe explains the early, common understanding of the Spirit, and how every evangelist necessarily relied upon it to explain the person of Christ. "The early church felt constrained to interpret Jesus in terms of deity 'coming down' to the human sphere in his person. It might be expected that the most appropriate concept for the expression of this image would be Spirit-possession. God's Spirit is his own active presence: God

---

99. E. Schweizer, *TDNT* 6: 438; cf. E. Käsemann, *The Testament of Jesus*, 20-26.

100. Barrett, *John*, 67; cf. S. Smalley, "Diversity and Development in John," *NTS* 17 (1970-71) 276-92.

himself reaching out to his creation."[101] To be sure, John understands this concept, as we see in the baptismal account (1:32-33) and in 3:34. But Lampe goes on to show how a Logos/Son christology (esp. as formulated in Alexandria) rests uneasily side by side with this concept. The Fourth Gospel clearly shows the strains of this tension. How can a preexistent Christ be anointed with the Spirit?

We will begin by looking for pneumatic signs in Jesus' works that might point to the Spirit. In the Synoptics these were vital in discovering the Spirit. We will then look at Johannine christology and examine texts which indicate the Spirit in the person of Christ. Finally, a prophet christology in John will be found to relate to the Spirit's revelatory role in the Fourth Gospel.

b. Works of Power

(1) Exorcisms and Satan

At the very outset we are struck by the absence of exorcisms in John. Jesus is anointed with the Spirit, but he does not immediately experience a satanic temptation or battle with demonic adversaries.[102] No miracle is ever connected to the destruction of Satan's power. Instead, Jesus is found converting a host of followers who in turn introduce the reader to an exhaustive list of high christological titles (1:35-51). But this is not to say that John is unaware of Jesus' war with darkness. This theme abounds in the Gospel (1:5; 8:12; etc.). In John, Jesus' fight is considerably different. There is only one place where Jesus directly battles Satan: the cross. The occurrences of John's terminology for Satan bear this point out. Σατανᾶς appears once (13:27), when he inspires Judas's betrayal. Of the three occurrences of διάβολος, two refer to the betrayal of Judas (6:70; 13:2). "The ruler of this world" (ὁ ἄρχων τοῦ κόσμου τούτου) is confronted and judged in Jesus' passion and death (12:31; 14:30; 16:11). John's dualistic language supports this point as well. After Satan's work in Judas, John suggestively remarks, "It was night." The women at the tomb likewise arrive early, "while it was still dark" (20:1). Luke 22:53 provides an interesting parallel: Jesus tells Judas and the arresting party, "This is your hour and the power of darkness."

One other area of satanic activity is apparent, however. In 8:44 Jesus is in the midst of a heated debate with the Jews and identifies his true opposition as stemming from his opponents' "father"—the devil (διάβολος)—whose work they are doing. In contrast, Jesus' "father" is God (8:38, 42). The disputed contention is the truth of Jesus, which, according to John, is the chief evil denial of the Father of Lies. The Devil, therefore, does not combat Jesus' power (as in the Synoptics) but denies his identity.

---

101. G. W. H. Lampe, "The Holy Spirit and the Pre-Existence of Christ," in *Christ, Faith, and History: Cambridge Studies in Christology*, ed. S. W. Sykes and J. P. Clayton (Cambridge: University Press, 1972) 117.

102. J. E. Davey demonstrates how temptation is actually experienced by the Johannine Christ, *The Jesus of St. John*, 56-72.

The result of this christological debate in John 8 is that Jesus is accused of having a demon. In the Synoptic record, such an accusation makes a single appearance (Mark 3:22 par.). In John it receives surprising attention. Δαιμόνιον and δαιμονίζομαι in the Synoptics commonly refer to unclean spirits confronted by Jesus.[103] These are John's only words for such evil spirits and each time they are applied to Jesus (7:20; 8:48, 49, 52; 10:20, 21, 31). Jesus is accused of being demon-possessed three times (7:20; 8:48; 10:20). We must not fail to miss the force of this accusation. In Jewish terms, "the reproach implies total rejection and dishonoring."[104] Even the Markan parallel is not a true parallel. There Jesus' show of power is said to stem from Beelzebul because Jesus is in league with him and has power over his demons. In John, Jesus is said to be subject to them.[105] Although the logical argument found in Mark 3:23ff. ("Can Satan cast out Satan?") is not represented in John,[106] another important response is evidenced. The affront is countered by Jesus' relationship to his Father (8:49-50, 52-53). The accusation in 8:52 is set in a discussion of Jesus' immunity from death and his knowledge of God. It is climaxed by the lofty affirmation, "Before Abraham was, I am." The accusation of demon possession is therefore centered on who Jesus is—"Who do you claim to be?" (10:53). It is not a conclusion reached by his display of power as in the Synoptics, but by his affirmations about himself. Thus the debate is again christological.

In comparison with the Synoptics, the Johannine picture of spiritual conflict is refashioned to serve two themes. First, the cross is the chief battlefield (although Satan has no power even here, 14:30). Second, the identity of Jesus is the defended concept (but Jesus turns the accusations back upon his accusers, 8:44). The image is not of evil and good powers contending for rulership (the Synoptic battle of the kingdom). Rather, the conflict is moral: truth opposes deceit. The true identity of Jesus and his glorification confront denial. The activity of Satan and demons is not evidenced in crippled, blind, or possessed people needing freedom from their bondage. None of the healing miracles allows this suggestion. Instead, Satan's only power is to effect a denial of Jesus among the Jews. The contest is not about pneumatic power but about Jesus' identity. The victory of this battle is not the successful emergence of the kingdom of God but the true revelation of the identity of the Son of God and his work.

(2) Miracles

We immediately notice a strict reduction of the miraculous in John. In Mark, for example, of 666 verses (to 16:8), 209 deal with miracles (31%). If the

---

103. Δαιμόνιον 11 times in Matthew; 11 times in Mark (or 13 times with the longer ending); 23 times in Luke; δαίμων occurs once, Matt. 8:31. Δαιμονίζομαι occurs 7 times in Matthew; 4 times in Mark; once in Luke. Other terms are also used for the same thought, e.g., πνεῦμα ἀκάθαρτον and πνεῦμα πονηρόν. Cf. Foerster, TDNT 2: 16ff.

104. Foerster, ibid., 19.

105. Cf. Lindars, John, 290.

106. John 10:21 pursues a different argument about the divine provenance of wisdom and miracles: Can wisdom come from a madman? Can good works come from evil?

passion is omitted, 200 of 425 verses deal with miracles (47%).[107] While Matthew and Luke tend to add to the number of miracles in Mark, John records only seven in Jesus' ministry (see the chart below). But this difference is entirely in line with John's intentions. John 20:30-31 tells that he knows more but has given a selective list with a purpose.

On the whole, these data strictly alter the image of Jesus. What possibilities the Synoptic writers left for seeing Jesus as a wonder worker John has all but removed.[108] Nowhere do crowds press near for his touch. Nowhere does he command disease and nature like a pneumatic. Πνεῦμα is never included in a miraculous account. Indeed, "John does not picture Jesus as performing his miraculous signs by the power of the Spirit."[109] But it is not entirely fair to say that John has no appreciation for the miraculous. Where his signs can be compared with a Synoptic account (esp. John 4:46ff.; 6:14ff.), John has heightened the miraculous by stressing some of the miracle's features.[110] Even the Johannine miracles have tremendous elements (e.g., 2:6, 120 gallons of wine). Thus each of the few signs are major and astonishing, yet Jesus is not depicted as displaying his power at every turn. The Fourth Evangelist is focusing on the significance of the *sign*, not on the personal powers of Jesus.

But power is still a feature of the Johannine Christ. Although he intentionally omits the frequent Synoptic term δύναμις, no doubt for christological reasons, he frequently employs δύναμαι.[111] The healing of the blind man makes Jesus' power apparent. The Pharisees are forced to admit, "How is a man who is a sinner able to do such signs?" (9:16). In the witness of the man himself we are told that Jesus' power comes from God (9:33). Finally, in

---

107. A. Richardson, *Miracle Stories*, 36; cf. M. E. Glasswell, "The Use of Miracles in the Markan Gospel," *Miracles*, 149-62.

108. See B. Vawter, "Johannine Theology," 833; Bernard, *John*, 1:clxxvi-clxxxvi; Brown, *John*, 1:525ff. This view is contrary to the arguments advanced by E. Lohse and R. H. Fuller, who believe John has thoroughly heightened the miraculous; R. H. Fuller, *Miracles*, 88-109; E. Lohse, "Miracles in the Fourth Gospel," in *What About the New Testament?* ed. M. Hooker and C. Hickling (London: SCM, 1975) 64-75. Cf. M. Appold, *The Oneness Motif in the Fourth Gospel* (Tübingen: Mohr, 1976) 88-94. Proponents of the Signs Source argue that John reinterpreted a document which presented Jesus as the Divine Man of Hellenism; see below, n.115.

109. G. Ladd, *Theology*, 288; cf. J. F. Walvoord, "The Holy Spirit in Relation to the Person and Work of Christ," *BSac* 98 (1941) 29-55, esp. 48ff.

110. See Lohse, "Miracles in the Fourth Gospel," 65-67; yet it must be noted that John does not use the astonishment and awe of the people as a frequent literary device. Notice its absence following every miracle except the feeding of the 5,000. For John the proper response is belief (2:11; 4:50; 9:37; 11:45), worship (5:14), or confession (6:14).

111. Δύναμις occurs 12 times in Matthew; 10 times in Mark; 15 times in Luke; 10 times in Acts; 49 times in Paul; thus a total of 119 times in the NT. Δύνατος occurs 3 times in Matthew; 5 times in Mark; 4 times in Luke; once in John; 6 times in Acts; 12 times in Paul; thus a total of 32 times in the NT. John's avoidance of these terms must have some significance. Jesus' miracles were undeniable, but for John they were vehicles of revelation, not power. Likewise, John omits other terms that denote might: ἰσχύς, ἰσχυρός (5 times in Matthew; 3 times in Mark; 5 times in Luke; once in John); ἰσχύω (4 times in Matthew; 4 times in Mark; 8 times in Luke; once in John [1:6]; 6 times in Acts; twice in Paul; a total of 28 times in the NT).

Δύναμαι occurs 27 times in Matthew; 33 times in Mark; 26 times in Luke; 21 times in Acts; 38 times in Paul; a total of 210 times in the NT. John uses this term 36 times, 10 of which refer to the mere ability of Jesus (see below, p. 77). Cf. the discussion of Grundmann, *TDNT* 2: 303-304.

FIGURE 2. MIRACLES IN THE FOURTH GOSPEL

Miracle	Text	Synoptic Parallel	σημεῖον "sign"	ἔργον ἐργάζομαι "work"	δόξα "glory"	Jesus as subject	"I am" saying	Associated Discourse
1. Cana Wedding	2:1-11	Mark 2:22*	2:11 first sign		2:11			
2. Nobleman's Son	4:46-54	Matt. 8:5ff.* Luke 7:1-10*	4:48, 54 second sign					Water of Life, John 4*
3. Lame Man	5:2-9	Mark 2:1ff.*		5:17, 20		5:19, 30		
4. Feeding 5,000	6:4-13	Mark 6:32-44 and par.	6:14, 26	6:27ff.		6:52	6:35	Bread of Life, 6:25ff.
5. Walking on Water*	6:16-21	Mark 6:45-52						
6. Blind Man	9:1-7	Mark 8:22ff.* Mark 10:46ff.*	9:16	9:3, 4		9:4, 16, 33 10:21	8:12 9:5	Light of the World, 8:12ff.
7. Lazarus	11:1-44	Mark 5:22ff.*	11:47		11:4, 40	11:37	11:25	Shepherd, 10:1-18*
8. Catch of Fish (A Resurrection Appearance)	21:4-14	Luke 5:1-11*	20:30*					

*Disputed

FIGURE 3. VOCABULARY STATISTICS OF THE MIRACLES IN THE FOURTH GOSPEL

Term	1	2	3	4	5	6	7	8	9	10	11	12	13	14	15	16	17	18	19	20	21
σημεῖον 17 occurrences (1 reference to Jesus)	11 18 23		2	48 54		2 14 26 30	31		16	41	47	**18** **37**								**30**	
σημαίνω 3 occurrences (all references to Jesus)												33						32			19
ἔργον 27 occurrences (19 references to Jesus)			19 20 21	**34**	**20** **36***	28 29	3 7 **21**	39 41	3 **4**	**25** **32*** **33** **37** **38**				10 11 12	24		4				
ἐργάζομαι 8 occurrences (5 references to Jesus)			21		17*	27 28 **30**	18*		4*												
δόξα 19 occurrences	14*	11			41 44*			50 54	24		4 40	41 43*					5 22 24				
δοξάζω 21 (22†) occurrences							39	54*			4	16 23 28*	31* 32†	13	8	14	1* 4 5 10				
δύναμαι 36 occurrences (7 references to Jesus)	46		2 3 4* 5 9 **27**		19 **30** 44	44 **52** 60 65	7 34 36	21 22 43	4 **16** **33**	**21** 29 35	**37**	39	33 36 37	17	4 5	12					
δύναμις No occurrences																					
ἐξουσία 8 occurrences (4 references to Jesus)	12				27					18*							2		10* 11		

Bold verse numbers indicate Christ reference

*Term occurs twice in this verse.

†Term occurs twice and perhaps a third time in this volume.

77

10:19-22, Jesus' powers refute the suggestion that he has a demon. Jesus is consistently shown to have unlimited powers (esp. at the raising of Lazarus, cf. 11:37) and that his power comes from God. The works of Jesus are simply the works of God which Jesus imitates—or better, participates in (5:17, 19-20). Therefore his power is God's power inherent in every aspect of his ministry. The authority (ἐξουσία) of Jesus bears this out. Every mention of Jesus' authority refers directly to the fact that his authority stems from God. Jesus' authority includes his judgment (5:27), his own death/resurrection (10:18), and the eternal life of his followers (17:2).[112]

John's stress on revelation amidst the powerful works of Jesus is seen in his special vocabulary for miracles. (See the chart above.)

(a) Sign (Σημεῖον)

This is the Johannine word for the Synoptic *"power"* (δύναμις). This correspondence is supported by the appearance of σημεῖον in the context of five of the seven miracles.[113] Furthermore, a parallel between σημεῖον in John and δύναμις in the Synoptics is found by comparing John 10:41, "John did no sign" ('Ιωάννης μὲν σημεῖον ἐποίησεν οὐδέν), and Mark 6:5, "Jesus could not do a mighty work" (οὐκ ἐδύνατο . . . ποιῆσαι οὐδεμίαν δύναμιν).[114] The parallel use of ποιεῖν is especially instructive.

A tremendous amount of discussion has surrounded John's use of this term and the possibility of finding a signs-source behind the Gospel.[115] We cannot discuss this theory but must move on to John's use of *sign* as a revelatory term.

Aside from a special eschatological usage (e.g., Matt. 24:3, 24, 30; cf. Acts 2:19), the Synoptics generally use σημεῖον for miracles demanded of Jesus by an unbelieving crowd (cf. Matt. 12:38-39 and Luke 23:8). Jesus consistently refuses to give such proof of his credentials (Matt. 12:39). The nearest John comes to this usage is in 2:18 and 6:30, but no rebuke follows this request,

---

112. J. E. Davey describes this as a part of John's christology of dependence, in this case, on God's power. See idem, *The Jesus of St. John*, 91-95; cf. 115.

113. 2:11; 4:48, 54; 6:14, 26; 9:16; 11:47; see R. E. Brown, "The Gospel Miracles," in *New Testament Essays*, 180-86; also W. Wilkens, *Zeichen und Werke* (Zürich: Zwingli, 1969) 30-45.

114. Rengstorf, *TDNT* 7: 245ff.

115. This was first suggested by E. Schwarz (1907) and J. Wellhausen (1908) and was given full treatment in R. Bultmann's commentary (1st ed., 1941). Recent major studies include J. Becker, "Wunder und Christologie zum literarkritischen und christologischen Problem der Wunder im Johannesevangelium," *NTS* 16 (1969-70) 130-48; R. T. Fortna, *The Gospel of Signs* (Cambridge: University Press, 1970); idem, "Source and Redaction in the Fourth Gospel's Portrayal of Jesus' Signs," *JBL* 89 (1970) 151-66; W. Nicol, *The Sēmeia in the Fourth Gospel: Tradition and Redaction* (Leiden: Brill, 1972); H. M. Teeple, *The Literary Origin of the Gospel of John* (Evanston, Ill.: Religion and Ethics Institute, 1974). A critique of Fortna and Becker is provided by Lindars, *Behind the Fourth Gospel* (London: SPCK, 1971) 28-37. It should be noted that (a) outside the hypothesized source in John there is no other evidence for it; (b) Johannine stylistic features cannot be determined with precision (despite Fortna; see esp. E. Schweizer, *Ego Eimi*; and E. Ruckstuhl, *Die literarische Einheit*; and (c) it is doubtful if such a miracle source would have existed without teachings or discourses by Jesus, presenting him purely as a divine man (contra Becker).

because in the Fourth Gospel people come to belief through signs.[116] To be sure, such belief is criticized as inferior (2:23-25; 4:48; 6:26), but it is a step in the right direction. Through the signs one can ultimately discover who Jesus is (20:30). But the opposite is also possible. In 7:1ff. Jesus' brothers believe in his works, but immediately John remarks that they did not "believe in him" (7:5).

In Johannine thought a miracle simply evokes the surface apprehension of power. After the feeding, the people are reproved (6:26) because they saw only the loaves and fish. Σημεῖον points to an awareness of what transpired and why.[117]

In this sense, John stresses the spiritual symbolism of the event. This emphasis is wholly in keeping with his incarnational theology. The material aspect has become secondary in that now flesh avails nothing (6:63). It is the spiritual presence that is all-significant.[118] John has advanced the Synoptic synthesis of miracle faith in his view that a miracle becomes a revelatory sign when it is apprehended by faith. The result is not merely a prodigy but an unveiling of Jesus. Unlike a miracle, a sign cannot be ignored. This is the nature of revelation. In it the viewer is confronted with a disarming penetration of his world: it compels one to make a decision about the revelation.[119] According to the Evangelist, only two options are open: offense or belief. After the raising of Lazarus, some Jews believe (11:45) while others conspire to kill Jesus (11:53). No one simply walks away.

This effect is chiefly because of what is revealed. The main purpose of the signs "is to bring out the revelation of Jesus' glory which is actually taking place."[120] Therefore both the faith and offense are directed at Jesus. The signs are singularly christological. We cannot agree with Bultmann that in the end Jesus reveals nothing other than that he is the Revealer.[121] The signs reveal the oneness and unity of God and Jesus in all that Jesus does. The signs are proof that the Father is working through Jesus.[122] They authenticate the revelation of the Son. The signs are John's conscious theological effort toward a oneness christology. John's special use of *work* (ἔργον) supports and develops this aspect further.

(b) Work (Ἔργον)

The Fourth Evangelist gives this word unique attention. It is a broader term than σημεῖον in that it more comprehensively describes the activity of Jesus. Of

---

116. John 2:23; 3:2; 6:2, 24; 7:31; 9:16; 12:18; many scholars argue that John is critically reinterpreting his signs source by showing up the inadequacy of miracle faith. See Nicol, *The Sēmeia*, 99-106; Appold, *The Oneness Motif*, 94-102.

117. A. Corell, *Consummatum Est*, 124; Nicol, *The Sēmeia*, 114.

118. Brown, "The Gospel Miracles," in *New Testament Essays*, 187; Brown uses the suggestive terms *signa efficacia* and *signa prophetica* to describe how the signs prophesy and contain the intervention of God. Cf. E. Haenchen, "Der Vater, der mich gesandt hat," *NTS* 9 (1962-63) 208-16.

119. R. Bultmann, *Theology*, 2: 44-49.

120. R. Schnackenburg, *John*, 1: 524; cf. E. Stauffer, *Theology*, 121-22.

121. *Theology*, 2: 62, 66.

122. W. Wilkens, *Zeichen und Werke*, 85-86; M. Appold, *The Oneness Motif*, 22-24; Rengstorf, *TDNT* 7: 248-50; Nicol, *The Sēmeia*, 90-94.

the 27 occurrences in John, most refer to the signs of Jesus.[123] A broader application is found in 14:10, where Jesus' words are works too. In 17:4 ἔργον is used to sum up the entire lifework of Jesus.

The importance of this word for us is the connection John makes between Jesus and God. Never are Jesus' works called his own (i.e., τὰ ἔργα μου). When Jesus refers to "the works which I do" (τὰ ἔργα ἃ ἐγὼ ποιῶ, 5:36; 10:25; 14:12), he always does so in the context of the full and vital relationship between himself and God.[124] Indeed, there is a particular Johannine stress on the role of the Father in inspiring and actualizing Jesus' works. God gives Jesus every work that he does.[125] Therefore the Johannine Jesus never stands autonomous from God. Through his mission, every act makes God transparent; God's glory became visible. Thus Jesus continually participates in God's self-revelation. John 10:37-38 stresses this relation well: "even though you do not believe me, believe the works [ἔργα] that you may know and understand that the Father is in me and I am in the Father" (cf. 14:11).

(c) Glory (Δόξα)

The signs of Jesus are also linked to revelation in that they reveal the glory of Christ.[126] A significant statement in the prologue affirms that the result of the incarnation was the visibility of the glory of the Word before human beings (1:14). Δόξα and δοξάζω are frequently used to explain the death and departure of Jesus (e.g., 7:39; 13:31-32).[127] After the prologue, however, δόξα is used only three times in connection with Jesus' earthly life—and all three refer to a miracle. In 2:11 the manifestation (φανερόω) of Jesus' glory is seen in the first sign. John 11:4, 40 (at the raising of Lazarus) is viewed in this same context of δόξα revelation. The signs therefore permit a unique revelation of Jesus' glory.[128]

Most scholars urge that an OT background of the "glory of the Lord [כבוד יהוה]" must be seen behind this Johannine idea. Brown aptly describes this OT concept adopted by John as "the visible manifestation of [God's]

---

123. 5:20, 36; 6:29-30; 7:3, 21; 9:3-4; 10:25, 32, 37-38; 14:10-11; 15:24; 17:4; in the Synoptics it occurs only twice for a miracle (Matt. 2:11 and Luke 24:19), but even its total Synoptic use is limited: 6 times in Matthew; twice in Mark; twice in Luke; a total of 169 times in the NT.

124. Rengstorf, *TDNT* 7: 248; cf. John 3:35; 5:20; 8:19; 12:45; 14:19ff.; 17:1ff.

125. 4:34; 5:17, 36; 9:3-4; 10:32, 37; 14:10; 17:4; further, according to 14:10 Christians will do greater works because Jesus is with the Father, and the Father will answer prayer.

126. See the excursus of Schnackenburg, "The Theological Significance of the Signs," *John*, 1:52-53; also, Rengstorf, *TDNT* 7: 253-54.

127. Δόξα occurs 7 times in Matthew; 3 times in Mark; 13 times in Luke; 19 times in John; (see the vocabulary statistics above, p. 77); 4 times in Acts; 77 times in Paul; a total of 165 times in the NT. Δοξάζω occurs 4 times in Matthew; once in Mark; 9 times in Luke; 22 times in John; 5 times in Acts; 12 times in Paul; a total of 61 times in the NT.

128. E. C. Colwell and E. L. Titus attempt to view all references to Jesus' glory as references to the Spirit (*The Gospel of the Spirit: A Study in the Fourth Gospel* [New York: Harper and Row, 1953] esp. 107-41, "The Descent of the Spirit"). But this interpretation uncovers the error of failing to read John in its own conceptual categories. Similarly, see L. Floor, "The Lord and The Holy Spirit in the Fourth Gospel," in *The Christ of John*, ed. A. B. DuToit (Potchefstroom: Pro Rege Press, 1971) 123-29.

majesty in acts of power."[129] Significantly, John has applied this glory to Jesus' earthly life. John records no transfiguration account, but to him, Jesus is transfigured—that is, his glory is made transparent, throughout his life and especially through his signs.

The language of glorification in John shows that there is functional reciprocity here between Jesus and God. The one reveals the glory of the other. In the Lazarus miracle (11:4) God is glorified and through this miracle so is the Son. John 13:31 and 17:1 point to the passion wherein the Son is glorified and through this event so is God. Jesus sums up his earthly works as a glorification of the Father (17:4) and then invokes God to glorify him. Mutual glorification is achieved, as it were, because of oneness—both functional and ontological. God and Jesus work in unison (5:17; 10:15; etc.) and are in fact one (10:30; 14:9).

* * *

To sum up, we have sought to establish that John's concern for this Synoptic category ("Works of Power") is strictly specialized. Although Jesus can be depicted as a miracle-working Messiah, the Synoptic understanding is entirely inappropriate. There, works of power were the inevitable result of that power Jesus carried (the messianic Spirit). In John, miracles become signs which reveal not Jesus' power but his glory. The question has changed from *what* Jesus has to *who* Jesus is. John has made the miracles intensely christological, and if one recognizes this divine identity, faith emerges. Thus the revelation of the signs is intimately related to salvation.[130]

Does the christology of John then hold no place for the Spirit? Does John anywhere represent the older tradition? To these questions we must now turn.

c. The Spirit and Johannine Christology

(1) Jesus, a Man Anointed

The Synoptic understanding of Jesus as a Messiah who is distinguishable from the Spirit and who acts in its power is found in John 3:34. Other passages and themes in distinctively Johannine idiom suggest the same.

(a) John 3:34

Two perplexing questions have always surrounded the context (vv. 31-36) of this verse.[131] First, who is speaking? The same problem arises in 3:16-21.

---

129. R. E. Brown, *John*, 1:503; cf. Kittel and von Rad, *TDNT* 2: 232-55.

130. Brown, "The Gospel Miracles," 186-87; cf. Schnackenburg, "The Theological Significance of the Signs," *John*, 1: 521-25.

131. One textual variant, not vital to our exegesis, appears in vv. 31b-32a. Most discussion involves the omission of ἐπάνω πάντων ἐστίν in p75 א* D λ 565 Origen Tertullian Hippolytus Hillary Ambrosianus; Barrett, *John*, 225-26; and esp. M. Black, *Aramaic Approach*, 147ff., persuasively show the importance of Semitic parallelism to confirm the antiquity of the longer reading.

> A. He who comes from above
>   **is above all**
> B. He who comes from the earth

Second, if Jesus is the speaker, has the text been transposed from its original setting in the Nicodemus dialogue? Bauer, Barrett, and Tasker find continuity with vv. 22-30 and believe John the Baptist to be the speaker. M. Black supports this view in his identification of Aramaisms common to both sections.[132] On the other hand, thematic parallels with the Nicodemus section (vv. 1-21) have led many others to nominate Jesus as the speaker (e.g., Schnackenburg, Brown, Bultmann, Bernard). Brown carefully outlines nine parallels which lead him to suggest that these six verses were originally part of the earlier discussion but now have been transposed by the Evangelist.[133] But Dodd points out that such an original setting is unlikely because vv. 31-36 are not "an appropriate continuation" of 3:21.[134]

Perhaps the best alternative is the third. Lagrange and others believe that 3:31-36 is the Evangelist's commentary on the preceding section, just as vv. 16-21 were his commentary on the Nicodemus dialogue.[135] This would make these words a "suitable appendix" (R. H. Lightfoot) to sum up chap. 3. To be sure, the Evangelist has hardly given many clues. As Dodd explains, this passage points to the more general problem in John of dramatic dialogue melting imperceptibly into monologue.[136]

This discussion is important for our exegesis because it determines the theological context in which 3:34 must be seen. Does it refer primarily to Jesus and the Spirit (recalling 1:32) or to the believer and the Spirit (recalling 1:33 and the Nicodemus section)? Because the subject of δίδωσιν (give) is not clear, scholars have sought to establish it by context.

In our view, 3:31-36 is the final Johannine examination of the Jesus-Baptist contrast. Christological ideas are summations from vv. 1-21 and this

---

is of the earth
and speaks of the earth
A'. And he who comes from heaven
is above all
and he testifies to what he has seen and heard.

A second variant appears in B syr⁵—both of which omit τὸ πνεῦμα from v. 34. Bultmann (*John*, 164n.1) is certainly wrong in following this reading and rejecting πνεῦμα here as "completely unjohannine." Perhaps these texts wanted to avoid a contradiction with 7:39, presuming Christ to be the subject of 3:34b; see R. Schnackenburg, *John*, 1: 387.

132. *Aramaic Approach*, 146-47; but there are thematic problems with this view, e.g., vv. 32b and 26; 3:22-30 appears to expand on the successes of Jesus, not on his rejection, so L. Morris, *John*, 243-44.

133. *John*, 1:159-60; Dodd, *Interpretation*, 108; among these parallels note the references to "from above" (vv. 3, 7, 31), "testimony" (vv. 11, 32), rejection (vv. 11, 32), the Spirit (vv. 5-8, 34), eternal life (vv. 15, 16, 36); but these could stem from a summary rather than a continuation of the thought in 3:1-21.

134. Dodd, *Interpretation*, 309; Brown mentions that J. G. Gourbillon solves this problem by placing it after 3:13, but this solution as well is not compelling. See J. G. Gourbillon, "La parabole du serpent d'airain," *RB* 51 (1952) 213-26; Porsch, *Pneuma*, 101-102, examines the arrangement of 3:11-12, 31-36, 13-21.

135. M. J. Lagrange, *St. Jean*, 96-97; that vv. 31-36 is the comment of the Evangelist is also held by R. H. Lightfoot, *John*, 120; Dodd, *Interpretation*, 309-10; A. M. Hunter, *John*, 43-44; L. Morris, *John*, 243; and G. Johnston, *Spirit-Paraclete*, 13-15.

136. *Interpetation*, 308.

accounts for the numerous parallels. In 3:22-30 the final transition has taken place from John to Jesus (πάντες ἔρχονται πρὸς αὐτόν, v. 26). It remains for the Evangelist to draw out the substantial differences. In this regard, two issues are discussed. What are these men's origins? What was the nature of their message? Jesus is from above, and John is of the earth.[137] John's message is earthbound, Jesus' message is from God. Jesus' teachings stem from what he has seen in the heavenly world. The Evangelist's chief interest is on the superiority of Jesus: both in who he is and what he does.

Verse 34 must therefore be seen as a part of this christology. John goes on to support his view of Jesus by describing the generosity of the Father to the Son: God has given all things (πάντα) into his hands (v. 35). John 3:34b fits this theme. Jesus speaks the words of God (v. 34a) by virtue of his unlimited anointing in the Spirit (v. 34b). Πνεῦμα is thus a part of the πάντα in 3:35.

The subject of δίδωσιν has been debated. One alternative has been to view Jesus as the subject,[138] confirming the expectation of 1:33b and 3:5 that Jesus is the one who generously gives the Spirit. The most recent advocate of this view is Felix Porsch. Porsch not only joins Schnackenburg and replaces the unit in the Nicodemus section (after 3:12), but he also underscores this alternative's two chief strengths. First, the gifts given by the Father to the Son in John are generally expressed by the perfect (17 times) as in 3:35 or by the aorist (8 times). Only once is the present used (6:37). Thus the use of the present tense in 3:34b suggests that the Son is the giver.[139] Second, a purely grammatical argument can be advanced. The subject of v. 34a is clearly Jesus. There may be no ground for assuming a new subject in v. 34b unless John has adopted a new subject from within v. 34a (ὁ θεός, God, the subject of the relative clause).[140] To make Jesus the subject is to say that he is the one who bestows the Spirit through his speaking the word of God. This thought, we might add, is not entirely foreign to the Fourth Evangelist (6:63b).

The attempts of scribes to provide a subject for δίδωσιν parallel the interpretations of most modern scholars.[141] Barrett tersely remarks that to make Jesus the subject "is to import alien ideas into the passage."[142] As we

---

137. ἡ γῆ in John is not pejorative (3:22, 31; 6:21; 8:6, 8; 12:24, 32; 17:4; 21:8, 9); ὁ κόσμος would have been.

138. See W. F. Howard, St. John, 73; W. Thüsing, Die Erhöhung und Verherrlichung Jesu im Johannesevangelium (Münster: Aschendorff, 1960) 154ff.; Lagrange, St. Jean, 96-97; Porsch, Pneuma, 101-105; cf. Dunn, Baptism, 20, 32.

139. This was first pointed out by Brown, John 1:158; cf. Porsch, Pneuma, 104.

140. Porsch, Pneuma, 104. But we might also argue that John's use of the conjunction γάρ (which is used least in the Johannine literature) forms a causal coordinating clause which can stand fully independent of the main clause. A subordinate causal clause would have properly been expressed with ὅτι, a subordinate conjunction, διά plus an articular infinitive, or a participle. See BDF, § 452; Robertson, Grammar, 962-66. The suggestion of Zahn and others to make "the Spirit" the subject is improbable in that there would no longer be a direct object for the verb.

141. Note the textual variants: ὁ θεός, D θ W it[a] vg syr[p] cop[sa] cop[bo] Origen; ὁ πατήρ, syr[c]; θεὸς ὁ πατήρ, syr[s]. Scholars who try to provide a subject include Schnackenburg, Barrett, Hill, Bernard, Lindars, Morris, Windisch, Cullmann, Bultmann, Hoskyns, Black, Hunter, Davey, R. H. Lightfoot, Strachan, Tasker, Marsh, and G. Johnston. Dodd and Brown remain unconvinced.

142. Barrett, John, 226.

have seen, the context and development of thought in John 3:31-32 is best served if here we allow John to complete his christological ascription to Jesus. The Spirit is one gift among many (3:35) that Jesus has in full. The reverse, that Jesus gives the Spirit without measure, would be a doubtful Johannine thought. Only the Son is anointed οὐκ ἐκ μέτρου.

A final difficulty deserving attention is the meaning of the phrase "without measure" (οὐκ ἐκ μέτρου). It is not a Greek expression (οὐ μετρίως or ἀμετρίως or οὐ κατὰ τὸ μέτρον would have been better) and has not been found elsewhere in Greek writing. But there is a possible parallel among the Rabbis. Rabbi Acha said, "The Holy Spirit, who rests on the prophets, does so only by measure."[143] If such a thought stands behind 3:34, Jesus is being compared with the prophets (cf. Heb. 1:1) in that his endowment with the Spirit is permanent, full, and eschatological. Thus οὐκ ἐκ μέτρου ties in with John's use of μένειν in 1:32, 33.

To argue that God is the subject of δίδωσιν is not to reject the pertinent observations of Porsch and Bultmann that Spirit and revelation are united in this passage. But Porsch would argue that Jesus' promise of Spirit baptism (1:33; cf. 3:5) is first defined here by John. Jesus' "Spirit baptism" is then "identical with his function as revealer."[144] Although this general conclusion is not compelling, 3:34 does indicate that the Spirit which Jesus immeasurably has will manifest itself in the words he speaks (6:63). That is, the truth of his revelation of the Father (ὃ ἑώρακεν καὶ ἤκουσεν) is grounded in his full anointing in the Spirit. John 3:34 links three important Johannine themes: Jesus' mission (ἀποστέλλω), Jesus' revelation (λαλέω, μαρτυρέω), and Jesus' anointing (τὸ πνεῦμα οὐκ ἐκ μέτρου). Jesus has been sent by God to reveal the very Father whose gift of the Spirit ascertains his revelation.

It is interesting to note in this connection that a similar relationship between Spirit and believer is anticipated. The Spirit will inspire the mission of the apostles (20:21-22) and reveal to them the identity and message of Jesus (14:26; 16:13).

(b) John 6:27, Σφραγίζειν

The word group surrounding σφραγίς receives only limited attention in the NT. Out of 32 appearances, 22 belong to the special usage of the Apocalypse.[145] Matthew's reference to sealing the tomb provides the standard meaning. Even in the Apocalypse, the seal is a mark of ownership or protection on an object or person. Paul develops a specialized usage. Following Jewish custom he labels circumcision a seal (σφραγίς, Rom. 4:11) but contrasts this seal with the seal of the Spirit that God has placed on believers (2 Cor. 1:22; Eph. 1:13; 4:30).

---

143. Midr. Rab. Lev. 15:2; Str-B, 2:431.

144. Porsch, *Pneuma*, 104-105; cf. Bultmann, *John*, 164-65.

145. Σφραγίζω occurs once in Matthew (27:66); not at all in Mark or Luke; twice in John (3:33; 6:27); 4 times in Paul (Rom. 15:28; 2 Cor. 1:22; Eph. 1:13; 4:30); 8 times in Revelation (7:3, 4 [bis], 5, 8; 10:4; 20:3; 22:10); a total of 15 times in the NT. Σφραγίς occurs 3 times in Paul (Rom. 4:11; 1 Cor. 9:2; 2 Tim. 2:19); 13 times in Revelation (5:1, 2, 5, 9; 6:1, 3, 5, 7, 9, 12; 7:2; 8:1; 9:4); a total of 16 times in the NT. Κατασφραγίζω occurs only in Rev. 5:1.

According to Paul, "In sealing believers God has made them his own inviolable possession; the pledge of this is the Spirit in their heart."[146]

Only in the Fourth Gospel is sealing applied to Jesus (6:27). The only other Johannine usage is in 3:33, where "a seal" is the testimony of the believer. The use of the aorist in 6:27 tempts one to look for a particular act of sealing. The incarnation, the image of the Father, and the seal placed on the sacrificial victims have all been suggested. But the best interpretation recalls the baptism/anointing of Jesus recorded in 1:32-33. Here the Baptist took this event as God's indelible messianic mark on Jesus. The Spirit was Jesus' σφραγίς.[147]

This understanding of 6:27 gains support when we remember two further developments. First, the Johannine Christians regarded seriously the notion that they bore the mark of the Spirit. Their idiom for Paul's sealing was χρῖσμα (anointing).[148] Χρῖσμα occurs only three times in the NT and is restricted to 1 John (2:20, 27), where it most likely refers to the indwelling presence of the Spirit.[149] This was the mark through which these believers claimed their identity and authority in Christ. If messianic anointing was indicative for them, it may have been an echo of the experience they understood to be upon Jesus.[150] Elsewhere in the NT, χρίω refers to the Spirit anointing/baptism of Christ (Luke 4:18; Acts 4:27; 10:38; cf. Heb. 1:9) which is normative for the Christian (2 Cor. 1:21).

Second, σφραγίζειν became a technical term in the postapostolic church to describe baptism. Both in Hermas and in the Acts of Paul and Thecla, baptism is called a σφραγίς.[151] Although the prominence of the Spirit has receded here, still the connection is made that at baptism one receives God's seal, the Spirit, which is the surety for redemption.

Thus the seal on Jesus in John 6:27 is the Spirit. John's double reference to God (θεός, πατήρ) is an emphatic way of stressing the divine origin of this seal. It is this seal which affirms that Jesus is the lifegiver. Just as elsewhere it is the Spirit alone that gives life (6:63), so here the food that endures to eternal life is supplied by the Son of Man because he carries the seal/Spirit of the Father.[152]

---

146. G. Fitzer, *TDNT* 7: 949; cf. G. W. H. Lampe, *The Seal of the Spirit*, 3-18; A. Richardson, *Theology*, 350-55.

147. Barrett, *John*, 287; Schnackenburg, *John*, 2:50; Bernard, *John*, 1: 191; Morris, *John*, 359; Dunn, *Baptism*, 184; Richardson, *Theology*, 135. BAG understands σφραγίζειν in 6:27 as "endue with power from heaven" (p. 796); but B. Lindars sees no need to refer to the baptism of Jesus. John 6:27 means that Jesus "has already been marked out" for the purposes of God. See his commentary, p. 225.

148. Paul parallels the two verbal forms in 2 Cor. 1:21-22: καὶ χρίσας ἡμᾶς θεός, ὁ καὶ σφραγισάμενος ἡμᾶς καὶ δοὺς τὸν ἀρραβῶνα τοῦ πνεύματος.

149. W. Grundmann, *TDNT* 9: 572; R. Schnackenburg, *Johannesbriefe*, 151-52, points out parallels between the promises of the Paraclete and this anointing (cf. John 14:17; 15:26; 16:8-10); Dodd, *Johannine Epistles*, 63-64, describes this χρῖσμα as the word of God. See below, pp. 174-75.

150. Cf. Grundmann, *TDNT* 9: 572.

151. Hermas *Sim.* 9:16; cf. 8:2, 3; Acts of Paul and Thecla 25; cf. Odes Sol. 4:8; 8:16; 2 Clem. 7:6; 8:6; see W. Bousset, *Kyrios Christos*, tr. J. E. Steely (Nashville: Abingdon, 1970) 295ff.; and Lampe, *Seal of the Spirit*, 97-148; complete references can be found in BAG, 796-97.

152. J. Dunn, *Baptism*, 184, suggests that in 6:27a we may have a reference to the coming gift of the Spirit.

(c) John 1:51

This verse presents the interpreter "with an almost bewildering complex of ideas and allusions."[153] Its analysis has a long history and for the most part remains uncertain. For numerous reasons commentators have viewed this verse as an independent logion later added to the conversion of Nathanael.[154] Above all, its reference to the Son of Man serves as a climax to the list of titles in chap. 1—but along with this important point is the perplexing question of the meaning of angels ascending and descending on him.

The allusion to the Jacob story (Gen. 28:12) seems unavoidable (pace Michaelis). The Rabbinic debate whether the angels were descending on the ladder or on Jacob is clearly brought out by Midr. Gen. Rab. 68:18.[155] Although this variation would solve the Johannine parallel (the angels descend on Jesus), we are still left with interpreting the meaning of this event for John. Numerous suggestions have been put forward. Jeremias points to Jewish myths about the stone of Bethel as the place of the presence of God. Similarly Fritsch aligns Jesus with Bethel as the house of God. McKelvey argues for a temple replacement motif. Odeberg and Bultmann point to Jewish mystical traditions which viewed the angels moving between Jacob's celestial ideal and earthly person (so Philo, De Somniis 1:22). Of special interest are the Targums (so Quispel), which refer to the shekinah of Yahweh in Gen. 28 as present on Jacob. Hence John 1:51 may reaffirm the prologue's statement that Jesus embodies the shekinah of God.

It is clear from these different interpretations that the Jewish use of the Jacob story was rich and varied. In this sense, many scholars point out the need of seeing a figurative image here.[156] But the Jewish interpretations and John have one image in common: Jesus (or Jacob/Bethel, etc.) "is the place of revelation, the place over which the heaven has been opened (Matt. 3:16; Rev. 19:11)."[157] Jesus is the locus of divine glory. In this general context it is possible

---

153. S. Smalley, "The Johannine Son of Man Sayings," NTS 15 (1968-69) 289. For attempts at analysis see C. F. Burney, Aramaic Origins, 115-16; J. Jeremias, "Die Berufung des Nathanael (John 1,45ff.)," Angelos 3 (1928) 2-5; H. Odeberg, Fourth Gospel, 33-42; H. Windisch, "Angelophanien um den Menschensohn auf Erden," ZNW 30 (1931) 215-33; idem, "John 1,51 und die Auferstehung Jesu," ZNW 31 (1932) 199-204; G. Quispel, "Nathanael und der Menschensohn (John 1,51)," ZNW 47 (1956) 281-83; I. Fritsch, "Videbitis angelos Dei ascendentes et descendentes super Filium hominis," VD 37 (1959) 3-11; W. Michaelis, "John 1,51, Gen. 28,12, und das Menschensohn-Problem," TLZ 85 (1960) 26-30; C. Colpe, TDNT 8: 468-69; S. Smalley, "Johannes 1,51 und die Einleitung zum vierten Evangelium," in Jesus und der Menschensohn. Für Anton Vögtle, ed. R. Pesch and R. Schnackenburg (Freiburg: Herder, 1975) 300-313; and R. J. McKelvey, The New Temple. The Church in the New Testament (Oxford: University Press, 1968) 77.

154. On the independence of the logion see Brown, John, 1: 88-89; Colpe, TDNT 8: 468n.461. The chief evidence is as follows: (a) v. 51 changes to the plural; (b) καὶ λέγει αὐτῷ appears editorial and repetitive; (c) ἀμὴν ἀμήν may serve to quote adopted tradition; (d) v. 50 would be a good introduction to the Cana miracle. Windisch, "Johannes 1, 51, und die Auferstehung Jesu," sought to identify its source in an angelophany tradition.

155. See the text, cited in Odeberg, Fourth Gospel, 33; Rabbi Hiyya and Rabbi Yannai dispute the antecedent of בו. The LXX, which John apparently did not use, is clear: ἐπ' αὐτῆς (i.e., the ladder, ἡ κλίμαξ).

156. So Bultmann, John, 106; Dodd, Interpretation, 294; Brown, John, 1:90.

157. Hoskyns, John, 189.

to see a distinctively Christian use of the imagery. For John, Jesus is the one before whom all heaven is open and who in turn reveals all that he sees.

Baptismal interpretations have also been applied to this verse (cf. Michaelis). Although the heavens are not mentioned in John 1:32-33, John's use of *heaven* here parallels that of Luke 3:21 at Jesus' baptism (both Matthew and Mark use the plural). Luke and Matthew also employ ἀνοίγειν (to open) with John to describe this theophany. Further, John 1:49 parallels the Synoptic baptismal proclamation, Son of God. Michaelis also cites (dubiously) the reference to angels paralleling the Synoptic temptation account.

Although John 1:51 is not a Spirit text, the above discussion leads us to believe that it is written in a distinctively Johannine idiom for coordinate concepts. The opened heavens and descending messengers recall baptismal images. But here the ἀνάβασις/κατάβασις (ascent/descent) deepens the thought, making Jesus the point of contact between heaven and earth.[158]

The chief Synoptic parallel to 1:51 is the Son of Man's promise of a triumphant eschatological return (Mark 13:26). But John 1:51 brings us to the heart of the Johannine Son of Man problem: this future expectation is given a present reality in John. The textual variant, ἀπ' ἄρτι,[159] though probably a conflation from Matt. 26:64, carries the same thought. From now on the glory of the Son of Man will be evident. It will not need to wait for his future exaltation.

The danger of drawing in passages such as 1:51 is that we may lose sight of our original goal. Texts dealing with the glory of the Son or with his role as revealer can be included only with care.[160] One is suddenly enmeshed in a discussion of christology and the Son of Man instead of the Spirit. As we shall see, however, this strictly Johannine peril arises out of a christology which at many points is indistinguishable from pneumatology. The unique glory and revelatory power of the Johannine Christ stems from his perfect union with the Spirit and with the Father—all of which John presents in the person of Jesus.

(2) Spirit Christology

The intimate union of Spirit and Christ is by far the most prominent theme in John's pneumatology. The Spirit is not a power impulsively resident in Jesus but an attribute of his own person. Johannine eschatology exhibits this relation by depicting the Spirit in terms reminiscent of Jesus' earthly ministry. John's christology brings out this relation with a special metaphor (living water) which serves in two ways. First, this is water which only Jesus may distribute

---

158. Cf. C. K. Barrett: "John surely is concerned not only to make a christological point in a straightforward ontological proposition, but to emphasize movement, traffic, intercourse." See his "Christocentric or Theocentric? Observations on the Theological Method of the Fourth Gospel," *Bibliotheca Ephemeridum Theologicarum Lovaniensium* 41 (1976) 370.

159. 'Απ' ἄρτι appears elsewhere in John at 13:19 and 14:7; this reading in 1:51 appears in a variety of codices, the Old Latin, Chrysostom, and Augustine; see Barrett, *John*, 187. Schnackenburg, *John*, 1:321, comments that the perfect of ἀνοίγειν "leaves the length of the vision undefined."

160. This is the major flaw in the study of Colwell and Titus, *The Gospel of the Spirit* (New York: Harper & Row, 1953).

(4:10, 14). Second, this is water which is alive within him (7:37-38) and may be dispensed only through his cross (7:39; cf. 19:34). John 7:37ff. defines this water as the Spirit. As 20:22 makes plain, this Spirit is none other than Jesus' own breath.

(a) John 7:37-39

These verses have been the subject of protracted scholarly debate. On the whole, two major interpretations usually reappear for discussion. The traditional view, called the Eastern Interpretation (following Origen, Athanasius, and the Greek fathers) understands the believer to be the source of living water:

37b ἐάν τις διψᾷ ἐρχέσθω πρός με[161]
    καὶ πινέτω.

37b If someone thirsts, let him come
    to me and drink.

38 ὁ πιστεύων εἰς ἐμέ,
   καθὼς εἶπεν ἡ γραφή,
   ποταμοὶ ἐκ τῆς κοιλίας αὐτοῦ
   ῥεύσουσιν ὕδατος ζῶντος.

38 He who believes in me,
   just as the scripture says,
   rivers of living water will flow
   from his belly

This view places a full stop after πινέτω (let him drink) and makes the participle, ὁ πιστεύων (the believer), the suspended subject (casus pendens) of the citation (resumed in αὐτοῦ). Although this interpretation results in an anacoluthon, it is common Semitic Greek and appears most often in John. This view has received much traditional and modern scholarly support.[162]

On the other hand, a second, Western or Christological Interpretation views Christ as the source of the living water:

37b ἐάν τις διψᾷ ἐρχέσθω πρός με
    καὶ πινέτω

37b If someone thirsts, let him come
    to me. And let him drink

38 ὁ πιστεύων εἰς ἐμέ.
   καθὼς εἶπεν ἡ γραφή,
   ποταμοὶ ἐκ τῆς κοιλίας αὐτοῦ
   ῥεύσουσιν ὕδατος ζῶντος.

38 who believes in me.
   Just as the scripture says,
   rivers of living water will flow
   from his belly.

---

161. ℵ* D p[66] omit πρός με, although both p[75] and B read ἐμέ. Bultmann (John, 303n.1) views this as an addition to expand the context. But its strong attestation elsewhere and its fully Johannine force (6:35; 5:40; 6:44, 45, 65; etc.) suggest its authenticity. Compare its use in parallelismus membrorum below.

162. On the grammar see Moulton, Grammar, 1:69, 225; BDF, § 466; on John, see Moulton Grammar, 2: 424; Abbott, Johannine Grammar, §§ 1921, 2129; Burney, Aramaic Origin, 64-65; cf. John 1:12, 18, 33; 3:26, 32; 5:11; etc. See also M. Balague, Barrett, Behm, Bernard, Cadman, Cortez, Freed, Hodges, R. H. Lightfoot, Lindars, Michaelis, Morris, Odeberg, Rengstorf, Schlatter, Schweizer, C. H. Turner, M. M. B. Turner, Westcott, Zahn; AV, RSV, NASB, UBS, Nestle 26th ed. On the patristic interpretation of John 7:37-39 see J. E. Menard, "L'interprétation patristique de Jean VII,38," Revue de l'université d'Ottawa 25 (1955) 5-25; F. D. Mattijs, "An Enquiry into the Patristic Exegesis of John 7:39," unpub. diss., Pontifical Gregorian University, Rome, 1959; also see Hoskyns, John, 365-66; and Schnackenburg, John, 2:211ff.

Here a full stop follows εἰς ἐμέ (in me). The participle then becomes the subject of πινέτω (let him drink; or both imperative verbs, so Kilpatrick),[163] and the rivers mentioned in the citation refer only to Jesus. In addition to patristic support (Justin, Hippolytus, Tertullian, Irenaeus), this view has also found modern scholarly consent.[164]

Three questions dominate this exegetical discussion: (1) punctuation; (2) the antecedent of αὐτοῦ (his); and (3) the source of the scripture citation. These issues are strictly interrelated and in reality to decide on one is to interpret all three. We support the christological view with the following considerations in mind.

(1) From a textual-critical perspective, it is true that p[66] and p[67] place a full stop after v. 37 (following πινέτω). Although this is weighty evidence, the use of such marks in p[66] may be arbitrary and theologically motivated.[165] The Western punctuation is evidenced only in the colometry of the Old Latin mss. d and e (fifth century) and in one Coptic ms. connecting πινέτω with the participle.[166] Grammatical arguments are similarly inconclusive. Brown's remark that in John a participle heads a sentence 41 times must be balanced against Kilpatrick's convincing discussion of καθώς clauses: when a scripture citation is involved, such clauses invariably follow their main clause (cf. John 6:31; 12:14).[167] The absence of exhaustive evidence for this pattern in John does not invalidate these points.

Most important here is the presence of *parallelismus membrorum*. In 7:37-38 many scholars have noted such parallelism if the Western reading is maintained.[168]

---

163. G. D. Kilpatrick, "The Punctuation of John 7:37-38," *JTS* 11 (1960) 340-42.

164. Abbott, W. C. Allen, Badcock, Bindley, Bishop, Boismard, Braun, Brown, Bullinger, Bultmann, Burney, Dodd, Dunn, Guilding, R. Harris, Hoskyns, Jeremias, Loisy, McKelvey, Mollat, Painter, Porsch, D. M. Stanley, Thüsing, N. Turner, Vellanickal, Zerwick; NEB, RSV mg.; Boismard has shown that this interpretation was popular not only in the West: the support of Cyprian, Aphraates, and Ephrem show this view in the Syriac and African churches. See his "De son ventre couleront des fleuves d'eau," *RB* 65 (1958) 523-46. Schnackenburg, *John*, 2:153, shows the same diversified patristic support.

165. J. J. Collins, "Papyrus Bodmer II," *CBQ* 20 (1958) 281-89.

166. K. H. Kuhn, "St. John 7:37-38," *NTS* 4 (1957-58) 63-64.

167. Brown, *John*, 1: 320-21; the use of the participle here is irregular, however; see Kilpatrick, "The Punctuation of John 7:37-38," 340-41; also, N. Turner, *Grammatical Insights into the New Testament* (Edinburgh: T. & T. Clark, 1965) 144-45; see further Mark 1:1; Luke 2:23; Acts 7:42; Rom. 1:17; Gal. 3:6; the criticisms of J. B. Cortez, the most forceful proponent of the traditional view, are unconvincing: "Yet Another Look at John 7:37-38," *JTS* 24 (1922-23) 66-70; and most recently Z. C. Hodges, "The Problem Passages in the Gospel of John. Part 7. Rivers of Living Water, John 7:37-39," *BSac* 136 (1979) 239-48.

168. For John's use of parallelism see C. F. Burney, *Aramaic Origin*, 109-11; idem, *The Poetry of Our Lord* (Oxford: Clarendon Press, 1925); M. Black, *Aramaic Approach*, 143ff.; cf. Abbott, *Johannine Grammar*, §§ 2554-57; and X. Léon-Dufour, "Trois chiasmes johanniques," *NTS* 7 (1960-61) 149-55. See also C. F. Burney, "Our Lord's Old Testament Reference in John 7:37-38," *Exp* 20 (1920) 385-88; W. C. Allen, "John 7, 37-38," *ExpTim* 34 (1922-23) 329-30; Abbott, *Johannine Grammar*, § 2556. For similar parallelisms, see 6:35; 7:24; 8:23; 16:23; 17:18, 23. Opposed to such a parallelism are Cortez, "Yet Another Look"; and Blenkinsopp, "John 7:37-39: Another Note on a Notorious Crux," *NTS* 6 (1959-60) 95-98.

a   If someone thirsts
b   let him come to me;
a'   and let him drink
b'   who believes in me.

Although this parallelism was originally identified as a chiasmus (abb'a'), a synonymous parallelism (aba'b') aligns precisely themes which are often juxtaposed in John (6:35; 4:14a; cf. Rev. 22:17). The objection of Cortez that we do not find verbal agreement here is resolved by the fact that Semitic parallelism does not require verbal exactitude but thematic precision. Further, all studies show that vv. 37-38 were probably an Aramaic logion.

(2) More important objections to the traditional reading come when we seek the antecedent of αὐτοῦ (his). Are there parallels to the believer being the source of living water? John 4:14 is often called into service here, but in this verse the spring of water does not become a source of water for others.[169] Similarly, 14:12 does not permit any direct parallel. OT passages often depict the believer as filled with water, meaning wisdom (Prov. 18:4) or Yahweh's blessing (Isa. 58:11), but generally such references do not have the eschatological force given by John of a superabundant spring with eternal supplies. Nowhere in John or the NT is the believer said to be the source of living water.[170] Such distribution (which v. 39 describes as the Spirit) is strictly a divine prerogative.

On the other hand, John clearly places Jesus in this role. Jesus offers the Samaritan woman his own living water (ὕδωρ ζῶν, 4:10) which removes all thirst.[171] John 6:35 offers a remarkable parallel to 7:37-38.[172] He who hungers, comes, and believes can taste of Jesus' bread. But in our context, 7:39 speaks of the Spirit. Jesus alone is the source of the Spirit (20:22; cf. 14:16). Most importantly, 19:34 provides an unavoidable allusion to what is predicted here (see further below). Finally, Rev. 22:1-2 depicts a river of life flowing from the throne of God and of the Lamb (Christ).[173]

(3) Another argument in favor of a christological understanding of 7:37-38 is the source of the scripture citation. Because this phrase does not appear in the MT or the LXX, most scholars believe that we are dealing with a composite quotation.[174] The most probable sources for this material all refer

---

169. Brown, *John*, 1:321; and M. E. Boismard, "De son ventre couleront des fleuves d'eau," 535; against Cortez, "Yet another Look," 79. A roughly parallel thought is found in the Midr. Sifre since a rule is "When a disciple is like a well, then just as the well flows out living water on all sides, so from that disciple there will come forth disciples and their disciples." See Str-B, 2: 493.

170. C. H. Dodd, *Interpretation*, 349n.2; Bultmann, *John*, 303n.2.

171. In this context "the gift of God" (4:10) could refer to the Spirit; cf. Acts 2:38; 8:20; 10:45; cf. also Dunn, *Baptism*, 187.

172. John 6:35: ὁ ἐρχόμενος πρὸς ἐμὲ οὐ μὴ πεινάσῃ, καὶ ὁ πιστεύων εἰς ἐμὲ οὐ μὴ διψήσει (he who comes to me shall not hunger, and he who believes in me shall not thirst).

173. R. J. McKelvey, *The New Temple*, 80.

174. See C. K. Barrett, "The OT in the Fourth Gospel," *JTS* 48 (1947) 155-69; E. D. Freed, *Old Testament Quotations*, 21-38. Freed notes the following list of possible sources: Deut. 18:15-16; Ps. 36:9-10; 46:5-6; Joel 3:18; Zech. 13:1; Prov. 5:15-16; 18:4 LXX; Sir. 15:3; 24:28-32; Cant. 4:15; Isa. 32:1-2; 35:5-7; 41:18; 43:19-21; 49:10; Jer. 2:13; 17:13; Ezek. 36:25-27; 47:1-12; Jub. 8:19; 1 En. 17:4;

to messianic visions and expectations of the coming age (Isa. 43:19; 44:3; Zech. 14:8; Ezek. 47:1-11). Here both the Spirit and living water are eschatological images. Boismard's theory that John is actually using a targum of Ps. 78:15 leads us to consider the chief water image.[175] John's frequent use of Exodus symbols (paschal lamb, bronze serpent, manna, etc.) suggests that here he has in mind the rock Moses struck in the wilderness to bring forth water (Num. 20:8ff.). That such an image was popular is evidenced by scores of prophetic and hymnic passages (Isa. 43:20; 44:3; 48:21; Ps. 78:15-16; 105:40-41). It should come as no surprise, therefore, to find the NT absorbing this identical tradition. Paul identifies Christ with the rock: "For they drank from the supernatural rock which followed them, and the rock was Christ" (1 Cor. 10:4). There is a substantial parallel between this thought and John 7:37-38: Jesus is the rock from the midst of which living water will flow.[176] He is the messianic bearer of God's Spirit and wisdom.[177]

An important principle in the exegesis of 7:37-39 is that it should not be interpreted out of context. We have already mentioned the Johannine Exodus motifs. Of Moses' wilderness miracles, the water from the rock and the manna were singled out and together given elevated status (Ps. 78:15-30; 105:32-45; cf. Neh. 9:20, Spirit, water, and manna). John takes these important eschatological images and finds their fulfillment in Jesus. In John 6 Jesus repeats the manna miracle and declares, "I am the bread of life" (6:35). In John 7 Jesus is in the midst of the Feast of Tabernacles and is found to be the source of living water (7:38). In the context of both he is hailed a prophet, recalling the prophet-like-Moses expectation (6:14; 7:40).[178]

In addition to Exodus motifs and the Meribah miracle, a second area of background is important. John 7 is the only unmistakable NT reference to the Feast of Tabernacles (but cf. 2 Cor. 5:1 and 2 Pet. 1:13-14). Originally an agricultural feast, Tabernacles readily became a Jewish pilgrimage festival which invoked God for badly needed rain and recognized the autumnal equi-

---

22:9; 96:6; Rev. 7:16-17; 21:6; 22:1, 17. To this list we would add from Qumran CD 2:11; 1QH 8:4, 16-17; 12:11. S. H. Hooke suggests (unsuccessfuly in our opinion) that the citation could be a reference to Jesus' own word as scripture in John 4:14; see "The Spirit Was Not Yet," *NTS* 9 (1962-63) 377.

175. "Les citations targumiques dans le quatrième évangile," *RB* 66 (1959) 374-75.

176. Ἐκ τῆς κοιλίας αὐτοῦ should be viewed as the Semite's seat of emotions; so Behm, *TDNT* 3: 787-88; cf. H. W. Wolff, *Anthropology of the Old Testament*, tr. M. Kohl (London: SCM; Philadelphia: Fortress, 1974) 63-64. Burney argues for a mistranslation of מִן־מְעֵי, "from the fountain"; see *Aramaic Origin*, 110-11; idem, "The Aramaic Equivalent of ἐκ τῆς κοιλίας in John 7,38," *JTS* 24 (1922-23) 79-80. R. Harris sees the Syriac term "throne" *(kursaya)* behind 7:38; see "Rivers of Living Water," *Exp* 20 (1920) 196-202. Cullmann suggests that in 1 Cor. 10:4 Paul may be dependent on a saying of Jesus recorded in John 7:37 (*TDNT* 6: 87).

177. Similar descriptions were applied to Qumran's Teacher of Righteousness; cf. CD 2: 11-12; 1QH 8:16ff.; 12:11ff.; Brown points to yet another parallel in the Gospel of Thomas, logion 13: Jesus says to Thomas, "You have drunk from the bubbling spring which I have measured out"; *John*, 1: 320; idem, "The Gospel of Thomas and St. John's Gospel," *NTS* 9 (1962-63) 162.

178. The major discourses in John 5-10 are all christological and are set in the context of the major Jewish feasts: Sabbath, Passover, Tabernacles, Dedication. In each, Jesus is found to be the feast's fulfillment.

nox.[179] Ceremonies of water and light accompanied these observances and during the later periods developed eschatological dimensions. Zech. 14 provides this Tabernacles setting and demonstrates how these desires for both abundant water and light were given eschatological significance.[180]

The water ceremonies in Jerusalem at the time of Jesus are of marked importance for John 7.[181] The Mishna tractate *Sukka* records that water was taken from the pool of Siloam and brought to the temple while worshipers sang the Hallel Psalms.[182] There it was poured onto the temple altar to signify the eschatological streams of the New Jerusalem that would replenish the world (Exod. 47:1-12; Zech. 13:1; 14:8).

Although the invocation for rain was continually understood in a literal fashion, Rabbinic sources show a symbolic understanding of the flowing water: this was also the eschatological pouring out of the Holy Spirit.[183] In arid Palestine, such an effluence was the perfect metaphor for the abundance of the divine Spirit in the messianic age: the life-giving properties of both were clearly understood (cf. Joel 3:18).

But these two traditions (the rock of Meribah and the paradisal streams of Jerusalem) are not mutually exclusive. Schnackenburg points to P. Grelot's evidence that in Tos. *Sukka* 3:3-18 the traditions were joined.[184] The miraculous wilderness stream was a type of the final waters flowing on the last day from the holy rock in Jerusalem. Similarly, the inextinguishable flaming pillar in the wilderness (Exod. 13:21) looked forward to endless day in the eschaton (Zech. 14:7). Both traditions were conjoined at Tabernacles: to recognize a slowly dying sun and the fear of drought.

The lectionary readings for Tabernacles identified by A. Guilding suggest this same synthesis in an eschatological setting.[185] She notes that in addition to the regular reading of Zech. 14 and 1 Kgs. 8, the triennial reading of the Pentateuch for Tabernacles was accompanied by special haphtarah readings in the time of Jesus. During the latter half of the feast (the Johannine context, 7:14, 37) the synagogues might have studied the following:

---

179. G. W. MacRae, "The Meaning and Evolution of the Feast of Tabernacles," *CBQ* 22 (1960) 251-76, esp. 258-59; also T. F. Glasson, *Moses in the Fourth Gospel*, 58-59.

180. At this time the Hallel Psalms were sung, and these give added background; cf. Pss. 113-118; cf. Ezek. 47:1-12.

181. See Str-B, 2: 774-812; Jeremias, *Golgotha* (Leipzig: Pfeiffer, 1926), 80-84; idem, *TDNT* 4: 277-78; MacRae, "Feast of Tabernacles," 270ff.

182. Danby, *The Mishnah*, 172-81.

183. Str-B, 2: 434; see the Jerusalem Talmud (*Sukka*, 55a): "Why was the place called the place of drawing? Because there the Holy Spirit was drawn in virtue of the Saying [Isa. 12:3]: with joy you shall draw water out of the wells of salvation." Cf. Midr. Rab. 70 on Gen. 29:2-3.

184. Schnackenburg, *John*, 2: 156; see P. Grelot, "Jean VII, 38: eau du rocher ou source du Temple," *RB* 70 (1963) 43-51.

185. *The Fourth Gospel and Jewish Worship* (Oxford: Clarendon Press, 1960) 92-120, esp. 105; although these Tabernacles parallels are instructive, the general thesis of Guilding seems unconvincing. See the persuasive criticisms of L. Morris, *The New Testament and the Jewish Lectionaries* (London: Tyndale, 1964).

Deut. 8:11-12	Beware lest you forget the Lord your God . . . who brought you water out of the flinty rock.
Zech. 14:8	On that day living waters shall flow out from Jerusalem.
Jer. 2:13	(Haphtarah to Deut. 9) For my people have committed two evils: they have forsaken me, the fountain of living waters, and hewed out cisterns for themselves, broken cisterns that can hold no water.
Isa. 43:20	(Haphtarah to Gen. 35:9) For I give water in the wilderness, rivers in the desert, to give drink to my chosen people.
Isa. 44:3	For I will pour water on the thirst land, and streams on the dry ground; I will pour my Spirit on your descendants, and my blessing on your offering.

John 7:37 records that Jesus spoke out "on the last day of the feast."[186] In the Tabernacles setting, on this day the water libations were increased significantly. But the Jewish prayers for water were answered in an unexpected way. The water which would flow from beneath the temple would now flow from Jesus, the new temple (cf. 2:18ff.). R. J. McKelvey remarks that "Jesus' claim to supply living water could not fail to challenge Jewish readers. It means that the centre and source of the world's life was no longer the temple of Jerusalem, but himself, the new temple."[187] The inexhaustible Mosaic supply of life-giving water in the wilderness could now be found in Jesus, the new prophet-like-Moses (7:40). Jesus is the source of the awaited eschatological stream. In the wilderness Moses supplied manna: Jesus is the bread from heaven (6:32ff.). Moses gave water: Jesus is the living water (7:38). Moses led with a pillar of fire: Jesus is the light of the world (8:12).[188] In Jesus' person one can find the fulfillment of all the Tabernacles expectations.

(b) John 19:34

No study of 7:37-38 is complete without an examination of John 19:34. The blood and water flowing from the side of Christ has often been viewed as a fulfillment of John 7:38. For example, Origen echoes many of the Church Fathers when he discusses the rock in the wilderness (*Homilies on Exodus* 11:2). Just as that rock was struck in order for it to yield life-giving water, so too Christ, when he was struck, caused streams of the new covenant to flow. Similarly, Cyprian (*Epistles* 63:8) finds the fulfillment of Isa. 48:12 in John 19:34.

---

186. Whether this was the seventh or the eighth day is unimportant. John's stress is that this was "the great day."

187. R. J. McKelvey, *The New Temple*, 81.

188. Glasson demonstrates how these three gifts—manna, water, and light—were often united in the OT (Neh. 9:12-15; Ps. 105:39-41) and given special emphasis in Rabbinic exegesis (Mekilta on Exod. 16:28-36; Num. Rab. 1:2. Song Rab. 1:2; Lev. Rab. 27:6). See *Moses in the Fourth Gospel*, 62-63.

We have argued that the formative traditions behind 7:37-38 included the Jewish Tabernacles ceremonies in conjunction with an eschatological view of Moses' water miracle. One chief obstacle in interpreting 19:34 in this context is that here not only water but also blood flows from Christ's wound. It is interesting, however, that later Jewish traditions also viewed blood as coming from the rock of Meribah. Glasson cites the Midrash Rabbah on Exodus wherein an interpretation of Ps. 78:20 is given: "Moses struck the rock twice, and first it gushed out blood and then water."[189] Similarly, the Palestinian Targum on Num. 20:11 records: "and Moses lifted up his hand, and with his rod struck the rock twice: at the first time it dropped blood, but at the second time there came forth a multitude of waters." This tradition is developed in the later Aggadah legends of the Midrash Petirat Aharon. There the blood is explained through the violence of Moses' striking it. Clearly, no interpretation of 19:34 is complete without reference to this tradition.[190]

Since our interest is in the theological significance of this event for John, we need not dwell on the historical credibility of the report. But current study demonstrates that it cannot be dismissed lightly. Moreover, the stress on the eyewitness in 19:35 strengthens this view.[191] But it is entirely unlike John to record a historical event which does not have some deeper symbolic value. One tradition dating back to Irenaeus (*Adv. Haer.* 3.22.2) has understood this text as an anti-docetic apologetic: that is, Christ was truly man and truly dead (cf. Acts of John 101).[192] Although this motive is clear in 1 John 5:6-8, the mention of water in John 19:34 makes this suggestion uncertain. On the other hand, some scholars seek a symbolic allusion to the sacraments of baptism and the eucharist (Bultmann, Corell, Hoskyns, Cullmann). Although baptism may have a secondary reference here (see below), "blood" undoubtedly refers to Jesus' death (as will be seen in 1 John 5:6-8; cf. 1 John 1:7). Another approach is to look for parallels to OT concepts concerning sacrificial victims. For example, the Mishna requires that the victim's blood not be congealed so that it may be sprinkled.[193] More recently J. M. Ford has applied these conclusions to the

---

189. Ibid., 54; see further L. Ginzberg, *The Legends of the Jews*, 6 vols. (Philadelphia: Jewish Publication Society, 1928, 1953) 5: 421n.132.

190. Ginzberg, ibid., 3: 320; this violence has suggestive meaning for the spearthrust at the cross. See also Glasson, *Moses in the Fourth Gospel*, 55; he cites Boismard, *RB* 63 (1956) 271-72; the rock/blood tradition may be evident in the Tabernacles tradition of pouring water and wine onto the altar.

191. Brown, *John*, 1: 946, details the chief arguments; see also P. Barbet, *A Doctor at Calvary* (New York: Kenedy, 1953) esp. 113-27; A. F. Sava, "The Wound in the Side of Christ," *CBQ* 19 (1957) 343-46; idem, "The Blood and the Water from the Side of Christ," *AER* 138 (1958) 341-45; M. Miguens, "'Salio sangre y agua' (John 19,34)," *SBFLA* 14 (1963-64) 5-31; F. T. Zugibe, *The Cross and the Shroud. A Medical Examiner Investigates the Crucifixion* (New York: Angelus, 1982) 118-30. Bultmann, *John*, 678-79, claims that this comment stems from his "ecclesiastical redactor."

192. Cf. G. Richter, "Blut und Wasser aus der durchbohrten Seite Jesu (Joh 19:34b)," *MTZ* 21 (1970) 1-21; Barrett, *John*, 556-57.

193. Brown, *John*, 1: 951, citing Miguens, "Salio sangre," 13-20; see Mish. *Pesahim* 5:3, 5; and *Tamid* 4:2.

Jewish Passover tradition: hyssop, unbroken bones, and mingled blood were all a part of that rite.[194]

On the other hand, it may be preferable to look within John for this symbol's meaning. John 7:37-38 anticipates a future time when rivers of living water will flow from Jesus' body. John 7:39 explicitly refers to Jesus' glorification. John 19:34 would then become a fulfillment text for this promise. As we have seen, both texts may employ imagery from the Jewish Meribah tradition. The eschatological waters expected from the temple thus flow from the cross. This fulfillment is further suggested by the note of triumph in vv. 35-37. The witness (the Beloved Disciple in our view) declares the truth of this report so that the reader might believe (v. 36).

We also noted that the later Tabernacles tradition saw the Spirit in this image of flowing water. Is this water from Jesus' side the Spirit? Later we will discuss the eschatological problem of Johannine pneumatology. At this point, however, we can draw out an important Johannine comment. John 7:39 links together cross and Spirit: "For as yet the Spirit had not been given, because Jesus was not yet glorified." The Spirit is thus closely connected with Jesus' death. Here in 19:34 is a proleptic symbol of the release of the Spirit. The actual bestowal of the Spirit upon the disciples is yet to come (20:22). But for the present symbolism, water flows, as it were, only when it joins the blood/death of Christ. Paradoxically, the spear thrust was meant to insure the death of its victim; yet instead it made available the living water within (hence, $\alpha \tilde{\iota} \mu \alpha$ must preceed $\H{\upsilon} \delta \omega \varrho$).[195] The living Spirit must seemingly await its host's death to be released. That is to say, the living Spirit is none other than the life of its Lord.

(c) 1 John 5:6-8

Although the interpreter of John can use 1 John exegetically only with care, the parallels between John 19:34 and 1 John 5:6-8 indicate that they are conceptually in the same school: blood, water, testimony, and the Spirit all converge.[196] While John 19 is chiefly concerned with Jesus' saving work on the cross, however, 1 John 5 is focused on the person of Jesus and right belief. Of course, this belief includes the cross, but as scholars generally indicate, the emphasis here is apologetic: false notions of the incarnation (1 John 4:2) held a subsequent danger to orthodox soteriology in the early church.[197]

---

194. J. M. Ford, "Mingled Blood from the Side of Christ (John 19:34)," *NTS* 15 (1968-69) 337-38; cf. McKelvey, *The New Temple*, 83.

195. The order of blood and water is reversed in a few mss. (579 it[e] cop[bo]) and some early Fathers, but this is no doubt a harmonization with 1 John 5:6; see Schnackenburg, *John*, 1: 191; Lindars, *John*, 586-87.

196. So Hoskyns, *John*, 635; Lindars, *John*, 588; Porsch, *Pneuma*, 334-37; M. Vellanickal, "Blood and Water," *Jeevadhara* 8 (1978) 221-22; and F. M. Braun, "L'eau et l'Esprit," *RevThom* 49 (1949) 5-30.

197. J. A. T. Robinson, "The Destination and Purpose of the Johannine Epistles," *NTS* 7 (1960-61) 56-65; I. H. Marshall, *Johannine Epistles*, 230-39; R. E. Brown, *The Community of the Beloved Disciple*, 93-144. Brown's view that the Epistles are a corrective to misinterpretations of the Fourth Gospel is important; herein lies a vital criticism of Käsemann's contribution, *The Testament of Jesus in John 17*. Käsemann fails to deal with the christology of the Epistles.

Various themes in these verses are important for Johannine pneumatology. We shall return to the theme of the Spirit as a witness. For the moment, we need to examine the use of water and blood:

6a   This is he who came by *water and blood,* Jesus Christ;
6b   not with water only, but with *water and blood.*
7   and the *Spirit* is the witness because the *Spirit* is the truth;
8   there are three witnesses, the *Spirit, the water, and the blood;* and
     these three agree.

The consistent reversal of the order of terms (from 19:34) is at once evident. In the apologetic setting sketched above, John first stresses the comprehensive duration of Jesus' ministry: the heavenly Christ did not descend on Jesus at his baptism and depart before the cross (a later Gnostic heresy); rather, the same Jesus who was baptized was also crucified (v. 6b, "and blood"). Thus he came (ἐλθών, aorist) in water and blood, and this fact continues to witness to an enduring incarnation.[198]

The blood in 19:34 therefore indicates the death of Jesus, which, as its sequential priority shows (blood, water), must accompany the release of the Spirit. "Water" in 1 John 5:6ff. points to Jesus' baptism, yet the baptism of the Spirit experienced by him would not come to believers till Jesus had been glorified (7:39), that is, till he shed his blood. The testimony of the Spirit depicted in 1 John 5 must therefore await the cross. It would seem then that the "water" in 1 John 5:6ff. also hints at the baptism of believers in water and Spirit in John 19:34 (cf. John 3:5). Once again, this is not the actual giving of the Spirit, but a proleptic symbol tying together cross and Spirit. In addition, this water is not a direct allusion to baptism, but rather serves John's living water/Spirit metaphor. As patristic exegesis makes clear, however, a secondary reference might be entirely permissible.

To sum up, we have seen that both 7:37ff. and 19:34 stress two themes. First, the Spirit is viewed as a feature of Jesus' own life. It is living water within him. To receive this water one must come to Jesus, believe, and drink. Second, the Spirit's release is dependent on Jesus' death. Thus cross and Spirit are interdependent. These passages bring together the major soteriological themes of John's Gospel: death, glorification, witness, and belief. The one who baptizes in Spirit (1:33) is also the lamb of God (1:29; 19:36) who dies not only to give life (3:16) but also to give the Spirit (16:17).

(d) John 4:7-15

If it is true that John defines living water in 7:39 as the Spirit, the only other reference to such water should come into our consideration. Apart from the

---

198. See the excursus of W. Nauck, "Geist, Wasser, und Blut," in *Die Tradition und der Character des ersten Johannesbriefes* (Tübingen: Mohr, 1957) 147-82. The attempts of Bultmann, Cullmann, Schnackenburg, and others to distinguish v. 6 and v. 8 and thereby seek a sacramental interpretation of 1 John 5:8 are unsatisfying. See the detailed criticisms of J. D. G. Dunn, *Baptism in the Holy Spirit,* 200-204.

Apocalypse (see Rev. 7:17; 21:6; 22:17),[199] John's Gospel is the only NT writing to mention living water, and only in two closely related references: 7:39 and 4:7ff. That these texts have much in common is clear. Both refer to thirst (4:7, 15; 7:37), drink (4:7, 9; 7:37-38), living water (4:10; 7:39), and the Spirit (4:23-24; 7:39). Both urge belief in Jesus (4:39, 41-42; 7:38) and coming to him (4:40; 7:37). Finally, both apply to Jesus the title of prophet (4:19; cf. 42, 44; 7:40). John uses "living water" in conceptually parallel ways. OT and Jewish monuments and institutions are contrasted with the gift of Jesus. In John 7 Jesus replaces the water expectation of Tabernacles, while in John 4 his water makes redundant the historic well of Jacob. Although remaining attached to the old institutions means death (6:58-59), coming to Jesus means life (4:14). According to the OT, the righteous individual does not need to thirst, but continually drinks from the fountain of God (Ps. 1:3; 92:12ff.; Exod. 19:10). On the other hand, Jesus leaves no room for thirst: those who come to him have a well of life within. This "new mode of expression corresponds to fulfillment which surpasses the prophecy."[200]

According to Strack and Billerbeck, Jewish interpreters viewed "living water" from two vantages: it could be the eschatological Spirit or the Torah.[201] As we will indicate below, John clearly knows both these perspectives and employs the latter fully. We are convinced that here, however, his primary reference is to the life-giving Spirit. The following considerations have been persuasive:

Water was a metaphor for the Spirit in both OT and Rabbinic thought.[202]

Qumran also used a water/Spirit metaphor, although in a ritual sense of purification (1QS 4:21).

John has already aligned water and Spirit in 3:5.

Jesus' second dialogue (4:16ff.) directly introduces the Spirit (4:23-24).

If this water leaps up to eternal life (4:14), it is the Spirit that gives life (6:63).

John's use of ἅλλομαι (to leap up) in connection with water (4:14) is unique. But it is found in the LXX for the Spirit's descent on OT figures (Judg. 14:6, 19; 15:14; 1 Sam. 10:10).

The "gift of God" (John 4:10) was a technical term for the Holy Spirit (Acts 2:38; 8:20; 10:45; 11:17; Heb. 6:4). Similarly, John uses δίδωμι (to give) with the Spirit (14:16; 3·34; 1 John 4:13).[203]

---

199. See the study of Goppelt, *TDNT* 8: 324-25.

200. Ibid., 326; see B. Olsson, *Structure and Meaning*, Excursus 2, 212-18.

201. Str-B, 2: 434-36; cf. the excellent discussion of Porsch, *Pneuma*, 139-45, although his stress on revelation is excessive.

202. See Ezek. 36:25ff.; Isa. 32:15ff.; Joel 3:1; Zech. 12:10. Cf. Porsch, *Pneuma*, 63-64; his criticism (p. 140) that the OT refers only to "water" and not to "living water" overlooks John's development and commentary: Jesus' water gives life. Cf. John's use of ζωή and ζάω elsewhere, esp. 6:51, 58; 7:38; 8:12.

203. See J. D. G. Dunn, "A Note on *dōrea*," *ExpTim* 81 (1969-70) 349-51; cf. Büchsel, *TDNT* 2: 167; B. Olsson, *Structure and Meaning*, 213.

Finally, the Spirit was the mark of the messianic age. Already the woman has mentioned the Messiah (v. 25) and Jesus has characteristically brought the eschaton into the present: the hour is coming and now is (4:23).

The living water of John 4:7-15 is therefore a metaphor for the Spirit.[204] But the same christological concentration we have seen elsewhere in John is apparent here. First, the explanation as to why Jesus' supply far exceeds that of any well is found in his greatness over patriarchal figures. His water is new and makes the Jewish water obsolete. As MacGregor points out, there may be a material comparison here between standing water (cistern water) and running water: to this day in the Middle East the latter is called a gift of God.[205] The OT frequently makes this contrast (Jer. 2:13; 17:13; Zech. 14:8) to depict the spiritual life which never grows stagnant. But John 4:10 stresses the identification of who Jesus is, not what he has (εἰ ᾔδεις . . . τίς ἐστιν ὁ λέγων σοι). This identification is framed around a contrast with Jacob, the patriarch of both Jews and Samaritans. A similar christological development is found in 8:48-59. The Jews ask, "Are you greater than our father Abraham?" (8:53), just as here the Samaritan queries, "Are you greater than our father Jacob?" Significantly, in John 8 Jesus flees the temple as the Jews attempt to stone him. In John 4 the woman accepts this offer of living water and proclaims Jesus while the village is converted. Conversion in Samaria is therefore paralleled by hostility in Jerusalem.

We might note that water plays a similar role of contrast elsewhere in the Gospel. As a metaphor it either depicts the valueless institution which Jesus replaces in his person or it signifies the newness he brings. In John 1 the Baptist baptized in water (v. 26), while Jesus will surpass this baptism with that of the Spirit (v. 33). At Cana Jesus transforms Jewish ritual water into new wine (a type of living water?). In John 3 Nicodemus must be born of water and spirit. While the lame look for cures in the water of the pool Bethesda (John 5), Jesus can cure directly—and he does. In John 9 the waters of the pool of Siloam do seem to heal, but Siloam means "sent one," which is virtually a christological title in the Fourth Gospel (3:17, 34; 5:36, 38; 8:29; etc.). Moreover, these very waters were used in Tabernacles, and as 7:37-38 makes clear, Jesus' living water replaces these waters.

The second christological emphasis is found in the missing climax of the passage. The woman's question in 4:11b is clearly inappropriate: Jesus cannot tell her where he draws such water because he is the water. Samaritan theology has important parallels here of which John may be aware. Citing Samaritan liturgies, J. MacDonald refers to their quest for wisdom and salvation: "I seek to drink now a little water from wisdom's fount, a well whose waters

---

204. Bernard, *John*, 1:139; Zahn, *Johannes*, 237-38; F. J. McCool, "Living Water in John," in *The Bible in Current Catholic Thought*, ed. J. L. McKenzie (New York: Herder, 1962) 226-33; A. Wurzinger, "Der Heilige Geist bei Johannes," *BLit* 36 (1962-63) 291; E. Stockton, "Living Water in John," *Australasian Catholic Record* 41 (1964) 217-26.

205. MacGregor, *John*, 98; cf. Bultmann, *John*, 182n.3.

bubble up from the depth of righteousness. All who drink these are filled with living water."[206] This water was offered by Moses and is expected in the coming *Taheb*, or Moses *redivivus*. However, the climax of our passage is not found in a further use of the water metaphor (cf. Cana, 2:1ff.), but in the revelation of Jesus' person as prophet and Messiah (vv. 19, 25). The Samaritan expectation of living water is fulfilled if one believes in Jesus. No doubt for the sake of the reader, there follows a comprehensive list of christological titles giving substance to this belief: prophet (vv. 19, 44), Messiah and Christ (v. 25), "I am" (ἐγώ εἰμι) (v. 26), and Savior of the world (v. 42). We are told not how to obtain this water but to believe in Jesus.

*   *   *

In sum, although there is not an abundance of Spirit passages which we can apply to Jesus' earthly ministry (no Gospel gives us that luxury), we seem to be able to detect in John a distinctive orientation. Although a "lower christology" is evident in which Jesus appears anointed by a distinguishable Spirit (1:33; 3:34; etc.), this thought is not primary. It stands second to John's "higher" christological formulations in which Christ and Spirit are unified especially in function. More precisely, the divinity of the Messiah has been heightened to the degree that the Spirit is difficult to recognize. We have already touched on this matter above[207] and can now develop it further.

We noticed in our examination of Jesus' works of power that the Johannine Christ is not a pneumatic. His miracles are revelatory and make glory evident rather than power. Thus they are christological in that they express who Jesus is instead of what he bears. In addition this Johannine theme serves a oneness christology in which we can say that works of power do not reveal the power of the Spirit but the presence of the Father. Thus in 10:37-38 John can argue from Jesus' works to the presence of the Father in Jesus. If the Spirit abides in Jesus, the Father dwells in him too (14:10). Similarly, the confrontation in John 8 is not resolved by the goodness of Jesus' works, but by Jesus' preexistence before Abraham (v. 58). It appears that the role of the Spirit is somewhat preempted by the presence of the Father in Johannine christology.

But the Spirit does have its unique place in John. Rather than being resident upon the person of the Messiah, the Spirit appears to be the life of the Messiah himself after and before the resurrection. This is most clear in Johannine eschatology and the eschatology of early Christianity (cf. Acts 16:7; 2 Cor. 3:17; 1 Cor. 15:45), where the presence of the Spirit is the presence of Jesus. It is most pronounced in the Johannine Paraclete, who compensates for Jesus' absence, or better, who extends and communicates the presence of Jesus while

---

206. MacDonald, *The Theology of the Samaritans* (London: SCM, 1964) 276. Cf. the messianic use of living water in Memar Markah (the Teaching of Markah) 2:1ff., found in MacDonald, 292, 435. Various scholars have noted significant Samaritan influence on John: Cullmann, *Johannine Circle*, 46-56; J. Bowman, "Samaritan Studies," *BJRL* 40 (1957-58) 298-329; W. Meeks, *The Prophet-King*, 216-57.

207. See above, pp. 71ff.

Jesus is away. Thus in John 14:18 Jesus can say, "I will come to you," and refer directly to the Spirit Paraclete.

John has taken this identification a step further. The Spirit was an integral and inseparable part of Jesus' earthly life. The living-water motif makes this clear. This water, which is the Spirit (7:39), is another gift just like light (John 8) or bread (John 6). To receive these is to believe, accept, and commune with Jesus. Nicodemus and the Samaritan woman do have access to this aspect of the Spirit in all its immediacy while Jesus is before them. But at the same time, the traditional forms must remain: the cross is the watershed that fully releases the Spirit. Again, Son and Spirit are inseparably bound in that John poetically depicts the advent of the Spirit in the death of Jesus (see below). The Spirit of Jesus which departs at the cross in death will be the same Spirit which brings life at Pentecost. Moreover, it appears that the presence of the Spirit is not merely overshadowed by the Father in a negative fashion, but that the Spirit is alive and vital positively in the life of Jesus. That is to say, the Johannine Spirit is the Spirit of Jesus.

C. F. D. Moule has recognized this peculiar christological formulation in John. He remarks that christology dominated pneumatology in early pneumatic experience: "The Spirit is Christified; Christ is Spiritualized."[208] We might add that the same formulation is accurate for John's view of the incarnation. Jesus is the visible presence of the Father, and the life and being of Jesus waiting to be poured forth into the world is the Spirit.

But this bold and exceedingly descriptive portrayal of Jesus may not serve the trinitarian systems. J. E. Davey rightly points out that John's christology implies a binity: "In John, Son and Spirit seem to be aspects of the one Incarnate Divine Life."[209] Son and Spirit cannot be experienced distinctly and simultaneously. Just as one may know the Father in his knowledge of Jesus (14:9), so too belief in Jesus is implicit in knowing the Spirit. Conversely, one cannot experience any Divine Spirit other than the Spirit of Jesus (who is the Spirit Paraclete).

This emphasis in John no doubt stems from the Fourth Evangelist's historical perspective. He writes from a situation in which the Spirit is central to Christian experience. For this reason the primary category for his doctrine of the Spirit is his present eschatology—and his christological emphasis there has no doubt contributed to his view of the Spirit before the cross. The Fourth Evangelist remains concerned for the historical and traditional understanding of Jesus and the Spirit, but he has highlighted his own interests: the interdependence and unity of Jesus and the Spirit.

John's first emphasis in pneumatology as it concerns Jesus' earthly life is christological. His second and equally important emphasis is on the place of revelation and the Spirit.

---

208. C. F. D. Moule, *The Origin of Christology* (Cambridge: University Press, 1977) 105; cf. A. Wurzinger, "Der Heilige Geist bei Johannes," 290; M. E. Isaacs, *Concept of Spirit*, 124.

209. *The Jesus of St. John*, 75-76; Davey notes that Son and Spirit were both names of the Logos in Philo; cf. Dodd, *Interpretation*, 66-73; and Schnackenburg, *John*, 1: 485-87.

d. Words of Authority

We discovered in the Synoptic portrait of Jesus and the Spirit that a second category was necessary to examine comprehensively the role of the Spirit. There the Spirit was seen not only in what Jesus did but in what he said. He was a prophet in that he bore the Spirit which revealed the will of Yahweh with unprecedented authority. John echoes this emphasis but adds his own unique nuance.

That Jesus is a revealer in Johannine christology is generally accepted. Even in the prologue, the incarnation is explained through the revealing functions of the Logos: the divine glory of God was visible in Jesus (1:14; 14:9). This Johannine theme has received immense attention, and Rudolf Bultmann stands out as a chief spokesman of this view. Bultmann explained the Johannine discourses as coming from a Gnostic Discourse Source, and in the second volume of his *New Testament Theology* he developed in full the Fourth Evangelist's use of revelation as a primary theological category.[210]

Our discussion cannot become involved in the functional role of Christ in John's theology except in one specialized aspect: How does the Spirit fit into this theme in the Fourth Gospel? Already we have encountered various emphases on revelation. The Spirit's descent at Jesus' anointing (1:32ff.) revealed the identity of Jesus to the Baptist. Similarly, the Fourth Evangelist redefined Jesus' miracles to incorporate unique revelatory concepts. But John has yet another stress. The language of the Spirit often lends itself to a sapiential interpretation, which is developed in two directions. First, the Spirit in Jesus' ministry is often evidenced in Jesus' teachings. John's metaphors often recall OT ideas of Wisdom and Torah. Furthermore, this relation parallels a Johannine emphasis on Jesus as a prophet who discloses teachings and wisdom in ways before unknown. Second, the eschatological Spirit (the Paraclete in particular) will likewise be a revealer in the Johannine church: he will unlock the significance of Jesus' words (14:26) and lead the disciples into all truth (16:13). For the present, we must draw attention to the first of these developments.

(1) Spirit and Word

We have already been introduced to the revelatory role of the Spirit in John 3:34. Here, in the context of affirming the veracity of Jesus' testimony, John remarks that Jesus speaks the words of God because he bears the Spirit of God. In addition, v. 34a bases this revelation in the mission of Jesus. Therefore the mission of Jesus for which he has been anointed includes this activity of revealing. Word and Spirit are interdependent.

But in addition 3:31-36 is replete with terms which characterize a revelatory discourse: coming from heaven, speaking, witness, testimony, truth, words of God, and giving. This is so much the case that Schnackenburg can argue for the unity of this section with 3:12-21 on just these grounds: the combined section almost becomes a cohesive presentation of John's theology of

---

210. "Jesus' activity is conceived strictly in terms of his revelation"; Bultmann, *John*, 252; cf. idem, *Theology*, 2: 33-69.

the eschatological revealer.[211] Although we do not find such a reorganization of chap. 3 compelling, still the point is made that John's christological discussion here turns on revelation. Jesus unfolds to Nicodemus "heavenly things" (3:12) because he is the descended Son of Man (v. 13). He is an eyewitness of heavenly things and can give witness to them with authority.

(2) Spirit as the Word

In the first instance, therefore, the Spirit can be found making Jesus' word authoritative. But there is a further development in John wherein the Spirit itself is identified with the Word. That is, the Spirit Jesus possesses and the Spirit he can offer are the words he speaks. Jesus as the Logos (the Word) becomes one with his mission and presents himself in the words he offers. This striking suggestion follows from John's metaphor for the Spirit, living water.

We noted earlier that water and living water were rich symbols in biblical thought.[212]. Although we argued that the living water in John 4 was the Spirit, this term had a broad sapiential usage. Therefore it comes as no surprise to find scholars arguing for a wisdom motif in these verses.[213]

Water is frequently a term for wisdom or the knowledge of God (Prov. 13:14; 16:22; 18:4; 20:5; Sir. 15:3; 24:21, 25-27, 30-33; Bar. 3:12; Cant. 4:18). The Targums understood the well-known Isa. 55:1 as referring to coming and drinking of wisdom and learning.[214] Similarly Ben Sirach could speak of the "water of wisdom" (Sir. 15:3) and Baruch of the "fountain of wisdom" (Bar. 3:12). 1 Enoch developed this theme in full: "And in that place I saw the fountain of righteousness which is inexhaustible: and around it were many fountains of wisdom; and all the thirsty drank of them, and were filled with wisdom" (48:1).[215] Likewise Qumran (1QH 4:11; 8:12) and Gnostic thought used this image (Odes Sol. 6:11, 18; 11:6; cf. 4:10; 28:15; 38:17).

Of special interest to H. Odeberg is the later development in which Judaism used water to depict the life-giving power of the Torah. It is here, in Judaism's Torah wisdom, that "living water" finds an important antecedent. Odeberg cites Yalkut Shemoni (1:480) in Pesiqta Rabbati: "Just as the waters descend in drops . . . so the words of the Torah . . . until it becomes a flowing spring."[216] Similarly, the Zadokite Fragment points to "living waters" and "water of life" as symbols of Torah or the knowledge of God (5:1, 3; 8:3-10; 9:28 as in Odeberg). Finally, at Qumran, water and life were conjoined to depict the esoteric teachings of that community (1QH 4; 8; 1QS 11:3ff.). But most importantly, at Qumran "living water" was used to describe the Torah (CD 19:34; cf. 3:16; 6:4-11).

---

211. Schnackenburg, John, 1: 380-81.

212. See above, pp. 96-99.

213. Str-B, 2: 435-36; Odeberg, The Fourth Gospel, 149-69; Schnackenburg, John, 1: 426-28; Porsch, Pneuma, 62-63, 139-45.

214. Str-B, 2: 435; esp. Targums on Isa. 12:3.

215. R. H. Charles, Apocrypha and Pseudepigrapha, 2: 216; see also 1 En. 49; 22:9; 65:11; 67:8, 11, 13; 96:6.

216. Odeberg, The Fourth Gospel, 160; cf. Goppelt, TDNT 8: 322.

If these images are in the background of John's thought in John 4:7ff. or 7:37ff., we could argue that what he offers in the Spirit are Jesus' words and teachings. In John 4 other features point to this conclusion. The gift of God (4:10) was a commonplace term for the Torah.[217] Ἄλλομαι in the Wisdom tradition was used to describe the word of God "leaping" from heaven onto people (cf. v. 29, "he told me all that I ever did").[218]

Jesus' living-water discourse at Tabernacles also invites this view. The difficult scripture citation in 7:38 echoes many wisdom texts.[219] Moreover, various wisdom themes abound: the looking/finding theme of 7:33ff. echoes the quest for wisdom (Wis. 6:12; Prov. 1:28-29); Jesus' "cry" in 7:37 (cf. 12:44-45) is the cry of wisdom (Prov. 1:20; 8:2-3); and the invitation to drink is also a sapiential theme (cf. Prov. 9:3; Sir. 51:23-24). Further, reference to Jesus' belly (7:38) could reflect Ps. 40:8: "your law is in my belly." Finally, this discourse of Jesus is framed by explicit references to the law (7:19, 49).

Yet these arguments do not invalidate our earlier conclusion that John's message concerns the Spirit. The criticism that nowhere in extrabiblical sources is "living water" aligned with the Spirit does not present an impasse.[220] "Living" depicts the distinctiveness of Jesus' gift. Jesus is not the bread (manna) but *living bread*. He is not Wisdom/Spirit, but *living Wisdom/Spirit*. In Sir. 24:21 Wisdom exclaims, "Those who eat me shall hunger for more; those who drink me will thirst for more." But Jesus' water is fully satisfying (John 4:14). If revelation is influential here, as most commentators admit, it fits well with John's theology. Jesus is consistently viewed as surpassing the Torah (1:17). His use of the water/Wisdom/Torah theme may then be his commentary: "The Evangelist takes over the standing equation of wisdom with the waters of the Old Testament, and identifies wisdom, not with the Torah, but with the Holy Spirit."[221]

Our ability to argue for both interpretations points to conclusions suggested by I. de la Potterie and F. J. McCool.[222] Contrary to Bultmann, the two interpretations (revelation and spirit) may not be mutually exclusive. McCool argues that John intends a synthesis. After all, the Wisdom tradition allows for this view as well. Wis. 9:7 identifies wisdom with the Spirit. Wis. 7:7 aligns them in parallelism: "Therefore I prayed, and understanding was given me; I called upon God, and the Spirit of Wisdom came to me" (cf. 7:22; 12:1-2). Wis. 7:25 refers to wisdom as "a breath of the power of God."

The significance of this correlation for John is later brought out in *Spirit*

---

217. Odeberg, ibid., 150-51; Str-B, 2: 492; Barrett, *John*, 233.

218. On the prophetic background of John 4, see W. C. van Unnik, "A Greek Characteristic of Prophecy in the Fourth Gospel," in *Text and Interpretation: Studies in the New Testament Presented to Matthew Black*, ed. E. Best and R. McL. Wilson (Cambridge: University Press, 1979) 211-29.

219. See above, p. 90n. 174.

220. As argued by F. Porsch, *Pneuma*, 140.

221. W. L. Knox as cited by E. K. Lee, *The Religious Thought of St. John*, 218.

222. I. de la Potterie, "L'onction du chrétien par la foi," *Bib* 40 (1959) 12-69; F. J. McCool, "Living Water," 226-33; also, B. Olsson, *Structure and Meaning*, Excursus 2, "Living Water in John," 212-15.

of Truth. In the Johannine church the Spirit was the power which recalled and interpreted all of Jesus' teachings (14:26; 16:13). Similarly, de la Potterie points to 1 John 2:27 in which the anointing of believers might be the word of revelation/illumination or the Spirit—possibly it is both. In this sense, such a "word" is not the word as it is preached externally in the community but as it is received in people's hearts in faith. The activity of the Spirit's power is found in the presence of the word in the believer, and this entire process brings life (4:14). Thus in John 5:38 Jesus criticizes the Jews because they do not allow his word to remain in them. In contrast, the words of Jesus should remain in the true disciple (8:31; 15:7). Likewise, the Spirit of Truth will dwell within them permanently (14:13-17). "He is the abiding principle who constantly and permanently vivifies the revelation of Jesus by recalling it, developing its potentialities and aiding Christians to practice it."[223] This revelatory word thus carries a substantial value for John. It is the word not about life but the word of life. Odeberg comments: "The teaching of Jesus is not a teaching merely *concerning* the spiritual realities and the eternal life, but it *is* the eternal life and the spiritual reality. In the same way the receiver of this teaching obtains, not a mere knowledge of the things taught, but these things themselves, that is the spiritual perception, knowledge, γνῶσις, does not consist in the acquisition of facts relating to outside objects, but in an assimilation with, a self-transformation into, the spiritual realities."[224]

The living water of John thus can be said to symbolize both: it is the life-giving word empowered by the Spirit. Together they are the power of life which reveals Jesus to the believer. That this synthesis is the express intention of the Evangelist is best seen in the conclusion of Jesus' bread of life discourse, John 6:60-65.

(3) John 6:63

At the conclusion of this discourse, John brings together Spirit and word directly.

> 6:63a   It is the Spirit that gives life, the flesh is of no avail;
> 6:63b   the words I have spoken to you are Spirit and life.

After a response of disbelief and dismay, many disciples turn away. Peter, however, gives an important, parallel confession.

> 6:68   Lord, to whom shall we go? You have the words of eternal life.

The importance of these verses for our study of the Spirit is obvious. But we cannot appreciate their significance outside of their context. John 6 and its host of problems are directly related to this comment on word and Spirit.

---

223. McCool, ibid., 232.
224. Odeberg, *The Fourth Gospel*, 168.

Indeed, we can agree with C. H. Dodd that 6:63 "is the clue that the reader must hold fast in attempting to understand this discourse."[225]

The current debate surrounding the discourse centers on two questions: the place of sacramentalism in the manna metaphor as the discourse develops; and, following on from this point, the possible interpolation of this conceivably eucharistic passage (vv. 51c-58). Our chief concern here involves the importance of 6:63 for the discourse and thus our comments must be brief. Suffice it to say, the role of the eucharist will emerge again (in detail) when we examine Johannine worship (see pp. 178-89 below).

First, we believe that the eucharist is absent from the discourse (or quite secondary) until Jesus gives the manna analogy a specific application in 6:51-58.[226] Above all, wisdom motifs appear to be central to vv. 26-51, and they even appear in vv. 51c-58 as a secondary theme.[227] Brown has effectively argued for wisdom throughout the discourse.[228] In Jewish thought "bread from heaven" could signify divine instruction, wisdom, or Torah.[229] Similarly, the eating/drinking motif suggests wisdom (Amos 8:11-13; Sir. 15:3; 24:21; Prov. 9:5) as does Jesus' OT citation of what precedes belief, "they shall all be taught by God" (John 6:45; Isa. 54:13).

It is important to note, however, that wisdom as distinct from Jesus is not implied here. Jesus is the bread of life (which formerly was wisdom or Torah). He is the descended food. The bread metaphor is therefore also christological in that Jesus is incarnate wisdom in John. But to the extent that the eucharist is also christological, the development in vv. 51-58 is fully permissible. In this section the language of the eucharist is employed in a metaphorical, negative sense. As Dunn has shown, 6:62-63 is a critique of the eucharist.[230]

Second, one should interpret the discourse as a unified whole and reject interpolation theories.[231] This point applies specifically to 6:51c-58, the Johannine character of which is beyond doubt.[232] P. Borgen has even shown that

---

225. C. H. Dodd, *Interpretation*, 341.

226. Contra Cullmann, *Early Christian Worship*, 93-102; A. Corell, *Consummatum Est*, 63-67; G. H. C. MacGregor, "The Eucharist in the Fourth Gospel," *NTS* 9 (1962-63) 114-16.

227. Contra Odeberg, *Fourth Gospel*, 235-69, who sees wisdom as the sole theme here. Lindars, *John*, 251, writes, "Thus the eucharistic interpretation is latent beneath the sapiential section (35-50), and the sapiential continues without any diminution in the eucharistic section (51-8)."

228. See his *New Testament Essays*, 84-85; idem, *John*, 1: 266-67, 272-74. Brown views vv. 35-50 as primarily sapiential and vv. 51-58 as sacramental.

229. Str-B, 2: 481; Dodd, *Interpretation*, 336; Schnackenburg, *John*, 2: 65-66; cf. Deut. 8:3; Wis. 16:20, 26; Neh. 9:20.

230. J. D. G. Dunn, "John VI: A Eucharistic Discourse?" *NTS* 17 (1970-71) 328-38; we will examine this suggestion of Dunn's in a subsequent chapter.

231. Bultmann, *John*, 234-37, finds here the work of his ecclesiastical redactor. The most plausible theory is that of Brown who finds in vv. 51c-58 a Johannine interpolation, i.e., a Johannine saying of Jesus transposed from another setting (possibly the Lord's Supper now in chap. 13). But the section is so well integrated (e.g., the numerous parallels between vv. 35-50 and 51-58) that it now cannot and should not be isolated.

232. E. Ruckstuhl, *Die literarische Einheit*, 220-71; cf. G. Richter, "Zur Formgeschichte und literarischen Einheit von Joh 6,31-58," *ZNW* 60 (1969) 21-55. H. Schürmann has even shown that

John here employs traditional homiletic forms which necessarily include the difficult eucharistic section.[233] As most commentators recognize, the theological development in the discourse has been carefully constructed and each unit plays a significant role.

These comments are important to 6:63 because its rejection of flesh (σάρξ) and elevation of Spirit and word provide the climax of the discourse. Jesus offers these words not to the masses but to the disciples, who are best able to grasp his meaning (but cf. vv. 64, 66). But even here, offense results.

The rejection of flesh can point in two directions. On the one hand, if the eucharistic themes are present in vv. 51-58, the parallel use of σάρξ (flesh) there makes this reference a criticism of the rite. John points not to the event itself but to union with Christ, which the event should portray. In this case, "the life-giving consumption of the Son of Man (v. 53) really refers to the reception of the Spirit of the exalted Jesus. For it is the Spirit who gives life (v. 63)."[234] On the other hand, Schnackenburg points to a broader force for σάρξ.[235] Although John puts great christological stress on the value of flesh (from the incarnation, 1:14, to Christ's death, 6:51c), it is not this flesh which ultimately gives life. The dominant stress in the Gospel is on the approaching death of Jesus and the life-giving bestowal of the Spirit. When Jesus descended into our world of flesh, he joined the sphere of humanity's weakness and limitation. This point is consonant with John's use of "flesh" throughout his Gospel (cf. 3:6). John is pointing to the ascension (v. 62), when true union with Christ and the appropriation of life are possible through the Spirit.

In what sense then are Jesus' words Spirit and life? Initially, "word" (ῥῆμα) must refer to the words which Jesus has just spoken.[236] His redirection away from material religion as found among Jews (6:26, 30) and possibly even Christians (6:51-58) is itself revelatory. John 6:63b is the summary of Jesus' authority in the discourse. His words come from the Father (12:49; 14:10, 24; etc.), are empowered by the Spirit (3:34), and therefore can give eternal life (5:24). Thus Jesus' words can and must be elevated—either in this Johannine setting or in the life of the believing community—to the status of scripture. Brown's remark that 6:63b points back to the wisdom motif is also sound. The manna—which could be God's word—is now Jesus' word. Because these words supremely reveal God, they can lead to life and the Spirit.

But there is another sense in which word and Spirit come together. The Fourth Gospel can depict union with Christ in terms of appropriation of and remaining in Jesus' word (5:24; 8:51; 14:23; 17:6). In this sense believers experience life and the Spirit if they take Jesus' word (in this case, the discourse or

---

6:51c belongs primarily to the preceding section, vv. 35-50; see "Joh 5,51c—ein Schlüssel zur grossen johanneischen Brotrede," BZ 2 (1958) 244-62.

233. *Bread from Heaven* (Leiden: Brill, 1958) 28-58; cf. the criticisms of G. Richter, "Zur Formgeschichte," 33-34.

234. Dunn, "John VI," 331.

235. Schnackenburg, *John*, 2: 72; cf. C. K. Barrett, *John*, 324-25.

236. The attempt to find a Semitism here, in this case דבר meaning "things" or "matters" (i.e., the eucharistic elements, vv. 51-58), is strained, esp. in the light of John's use of ῥῆμα elsewhere and its appearance in v. 68; cf. Dodd, *Interpretation*, 342n.3.

wisdom) and believe it (v. 64; cf. 6:29, 35, 36, 40, 47) and allow it to develop into a source of life within them (see 4:14). This meaning is carefully portrayed in the revelatory role of the Paraclete. He is not just the Spirit, but the Spirit of Truth who exists in union with Jesus' word (14:26).

(4) The Johannine Prophet Christology

This conjunction of word and Spirit makes it entirely unnecessary to find the antecedent for John's christology in speculations concerning proto-Gnostic revealers. As in the Synoptics, a prophet christology has also served in John's background. Needless to say, the Fourth Evangelist has developed it, but his starting point was the same. Jesus' words, now authorized by the Spirit, are prophetic words in the mainstream of OT prophetism.

Numerous scholars have pointed to John's prophet christology. For this reason Longenecker and Cullmann include John in the mainstream of Jewish Christianity's christological development. In particular, Glasson, Meeks, and deJonge have carefully examined the Fourth Gospel in analyzing this theme.[237]

(a) Jesus as Prophet

On the one hand, Jesus calls himself a prophet in 4:44, using the Jewish proverb also found in the Synoptics (Mark 6:4). Although this reference has minimal christological significance, the two times that Jesus is labeled "a prophet" by others who have recognized his secret are important (4:19; 9:17). Both this labeling and the Jews' denial of prophetic status to Jesus (7:52; 8:52, 53) uncover the Evangelist's interest in this title for Jesus.

Even more evident are the prophetic characteristics of Jesus' ministry. Dodd claims that John's sonship christology was even formed on a prophetic model. "The human mould, so to speak, into which the divine sonship is poured is a personality of the prophetic type."[238] The best means to examine this model is by viewing Jesus as God's agent in John.[239] First, this characteristic is found in the many instances that Jesus is said to be sent by God. If one takes into account equivalent statements, John affirms this 16 times.[240] Similarly Jesus repeatedly refers to God as "he who sent me."[241] John also stresses that Jesus never comes "of himself" (ἀφ' ἑαυτοῦ). He comes in his Father's name (5:43) and seeks only his glory (7:18; 8:49; cf. 11:4).

Second, Jesus' role as God's agent is further seen in his subordination to

---

237. R. Longenecker, *Christology*, 36-41; O. Cullmann, *Christology*, 49ff.; see esp. F. Schnider, *Jesus der Prophet*, 191-231; H. M. Teeple, *The Mosaic Eschatological Prophet* (Philadelphia: Society of Biblical Literature, 1957); T. F. Glasson, *Moses in the Fourth Gospel*; W. Meeks, *The Prophet-King*; idem, "The Man from Heaven in Johannine Sectarianism," *JBL* 91 (1972) 44-72; F. Hahn, *The Titles of Jesus in Christology*, Appendix, pp. 352-58. For criticisms of Meeks, see M. deJonge, "Jesus as Prophet and King in the Fourth Gospel," *ETL* 49 (1973) 160-77. See esp. the bibliography of Meeks, *The Prophet-King*, 320-35.

238. Dodd, *Interpretation*, 255.

239. Bultmann, *Theology*, 2: 50ff.; Meeks, *Prophet-King*, 301-302.

240. 3:17, 34; 5:36, 38; 6:29, 57; 7:29; 8:42; 10:36; 11:42; 17:3; 18:18, 21, 23, 25; 20:21.

241. 24 times: 4:34; 5:23, 24, 30, 37; 6:38, 39, 44; 7:16, 18, 28, 33; 8:16, 18, 26, 29; 9:4; 12:44, 45, 49; 13:20; 14:24; 15:21; 16:5.

God in both his words and his deeds. In this sense Jesus' authority is dependent and derivative like that of a prophet. He completes the works assigned him by his Sender (4:34; 5:30; 6:38-39; 9:4; 10:32, 37; 17:4). Likewise he speaks only those words given him to say (3:34; 7:16, 18; 8:26; 12:49; 14:10, 24; 17:8, 14). The demand of Jesus is that one believes God has sent him (11:42; 17:8, 21; cf. 17:23, 25). Belief in the Sent One is thus the same as belief in the Sender (12:44-45; 17:3; 5:24; cf. 5:23, 38; 8:19).

Finally, other prophetic characteristics abound and we need only mention them in passing. The extraordinary knowledge of Jesus in 4:19 is surely a prophetic ability.[242] Meeks believes that the accusations found in 7:14-18 are against a false prophet: Jesus leads people astray and performs "signs and wonders" (see Deut. 13:2-6; 18:18-23).[243] Hill points to the difficult text of John 10:34-36 and recalls the prophetic vocations of Jeremiah and Moses.[244] It is clear that John's distinctive use of "sign" (σημεῖον) for Jesus' miracles bears a prophetic meaning.[245] Each time Jesus is called a prophet (or "the prophet"), a miraculous deed (4:19; 6:14; 9:17) or utterance (7:40) follows.

(b) Jesus as the Eschatological Prophet

One characteristic theme of this Gospel is its attempt to depict Jesus clearly in terms that exceed OT prophetism and find in Jesus the fulfillment of the Deut. 18 expectation. The polemic that the Baptist is not "the prophet" (John 1:21, 25) is John's way of emphasizing that Jesus is the prophet.[246] The specific christological use of this title in 6:14 and 7:40 centers on the expectation of the coming prophet-like-Moses. He was to repeat Moses' miracles of water and manna. Further, the titular significance of "he who comes" (ὁ ἐρχόμενος) in Synoptic passages such as Matt. 11:3 (par.) also appears in John with parallel messianic force (esp. 6:14; cf. 11:27; 12:13).

But titles are not the only feature John employs to complete this picture. As in the Synoptics, the Moses typology appears throughout, as Glasson, and more cautiously Meeks, have shown. But John's intention is not to depict Jesus as a second Moses. This is chiefly an antithetical typology. Jeremias aptly remarks, "In general it is a mark of the Moses/Christ typology in John's gospel that it emphasizes more strongly than other early Christian literature the contrast between Moses and Christ."[247] Moses may have given manna, but Jesus is the true bread from heaven.

Two features established Moses as Israel's chief prophet: he revealed the name of Yahweh and he gave Israel the Torah. Jesus' high-priestly prayer in

---

242. See Friedrich, *TDNT* 6: 844; Schnider, *Jesus der Prophet*, 194-95; see also John 1:42, 45-48; 11:11, 14.

243. Meeks, *Prophet-King*, 47; cf. A. E. Harvey, *Jesus on Trial*, 83-87.

244. D. Hill, *New Testament Prophecy*, 54-56.

245. C. K. Barrett, *John*, 76; Dodd, *Interpretation*, 141-42, 254-55; Nicol, *The Sēmeia*, 81-82, 116-17.

246. O. Cullmann, *Christology*, 28-29, 49.

247. Jeremias, *TDNT* 4: 873. Moses appears 11 times in John, frequently in a contrast motif: 1:17, 45; 3:14; 5:45, 46; 6:32; 7:19, 22, 23; (8:5); 9:28, 29. Cf. J. L. Martyn, *History and Theology*, 102-28.

John 17 also serves as a résumé of his earthly ministry and here these two features also appear: "I have manifested [ἐφανέρωσα] thy name to the men whom thou gavest me out of the world" (17:6). But John goes a step further. Jesus not only reveals the name of God but also manifests God in his own person. Whoever has seen him has seen the Father (14:9; cf. 1:18).

The second element (Jesus and the Torah) is also given careful attention. The prophetic revelations enjoyed in Moses are now surpassed in Jesus. John develops this contrast along three lines. First, Jesus' word and the Torah are contrasted. This point is especially evident in 1:17, where the ministries of Jesus are juxtaposed to the law of Moses. But further, Jesus speaks as one outside the law, calling it "your law" before the Jews (8:17; 10:34; cf. 7:51; 15:25). Likewise the Jews oppose him, referring to "our law" (19:7). Finally, the law is said to serve Jesus: through it Moses wrote of him so that the true Israelite would recognize the Christ (1:45; 5:46; cf. 5:39, 46-47).

Second, Jesus' words are functionally equivalent to scripture. Initially Glasson points out how John makes use of Deut. 18:18, "and I will put words in his mouth and he will speak."[248] John 4:25; 8:28; and 12:49-50 are model examples which hint at the strong OT undercurrent behind this Gospel when Jesus speaks—or reveals—like a prophet. Jesus says, "I do nothing of myself, but as the Father taught me, I speak these things" (8:28). Moreover, the OT scripture fulfillment formula employed by John (ἵνα πληρωθῇ)[249] is twice used directly of Jesus' own words (18:9, 32). Meeks adds that John 17:8 is almost identical with the transmission of the Torah on Sinai to Israel through Moses (Deut. 10:4 and 5:5 LXX).[250]

But there is a final step which is inevitably Johannine. Jesus himself *is* the new Torah in his own being. In the prologue the Logos is the counterpart to Jewish concepts of Torah.[251] Jesus is also symbolized through Torah metaphors (manna, water, light). Above all, this parallel claims a centrality for Jesus which was held for the Torah by the Jews (cf. 5:39-47). For John, Christ's revelation offers in reality what Judaism had failed to do: provide a genuine, life-giving knowledge of God.

* * *

In sum, we have seen that John's interest in word and Spirit follows from a christology developing the motif of the eschatological prophet. Through the Spirit Jesus reveals the word—and this enables his message to bring the knowledge of God and life. The bringing together of word, Spirit, and prophet firmly places John in the Jewish tradition and obviates the need to discover revealer/redeemer concepts here.

But we have also seen that the prophetic vessel John has chosen to depict

---

248. T. F. Glasson, *Moses in the Fourth Gospel*, 30.

249. See 12:38; 13:18; 17:12; 19:24, 36; note the nearly perfect parallel in the formula of 12:3 and 15:25 with 18:9, 32.

250. *Prophet-King*, 289-91.

251. See esp. E. K. Lee, *The Religious Thought of St. John*, 101-102; Dodd, *Interpretation*, 85-86; Glasson, *Moses in the Fourth Gospel*, 86-94.

his Messiah bursts when filled with its new content. "The prophet," though an effective title to describe Jesus' relation to the word, does poor justice to the intimate association of Jesus with the Father. Jesus does not merely speak the word—*he is the word.* Thus in the Johannine christology this title must remain secondary and serve only to supplement the fuller titles Son of Man and Son of God.[252]

3. Conclusion

Two primary themes emerge in the christology of John when we explore the role of the Spirit in Jesus' ministry. First, John develops the importance of revelation within the primitive scheme of the Spirit. Second, John offers a unique and unparalleled emphasis on the interdependence of Christ and Spirit.

Former Synoptic acts of power now play a revelatory role. Satanic battles and demonic accusations now challenge the identity of Jesus—not his power. Miracles become signs which depict the inner meaning of this Messiah. They show that the Father is at work within the Son and that each brings reciprocal glorification of the other. Even so, only those with eyes of faith can penetrate this mystery.

But John goes beyond this point. The Spirit in Jesus' ministry evokes images of OT wisdom. Jesus brings the eschatological Spirit, but more, he brings the knowledge of God in his words. "The words I have spoken to you are Spirit and Life." Word and Spirit exist together and must be experienced in tandem in the life of the believer. Thus Jesus can correctly be labeled a prophet as he does this work. But even this title misses the mark. Jesus is set above Moses as the bearer of the new Torah. He has revealed a foundation for something entirely new. "For while the law was given through Moses, grace and truth came through Jesus Christ." Jesus is a revealer who has seen into and exposed the very heart of God. The experience of this revelation brings Spirit and life.

From the above, the emphasis on Christ is at once evident. John gives limited attention to the "lower" christological form of inspiration or anointing because for him there is an intimate unity between Christ and Spirit. The Spirit is the life of Jesus. As in John's eschatology, where the Spirit assumes the features of Christ, so here, Christ is "spiritualized." This relation obscures the distinction between Jesus and the Spirit such that pneumatology almost gets lost in christology, but the message that emerges is one of expectation. No other Gospel anticipates Pentecost like the Fourth Gospel. Jesus' own Spirit awaits release through the cross, where in John's climactic theological unity of Christ's death-resurrection-ascension, the Spirit is finally given to comfort, defend, instruct, and direct the disciples.

---

252. This is the fair criticism of Meeks's work, *The Prophet-King*, as brought out by M. de-Jonge, "Jesus as Prophet," 161ff.

Virgin Birth or Preexistent Logos? The Spirit and Jesus' Origins

A serious problem facing any study of the Spirit in John is found in the Johannine prologue. Can it be said that the meaning of the Logos contributes to the meaning of the Spirit in John? We cannot be concerned here with the complex questions of the structure or message of the prologue, much less with the background and origin of the term λόγος. In early thought, however, the Spirit was used to explain the pressing question of Jesus' origins. For John, the Logos hymn answers this problem.

Modern study of the Virgin Birth as well as current approaches to christology have shown that the birth narratives answer the question of the pre-baptismal nature of Jesus.[1] We are told that this view was the end result of early christological thinking that worked "back to front." Jesus' identity was first found in his coming parousia, then in his vindicating resurrection, and then (after other such strata) in his relation to God before his baptism and ministry. If the baptism pronouncement of Mark 1:11 left early Christianity open to the heresies of the adoptionists, Matthew and especially Luke answer the problem by moving a step backward: Jesus was born of the Spirit (Matt. 1:20; Luke 1:35).

---

1. On the virgin birth see O. Piper, "The Virgin Birth: The Meaning of the Gospel Accounts," *Int* 18 (1964) 132-48; H. von Campenhausen, *The Virgin Birth in the Theology of the Ancient Church* (London: SCM, 1964); W. C. Robinson, "A Re-Study of the Virgin Birth of Christ," *EvQ* 37 (1965) 198-211; J. A. Fitzmyer, "The Virginal Conception of Jesus in the New Testament," *TS* 34 (1973) 541-75; R. E. Brown, *The Virginal Conception and Bodily Resurrection of Jesus* (London: Chapman, 1974); idem, *The Birth of the Messiah* (London: Chapman; New York: Doubleday, 1977), esp. Brown's bibliography, 531-33. M. Miguens, *The Virgin Birth* (Westminster, Md.: Christian Classics, Inc., 1975). On christology see R. H. Fuller, *Christology*; and F. Hahn, *Christology*; cf. R. E. Brown, *The Birth of the Messiah*, 29-32, 140-41, 313.

In John this thought is absent. "Born of the Spirit" is restricted to something experienced by believers in the Fourth Gospel (1:13; 3:5ff.).[2] But if the question of divine origins is at issue, the Johannine Logos provides an answer not entirely dissimilar from Matthew and Luke. To be sure, John does go one step further. He pushes his christology back prior to creation while Matthew and Luke leave it at conception. But the latter thought could have led to the former. Both images portray a suprahuman divine connection which, as the second-century Fathers showed (e.g., Ignatius; cf. Aristides), could be harmonized. The Spirit, just like the Logos, was believed to exist above history.

Some scholars object that John's preexistence christology is incompatible with the earlier conception christology. For example, Wolfhart Pannenberg argues that "in its content, the legend of Jesus' virgin birth stands in an irreconcilable contradiction to the christology of the pre-existent Son of God found in Paul and John."[3] True, John has developed the earlier idea, but both conceptions are different (though related) answers to the same problem (so R. E. Brown).[4] This difference should not obscure their similarities. Because they share a developmental connection, much of what Matthew and Luke say may be found buried in John.

Therefore, if John developed the tradition he received, what was his aim? Simply to stress that the Son's sonship did not begin on earth but began in his prior relation with the Father in heaven. Only his earthly career began at the incarnation. This is a consistent Johannine theme (1:1; 8:38, 58; 17:5; cf. Phil. 2:6-7; Col. 1:15-17). The Johannine Jesus was not merely begotten on earth, he has "come down from heaven" (6:38). Yet as Kittel has rightly seen, although the Logos is preexistent, the focal point of the prologue is not here but on the transition of this preexistent One into history: "and the word became flesh" (1:14).[5] This is, as it were, the Spirit of God joining with the humanness of the young woman Mary. This is the Johannine "immaculate conception."

Certainly we cannot deny that John is far beyond the picture of his Synoptic peers. But there is still a significant parallel. Jesus' birth by the Spirit is substantially related to the *incarnation* of the Logos. Both speak, albeit in different ways, of divine origins and divine union with humanity. Both Spirit and Logos are thus similarly "preexistent" (pace Pannenberg). Both therefore

---

2. Some have argued that a variant reading in John 1:13 (ὅς οὐκ . . . ἐγεννήθη) refers directly to Jesus' virgin birth. But no single Greek ms. provides evidence for this reading, and most scholars discount it as a theological development promulgated among the early Fathers; cf. Burney, *Aramaic Origins*, 43-48; Brown, *John*, 1: 11-12; idem, *The Birth of the Messiah*, 520-21; J. Schmid, "Joh 1,13," *BZ* 1 (1957) 118-25; J. Galot, *Etre né de Dieu: Jn 1,13* (Rome: Pontifical Biblical Institute, 1969). Likewise John 18:37 and 1 John 5:18 have a disputed application to our subject.

3. Pannenberg, *Jesus—God and Man*, tr. L. L. Wilkins and D. A. Priebe (London: SCM; Philadelphia: Westminster, 1968) 143, as cited by Brown, *The Birth of the Messiah*, 529n.30; also of this view is Windisch, *Spirit Paraclete*, 29; cf. Brown, *Virginal Conception*, 43-45; and T. W. Manson, *On Paul and John* (London: SCM, 1963) 134-35.

4. *The Birth of the Messiah*, 141-42; cf. W. R. Hutton, "The Johannine Doctrine of the Holy Spirit," *CrozQ* 24 (1947) 339-40; and the full discussion of Dunn, *Christology in the Making* (London: SCM; Philadelphia: Westminster, 1980).

5. *TDNT* 4: 129-30.

refer to the movement of God in his powerful entry into human history, and both lead to the conclusion that Jesus is the Son of God (John 1:14, 18; Luke 1:32, 35).

What John has done is to clarify and intensify the meaning of the primitive Spirit, and in doing so he has employed an entirely new category. This clarification is likewise done for the coming eschatological Spirit. No longer is it an untamed rushing wind, but the Paraclete, patterned after the personality of Jesus. Similarly, the Logos defines Jesus' Spirit origins and also makes it intensely christological. Jesus originated as the Logos (1:1ff.), he returns as the Spirit (14:18; etc.), and therefore Logos and Spirit are virtually two ways of expressing a similar thought.[6]

But what is the contribution that the term *Logos* makes here? Despite the endless possibilities for the word, it can at least be said that the Fourth Gospel wishes to unite revelation and incarnation. Being the Logos, Jesus is the word of the Lord made flesh.[7] He may reveal OT wisdom, the living Torah, or even the personal name of God. But in essence he is God's word incarnate. Therefore if Jesus' origins are to be found in the Spirit, and the Logos is John's unique term for this fact, the Being of the Johannine Jesus must be found in the Spirit of revelation. Spirit and word work together to define the Messiah's origins, nature, and work on earth. As we have seen, this Spirit manifested itself in the career of the Messiah through works of power such as we find in the Synoptics. For the Johannine Jesus, the *words* he speaks are Spirit and life.

It would be simplistic to say that Jesus' Logos origins and Spirit birth are merely two sides of the same coin. There are vast differences. But at their heart they are wrestling with the same problem: How has God substantially expressed himself in the man Jesus? Matthew and Luke are compelled at the outset to introduce the Spirit in order to cope with this problem. John must likewise begin here, but with further reflection and characteristic terms.

---

6. W. H. Cadman, *The Open Heaven* (Oxford: Blackwell, 1969) 8, shows how the early Fathers united the meaning of Logos and Spirit. The "preexistence language" in John 1 spills over to influence the understanding of Jesus' Spirit origins. Cf. Justin Martyr (*1 Apol.* 33), the Shepherd of Hermas (*Sim.* 5.6.5), and 2 Clem. 9:5. Dodd points out how Philo's Logos closely parallels the Spirit in John (*Interpretation*, 68; cf. 65-72).

7. E. M. Sidebottom, *The Christ of the Fourth Gospel*, 26-68.

CHAPTER THREE

SPIRIT AND ESCHATOLOGY: JOHN 20:22

A. THE PROBLEM

1. ESCHATOLOGY

Rudolf Schnackenburg presents the problem of Johannine eschatology which so often troubles interpreters: "The phrase 'the eschatology of the fourth gospel' is misleading to the extent that it might be taken to mean the expectations for the future mentioned in this gospel. To do that, however, would be to narrow the perspective in advance; John shifts the focus from the future to the present, and even where the Johannine Jesus is apparently talking about the future (in the Farewell Discourses), in reality what is being talked about is the life of the community in the present, the presence of the Paraclete."[1] John seems to have rethought the horizontal historical perspective of early Christianity and presented it in vertical terms. So serious a concern is this subject that Robert Kysar has chosen to call it "a storm centre of scholarship" which receives regular scholarly attention.[2]

---

1. R. Schnackenburg, *John*, 2: 426, Excursus 14, "Eschatology in the Fourth Gospel."

2. R. Kysar, *The Fourth Evangelist and his Gospel*, 207; cf. his excellent discussion also in *John: The Maverick Gospel*, 84-110. Among the esp. important studies, note R. Bultmann, "The Eschatology of the Fourth Gospel" [1933] in *Faith and Understanding I*, tr. L. P. Smith, ed. R. W. Funk (London: SCM, 1969) 165-83; idem, *Theology*, 2:33-69; W. F. Howard, *Christianity According to St. John*, 106-28; G. R. Beasley-Murray, "The Eschatology of the Fourth Gospel," *EvQ* 18 (1946) 97-108; C. K. Barrett, "The Place of Eschatology in the Fourth Gospel," *ExpTim* 59 (1947-48) 302-305; M. V. Scott, "The Eschatology of the Fourth Gospel and the Johannine Epistles," unpub. diss., Edinburgh University (1952-53); E. Stauffer, "Agnostos Christos: John 11, 24 und die Eschatologie des vierten Evangeliums," in *The Background of the New Testament and Its Eschatology*, 281-99; A. Corell, *Consummatum Est*; M. E. Boismard, "L'évolution du thème eschatologique dans les traditions johanniques," *RB* 68 (1961) 507-24; L. vanHartingsveld, *Die Eschatologie des*

Those who have viewed apocalyptic as an early Christian accretion requiring removal (C. H. Dodd; E. Stauffer; J. A. T. Robinson) have often looked to John for support. The realized eschatology of the Fourth Gospel is so apparent that it is difficult to determine when the eschatological age begins.[3] What is future for the Synoptics is often present for John. Judgment (Matt. 25:31ff.; John 3:18-19), eternal life (Mark 10:30; John 5:24), the promise of sonship for the believer (Luke 6:35; John 1:12), and the anticipated glory of Jesus (Mark 13:26; John 1:14; 13:31-32) all fit this pattern. For John the future is swept into the present—"the hour is coming . . . and now is" (4:23; 5:25; cf. 16:32).[4] Had they asked Jesus, Nicodemus presumably would have been born anew, the Samaritan woman would have discovered living water, and the worshipers at Tabernacles would have found the drink of life. C. H. Dodd, consistent with his view of realized eschatology, even includes Jesus' ministry of the Spirit in these terms. The isolated references in John 3:22 and 4:1 to the fact that Jesus baptized are for him a fulfillment of the Baptist's prophecy in 1:33.[5]

This view has two problems, however. First, unless we join Bultmann and excise a considerable portion of futurist expectation in John (notably 5:28-29; 6:39-40, 44, 54; 12:48), there is no denying that John expects a future consummation. "If it is the essential nature of all primitive Christian eschatology to give expression to God's saving activity in Christ in the present and the future, then for John the eschatology of the final scenes has a very important function."[6] He does not present us with apocalyptic hopes, but he does point forward to an age when Christ's work will be complete and the present world ended.

Second, this interpretation must also deny a genuine salvation-historical perspective on John's part. But the Fourth Evangelist does not sweep eschatological themes (judgment, eternal life, etc.) into the ministry of Jesus without regard for Christ's glorification. The work of Christ is pivotal in John especially as it proceeds through the various stages of death, resurrection, and

---

Johannesevangeliums (Assen: Van Gorcum, 1962); J. Blank, *Krisis: Untersuchungen zur johanneischen Christologie und Eschatologie* (Freiburg: Lambertus, 1964); P. Ricca, *Die Eschatologie des vierten Evangeliums* (Zürich: Gotthelf, 1966); R. E. Brown, *John*, 1:cxv-cxxi; C. F. D. Moule, "A Neglected Factor in the Interpretation of Johannine Eschatology," in *Studies in John Presented to Professor J. N. Sevenster on the Occasion of His Seventieth Birthday*, NovTSup 24 (Leiden: Brill, 1970) 155-60; W. Thüsing, *Die Erhöhung und Verherrlichung Jesu im Johannesevangelium* (Münster: Aschendorff, 1960); R. Kysar, "The Eschatology of the Fourth Gospel: A Corrective of Bultmann's Redactional Hypothesis," *Perspective* 13 (1972) 23-33; G. Ladd, *Theology*, 298-308; C. K. Barrett, *John*, 67-70.

3. Brown, *John*, 1: cxvii, remarks, "In many ways John is the best example in the New Testament of realized eschatology."

4. One of the most eloquent expositions of this view is in R. Bultmann's essay, "The Eschatology of the Fourth Gospel."

5. "The implication is that the water-baptism administered by Jesus . . . is also baptism ἐν πνεύματι," Dodd, *Interpretation*, 310; also MacGregor, *John*, 89; R. H. Lightfoot, *John*, 119. J. E. Yates has argued similarly for Mark in *The Spirit and the Kingdom* (London: SPCK, 1963).

6. W. G. Kümmel, "Die Eschatologie der Evangelien," *Theologische Blätter* 15 (1936) 239, as cited by W. F. Howard, *Christianity According to St. John*, 121; the study of vanHartingsveld (1962) swings wrongly to the other extreme of seeing John as chiefly futurist.

ascension. In this sense it is questionable if anyone achieves authentic faith before the cross. True believers belong especially to the later age (20:28).[7] As might be expected, O. Cullmann has made this his own complaint against many interpreters of the Fourth Gospel.[8] It is true that John has presented us with a more realized eschatology, but this development is still coordinate to his expectation. "The hour is coming."

Whereas a mere cursory study of the Synoptics at once makes evident their interest in apocalyptic expectations, in John such strains are hidden and must be sought. John possesses no equivalent to Mark 13; yet as we have said, John does represent a futurist eschatology which runs parallel to the Synoptic portrait (with distinctive nuances). Of marked importance is how John has developed the understanding of the intervening age between the cross and the parousia. The extensive farewell discourse in John 14 finds no parallel in the Synoptics; however, it stands at a point in John which is similar to (though distinct from) Mark's eschatological discourse.[9] This point highlights an aspect of John's intentions. His expectation of the Spirit and his highly descriptive portrayal of the Paraclete suggest features reminiscent of the awaited, returning Christ. Thus C. K. Barrett can find emerging from John 14 varying "stages" of thought, some looking to the parousia, others to the Spirit.[10] Of course, the more extreme critic would claim that John has discarded the "naive" primitive expectation and replaced it with something more mystical or existential.[11] But something else may be at work here. John may be interpreting the church age as centrally eschatological. That is to say, today through the presence of the Spirit the effects of the Last Day are with us.

There is therefore a certain elasticity in John's presentation of the eschatological age. It is effectively present in John 1–19; but it has further emerged through the Spirit in the present age (John 20–21). But this is not to say that John ignores the historical chronology of the other NT writers in order to develop his theology. It would be more accurate to say that John's chief concern is not the past or the future but the present. His is an eschatology shaped by the presence of Christ in the believer's present existence. His emphasis on the Spirit is the means by which this presence is realized. Barrett remarks that the Spirit "is the means by which the historical past and the historical future (in the two 'comings' of Jesus) are brought to bear upon the present in such a way as to determine the significance of the immediate, spiritual presence of Jesus."[12]

2. John 20:22

Few passages in John present the interpreter with so many problems and options as are inherent in 20:22. This passage incorporates all the difficulties

---

7. J. Painter, *John: Witness and Theologian*, 83-85; 89-90.

8. O. Cullmann, *Salvation in History*, tr. S. G. Sowers (London: SCM, 1967) 268-91.

9. C. K. Barrett, *John*, 454-55. That such a discourse here is not necessarily a Johannine creation is suggested by Luke 22:21-38, where Jesus gives the disciples warnings about the future and general directions. Cf. the prayer of Jesus in Luke 22:39 and John 17.

10. C. K. Barrett, "The Place of Eschatology in the Fourth Gospel," 304.

11. Bultmann, "The Eschatology," 175-76; cf. E. Käsemann, *The Testament of Jesus*, 13-17.

12. Barrett, "The Place of Eschatology," 304; cf. Schnackenburg, *John*, 2: 426.

connected with eschatology. Is this the *terminus a quo* of the eschatological age? Is this another step in the work of Christ begun on the cross? Is traditional futurist eschatology here given a complete redefinition in realized form? That is, has John brought together his expectations of Pentecost and parousia if this is the advent of the Spirit Paraclete?

Two concerns are associated with this *crux exegetica*. First, what is the historical relation of 20:22 to the Lukan Pentecost of Acts 2? Can (or should) the passages be dovetailed? Surely John was aware of the stupendous event of Pentecost, and it is only reasonable to expect him to mention it. If John 20:22 is his account (or interpretation) of Pentecost, however, formidable historical problems arise.[13] Jesus had not yet ascended (apparently), and this event is clearly on Easter day instead of fifty days later on Pentecost.

A second concern is equally important. What is the relation of 20:22 to the context of Johannine theology? Are the immense expectations of the Farewell Discourses fulfilled here? Is this the advent of the Paraclete? For John, one clear prerequisite for the coming of the Spirit is Jesus' glorification (7:39), which many have argued is not complete by 20:22. If this interpretation is true, does John not record the anointing that his Gospel so urgently promises?

To examine how John intends us to interpret 20:22 in the context of his eschatological expectations, we shall first discuss alternative interpretations which have attempted to resolve the problem.[14] Is John consistent with the chronology of Luke-Acts or not? Or does he interpret it within his theology of the cross?

B. INTERPRETING JOHN 20:22

1. JOHN 20:22 AS SYMBOL

The most attractive feature of this approach to the text is the ready harmonization that results with Luke-Acts. In John 20 Jesus does not impart any gift of the Spirit but performs a sign—much like his others—which will indicate to the disciples on Pentecost that the gift of that day is from him. Although this view has the distinction of being officially condemned in A.D. 553 (it was defended by Theodore of Mopsuestia at the Second Council of Constantinople), it is often supported by conservative scholars and for good reason.[15] (a) John stresses the symbolic nature of Jesus' acts. His miracles are signs, but even in

---

13. Of course, the entire problem is resolved if Luke is deemed unreliable historically. C. S. Mann argues this position and claims that John possesses the only accurate account; see "Pentecost, the Spirit and John," *Theol* 62 (1959) 188-90; see also A. Richardson, *Theology*, 116-17.

14. In addition to those positions listed below, one other hypothesis is that ἐνεφύσησεν means simply that Jesus expelled a deep breath. But this interpretation is extremely doubtful. (1) Ἐμφυσᾶν (a NT hapax) would have to have lost the force of its prefix, which, as most LXX usage shows, was not the case (3 Kgs. 17:21; Job 4:21; Nah. 2:2; Ezek. 21:31, 36; 22:30; 37:9; Wis. 15:11; Tob. 6:8; 11:11). The scribal addition of αὐτοῖς thus interprets ἐμφυσᾶν correctly (D syr). (2) If this were John's thought, ἐκπνεῖν would have been better (cf. Mark 15:37, 39). (3) This interpretation fails to explain the meaning of πνεῦμα ἅγιον in v. 22b.

15. G. Ladd, *Theology*, 289; D. Guthrie, *Theology*, 533-34; D. Carson, "Spirit and Eschatology in the Gospel of John," Tyndale Study Group Paper, Cambridge, 1975, 8; J. Painter, *John: Witness and Theologian*, 70; W. Hendriksen, *John*, 461; T. Zahn, *Johannis*, loc. cit.

his other actions a parabolic undertone is evident (e.g., washing the disciples' feet, John 13). Just like the Synoptic cursing of the fig tree, this may be an eschatological sign depicting a climactic event to come.

(b) Elsewhere in his ministry Jesus used imperatives which cannot be fulfilled immediately. "Come and drink" in 7:37 may parallel "receive (the) Holy Spirit" in 20:22. Both exhibit that peculiar tension in John where future possibilities are viewed as realities of the present.

(c) Scholars often point to the parallels between John 20 and Luke 24.[16] Luke records an expectation of the Spirit mentioned on Easter day (24:49) which may be the source for John.[17] Similarly, Matthew records a promise of the sustained personal presence of Jesus (28:20) which as we shall see plays an important role for the Fourth Evangelist. Thus other primitive traditions may have held the raw materials from which John developed this episode.

But this option is just as vulnerable as it is attractive. Although it fits John into the historical schema of Acts, it does scant justice to Johannine theology itself. (a) J. D. G. Dunn has rightly observed that whatever we make of John 20:22, it is clearly a determinative event for John.[18] The background of ἐμφυσᾶν is to be found in the divine creative breath (cf. Gen. 2:7). In addition, as Bultmann has stressed, John's use of λαμβάνειν (receive) accords with early Christian terminology for receiving the Spirit.[19] The symbolic interpretation gives no genuine significance to the event within the Johannine economy.

(b) But this is not even to mention Johannine expectation. The Paraclete and the Holy Spirit are clearly bound together in the Farewell Discourses. Thus we cannot disassociate the promise in 14:26 from the event in 20:22. Whereas the world cannot receive the Spirit Paraclete (λαμβάνειν, 14:17), the disciples will (λαμβάνειν, 20:22). But these connections between the farewell expectation and the insufflation are extensive and we shall return to them later.

(c) It is true that some imperatives in the Fourth Gospel do point to a later time of fulfillment (7:37ff.), but it is incorrect to apply this interpretation to John 20:22.[20] The "anticipatory imperative" in John points to the time of Jesus' glorification; but in chap. 20 this process is already underway. Thus the Spirit insufflation stands at the opposite side of the crucial theological midpoint for John. For these reasons, therefore, we must reject the symbolic interpretation as being unnatural to the text.[21]

---

16. Note that both traditions show Jesus standing in their midst (μέσος, John 20:19 par. Luke 24:36); Jesus displaying his wounds (John 20:20 par. Luke 24:39); the disciples rejoicing (John 20:20 par. Luke 24:41); a Spirit reference (John 20:22 par. Luke 24:49; cf. Acts 1:8); a reference to sin and forgiveness (John 20:23 par. Acts 24:47); mission (John 20:21 par. Luke 24:46-49; cf. Acts 1:6-11). See Porsch, Pneuma, 354-55; J. A. Bailey, Traditions Common to Luke and John, 85-102; see below, p. 129.

17. Porsch, Pneuma, 355, believes that Luke's promise was in John's source, but that the Fourth Evangelist altered it.

18. Dunn regards the symbolic interpretation as "an unsupported speculation which does too little justice to the text" (Baptism, 178).

19. Rom. 8:15; 1 Cor. 2:12; Acts 8:15; etc. See Bultmann, John, 616n.3; Delling, TDNT 4: 7; Porsch, Pneuma, 356.

20. As does Carson, "Spirit and Eschatology," 9.

21. Hoskyns, John, 547, refers to this view as "merely a subterfuge." Cf. also Westcott, John,

2. John 20:22: A Pre-Pentecost Anointing

This alternative still retains chronological harmony with Luke-Acts but has the advantage of taking seriously John's theology. Its chief obstacle is that no other writer seems to be aware of or make allowance for this preliminary event. No less an exegete than Raymond Brown regards this criticism as decisive.[22]

In general, scholars who support this view agree on three major issues. First, this work of Christ is a determinative event for John which directly relates to his theology of the cross. For some, this is the *terminus a quo* of the eschatological age complete with authentic belief (e.g., 20:28-29). Second, although this event is important, it is not the fulfillment of the Paraclete promises. As Dodd points out, the Paraclete promises are personal, yet the concept of the Spirit here is impersonal.[23] Thus many would urge that the expectation of 7:39 is fulfilled here (and perhaps stems from the same pre-Johannine tradition as 20:22). Third, Jesus has not yet ascended by 20:22. This further buttresses the pre-Pentecost date of the event, but it also thoroughly disqualifies this event as John's version of Acts 2.[24]

To disqualify John 20:22 as a symbol and yet to object that it is not the "Johannine Pentecost" presents the problem of explaining just what the insufflation does mean. In order to clarify the problem, three different approaches may be distinguished.

a. An Ordination Gift

Rather than an anointing for the church universal, it may be that John wants to make a qualitative distinction: this is a special equipping for the apostolic work of ministry. Taking John 20:21, 23 as a lead, Holwerda points to the call to mission and the ability to forgive sins: "This special gift of the Spirit was received by the apostles alone . . . and thus these verses report the renewal of the apostolic office and the power of keys" (cf. Matt. 18:18).[25] It follows from this view that the gift is not universal and therefore 20:22 cannot refer even to the promise of 7:39 which all believers can anticipate.

But these are doubtful conclusions to be drawn from 20:22. First, the suggestion that this gift belongs exclusively to the apostolic circle is nowhere urged (20:10, 17, 18-19, 24, 25). Moreover, John is particularly interested

---

295: "To regard the words and act as a promise only a symbol of the future gift is wholly arbitrary and unnatural."

22. R. E. Brown, *John*, 2: 1038-39; cf. Barrett, *John*, 570.

23. C. H. Dodd, *Interpretation*, 430; idem, *Historical Tradition*, 144n.1. Schnackenburg argues from the absence of Paraclete functions here: "But the functions which the Paraclete is to take over after Jesus' departure (reminding and teaching the disciples, witness to others and conviction of the world), do not yet come into view in 20:22" (*John*, 3:326); cf. D. E. Holwerda, *The Holy Spirit and Eschatology*, 21ff.

24. Holwerda, ibid., 1-24, works exhaustively to demonstrate this point.

25. Ibid., 24; H. Thyen would refer to this as "Ordinationritus"; see *Studien zur Sündenvergebung* (Göttingen: 1970) 248, as cited by Schnackenburg, *John*, 3:472n.82; also H. Windisch, *The Spirit Paraclete*, 33-34; H. B. Swete, *The Holy Spirit*, 166-68; L. Floor, "The Lord and the Holy Spirit in the Fourth Gospel"; see the exposition of Temple, *Readings*, 386.

throughout his Gospel to reduce the significance of the Twelve.[26] Even in these verses, Jesus' model relationship with his Father (20:21) is the regular formula for every Christian, not simply the apostles. Even such a mission (ἀπο- στέλλειν) is meant to be universal (17:18ff.). In addition, the authority to forgive sins is best seen as not the ability of any one person. The parallel of 20:23 with Matt. 18:18 suggests that this forgiveness is a community func- tion.[27] If this is an explication of the earlier mission (v. 21), it should be seen in the light of John's understanding of judgment. The authority is a consequence of Christian witness. The announcement of truth brings immediate judgment (John 3:18; 9:40): people either come to the light and find forgiveness or turn away and are condemned.

Second, the tasks of mission and judgment are Paraclete tasks (15:26, 27; 16:7-11).[28] As most scholars agree, the Paraclete is intended to be the posses- sion of the entire community. We shall return to this point concerning the relation of the Paraclete promises to 20:22. If the connection is valid, however, the narrow limits imposed by this interpretation must disqualify it.

b. The Power of Life

This interpretation argues that it is unnecessary to choose between Acts 2 and John 20; rather, the two events are complementary. This view stresses that the Spirit came in a dynamic fashion giving different gifts at different times. Here in 20:22 the power of life "is experienced" (an impersonal force), while in Acts 2 the Paraclete "is sent" (personal).[29] Already students of the history of religions (e.g., O. Betz) maintain that John was aware of this distinction. For example, the Qumran community knew of the impersonal spirit of truth, yet also held a similar role for the personal angelic warrior Michael (1QS 3:18ff.; 1QM 13:10; 17:6-8).[30] Although the specific parallels with Qumran's dualism

---

26. Ἀπόστολος appears only once in a nontechnical sense (13:16). The Twelve are referred to in 6:67, 70, 71; 20:24 (cf. Rev. 21:14), but no negative overtones are present. John does not want to demote the Twelve, but to emphasize the general importance of individual believers. Note how all three Synoptics echo a reference to the Eleven in this context (Mark 16:14; Luke 24:33; Matt. 28:16) which John does not reflect in his parallel account. Cf. Brown, *John*, 2: 1033-35; idem, *The Community of the Beloved Disciple*, 81-88 (which is very speculative); K. Rengstorf, *TDNT* 1: 434ff.; and D. Müller, *NIDNTT* 1: 128-35.

27. Note how this text is followed by a promise of Jesus' personal spiritual presence among the apostles, v. 20. cf. 1 Cor. 5:1-11; 2 Cor. 2:5-10; 1 John 5:16ff.; 2 John 10; so M. M. B. Turner, "The Concept of Receiving the Spirit in John's Gospel," *Vox Evangelica* 10 (1977) 32-33; J. Marsh, *John*, 640-41.

28. Lindars, *John*, 613; F. Beare, "The Risen Jesus Bestows the Spirit," *CJT* 4 (1958) 98.

29. Thus L. Morris, *John*, 847: "It is false alike to the New Testament and to Christian experience to maintain that there is but one gift of the Spirit. Rather the Spirit is continually manifesting Himself in new ways. So John tells us of one gift and Luke another." Also, Hoskyns, *John*, 546-47; Westcott, *John*, 295, "the power of new life"; similarly, P.-H. Menoud, "La Pentecôte lucanienne et l'histoire," *RHPR* 42 (1962) 141-47, as summarized in *NTA* 7 (1962) 202.

30. O. Betz, *Der Paraklet*, passim; on Michael, pp. 66-69, 149-58; also see A. R. C. Leaney, "The Johannine Paraclete and the Qumran Scrolls," in *John and Qumran*, ed. J. H. Charlesworth (London: Chapman, 1972) 38-61; see above, pp. 16-23.

are not compelling, the distinction may be true for John. John 20:22 would then be a universal outpouring of the Spirit without Paraclete functions.

This distinction may be sound if the Pneuma texts could be shown to stand apart. But evidence for this separation is difficult to find. M. M. B. Turner, while not giving such evidence, provides us with essentially equivalent conclusions. Using OT examples of an irregular dynamic Pneuma, he draws an alignment between Spirit and life in John. This link is evident in 6:63 of course, but it is also implicit in the Nicodemus dialogue (3:1-15). To have the Spirit is to be born into new life. But Turner goes too far in figuring that belief and Spirit have a similar association. For him, the process of developing belief is a work of the Spirit in the Gospel—and within this process, John 20:22 is a "climacteric" of experience. "The words 'receive the Spirit' would then stand 'in parallel to' (and be interpretive of) the appearance, the greeting and the commission . . . rather than being 'in series' (or additional) to them."[31] The expectation that the faith experience of the disciples will "peak" in 20:22 is further found in 17:17-19. The themes of sanctification, mission, and sacrifice all (apparently) converge.

John certainly understood the Spirit in 20:22 to be a life-changing power. But various problems of eschatology arise when we bifurcate Spirit and Paraclete. First, Turner's hypothesis obstructs the expectation of an ultimate giving of the Spirit. Not only are there limited NT examples (outside of Luke) of pneumatic activity among Jesus' followers before Pentecost, but here we are dealing with a climactic giving to which even Luke points. To argue for "penultimate experience" from OT parallels is dubious at best.

Second, this view rides the realized eschatology of John too hard. John would say that "incipient faith" was present, but hardly that Jesus' followers were experiencing the eschatological Spirit. This is the very least that the "not yet" (οὔπω) in 7:39 can mean. Moreover, this interpretation overlooks the continual forward orientation to the cross and glorification.

Finally, this view does not genuinely help us explain the relation of John 20 and Acts 2. Is John 20:22 a permanent gift? OT and Synoptic (Luke 24) precedents would urge a negative response. If it is, as Turner must argue, one must explain how any Spirit can be given before Jesus' ascension. To urge that Spirit and life must be aligned is correct. But to separate this alignment from the full presence of the Spirit is to invite confusion. After the ascension, were these two experiences synthesized into one? Does Acts 2 give no indications of a life-changing Spirit?

Very similar conclusions are reached by J. D. G. Dunn, whose discussion is unmatched for its critical penetration of the problems here.[32] Although he confesses to being torn between viewing this as John's Pentecost or as a fulfillment of the Pneuma passages, he finally opts for the latter. His reasons are surprising, however. If John's theology had completely swamped the chronol-

---

31. M. M. B. Turner, "Receiving the Spirit," 34: "The Fourth Gospel appears to depict this new birth of the disciples as a process (corresponding to their growing belief) which reaches a climax in the revelation of Jesus through his death and resurrection."

32. *Baptism*, chap. 14, "The Johannine Pentecost?" 173-82; idem, *Jesus and the Spirit*, 135-56; similarly, B. F. Westcott, *John*, 294-95.

ogy, there would be both a greater development of the Spirit/ascension/cross unity and a reduction of chronological awareness in John 20 (οὔπω, 20:17; time lapses, vv. 1, 19, 26). But this is to say only what the Evangelist might have done.[33]

More importantly, Dunn rightly develops the theme of life within 20:22. The key is correctly seen as Gen. 2:7—"Jesus is the author of a new creation as he was of the old (1:3)."[34] Thus John 20:22 is the *terminus a quo* of the age when authentic faith is possible. But this is not to say that the apostolic experience was paradigmatic. Dunn provides answers to the problems left in tension by Turner. The dawning of the new age could only be experienced as it unfolded. The incarnation, the cross, and the gifts of Pentecost were all steps progressing to a goal realized later. "The disciples lived through this transition period, and during it their spiritual experience was limited to that which was appropriate and possible at each new stage."[35] Therefore Dunn helpfully insists on the pivotal nature of 20:22. It is not a climacteric within a process, but the inauguration of a new era in the work of Christ.

c. The Embryonic Paraclete

Again and again we have come up against a problem. On the one hand, there is no room in John's thought for a second anointing of the Spirit (Acts 2). The Johannine horizon stops here. On the other hand, the Paraclete does not seem to be evident in 20:22. If John has fallen heir to two Spirit traditions, 20:22 must tie up with the Pneuma texts while the Paraclete passages are left to one side.[36] Most scholars resolve this tension by denying one of these two problems.

One writer has posed a synthesis. Felix Porsch readily admits both these problems. For him the solution is found in holding fast to both truths. In 20:22 the physical presence of Jesus disqualifies this event as a fulfillment of the Farewell Discourses.[37] According to 16:7 Jesus apparently must go away first. Yet 20:22 is a central event in John's theology that expects no later completion (contra Turner, Dunn). Porsch believes John did not possess an account such as Acts 2, but he had before him something like Luke 24, which he developed into the present text. For Porsch, the Spirit is given here definitively, yet only later will it become the Paraclete. "As the departing Lord—who is not yet glorified but who already stands in the splendor of his glorification, Jesus gives the Holy Spirit. But because Jesus himself abides in the midst of the disciples, this Pneuma cannot exactly be designated as Paraclete. The functions of the

---

33. For example, it is not compelling to suggest that ἀναβαίνω would appear on Jesus' lips on the cross. See Dunn, *Baptism*, 177.

34. Ibid., 180; cf. Hoskyns, *John*, 547; Schnackenburg, *John*, 3:325; also Hoskyns, "Gen. 1–3 and St. John's Gospel," *JTS* 21 (1920) 210-18.

35. *Baptism*, 181; in a personal communication J. Dunn has remarked that he is now inclined to see John 20:22 as John's theological commentary on the Pentecost event of Acts 2; cf. the view of Thüsing, *Die Erhöhung und Verherrlichung Jesu*, as outlined in Porsch, *Pneuma*, 343.

36. Dodd, *Interpretation*, 430.

37. Porsch, *Pneuma*, 375.

Spirit Paraclete are not yet assumed by this Spirit. It is rather the Pneuma which will *in the future be a Paraclete and work as such.*"[38]

Within the Farewell Discourses John wants to stress the unity and continuity between Jesus and the Paraclete. If Jesus were away, the continuity would be lost. Yet since he is still present the full installation of the Paraclete is not evident.

At once it is clear that Porsch has jettisoned the tension with Acts 2. John shares no chronology with Luke.[39] But more problematic is our understanding of how this metamorphosis will transpire. Porsch gives us no substantive clues. Apparently the apostles have received the eschatological Spirit—but not entirely; yet no further event is expected. This theological construction thus creates more problems than at first glance it seems to solve. In the end, one wonders if Porsch can have it both ways: to deny that the Paraclete comes in 20:22 and yet not provide a harmonization with Acts 2 (nor provide for any later pneumatic event). Porsch's creativity is as intriguing as the paradox with which he leaves us.

3. A Johannine Pentecost

The cavalier dismissal of this alternative by some scholars and the unqualified acceptance of it by others[40] is surprising in view of the complexities involved. The starting point for this interpretation is that in 20:22 John records the full giving of the Spirit Paraclete, and this passage corresponds with Luke's account in Acts 2. John is either using a different chronological tradition in his sources or he has disregarded chronology altogether for the sake of theological emphasis.[41] To be sure, nothing in John forces us to call 20:22 partial or provisional. In addition, as Raymond Brown has remarked, it may be poor

---

38. Ibid., 376.

39. This is interesting in view of John's apparent acquaintance with so many other Lukan traditions; see J. A. Bailey, *The Traditions Common to Luke and John*.

40. Those who dismiss the alternative include M. M. B. Turner, "Receiving the Spirit," 28-29; D. A. Carson, "Spirit and Eschatology," 4-6; Morris, *John*, 847. Those who accept it include Marsh, *John*, 639; Käsemann, *Testament of Jesus*, 28-29.

41. For the former view see C. H. Dodd, *Historical Tradition*, 144n.1: "It is in some sort an alternative version to the story in Acts ii, and in a very broad sense a common tradition of an event remembered in the church may lie behind both. But that event is conceived in entirely different ways, and there is no manifest contact between John and Acts, or the form of the tradition which each represents"; cf. C. K. Barrett, *John*, 570. For the latter view see A. Corell, *Consummatum Est*, 38: "[The problem of John 20:22] need not surprise us, however, for St. John thinks theologically, not chronologically." Cf. R. E. Brown, *John*, 2: 1014; J. D. G. Dunn, *NIDNTT* 3: 704; B. Vawter, "John," in *The Jerome Biblical Commentary*, 2: 464. The tendency among some scholars is to admit the theological unity of Jesus' glorification, yet use excessively vague language to define the relation between history and theology. See D. A. Carson, "Spirit and Eschatology," 7: "The sequential arrangement and time lapses [in John 19–20] relate to history; the unity of the saving event relates to theology. Theologically, the constituent parts of this saving work of Jesus are not 'chronologically disposed,' while historically they are." Does this mean that John 20:22 is historical, yet not chronological?

methodology to invent harmonizations when there are so many pointers to the contrary.[42]

One approach has been to bypass the chronological problem with Luke and yet achieve a sequential harmony by suggesting that Jesus has ascended before 20:22 (as Acts 1:9 precedes 2:2).[43] In this case, Jesus' unusual discussion with Mary in 20:17 and especially his direct mention of ascension may be John's hint that Jesus has ascended before the appearance in 20:19. The language is clearly provocative. Jesus said to her, "Do not touch me, for I have not yet ascended [ἀναβέβηκα] to the Father; but go to my brethren and say to them, 'I am ascending [ἀναβαίνω] to my Father and your Father, to my God and your God.'" The basis of Jesus' prohibition seems to be linked to his ascension. Yet in the later encounter with Thomas, the skeptical apostle is urged to touch Jesus. Has the ascension been completed?[44]

C. F. D. Moule has pointed out that the contrast between 20:17 and 20:27 may stem from the differing needs of the two disciples.[45] Mary is redirected toward a new type of relation with Jesus in the Spirit (NEB: "Do not cling to me"), while Thomas seeks confirming evidence of the resurrection. Moreover, ἀναβαίνω could convey the future: "I am going to ascend" or "I am about to ascend."[46] Finally, the appearances after v. 19 are not much different from his appearance to Mary. If anything the tangibility of Jesus' appearance is stressed.[47] Therefore, although John is undoubtedly working with the motif of the ascension in this passage, the evidence is too tenuous to identify when this event occurred. Attempts at rearrangement, such as placing vv. 21-23 after v. 29 to allow for the ascension and a time lapse, are speculative and without evidence.[48]

---

42. Brown, *John*, 2: 1038; cf. R. H. Fuller, "John 20:19-23," *Int* 32 (1978) 181: "It would be naive historicism to try and harmonize Luke's Pentecost with this 'Johannine Pentecost' as it is sometimes called. They are variant expressions of the same basic mystery."

43. Another approach we will not study is that of Cassian, who argues that John's use of τῇ ἡμέρᾳ ἐκείνῃ (in that day) in 20:19 is exclusively eschatological instead of chronological so that 20:19-23 refers not to Easter but to Pentecost some 50 days later. This is very speculative and still leaves unsolved the later appearance to Thomas, vv. 26ff. See Cassian [The Archimandrite], *La Pentecôte johannique (Jn 20, 19-23)* (Paris: Editeurs Réunis, 1939) 35-54.

44. Among those scholars supporting this view are J. S. Billings, "The Ascension in the Fourth Gospel," *ExpTim* 50 (1939) 285; J. Moffatt, *Introduction to the Literature of the New Testament* (New York: Scribner's, 1915) 536; E. F. Scott, *The Fourth Gospel*, 307; S. H. Hooke, "The Spirit Was Not Yet," *NTS* 9 (1962-63) 379; MacGregor, *John*, 359-60; Marsh, *John*, 639; Strachan, *John*, 328; Braun, *Jean*, 3: 225-28.

45. C. F. D. Moule, "The Individualism of the Fourth Gospel," *NovT* 5 (1962) 175-76; also Brown, *John*, 2: 1011. Note that the verbs of touch are different in each episode. The further suggestion applauded by Dunn, *Baptism*, 176-77, and Barrett, *John*, 565-66, that οὔπω γὰρ ἀναβέβηκα (for I have not yet ascended) is not the ground of the refusal to touch but a part of the message (πορεύου δέ), seems like extraordinary syntax.

46. So BDF, § 323.3; cf. also Barrett, *John*, 566; Morris, *John*, 841; Porsch, *Pneuma*, 344.

47. W. Grundmann, "Zur Rede Jesu vom Vater im Johannesevangelium; Eine redaktions- und bekenntnisgeschichtlich Untersuchung zu Joh 20,17 und seiner Vorbereitung," *ZNW* 52 (1961) 213-30. It is possible that John is working with an anti-docetic theme here in his stress on the physical tangibility of Jesus' resurrected body. Within this emphasis, John's later stress on the Spirit in no way nullifies his stress on the physical reality of the resurrection.

48. This is the solution of Strachan, *John*, 312; and MacGregor, *John*, 361; no recent commentators seem to take this suggestion seriously.

The most common view is to say that either Jesus is in the process of ascension or that the event cannot be determined because John has redefined it.[49] We shall return to this theme because of its importance in Johannine thought with regard to the continued presence of Jesus after his glorification. Suffice it here to say that John has compressed historically separate events into a theological unity: the death, resurrection, and ascension of Jesus as well as the gift of the Spirit all constitute a single movement in the Johannine economy. Our problem may be that we have not tried to discover *John's* message about Jesus' glorification. Instead we have worked to fit John into a non-Johannine chronology. But already we are ahead of ourselves. Our task now is to examine the evidence which argues that 20:22 is John's record of the ultimate giving of the Spirit Paraclete which corresponds with Acts 2. This view has many strong features which demand serious consideration.[50]

1. If the Pneuma and Paraclete passages are taken together, John 7:39 should serve as a primary indicator to tell us if the eschatological Spirit has been given in full. As we shall see later, the process of glorification is complete in 20:22 by virtue of Jesus' giving the Spirit. But since the meaning of the ascension is controversial, we should move on.[51]

2. John's use of ἐμφυσᾶν (to breathe) deliberately echoes Gen. 2:7 (LXX) and emphasizes Jesus' role as creator (cf. Ezek. 37:9). This is the same theme found in the prologue (1:3) and as Schulze-Kadelbach has remarked, 20:22 is the Gospel's closing frame: Jesus is also the re-creator.[52] This conclusion is further supported by the LXX use of ἐμφυσᾶν. It is generally the divine breath of Yahweh, and here, significantly, John has made Jesus its source.[53] We shall note Luke's use of this motif in a moment.

---

49. For the former view see Bultmann, *John*, 691: "That Jesus in the meantime [before v. 19] had ascended to the Father, as he had said to Mary that he would, and has now again returned to earth would be a false reflection. . . . Rather, the sense is that he *has* ascended, and even *as such* he appears to the disciples." For the latter view see R. E. Brown, *John* 2: 1012-17, who refers to P. Benoit, "L'Ascension," *RB* 56 (1949) 161-203; also A. M. Ramsey, "What Was the Ascension?" in *History and Chronology in the New Testament*, ed. D. E. Nineham (London: SPCK, 1965) 135-44; cf. Dunn, *Jesus and the Spirit*, 114-15, 135-46.

50. Among the scholars who see the fulfillment of the Paraclete promises in 20:22 are Bultmann, *John*, 691; Barrett, *John*, 570; Dodd, *Historical Tradition*, 144; idem, *Interpretation*, 430; 442; Bauer, *John*, loc. cit.; C. S. Mann, "Pentecost," 188-90; Isaacs, *Concept of Spirit*, 94, 122; Hill, *Greek Words*, 287-88; Lightfoot, *John*, 331; Betz, *Der Paraklet*, 165-69; Schlier, "Der Heilige Geist als Interpret nach dem Johannesevangelium," *Internationale Katholische Zeitschrift* "Communio," 2 (1973) 102; G. Schulze-Kadelbach, "Zur Pneumatologie des Johannesevangeliums," *ZNW* 46 (1955) 279-80; F. Filson, *The New Testament Against Its Environment*, SBT 1/3 (London: SCM; Naperville: Allenson, 1950) 75; E. Stauffer, *TDNT* 2: 537; Sanders and Mastin, *John*, 433; Leaney, "The Johannine Paraclete," 50; Kealy, *John*, 161; Hunter, *John*, 187-88; also those authors listed above on p. 124n.44. See further F. E. Scholte, "An Investigation and an Interpretation of John 20:22," unpub. diss., Dallas Theological Seminary, 1953; and H. Thyen, "Aus der Literatur Zum Johannesevangelium," *TRu* 44 (1979) 127-28.

51. Porsch, *Pneuma*, 353, rightly points out that we must beware of arguing in a circle here: on the one hand, Jesus is the Glorified One *because* he has given the Spirit; and on the other, this *is* the Paraclete, because Jesus has glorified.

52. "Zur Pneumatologie," 280.

53. Ἐμφυσᾶν appears 11 times in the LXX (Gen. 2:7 [נפח]; 3 Kgs. 17:21; Tob. 6:8; 11:11; Job 4:21; Wis. 15:11; Sir. 43:4; Nah. 2:1; Ezek. 21:31 [פוח]; 22:20 [נפח]; 37:9 [נפח]). As the breath of

3. The absence of the definite article in 20:22 (simply πνεῦμα) does not mean that John intends only "a gift" of the Spirit (so Westcott, Swete); rather, it may point to the parallel usage in the Baptist's prophecy (1:33, οὗτός ἐστιν ὁ βαπτίζων ἐν πνεύματι ἁγίῳ). This connection would suggest that 20:22 fulfills 1:33, which can refer only to Pentecost (so the Synoptics). Moreover, numerous other NT texts omit the definite article and still understand the Holy Spirit in the full sense (Acts 2:4; 8:7, 15).

4. Our earlier mention of the use of "receive" (λαμβάνειν) should be repeated. The use of this verb in conjunction with "Holy Spirit" (πνεῦμα ἅγιον) appears to have been an early Christian formula. John uses it three times (7:39; 20:22; note esp. 14:7), and it frequently appears in Paul (Rom. 8:15; 1 Cor. 2:12; 2 Cor. 11:4; Gal. 3:2, 14). More interesting is its frequent use in Acts (1:8; 2:38; 8:15, 17, 19; 10:47; 19:2).[54]

5. Although the full catalogue of tasks assigned to the Paraclete in the Farewell Discourses is not listed here, it may be invalid to use this as an argument against the fulfillment of the Paraclete promises.[55] As we have noted already, it is at least incorrect. The tasks listed in 20:21, 23 may apply to the Paraclete. But the larger question is whether we are asking too much. Once again we are looking for what John should have done. The Fourth Evangelist's theological aim may have been different. As we shall see, christological interests are his chief concern.

Another aspect of this passage often escapes notice. One of the important themes of John 14 and 16 is the grief brought on by Jesus' departure (death). The coming of the Paraclete will restore the disciples' peace (14:27; 16:33) and joy (16:20, 21, 22). In our text Jesus gives a threefold blessing of peace (20:19, 21, 26)—a term which occurs elsewhere only in the earlier promises (14:27; etc.). This is more than just a Semite's greeting. Moreover, the disciples' response to their returned Lord is joy (v. 20). These terms point to an eschatological fulfillment of the earlier expectation.[56]

6. It appears that Jesus anticipated and the early church recalled only one climactic giving of the Spirit to inaugurate the church.[57] The event which John compressed Luke may have schematically developed into epochs of redemp-

---

Yahweh its role in creation is developed by Ezekiel to represent the eschatological rebirth. This is known to John (John 3), but it is possibly used by Luke in Acts 2. Hoskyns, *John*, 547, notes how this word was employed in early Christian baptismal rites.

54. Cf. Bultmann, *John*, 616n.3; Delling, *TDNT* 4: 7; E. A. Russell, "The Holy Spirit in the Fourth Gospel," *IBS* 2 (1980) 86. Cf. 1 Pet. 4:10 and 1 John 2:27, which use χρίσμα. This usage corresponds to the similar use of διδόναι plus πνεῦμα ἅγιον, Rom. 5:5; 2 Cor. 1:22; Acts 8:18; 1 John 2:24; 4:13.

55. Turner, "Receiving the Spirit," 29: "Very little if anything corresponds to the Paraclete." Cf. Schnackenburg, *John*, 3: 326. To argue further that "from 20:22 to the end of John's gospel there is no trace of Paraclete activity" is unpersuasive if this were not the Evangelist's aim. That Jesus fails to say "receive the Paraclete" is insignificant (pace Turner, "Receiving the Spirit," 40n.40).

56. Cf. Hunter, *John*, 187; Brown, *John*, 2: 1021; Lindars, *John*, 610; Swete, *The Holy Spirit*, 165.

57. L. Goppelt, *Apostolic and Post-Apostolic Times*, tr. R. A. Guelich (London: A. & C. Black, 1970; repr. Grand Rapids: Baker, 1977) 20-24; cf. Dunn, *Baptism*, 38-54; idem, *Jesus and the Spirit*, 136ff.

tive history. John is no exception to this single expectation. His Gospel expects one anointing which will climax Jesus' relations with his disciples. Moreover, only Luke carefully distinguishes between Easter and Pentecost. The longer ending of Mark records an Easter ascension (16:19) and implies that after Jesus' commission (cf. John 20:21) "the Lord was working with them." Luke 24:46-49 similarly records an Easter commission conjoined with a ministry of forgiveness which is dependent on the presence of the Spirit.[58] Further, the longer reading of Luke 24:51 actually records an Easter ascension and is not without some substantial support (p^{75} ℵ^c A B Θ W f^1 f^{13}).[59]

7. One consideration is rarely used in support of this interpretation. A cursory study of the NT record of resurrection appearances shows the divergent accounts presented by each author. This was a very fluid historical period. For example, were the first resurrection appearances in Galilee (Matthew, Mark) or Jerusalem (Luke)? As we noted above, when John 20 is compared with these accounts there are striking parallels with Luke 24. If John is recording the event of Pentecost which Luke recounts in Acts 2, however, we should expect to find some parallels here as well. (See Figures 4 and 5.)

While the parallels with Luke 24 are well known,[60] a comparison of John 20 and Acts 2 bears the following results.

The Setting. Both events occur at Jerusalem and are set in seclusion. John remarks that the disciples were gathered together behind closed doors for "fear of the Jews" (20:19). Luke's Pentecost company is similarly gathered (Acts 2:1), no doubt in their Jerusalem upper room (1:13). The motive for their seclusion here, however, is probably prayer (1:14), although fear may not be entirely excluded.

The Commission. The commission of Jesus in John 20:21 is basic to the narrative of Acts 1–2. Acts 1:8 is an anticipation of the witness again hinted at in 2:5 and later fulfilled in Peter's speech (cf. 2:32). Although John does not record the work of witness taking place, he presents the charge to do so.

The Ministry. We have noted that John views apostolic mission as a commission to witness and as a ministry of forgiveness (ἀφίημι, v. 23). In the speech of Peter the work of witness takes place, but it is climaxed with an appeal for reconciliation, "repent and be baptized for the forgiveness [ἄφεσιν] of your sins" (2:38).

The Wind/Breath. These are the most characteristic images employed by

---

58. Note Luke's use of the present here (ἐξαποστέλλω) and the term "promise" (ἐπαγγελία), which for him can imply both promise and fulfillment. Cf. Marshall, *Luke*, 907; Schniewind and Friedrich, *TDNT* 2: 582.

59. The grounds for retaining the longer ending are compelling: (1) The textual evidence for omission is weak (ℵ* D it syr^s); (2) the omission of the words would be more likely in order to create a harmony with Acts 1:9; (3) the Western non-interpolation argument for authenticity should be questioned (see A. Plummer, *Gospel According to St. Luke*, ICC [Edinburgh: T. & T. Clark, 1922] 566-69; and Metzger, *Textual Commentary*, 191-93); (4) the use of ἀναφέρειν is unusual and is an unlikely copyist's addition; (5) the literary structure of the passage (3 coordinate clauses) requires the clause (so Marshall, *Luke*, 909); and (6) even without v. 51b, διέστη ἀπ' αὐτῶν may already imply the ascension (so Plummer, ibid., 564). In Acts 1:2 Luke even suggests that he has dealt with the ascension in his first volume (see ἀνελήμφθη).

60. Bailey, *Traditions Common to Luke and John*, 85-102.

FIGURE 4. THE RESURRECTION APPEARANCES IN THE GOSPELS AND ACTS

	Mark 16*	Matt. 28	Luke 24	Acts 1-2	John 20-21
Easter	**Tomb** young man, v. 5 Mary Magdalene, v. 9	**Tomb** angel, v. 5 two women, vv. 1-10 grasp . . . feet, v. 9	**Tomb** two men, v. 4 various women, v. 10		**Tomb** two angels, 20:12 Mary Magdalene, 20:17 "Don't cling," 20:17
	Galilee promise, v. 7 **Country road** "two of them," v. 12 **Jerusalem** to eleven v. 14 Commission (at table). vv. 15-16 cf. v. 20	**Galilee promise,** v. 7 cf. v. 19 cf. v. 20	[Simon? v. 34] **Galilee reference,** vv. 6-7 **Emmaus road** "two men," vv. 13-27 **Jerusalem** to eleven, vv. 36-49 Commission, v. 48 Promise of Spirit, v. 49a Repentance/forgiveness, v. 47 Reference to Ascension, v. 51 (chronology vague)		**Jerusalem** to ten, 20:19-23 Commission (in evening), 20:21 Gift of Spirit, 20:22 Forgiveness, 20:23
	Reference to Ascension? v. 19				
After Easter	**[Galilee]** no reference; cf. 14:28 "The Lord was working with them," v. 20 **Ascension** cf. v. 19	**Galilee** on mount, v. 16 Commission, v. 19 Promise of sustained personal presence, v. 20	cf. v. 49a **Ascension** cf. v. 51	**Ascension,** 1:9 two men, 1:10 **Pentecost** Gift of Spirit, 2:1ff.	**Jerusalem** Thomas, 20:26-29 **Galilee** ch. 21 cf. 20:21

*The possible dependence of Mark 16:9-20 on Matthew and Luke reduces the value of its parallels.

FIGURE 5. PARALLELS LINKING LUKE 24, JOHN 20, AND ACTS 2

John 20:18-23	**John 20** Easter Sunday Jerusalem — John 20:24-27	**Luke 24** Easter Sunday Jerusalem	**Acts 2** Easter Sabbath Jerusalem
18 "I have seen the Lord"	"We have seen the Lord," v. 25		
19 doors shut; disciples inside; Jesus stands in their midst (μέσος); "Peace be with you"	doors shut, v. 26; disciples inside, v. 26; "Peace be with you," v. 26	eleven gathered with two from Emmaus and others, v. 33; Jesus stands in their midst (μέσος); "Peace be with you," v. 36 (p75 א A B)	disciples gathered "in one place," v. 1
20 Jesus displays hands, side; cf. v. 25; Disciples' joy	Jesus displays hands, side, v. 27; Disbelief, v. 25	Jesus displays hands, feet, v. 39; Disbelief, vv. 36-39, 41; Disciples' joy, v. 41	(Many proofs, 1:3)
21 "Peace be with you" (cf. v. 19); Commission		Commission, v. 47	(Commission, 1:8)
22 Jesus breathes "Receive Holy Spirit"			Rush of wind, v. 2; "filled with Holy Spirit," v. 4
23 Ministry of forgiveness		Ministry of forgiveness, v. 47	Forgiveness of sins, v. 38

John and Luke. The two accounts are less dissimilar than they might at first seem. First, the imagery itself is parallel. Luke could have correctly used πνεῦμα rather than πνοή in Acts 2:2 because both terms can refer to the wind.[61] The reverse is also the case. Πνοή (wind) in Acts 2:2 most likely refers to the breath of Yahweh.[62] Further, John has elsewhere depicted the spiritual rebirth using wind imagery. In John 3 it is the wind which blows freely (πνέω), and this image symbolizes the Spirit. It is interesting that the note of sound which Luke records in Acts 2:2, 33 is also picked up in John 3:8. The full image given to Nicodemus is fulfilled at Pentecost (esp. as recorded by Luke).[63]

Second, although Luke's account of the wind/breath tradition first echoes the prophecy of the Baptist (Luke 3:16), it is clear that he is aware of a firm OT tradition wherein God's Spirit is experienced as wind and power (cf. Elijah, 1 Kgs. 19:11; Ezek. 19 and 20). An important image for this tradition is found in Ezek. 37:8-10. Here Ezekiel has developed the Gen. 2:7 story where God breathed (נפח) into Adam: in the eschaton Ezekiel prophesies a re-creation when God will again breathe (נפח, 37:9) on human beings. John's use of the LXX of this Ezekiel passages seems certain (πνεῦμα, ἐμφυσᾶν, Ezek. 37:9; ἐμφυσᾶν, Gen. 2:7 LXX). Although Luke has no direct literary dependence on this passage (cf. πνοή, Gen. 2:7 LXX), it probably contributed to his background.[64] Both Luke and John play on the breath/wind metaphor to denote the life-giving power of Yahweh. They note the result of new life incorporating the concept of Spirit entering into the disciples (εἰσέρχομαι, Ezek. 37:10; πίμπλημι, Acts 2:4), and they develop the eschatological context.

Finally, one remarkable feature about the wind/breath metaphor is that both writers take pains to show that the origin of this divine Spirit is Jesus. This is most clear in John. In Acts 2:33, however, Luke records that Jesus "has poured forth this which you see and hear." Moreover, Jesus himself has received the Spirit (v. 33b) and is its custodian and dispenser. This parallels much in John's Farewell Discourses (16:7).

Anointing and Resurrection Appearance. One final consideration of a far more speculative nature can now be raised. A major problem in John 20:19-23 is that this anointing transpires in the context of a resurrection appearance. The thesis has been frequently advanced that Acts 2 was a resurrection appearance, which would explain Paul's account in 1 Cor. 15:6 of Jesus' appear-

---

61. Thus πνεῦμα in Wis. 5:23; 7:20; 13:2; 17:18; Sib. Or. 3:102; Philo V. Mos. 1:41, 179; 2:104; John 3:8; Heb. 1:7; 1 Clem. 36:3 (see Isaacs, Concept of Spirit, 150, 154). Thus πνοή in Job 37:10; 2 Sam. 22:16; Ezek. 13:13; Sib. Or. 5:375; Acts 2:2 (TDNT 6: 453).

62. Thus its use in Gen. 2:7; 7:22; Prov. 24:12; Acts 17:25; 1 Clem. 21:9; 57:3.

63. P. Parker, "The Kinship of John and Acts," in Christianity, Judaism, and Other Greco-Roman Cults, ed. J. Neusner (Leiden: Brill, 1975) 1: 191-93.

64. F. F. Bruce, The Acts of the Apostles: The Greek Text with Introduction and Commentary (Grand Rapids: Eerdmans, 1952) 81; R. P. C. Hanson, Acts (Oxford: New Clarendon, 1967) 63; note the use of the Ezek. 37:8-10 tradition in Rev. 7:1; 11:11; I. H. Marshall, Acts, Tyndale New Testament Commentaries (Leicester/Downers Grove: IVP, 1980) 68, refers to 2 Sam. 22:16; Job 37:10; and Ezek. 13:13.

ing to more than 500 people.[65] Althouth the parallel of 1 Cor. 15:6 and Acts 2 is not compelling,[66] the fact remains that some type of resurrection appearances did occur after the ascension mentioned by Luke. The appearance to Paul, long after the ascension (cf. 1 Cor. 9:1; 15:5-8; and the use of ὤφθη for all appearances), opens the way for other appearances and even that of the 500. The point for John is that Jesus appeared quite independently of the apparent terminus found in Acts 1:9. Therefore some may have believed that Jesus appeared in and through the Acts 2 experience. This thought is further supported by the frequent combination of christophany and experience of the Spirit. To experience the Spirit was in some measure to experience the reality of the present Jesus (Rom. 8:9; Gal. 4:6; Phil. 1:19; 1 Cor. 15:45). This is not to say that a resurrection experience and the Spirit could not be distinguished, but that there was a similar dynamic between them. As we shall see, this very association of Christ and Spirit is chief among John's concerns.

We have discussed at length the numerous pieces of evidence suggesting that John 20:22 possibly records the giving of the Paraclete and may be a parallel tradition to Acts 2. But one wonders if even these are convincing. Could John be so oblivious to the traditional chronology? Is he presenting a rival tradition? To be sure, the parallels between John 20 and Acts 2 (above) are not conclusive. If anything, the parallels with Luke 24 are far stronger: the setting (Luke 24:36), Jesus' greeting (v. 36), disbelief (vv. 38, 41), joy (v. 41), forgiveness (v. 47), the commission (v. 47), and the promise of the Spirit (v. 49). The three themes of John 20:21-23 are all here: the Spirit, the ministry to sin, and the charge to mission. This correspondence would then suggest that John has developed a traditional resurrection scene into a singular event uniting the return, the ascension, and the Spirit (so F. Porsch). Or John may have joined the events recorded in Acts 2 and Luke 24. Evidence for this theory, however, is only speculative and far from persuasive.

Another approach may aid our enquiry. *What was the Johannine expectation?* If we cannot determine the exact relationship with Acts 2, perhaps we can discover the Fourth Evangelist's intention. Is this John's record of the coming of the Paraclete? We shall first explore how John has collapsed and unified the various events of the "hour." Then we shall examine the relationship between Christ and Spirit in John's eschatological perspective.

C. THE JOHANNINE EXPECTATION/INTERPRETATION

John's expectation of the Spirit can be discussed in two ways. First, how does John view the events within the hour of glorification and how is the Spirit incorporated into these? Second, what is the relation between the expectation of the Spirit and the parousia of Christ? In other words, is Pentecost the final horizon for John's futurist eschatology?

---

65. This was advanced by E. von Dobschütz, *Ostern und Pfingsten* (Leipzig: Hinrichs, 1903) 31-43; see the excellent discussion of Dunn, *Jesus and the Spirit*, 142-46. Recent advocates include Jeremias, *Theology*, 1: 30-31; see 308n.1; S. M. Gilmour, "Easter and Pentecost," *JBL* 81 (1962) 62-66.

66. See the accurate criticisms of Dunn, ibid., 145-46.

1. THE UNIFIED EVENTS OF THE HOUR

Our first task is to explore the possibility that John collapsed the historical events of the cross (death, resurrection, ascension, anointing) into a single movement of Jesus' life-giving work. The importance of this work is stressed by 7:39, in which the glorification of Jesus is the prerequisite for the coming of the Spirit. This verse, however, should only be viewed functionally. The Spirit was upon Jesus (1:33; 3:34) while it was not yet active among his followers. But the question still remains: what does it mean for Jesus to be glorified?

a. Glorification

That John conceives of Jesus' glorification as a complex of events is shown by his use of *glorify* (δοξάζειν).[67] The reader is pointed forward to the hour of divine action (2:4; 7:30; 8:20; 12:23, 27; 13:1; 17:1), which includes not only Christ's death but his resurrection and ascension. Thus in 12:23; 13:31; and 21:19 John is primarily thinking of Jesus' death. In 7:39 and 12:16 the Spirit is considered.[68] In 17:5 it is clearly the ascension which is in view.

John's use of *exalt* or *lift up* (ὑψοῦν) supports this same conclusion. G. Bertram remarks that in John this verb "has intentionally a double sense in all the passages in which it occurs (3:14; 8:28; 12:32, 34). It means both exaltation on the cross and exaltation to heaven."[69] "Lifting up" is therefore the comprehensive event of salvation. While Luke uses ὑψοῦν for ascension in Acts 2:33 and 5:31, John is enjoying the irony of the term's double meaning (to crucify, to exalt; cf. רום). The movement up to the cross is a heavenward movement which is the first step back to Jesus' former glory with God. The confirmations expected in 8:28 and 12:32-33 will not come on the cross but after the cross in resurrection and ascension. Brown even compares the three passion/resurrection predictions in the Synoptics (Mark 8:31; 9:31; 10:33-34 and par.) with these three statements in John employing ὑψοῦν and concludes that there is a definite correspondence.[70] The Johannine Jesus does not predict his resurrection but only his "lifting up."

Spirit and ascension are unified in still other passages. In Jesus' discourse with Nicodemus the new birth is described as a consequence of believing on the Son of Man "lifted up" (3:14). This thought follows from 3:13, which affirms the coming ascension (ἀναβαίνειν). This relation implies that "birth ἐκ πνεύματος [of/by Spirit] is the consequence of the Son of Man's ascension and of faith in him thus exalted."[71] Ascension and Spirit are likewise conjoined

---

67. We have discussed δοξάζειν in the previous chapter (pp. 80-81) where it interpreted the signs of Jesus. Here we will concentrate on John's second usage when he anticipates the ultimate sign, the cross. See Dunn, *Baptism*, 173-76.

68. In 12:16, the "remembering" resulting from the glorification is a work of the Paraclete (14:26).

69. *TDNT* 8: 610; cf. R. Bultmann, "Zur Interpretation des Joh. Evangelium," *TLZ* 87 (1962) 1-5; E. K. Lee, *Religious Thought of St. John*, 145-52; and D. A. Mealand, "The Christology of the Fourth Gospel," *SJT* 31 (1978) 453-54.

70. Brown, *John*, 1: 146.

71. Dunn, *Baptism*, 175.

in John 6:62-63. The vision of life given by the Spirit is hinged to Jesus' ascent to the Father.

Nowhere is this thought more clearly expressed than in the Farewell Discourses. D. E. Holwerda rightly links the departure/return (ὑπάγω, πορεύομαι) language to the ascension/Spirit complex, but he draws the wrong conclusion.[72] The Paraclete is not merely a "post-ascension" figure, but more precisely he is involved in the dynamic of the ascension itself. Jesus must go away (go to the Father; be glorified; ascend) before the Paraclete can come (16:7; etc.). *The prerequisite departure of Jesus does not refer to his necessary absence when the Paraclete appears. It refers to the preliminary death and glorification of Jesus for which the Spirit must wait (7:39).* Thus John stresses the continuity of Paraclete and Christ: the disciples are saved from becoming orphans (ὀρφανοί) because of the immediacy of the exchange (14:15-24; 16:7). But unlike Luke, who separated Spirit and ascension and thereby breaks the Christ/Spirit dependence, John shows Jesus making a provision for his followers in the context of his departure.[73]

To sum up, although John is aware of the separate historical events of "the hour," he conceives of them theologically as a unified whole. In particular, ascension and Spirit are now linked to the cross. "To be lifted up" is a comprehensive term describing Jesus' heavenly return. Jesus begins his return as he approaches death (13:1), and even in the course of the Farewell Discourses he can speak as if his return were already underway (14:4, 28; 16:28). The first definite step brings him resurrection life. The final step is when he is lifted up to heaven. Within this process, when Christ makes his return, the Spirit emerges (3:13ff.; 6:62-63). This understanding alone explains the claim of 12:32, "When I am lifted up from the earth, I shall draw all men to myself." This "drawing" is the mission achieved by the Spirit Paraclete.

b. John 19:30, 34

Just as John relates the ascension of Jesus to the whole work of the cross, he views the Spirit as similarly dependent. Death and resurrection are movements in Jesus' ascension; so too the Spirit is linked to Jesus' death. John has provided fascinating clues suggesting this connection in 19:30 and 34.

On the one hand, παρέδωκεν τὸ πνεῦμα (he gave over/up his spirit) in 19:30 could refer to the anthropomorphic πνεῦμα, that is, Jesus here gives up his life force.[74] This reference would then compare with πνεῦμα in John 11:33

---

72. *The Holy Spirit and Eschatology*, 17-24; cf. p. 21: "as in 7:39 so here also, the Spirit is described as a post-ascension figure." But 7:39 (and his other texts) does not prove this; the departure theme closely follows the verbs ὑπάγειν (13:3, 33, 36; 14:4, 5, 28; 15:16; 16:5, 10, 17) and πορεύομαι (14:2, 3, 12, 28; 16:7, 28).

73. Note how Paul joins ascension and the Spirit in his citation of traditional materials in Eph. 4:8: "Therefore it is said, 'When he ascended on high, he led a host of captives, and he gave gifts to men.'" In the East Syrian and Palestinian churches the Ascension was celebrated on the fiftieth day after Easter until the 4th century. Cf. I. H. Marshall, "The Significance of Pentecost," *SJT* 30 (1977) 363, citing G. Kretschmar, "Himmelfahrt und Pfingsten," *ZKG* 66 (1954-55) 209-53.

74. Porsch, *Pneuma*, 327ff.; Schweizer, *TDNT* 6: 43n.714; Tasker, *John*, 217; Barrett, *John*,

and 13:21. In addition, John 19:30 would be another account of Matthew's ἀφῆκεν τὸ πνεῦμα (27:50), and especially Luke's παρατίθεμαι τὸ πνεῦμά μου (23:46). But it is clear that John's record stands apart. Παραδίδωμι is an unnatural term for this giving up. Nowhere in Greek literature is παραδίδωμι τὸ πνεῦμα used as a description of death.[75] To be sure, Matthew's use of ἀφίημι is more natural. If John meant to say that a gift (the Spirit) was being given back to the Father (so Luke), ἀποδίδωμι would have been most appropriate.[76] Παραδίδωμι often refers to the handing on of something to a successor.[77]

Other scholars find in 19:30 an actual giving of the Spirit.[78] This interpretation is doubly improbable, however. First, the language of John may be explained from Luke 23:46, or παραδίδωμι may stress the voluntary giving of Jesus' life, much like Isaiah's Servant (Isa. 53:12 LXX, παρεδόθη εἰς θάνατον ἡ ψυχή αὐτοῦ).[79] Second, this interpretation has to reckon with 20:22, where John makes the anointing obvious.

In 19:28-30 John's expression may convey a characteristically Johannine double meaning. The chief focus of the passage is not on παρέδωκεν τὸ πνεῦμα but on τετέλεσται (it is finished). This cry is not an anticipation of imminent death but the announcement of victory (cf. 4:34; 17:4). Loisy remarks, "The death of the Johannine Christ is not a scene of suffering, of ignominy, of universal desolation (as in the Synoptics)—it is the beginning of a great triumph."[80] There is no defeat. The work Jesus set out to do is now complete. Yet even death does not overtake him. Jesus pulls death upon himself. Jesus continues to be the subject of active verbs (κλίνας, παρέδωκεν). "No one takes [my life] from me, but I lay it down of my own accord" (10:18).

While the first level urges the voluntariness of Jesus' death, John's suggestive language also points in another direction. Unlike Luke, John nowhere describes the recipient of Jesus' giving (e.g., the Father), and he even implies that those beneath the cross (Mary and the Beloved Disciple) toward whom he

---

554; Bultmann, John, 675. John 13:21 (πνεῦμα) is paralleled by 12:27, which employs ψυχή. Of the 14 appearances of παραδίδωμι in John, no other refers to the Spirit. Ten refer to Judas's betrayal.

75. So Porsch, Pneuma, 328, who refers to I. de la Potterie, Passio et Mors Christi: Jo 18–19 (Rome: Pontifical Biblical Institute, 1964-65) 129; cf. W. Popkes, Christus Traditus, Eine Untersuchung zum Begriff der Dahingabe im Neuen Testament (Zürich: Zwingli, 1967) 141; cf. 40-41. Similar expressions include παραδῶ τὸ σῶμά (1 Cor. 13:3); τὰς ψυχάς (Acts 15:26); and ἑαυτόν (Gal. 2:20), which stress the willingness of death. The parallels cited by Bultmann (John, 675n.1) are of little help since παραδίδωμι is absent from them.

76. Matt. 5:26; 18:25ff.; Luke 4:20; 7:42; 9:42; 12:59; Hermas Mand. 3:2; Sim. 2:7; Diog. 1:5.

77. Dodd, Interpretation, 428n.3; see the many references in BAG, 614-15; and Büschel, TDNT 2: 169-72.

78. Hoskyns, John, 532; Lightfoot, John, 319; Braun, Jean, 3:168; It is generally argued that the symbolism employed involves Jesus giving the Spirit to the Beloved Disciple (the symbol of the model Christian) and to Mary (the church).

79. On the former view see Bailey, Traditions Common to Luke and John, 81-82; Barrett, John, 554. On the latter view see Ps. 30:5 LXX (Eng. 31:5); so Büschel, TDNT 2: 170; Bernard, John, 2: 641, shows how Isa. 53:12b was used as a passion prophecy (Luke 22:37); cf. Schnackenburg, John, 3:284-85; contra Bultmann, John, 675n.1; and W. Popkes, Christus Traditus, 41.

80. Le Quatrième Evangile, loc. cit., as cited by Brown, John, 2: 930.

bows his head are the aim of this "handing over" (Barrett). This creates the general impression that the gift of the Spirit is active at the time of the cross. The gift is, as it were, a fruit of the cross.[81] The loosing of Jesus' Spirit is part of the overall theological image given by John. This theme should not take us by surprise here, but rather support our other evidence that John has interlocked the Spirit and the "hour." The Spirit is not actually given (cf. 20:22), but in a symbolic, proleptic fashion—at the shifting of the eras when the moment of sacrifice comes—the movement of God toward humanity is the Spirit.

It is not overly subtle to interpret Jesus' cry of thirst in this way (19:28).[82] Within the Johannine framework this cry is initially a fulfillment of various prophecies concerning messianic suffering (Ps. 69:22; 22:16). This theme is obvious to John (18:11). On another level, διψῶ is Johannine irony echoing 7:37ff. The source of living water now thirsts. John's only other uses of διψῶ bring forward this same suggestion (4:13, 14, 15; 6:35; 7:37). Further, the OT texts which probably lie behind 7:37 (Ezek. 47:1-11; Zech. 14:8) conjoin the motifs of Spirit and thirst.

In an even more enigmatic way, John 19:34 presents the same theme. We have discussed 19:34 and its background in the previous chapter and here will only briefly recall our conclusions.[83] First, water flowing from the side of Jesus is a direct allusion to the living water expected to flow from his κοιλία. This flow, as we saw, is a symbolic representation of the Spirit (John 4:7-15; 7:37-39). Second, the background of John's living-water tradition is strictly eschatological. The rock of Meribah and paradisal streams from Jerusalem as portrayed at the Feast of Tabernacles have shaped John's imagery. Furthermore, he is aware of Rabbinic traditions which once again interpreted this effluence as the Spirit.

Therefore, while the blood from Jesus' side points either to his certain death or to the acceptable nature of his sacrifice,[84] the water evokes images of the Spirit. It is through the death of Jesus that the Spirit is given. This death opened the way for Jesus' return to his glory, and this event, as it were, makes possible the birth of the Spirit. Brown sums up: "The symbolism here is proleptic and serves to clarify that, while only the risen Jesus gives the Spirit, that gift flows from the whole process of glorification in 'the hour' of the passion, death, resurrection, and ascension."[85]

---

81. F. Porsch, *Pneuma*, 330-31; S. Karotemprel, "The Glorification of Jesus and the Outpouring of the Spirit," in *The Promise of Living Water* (Bombay: Asian Trading Company, 1977) 63-82; E. A. Russell, "The Holy Spirit in the Fourth Gospel," 90; T. Smail, *Reflected Glory: The Spirit in Christ and Christians* (London: Hodder and Stoughton, 1975) 106-107.

82. Brown, *John*, 2:930; Lindars, *John*, 581.

83. See above, pp. 93-95.

84. We have elsewhere shown the background material (e.g., the prohibition against congealed blood, Mish. *Pesahim* 5:3, 5) at work here. John has made evident in other ways in this episode that Jesus is the paschal lamb. Both the satisfaction of Jesus' thirst using ὕσσωπος (synonym of κάλαμος; LXX Exod. 12:22, δέσμη ὑσσώπου) and the failure to break legs (cf. Exod. 12:46; Num. 9:12; Ps. 34:20) evoke further Passover images. Cf. J. M. Ford, "'Mingled Blood' from the side of Christ (John 19:34)," *NTS* 15 (1968-69) 337-38; G. Richter, "Blut und Wasser aus der Durchbohrten Seite Jesu (Joh 19,34b)," *MTZ* 21 (1970) 1-21.

85. Brown, *John*, 2: 951; Barrett, *John*, 557; Hoskyns, *John*, 532-33.

c. The Ascension and John 20:17ff.

We have discovered that John has united the various events of the "hour." Ascension is linked to the cross; resurrection is a step in the ascension process; the Spirit is a result of Jesus' death; and the Spirit appears while Jesus is departing. One feature of this glorification process is still unresolved. The various attempts at interpreting 20:22 generally come up against the problem of Jesus' reference to ascension in 20:17-18. Has John employed a different conceptual framework in his view of the ascension? Is he at odds with Luke's very material rendering in Acts 1? Is "ascension" the terminus which must be final before the Spirit can be sent (so Luke)?

A helpful discussion concerning the concept of "ascension" can be found in the writings of R. E. Brown, P. Benoit, P.-H. Menoud, and A. M. Ramsey.[86] Two problems face us in this area: the materializing tendency of Luke in Acts 1, and the "local" problem of the resurrection.

In Acts 1 Luke describes the ascension as a levitation terminating the presence of Jesus. But this spatial language presents the question, Where did Jesus go? Does Luke expect a material or spatial answer to this question? Is this when Jesus first enters the Father's presence?

This question leads to a second problem. The resurrection must have been a glorification before the Father. Luke at least implies this correlation in Acts 2:32-33, "God raised Jesus up . . . being therefore exalted at the right hand of God" (cf. Acts 5:30-31). If this is true, "ascension" is "merely the use of spatial language to describe exaltation and glorification."[87] And it is strained language at that. Jesus' resurrection/ascension moved in spatial and local categories beyond our material conceptualizations. Whenever Jesus appeared as the Resurrected One, he necessarily appeared from heaven. Far from implying that Jesus dwelt with the apostles for forty days, Acts 1 suggests the fleeting, occasional nature of the appearances (ὀπτάνομαι, συναλίζω, 1:3, 4; cf. ὁράω, 1 Cor. 15:5-8). Therefore it is best to view the ascension of Acts 1:9 as simply a dramatic terminus of the type of relation Jesus had been enjoying with the disciples after the resurrection.

It is evident that John is working with this definition of ascension as "glorification." Rather than a terminus of Jesus' earthly appearances, it is an exaltation before the Father. Hence the entire upward movement beginning with the cross can be viewed as ascending. Ascension for John is more precisely

---

86. Brown, *John*, 2: 1012-14; P. Benoit, "L'Ascension," *RB* 56 (1949) 161-203 (English summary, *TD* 8 [1960] 105-10); P.-H. Menoud, "La Pentecôte lucanienne et l'histoire," *RHPR* 42 (1962) 141-47; A. M. Ramsey, "What Was the Ascension?" in *History and Chronology in the New Testament*, 135-44; most recently, see T. F. Torrance, *Space, Time, and Resurrection* (Edinburgh: Handsel Press; Grand Rapids: Eerdmans, 1976) 106-58.

87. Ramsey, ibid., 141; cf. Rom. 8:34; Eph. 1:20; Phil. 2:8-9; 1 Pet. 3:21-22; in Matt. 28:16-20 the resurrected Jesus has already been given all power on heaven and on earth. Ramsey writes that when Jesus names "the Father as the goal of his journey ('going' in John 14–16) he is predicting the death, resurrection, and the ascension drawn together as in a single act." Cf. I. H. Marshall, "The Resurrection in the Acts of the Apostles," in *Apostolic History and the Gospel: Biblical and Historical Essays Presented to F. F. Bruce on His Sixtieth Birthday*, ed. W. W. Gasque and R. P. Martin (London: Paternoster; Grand Rapids: Eerdmans, 1970) 92-107.

the terminus of "the hour" in which Jesus completes the various steps of glorification. John does not describe another terminus for the earthly appearances. He leaves this chapter in his account open. Could this be a suggestive allusion to the nearness of Jesus to the believing community? Of this we shall have more to say in a moment.

We can return from here to John 20:17ff. and pick up the difficult story of Mary with a new perspective. It is true that Jesus has not yet ascended (ἀνα-βέβηκα, v. 17); but this fact points to the incomplete process before him. The gift of the Spirit still lies ahead. Therefore Jesus is redirecting Mary to a new type of relation with him which will come only through the Spirit. Then again, it is still correct to say that Jesus is in the process of ascension (ἀναβαίνω as a true present). The final step within that process when the Spirit comes follows directly on this section (vv. 19-23). Hence the Magdalene story is an *interpretative vehicle* designed to stress the transition already underway and to anticipate the coming Spirit. The criteria for the Paraclete are now satisfied. Jesus has gone away (16:7) in that the cross is behind him. He has gone to the Father (14:28) in that ascension is incorporated into the resurrection and glorification. Jesus has been glorified (7:39) since ascension finally terminates "the hour." The first half of 14:28 is therefore complete, "You heard me say to you, 'I go away.'" The second half now involves the resurrection and awaits the coming Spirit, "I will come to you."

2. THE UNITY OF CHRIST AND SPIRIT

Bultmann has made the penetrating observation that the "not yet" of 20:17 really refers to Mary's desire and echoes the "not yet" of 7:39.[88] If this interpretation is true, the satisfaction of her desire for nearness to Jesus is found in the Spirit. This proximity is John's second stress. Spirit and Christ work in close correspondence within the church age. Some would even argue that the Spirit fulfills the return of Christ for John's future eschatology as well.[89] This correspondence is evidenced in three ways. First, the expectation of the Farewell Discourses moves between the coming of Jesus and the coming of the Spirit in oblique yet purposeful ways. Second, John depicts a functional correspondence between the Paraclete and Christ. Third, John heightens the personal features surrounding the expected Spirit.

a. The Johannine Expectation

The coming/going of Jesus (and his ascent/descent) is one of John's most frequent images in his theology of the incarnation.[90] This image finds full expression in the Farewell Discourses. But here the "going" of Jesus rarely

---

88. Bultmann, *John*, 687; as cited in Brown, *John*, 2: 1012.

89. E. F. Scott, *The Fourth Gospel*, 348; E. K. Lee, *The Religious Thought of St. John*, 210; Bultmann, *Theology*, 1: 153-64; 2:57; cf. H. Schlier, "Zum Begriff des Geistes," 268.

90. See the recent study of J. V. Dahms, "Isa. 55:11 and the Gospel of John," *EvQ* 53 (1981) 78-88.

refers to the ascension and his "coming" rarely refers to the parousia. None of the uses of πορεύομαι and ὑπάγω in John 14–16 requires a reference to an ascension which is distinct from the glorification of the cross.[91] Similarly, within the many appearances of ἔρχομαι in these chapters the chief uses refer to the resurrected Jesus (14:18, 23, 28) or to the coming Spirit (15:26; 16:8, 13), *not* to the parousia.[92] To assuage the disciples' fear of the impending hour of darkness Jesus refers to his resurrection/return as their glorified Lord and to the coming of the Spirit. While some scholars debate whether this return refers to the resurrection (Lindars, Hoskyns, Barrett) or the Spirit (Holwerda, Bauer, Brown), the truth of the matter is that the two concepts spill into one another.[93] "I will come to you" in 14:18 initially refers to the return from death; but John develops this reference into a doctrine of personal indwelling. Now the relationship expected between Jesus and his disciples will have a permanency.

The return of the resurrected Jesus from death is given marked attention in the Farewell Discourses: "I will not leave you desolate, I will come to you" (14:18). "You heard me say to you, I go away, and I will come to you" (14:28). "A little while and you will see me no more; again a little while and you will see me" (16:16). Expressions such as "in that day" (14:20; 16:23, 26) and "the hour is coming" give these passages an eschatological tenor such that "I am coming to you" could indeed sound like the second advent. If this interpretation is accurate, John has dramatically heightened the eschatological dimensions of the resurrection appearance and the coming of the Spirit.

This refashioning of the Easter expectation is most apparent in 14:15-24. It turns out that Christ's coming again to the disciples implies four things: the Paraclete will dwell in them (vv. 15-17); they will live by virtue of the living Christ (v. 19); they will live in a continual interchange of ἀγάπη with Christ (v. 21); and Christ will manifest (ἐμφανίζειν; cf. Exod. 33:13 LXX) himself to them. This mutual indwelling finds sharp expression in 14:23. The climax of Jesus' coming to a believer is found both in Jesus and in the Father coming to the believer (cf. 14:18, ἔρχομαι) and making a home with him. Thus the coming of Jesus is portrayed as a tangible resurrection appearance, but it includes a personal epiphany of Christ to the believer in the Spirit. Just as Christ will be "in you" (ἐν ὑμῖν, 14:20), so too the Paraclete dwells with you and will be "in you" (ἐν ὑμῖν, 14:17).[94] Ἔρχομαι thus involves the dual movement,

---

91. See πορεύομαι in 14:2, 3, 12, 28; 16:7, 28; ὑπάγω in 13:3, 33, 36; 14:4, 5, 28; (15:6); 16:5, 10, 17; 14:2-3 is the sole exception, but see our discussion below. "Going to the Father" is John's idiom for Jesus' death as seen in the context of sorrow here (14:27-28; 16:27) and as interpreted in 16:17-24.

92. This corresponds to the Synoptic expectation of the coming of the Son of Man in glory, Mark 13:26 par.

93. Dodd, *Interpretation*, 395, comments: "In fact it would appear that the distinction drawn . . . between predictions of the death and resurrection of Christ and predictions of the second advent, though it is quite clear in the synoptics, is a vanishing distinction in John."

94. Ἔσται appears for ἐστιν in p66c p75 ℵ A D2 Δ vg cop (against p66* B D* W) and should be regarded as original (the theological context requiring it) or as the *lectio difficilior* after two verbs in the present; so J. Rieger, "Spiritus Sanctus suum praeparat adventum (Jo 14,16-17)," *VD* 43 (1965) 20, as cited in Brown, *John*, 2: 640. J. E. Morgan-White has argued that the two halves of

first of God in Christ (resurrection), then of Christ in believer (indwelling).[95]

Brown has taken this identification a step further by showing a formal parallelism between the role of Christ in 14:18-21 and the Paraclete in vv. 15-17.[96] Both units show similar features.

FIGURE 6

	The Paraclete vv. 15-17	Christ vv. 18-21
Necessary conditions; love Jesus/keep his commandments	v. 15	v. 21 (23)
Giving of the Paraclete/coming back of Jesus	16	18
The world will not see the Paraclete nor Jesus	17	19
The disciples will recognize the Paraclete and see Jesus	17	19
The Paraclete and Jesus will dwell in the disciples	17	23

Therefore the vindication of "the hour" from the disciples' point of view is found first in the resurrection (without reference to the parousia). Here Jesus will bring comfort to the disciples. But this event will also include a mystical experience of Christ dwelling within them. And all of this accords with the account in John 20. When the disciples meet the resurrected Jesus (20:19ff.) they encounter the Spirit. The Spirit, therefore, is a dimension of the resurrected, glorified Christ. Since the Spirit is the vehicle of this indwelling, the identification is made explicit: *the indwelling Paraclete is the indwelling Jesus.* The Farewell Discourses focus on the movement of Jesus out of the world and the transition of his personal presence with the disciples from bodily form to that of the Paraclete. Jesus "promises that he will come himself, showing that the Spirit is not something other than what he is himself" (Cyril of Alexandria).[97]

---

the ὅτι clause should be treated as separate ideas, thus allowing the future; see "A Note on John 14:17b," *BZ* 23 (1979) 93-96, as cited in *NTA* 23 (1979) 295.

95. E. K. Lee, *The Religious Thought of St. John*, 204-206; A. Nossol, "Der Geist als Gegenwart Jesu Christi," in *Gegenwart des Geistes*, ed. W. Kasper (Freiburg: Herder, 1979) 140-43.

96. Brown, *John*, 2: 64-65, also finds these themes in 1 John generally stressing the Father:

Necessary conditions: love one another, keep the commandments	1 John 3:23-24
Revelation of God	3:2
Opposition between the Father and the world	2:15-17
Christians will see him as he is	3:2
God abides in Christians	3:24

97. Cited by Hoskyns, *John*, 459; in our view it is unnecessary to choose as Morris (*John*, 651) and Hoskyns do whether this "coming" of Jesus refers to the resurrection or to the Spirit—it refers

b. Parallels: Christ and the Paraclete

The second means employed by the Fourth Evangelist to show a correspondence between Jesus and the Paraclete is found in the numerous passages which parallel features of both. Initially this functional correspondence means that for John the Paraclete will continue the work Jesus has begun. He is therefore subordinate to Jesus. As Jesus witnessed to and glorified the Father (17:18; 13:31), the Paraclete's chief task will be to continue the witness to Jesus (15:26) that began with the Baptist (1:7-8). Through the Paraclete the words of Jesus will still be audible (16:13). The Spirit Paraclete both will recall what Jesus has said (14:26) and will give fresh words from the still present, authoritative Christ (16:13). The correspondence between Paraclete and Christ is so strong that the Spirit is said to have no autonomous authority: as the work of Jesus is the work of the Father (5:17), the work of the Paraclete is that of Jesus (16:14-15).[98]

A strong possibility for the origin of this correspondence between Jesus and the Paraclete may be that John conceives of his Logos christology as the model for the Paraclete/Christ relation. The Paraclete is thus to Christ as Christ is to the Father. This relation means that the two figures are separate and distinguishable yet closely associated (cf. 10:30). As one sees the Father in Jesus (14:9), so one experiences Jesus in the Paraclete (14:15ff.). Jesus says and does only what he sees and hears the Father doing (8:28; 5:19-20). Similarly, the Paraclete says only what he hears from Jesus (16:13). Jesus' chief aim was to glorify the Father (17:4), while the Paraclete lifts up Jesus (16:14). The incarnation for John is God reaching into creation and revealing himself. In the Paraclete God reaches again, still glorifying Jesus (and himself), and through the Paraclete he reveals even more of himself (16:12).[99] Beyond their "upward" relation to the Father and Jesus, Christ and the Paraclete have numerous functions which parallel one another. A list of the most accepted correspondences[100] is given in Figure 7.

We can note an additional feature of this correspondence which is less obvious but equally significant. Scholars have rightly identified the "trial motif" which runs through the Fourth Gospel.[101] The climactic judgment

---

to both. Within the context of the resurrection, John portrays the coming of the Spirit (20:22); so Bultmann, *John*, 617-18; and Brown, *John*, 2:644-47. Cf. Barrett, *John*, 464: "we ought not to suppose that John simply confounds Jesus with the Holy Spirit." Cf. also W. R. Hutton, "The Johannine Doctrine of the Holy Spirit," *CrozQ* 24 (1947) 334-43, who looks closely at the Christ/ Spirit relation in John.

98. Note how the Father/Son model in John consistently informs the Christ/Paraclete relation. See further below.

99. J. M. Boice, *Witness and Revelation*, 152-53; cf. Painter, *John*, 66.

100. These parallels are well known. See G. Bornkamm, "Der Paraklet im Johannesevangelium," 79-81; E. Schweizer, *TDNT* 6: 442-43; Bultmann, *John*, 566ff.; R. E. Brown, "The Paraclete in the Fourth Gospel," 126-28; idem, *John*, 2: 1140-41; A. M. Kothgasser, "Die Lehr-, Erinnerungs-, Bezeugungs-, und Einführungsfunktion des Johanneischen Geist-Parakleten Gegenüber der Christus-Offenbarung," *Salesianium* 33 (1971) 570-75; Porsch, *Pneuma*, 239, 322-24; J. L. Martyn, *History and Theology in the Fourth Gospel*, 148-49.

101. See above, pp. 37ff., and below, pp. 204ff.

FIGURE 7

The Paraclete		Christ
14:16	given by the Father	3:16
14:16-17	with, in, by the disciple	3:22; 13:33; 14:20
14:17	not received by the world	1:11; 5:53; (12:48)
14:17	not known by the world (only believers know him)	16:3; 8:19; 10:14
14:7	not seen by the world (only believers see him)	14:19; 16:16-17
14:26	sent by the Father	cf. chs. 5, 7, 8, 12
14:26	teaches	7:14-15; 8:20; 18:19
15:26; 16:7, 13	he comes (from the Father into the world)	5:43; 16:28; 18:37
15:26	gives testimony	5:31ff.; 8:13ff.; 7:7
16:8	convicts the world	(cf. 3:19-20; 9:41; 15:22)
16:13	speaks not of self but of what is heard	7:17; 8:26ff.; 14:10
16:14	glorifies the Sender (Jesus/Father)	12:28; 17:1, 4
16:13ff.	reveals, discloses, proclaims	4:25; (16:25)
16:13	leads into the fullness of truth	18:37; 14:6
15:26; 14:17; 16:13	is the Spirit of Truth; Jesus is the Truth	14:6
14:16 (etc.)	a Paraclete	(14:16); 1 John 2:1

(John 19) is foreshadowed in the entirety of Jesus' ministry. Witnesses come and go while judgments on Jesus are passed.[102] Jesus is continually on trial before the world, but ironically, the reverse is the case: the world is on trial before God. The world's response to Jesus determines its judgment (3:18-19).

The most attractive explanation of John's use of παράκλητος is precisely this forensic setting. The Paraclete is the other advocate who will carry on the trial even though the church now receives the persecution of the world. The explicit warning of this conflict in 15:18-25 is followed immediately by the third Paraclete promise (vv. 26-27). Within this conflict (which the Johannine church was having with the Jews) the Spirit Paraclete is the church's advocate. He defends Jesus (15:26) in the testimony of the church (v. 27) and thereby defends the church as well.[103] This posture of the Spirit as witness and advocate even appears in the intra-church dispute evidenced in 1 John. "And the

---

102. See J. Boice, *Witness and Revelation*, 75-142; A. A. Trites, *The New Testament Concept of Witness*, 78-129, esp. 113-24; S. Pancaro, *The Law in the Fourth Gospel* (Leiden: Brill, 1975).

103. A. E. Harvey, *Jesus on Trial*, 115, writes: "Any particular occasion on which a disciple is actually brought to trial is only an instance and continuation of that eternal 'trial' in which Jesus, and then his followers, are inevitably involved before the judgement of the world." Cf. J. Boice, *Witness and Revelation*, 143-58.

Spirit is the witness, because the Spirit is the truth" (1 John 5:6; cf. 4:1ff.). The Paraclete, who originally worked against Jewish hostility, is later found confronting Christian heresy. Therefore the trial motif in which Jesus was the central character continues, but now the Paraclete enters as the new (ἄλλος) advocate.

c. The Personalization of the Paraclete

A third and final aspect links together Jesus and the Spirit: namely, the "personal" features of the Spirit Paraclete. This is the most readily recognized feature of John's pneumatology. As we have argued above (chapter 1), these personal images employed in the Farewell Discourses do not stem from angelic forms of the intertestamental period. The Johannine Paraclete is personalized, but this stems from the person of Jesus.[104] Above all, this personalization is apparent from the functional parallels shown above. But John also makes his point in other ways.

It must not be overlooked that the Holy Spirit is identified as the Paraclete (a masculine noun). Although many scholars would not agree with this conclusion (Bultmann, Betz, Sasse, Spitta, Windisch), the alignment in 14:26 is indisputable.[105] Johnston's arguments for the rejection of τὸ ἅγιον in this passage are unconvincing in view of the very strong attestation for the longer reading.[106] It is true that this is the only appearance of the definite article with ἅγιον in John but he freely employs πνεῦμα ἅγιον in 1:33; 20:22, and possibly 7:39.[107] This argument may be superfluous, however; John is not tied to a formula for the Spirit (e.g., "the Spirit of Truth"), and any alignment of πνεῦμα with παράκλητος emphasizes the personal nature of the Johannine Spirit.

More important are grammatical indicators where masculine personal pronouns are associated with the neuter πνεῦμα. Here we have the use of ἐκεῖνος in 14:26; 15:26; 16:8, 14 and αὐτός in 16:7. Although these masculine pronouns could arguably be attributed to their masculine antecedent (ὁ παράκλητος), the use of ἐκεῖνος in 16:13 is significant in that ὁ παράκλητος is dropped and only the neuter τὸ πνεῦμα τῆς ἀληθείας is employed. Bernard comments: "[this use of ἐκεῖνος] shows that for Jn. τὸ πνεῦμα τῆς ἀληθείας meant more than a mere tendency or influence."[108]

---

104. Brown, "The Paraclete in the Fourth Gospel," 124, 126-27; E. J. Dobbin, "Towards a Theology of the Holy Spirit," HeyJ 17 (1976) 17-19.

105. Barrett, John, 91, remarks, "The noun παράκλητος (unlike πνεῦμα which is neuter) is masculine; thus in its grammatical form alone it tends to remove the Spirit from the sphere of abstract, impersonal force into that of personality." Brown argues (John, 2:639) that this is the only passage that makes the identification of Paraclete and Pneuma explicit. Cf. Marsh, John, 515.

106. Only the Sinaitic Syriac omits τὸ ἅγιον; a few minor mss. read τὸ πνεῦμα τῆς ἀληθείας (from v. 17; cf. 15:26; 16:13). Barrett, John, 467, favors the shorter reading (cf. Lindars, John, 484). The texts of UBS, Nestle 25th and 26th ed., and Westcott and Hort support the longer text.

107. Πνεῦμα ἅγιον in 7:39 is found in p66* B L W X Δ 0105 f¹ f¹³ various minuscules and the Fathers; τὸ πνεῦμα ἅγιον ἐπ' αὐτοῖς is found in D*.

108. Bernard, John, 2:500; cf. Morris, John, 699n.26.

The use of ἄλλος in 14:26 is generally thought to indicate that for John Jesus is also a type of Paraclete (as is made clear in 1 John 2:1). But the reverse is also true; the Spirit Paraclete is also a type of Jesus. The identification of their roles suggests the identification of their personal functions. Where John does not use ἄλλος, he always draws the connection between Christ and the Paraclete (14:26; 15:26; 16:7, 14).

Finally, the image used in 20:22 moves in opposite directions from the impersonal Spirit. This Spirit is the breath of Jesus; or as a Semite might understand it, this Pneuma is his life force (symbolized by breath). Again we see that whenever the Spirit is given personal features, these point to the personality of Jesus.

d. The Problem of the Parousia

If we are correct in our assessment that in his eschatology John carefully associates Christ and Spirit, then we are confronted with the problem of Jesus' independent activity in the coming eschaton: namely, the parousia. This is, of course, the very problem emphasized by Dodd, that John has consistently refined away the apocalyptic expectation in preference for a Christ-mysticism.[109] While scholars have not generally agreed with Dodd's "realized eschatology" for the whole of Jesus' teachings, this reorientation identified in John is accurate. A more balanced view of the Fourth Gospel has been expressed by David Mealand: "The author of this gospel faced up to the challenge of the disappointment of apocalyptic hopes. He retained a future hope, but one purged of lurid apocalyptic, and based on the experience he and his readers had of what Jesus had already achieved."[110]

While it is doubtful that John has expunged the traditional hope altogether, it is quite another matter to say that he has refocused the emphasis of his expectation. The present is constantly in view. Another more likely explanation is that John is dealing with the delay of the parousia not by removing the hope but by stressing the present experience of the Spirit.[111]

The problem of the delay is evidenced in the Farewell Discourses and in chap. 21. First, in 14:19-20 Jesus alludes to his departure and return in spiritual terms. This at once presents difficulties which Jude voices: "Lord, how is it that you will manifest yourself to us and not to the world" (v. 22)? The expectation of a visible, public return of Jesus is clearly at issue. Rev. 1:7 represents well the expectation which the Johannine community certainly knew: "Behold, he

---

109. Dodd, *Apostolic Preaching*, 65, 148; cf. E. F. Scott, *The Fourth Gospel*, 348; E. Schweizer, *TDNT* 6: 437, comments, "The primary distinction [of John] from the Synoptists and Paul, then, is that the older ideas are more consistently eliminated." See also Bultmann, *Theology*, 1: 153-64; 2:52.

110. D. L. Mealand, "The Christology of the Fourth Gospel," *SJT* 31 (1978) 466; cf. C. K. Barrett, "The Holy Spirit in the Fourth Gospel," *JTS* 1 (1950) 3-4; W. R. Hutton, "The Johannine Doctrine of the Holy Spirit," *CrozQ* 24 (1947) 336ff.

111. See R. Kysar, *John: The Maverick Gospel*, 96; R. E. Brown, "The Paraclete in the Fourth Gospel," 130-31; C. K. Barrett, op. cit.; but cf. R. J. Bauckham, "The Delay of the Parousia," *TynBul* 31 (1980) 1-36.

comes in the clouds and every eye will see him." But John 14 presents a new definition. Jesus' personal indwelling along with the Father (14:23-24) will be Jude's own personal epiphany.[112]

Another important discussion occurs in 16:16ff. Jesus remarks that "a little while" (μικρόν) after his departure his disciples will see him once more. It is certain that the early Christians expected a brief interval between the ascension and the triumphant return. Yet when this "little while" grew, some despaired, as the ensuing conversation showed (16:17-24). The problem is not what Jesus means by "seeing," but rather what he means by "a little while" (v. 18). Again, the answer is in terms of an inner apprehension of Christ, which, as we have suggested above, refers to the Spirit.

Finally, 21:21ff. brings out the problem reflected elsewhere in the NT that the first generation of Christians might not die before the parousia (cf. 1 Thess. 4:15; 1 Cor. 15:51). Within the Johannine community, the death of the Beloved Disciple posed an apparent crisis: was John to remain "until Jesus comes" (v. 22)? This suggestion is denied (v. 23), but it once again stresses the eschatological adjustment transpiring in the community.

To stress the realized eschatology of John and the fact that this Gospel is responding to the problem of the delay is not to say that it holds no future hope. The expressions of futurist eschatology found in 5:28-29; 6:39-40, 44, 54; and 12:48 are not later additions[113] but traditional themes retained by the Evangelist. But it is correct to note the severely reduced role of Jesus in the future. John has no text which corresponds to Mark 13:26, though John 14:1-3 does reflect the parousia hope.

Raymond Brown has labeled 14:2-3 "extraordinarily difficult" due to the fact that Jesus' solution to the disciples' despair is virtually apocalyptic. Here Jesus will remove the believers from the world, while elsewhere he comes to aid them in the world through the Paraclete (14:18ff.; cf. 17:15). Dodd remarks, "Here we have the closest approach to the traditional language of the church's eschatology."[114]

Literary features point to peculiarities as well. Several scholars have identified 14:1-3(4) as a traditional, independent unit used by John in the development of the discourse.[115] C. F. Burney even identified in 14:1-10 a "characteristic rhythm" in Aramaic that suggests traditional materials.[116] In addition, the structure of the passage stands out: Jesus' assertion is made (vv. 1-4), then through the Johannine technique of misunderstanding three disci-

---

112. Mockers of futurist expectation are evidenced in 2 Pet. 3:4; ct. 1 Clem. 23:2; 2 Clem. 11:2-4; Barn. 21:3.

113. So Bultmann, *Theology*, 2: 37-39; Käsemann, *Testament of Jesus*, 14, 72-73.

114. Dodd, *Interpretation*, 404; cf. 393; Brown, *John*, 2:625; on the various interpretations of 14:3 see D. Aune, *The Cultic Setting of Realized Eschatology in Early Christianity*, 129-30.

115. See the discussion of Brown, *John*, 2: 622-24; M.-E. Boismard, "L'évolution du thème eschatologique dans les traditions johanniques," 518-23; Bultmann, *John*, 598-603; V. Estalayo Alonso, "La Vuelta de Christo en el Evangelio de Juan. Analisis Literario de John 14:1-3," *Estudios Teologicos* [Guatemala City] 5 (1978) 3-70, as summarized in *NTA* 24 (1980) 144; and D. B. Woll, "The Departure of 'The Way': The First Farewell Discourse in the Gospel of John," *JBL* 99 (1980) 225-39.

116. C. F. Burney, *The Poetry of Our Lord*, 126-29.

ples (Thomas, Philip, Jude) ask deliberate questions elucidating the intention of the original assertion.

Various items indicate that here we are dealing with the second advent. In brief, they include "my Father's house," which, as parallels show, points to heaven.[117] More important is the room (μόνη) which awaits the believer in the other world. In common usage this word had a local sense of a position in heaven (1 Macc. 7:38; cf. 1 En. 39:4; 2 En. 61:2) which the believer obtained either in death or in the final day of the Lord.

The verbs used in Jesus' coming likewise point to the future. Πάλιν ἔρχομαι occurs only here, and the use of the future παραλήμψομαι suggests that the future should be read for ἔρχομαι also. Bernard notes that παραλήμψομαι ὑμᾶς πρὸς ἐμαυτόν suggests a dramatic meeting with Jesus which recalls 1 Thess. 4:16-17 ("we shall be caught up together to meet the Lord").[118] The thrust of these passages is that the disciples will be taken to be where Jesus is (an apocalyptic notion) and not the reverse.

While it is certain that the original intention of John 14:1-3 pointed to the parousia, even this passage hints at the eschatological transition. John's one link with the traditional expectation can be shown to be already conformed to the subsequent adjustment. Whereas μόνη does point to heaven, in the only other NT use (14:23) John has reinterpreted it. Places of dwelling now are places of indwelling. Therefore the best interpretation of μόνη should reflect the regular Johannine verb μένειν (abide). To remain in Christ is John's description of union with Christ.[119] The μόνη is the place where Jesus and the Father meet the believers in their own spiritual life. Significantly, μένειν is used in 14:17 for the indwelling of the Paraclete.

Robert Gundry argues that in 14:3 Jesus does not actually say that he will come and rescue believers. He says he will take them "to himself" (πρὸς ἑαυτόν). This is a marked departure from, say, 1 Thess. 4:17. Hence the goal of this rendezvous is "not mansions in the sky, but spiritual positions in Christ."[120] Therefore it is not absolutely necessary to point to an "otherworldly" locale for this meeting.

The second level of meaning which surrounds 14:1-3 becomes even clearer as the dialogue develops.[121] The interlocutors Thomas, Philip, and Jude

---

117. See Philo De Somniis 1:256; cf. Eccl. 5:1.

118. Bernard, John, 2:535; John uses παραλαμβάνειν in this sense also in 19:17, "to seize."

119. John uses this term 40 times compared with 3 times in Matthew; twice in Mark; and 7 times in Luke; the Johannine Epistles use it 27 times; note the usage in John 15:1-17 (11 times), where union with Christ is explained and developed. See further our examination above, pp. 54-56.

120. R. Gundry, "'In My Father's House are Many Monai' (John 14:2)," ZNW 58 (1967) 70; contra A. L. Humphries, "A Note on πρὸς ἐμαυτόν (John 14:3) and εἰς τὰ ἴδια (John 1:11)," ExpTim 53 (1941-42) 356, who argues for: "take you along with me to my home." Cf. M. McNamara, "'To Prepare a Resting Place for You,' Targumic Expression and John 14:2f," Milltown Studies [Dublin] 3 (1979) 100-108.

121. The problem of the incompatibility of the futurist/realized eschatology in 14:1-31 has often been pointed out. Against Windisch's solution of excising the Paraclete passages themselves stands Woll's successful case that the discrepancy extends beyond the Paraclete texts into the other discourse material (vv. 12-17); see Woll, "The Departure of 'the Way,'" 233. The key to the problem, however, is not to be found in viewing the disciples as the successors to Christ in John and then the

advance the redefinition. The first establishes the "way" (ὁδός) of Jesus' departure and the "way" (ὁδός) which the disciples must follow. Jesus is going to be with the Father, and Christ himself is the way which the disciples must go to reach this same goal. This means that Jesus mediates the knowledge and presence of God. To go to the "place" of the Father is therefore not a transference of locale but a union of knowledge (as finally clarified in vv. 23ff.). Philip brings this point into even sharper focus. Even though Jesus is going (future) to the Father, he is already with the Father in spiritual union. "Do you not believe that I am in the Father and the Father is in me" (v. 10)? This same present experience is possible for the believer through love and obedience: through the Paraclete Jesus will bring this same spirtual union to the disciples. Finally, Jude makes the deflected answer explicit. The way (ὁδός) to the Father is the indwelling of the Father and Son within the believer (v. 23). Again, this indwelling is viewed in the context of the Paraclete (vv. 25-26).

We can conclude with two observations. First, even though John retains the futurist eschatology, in the Fourth Gospel this hope is in transition to a more realized eschatology. But John finds no problem with holding these two perspectives side by side even in contiguous passages (5:19-25, 26-30). This careful admixture of realized/futurist perspectives is reflected throughout Jesus' teaching in the Synoptics. Each Evangelist no doubt selected and emphasized that theme most important to him.

Second, the future hope had not died away in the Johannine community. The resurgence of futurist expectation is alive and well in 1 John, where the parousia is clearly anticipated (1 John 2:28; 3:2).[122] Similarly, the place of the Apocalypse and the Johannine community should also come into view.[123]

* * *

In sum, our examination of the unity of Christ and Spirit has suggested two general results. First, the Paraclete has been personalized and in function paralleled with Jesus. The "personality" of the Paraclete does not stand on its own but reflects entirely the person of Christ. Therefore any experience of the Spirit in the Johannine economy which is not also a Jesus experience is rendered inauthentic. The Paraclete's raison d'être is precisely the glorification of Jesus. But at the same time, the Paraclete and Jesus are not indistinguishable, as if this were Jesus' new mode of existence.[124] In that Jesus in fact ascends to the Father (14:2-3; 20:17-18) and is expected in the parousia (14:3; 21:22; 1 John;

---

apostle having to correct an abuse of this belief (contra Woll). Rather, John is highlighting the christocentric nature of the Spirit, and this emphasis could lead to the later identification suggested by Woll.

122. See the discussion and bibliography of this subject in A. D. Edwards, "Spirit and Eschatology in First John," Tyndale Study Group Paper, Cambridge (Tyndale Fellowship for Biblical Research), 1975.

123. See E. S. Fiorenza, "The Quest for the Johannine School: The Apocalypse and the Fourth Gospel," NTS 23 (1976-77) 402-27; also A. Satake, Die Gemeindeordnung in der Johannesapokalypse (Neukirchen Vluyn: Neukirchener Verlag, 1966); and D. Hill, "Prophets and Prophecy in the Revelation of St. John," NTS 18 (1971-72) 401-18.

124. This has been the solution suggested by E. F. Scott, The Fourth Gospel, 348; and R. Bultmann, Theology, 2: 57; cf. J. L. Martyn, History and Theology, 150.

Revelation), while the Paraclete is on earth in the interim, John has distinguished them. To use Lampe's term, John also believes in "the post-existent Christ." The functional parallel simply means that the Paraclete serves as the presence of Jesus while Jesus is away.

Yet more can and must be said. The image in 20:22 urges that this Spirit is the Spirit which stems from Jesus. One might even argue that this is the Spirit of Jesus. The going/coming texts of John 14 stress that Jesus himself is experienced in the Spirit. Therefore in his eschatology John moves very close to a binitarian theology. To have the Spirit is to have Jesus (and the Father) dwelling within (14:23; cf. 1 John 4:12ff.).[125] But this binitarian danger is only apparent. John understands the persons of the Godhead as closely unified. The unity and distinction of Jesus and the Spirit is paralleled by the same close relationship between Jesus and the Father. There is oneness (10:30; 14:18, 23) and at the same time there is separation (14:28; 16:7).

This leads us to our second conclusion. Two shifts in the traditional expectation are evidenced. Initially the resurrection return has taken on eschatological dimensions. For Jesus to come back from death is given undertones of the parousia and is examined in terms of the experience of anointing/indwelling. The Spirit, therefore, is a part of the community's experience of the physically resurrected Jesus. But John has also pulled in the future hope. The Fourth Evangelist's one contact with the parousia (14:1-3) is in transition and is reinterpreted. We might diagram this dual movement (of resurrection and parousia) thus:

The Resurrection	The Spirit	The Parousia

Yet John has not achieved this shift at the expense of the two traditional endpoints (pace Dodd, Scott, Schweizer). The resurrection is not spiritualized nor is the parousia lost. On the contrary, John's chief concern is to show how these two events have direct implications for the believer's present experience (so Barrett). The climax of the Gospel is the believer's personal experience of Jesus. John writes so that the reader may have life and faith (20:31), but more, that through the Spirit both Jesus and the Father might dwell within the disciple in a relationship of love. Therefore within John's present eschatology the Spirit assumes the role of Christ and effects a personal epiphany of Jesus to the believer.

D. CONCLUSION

It is now necessary for us to apply our conclusions to John 20:22. Have we shed any light on the relation of this passage to the historical framework of Luke? Is this the climax of the Johannine expectation of the Spirit Paraclete?

---

125. See the conclusions reached by the provocative study of G. W. H. Lampe, "The Spirit of God and the Spirit of Christ," in *God as Spirit*, 61-94; cf. M. V. Scott, "The Eschatology of John's Gospel and the Johannine Epistles," unpub. diss., Edinburgh, 1953: "If we speak theologically, we shall differentiate between the Son and the Paraclete; if we speak experientially, we shall say the Paraclete is the Son" (p. 158).

To have an absolute confirmation that 20:22 fulfills the Paraclete promises and duplicates the Acts 2 event, we would need a more specific allusion to the Paraclete in John 20 and stronger parallels with Acts 2. Although many items point in this direction, we are still left with the insuperable problem of chronology. What Luke records on Pentecost, John refers to Easter.

Yet Luke evidences a similar chronological shift in other ways. Luke makes all the resurrection appearances seem to occur on Easter. He then records a description of the ascension on Easter when he knows that the event will occur forty days later. Thus for Luke, if 24:51b is authentic, there would appear to be a conflict with Acts 1:9, but this apparent conflict gives the Third Evangelist no problems. Possibly we should say that John has done something similar. Knowing his Gospel would have no sequel, he has drawn the appearances, ascension, and Pentecost into Easter. Yet for him, this is not simply a matter of literary convenience. As we have seen, John weaves these events into "the hour" with explicit theological intentions.

On the historical level, John has at least given weighty significance to the fact that from the moment of Jesus' resurrection the disciples were experiencing his power in significant ways. This is certainly part of Luke's message in 24:13-35. John has focused on this aspect and found warrant for the development of his own emphasis. Themes from both Luke 24 and Acts 2 converge in John 20. Thus it seems that in some fashion the disciples were experiencing in John 20 the eschatological Spirit predicted in 1:33.

On the other hand, to invalidate this result we would want some hint that John is aware of the Pentecost to come. Or, conversely, we would expect Luke to suggest that the disciples experienced the Spirit before Acts 2. The silence of both Evangelists leaves us in a quandary.

But unlike our historical dilemma, greater certainty surrounds the expectation of John. First, within his theology John has made the coming of the Spirit a result of the sacrifice of the cross. The Fourth Evangelist works to show the unity of the diverse events of "the hour." If this is true, it comes as no surprise to see that John has a clear motive for bringing the Spirit into Easter. Death, resurrection, ascension, and anointing are all components of the single event of glorification. Thus in John 20 it is the *ascending* Jesus who must distribute the Spirit before he finally departs. It is also the *resurrected* Jesus who, having been with the Father, now bestows the Spirit as an effective encounter with himself. Ἔρχομαι πρὸς ὑμᾶς moves between the appearance of the risen Jesus and the indwelling of the Spirit.

Second, this unity means John has associated—or better, identified—the believer's experience of the Spirit with his experience of Jesus. Too often the reverse has been argued for this Gospel: that this Evangelist so understands realized eschatology that he has completely spiritualized the parousia. John's comment is not so much on Jesus (and concerns about the future, although they are there) as it is on the Spirit and the immediacy of the present. To have the Spirit and to have eternal life are various ways of saying that Jesus (and the Father) dwells within. John has not lost faith in the second coming, but he does comment that many of the features associated with that day are now present realities. In a very real way, in the Spirit Jesus has come back.

Therefore whatever may be our judgment about Acts 2, one emphasis is certain: the Fourth Evangelist considered John 20:22 to be the fulfillment of his expectation so carefully developed in the Farewell Discourses (contra Porsch, Holwerda, Carson). If Acts 2 in fact refers to this expectation of the Farewell Discourses, then the alignment of John 20:22 and Acts 2 is once again suggested. The insufflation is the climax of the disciples' relation with Jesus. This is the time of their "re-creation" and new birth. This is the advent of the Paraclete. This is the first opportunity for authentic faith. Thomas is the only one absent, and he doubts because of the lack of the experience. Yet even to Thomas, Jesus points beyond the tangibility of his presence as a basis for faith (v. 29). Perfect faith stems from a spiritual apprehension of Christ (indeed: faith, v. 28), not from physical or rational certainties.

Finally, this dual message of John—that the Spirit is released through the cross and that Christ and Spirit must never be separated—has an important contemporary relevance. Any theology which separates salvation from the life-creating Spirit is inadequate (contra many "second-blessing" theologies). Any theology which separates the acceptance of Jesus from the gift of the Spirit is incorrect. Our experience of the Spirit is wrapped up in our experience of Christ's sacrifice on the cross. Similarly, the anchor for unbounded enthusiasm must be the glorification of the historical person of Jesus.

But at the same time the reception of grace and the birth of a Christian cannot be devoid of pneumatic experience (contra many non-Pentecostal theologies). The encounter with Jesus must be accompanied by an encounter with the dynamic Spirit. No doubt in their secluded room the disciples would have been satisfied with the fellowship of Jesus alone. But his desire was for a permanency in the relationship through the Spirit. The interior dwelling of Christ is one of John's most important themes and carefully defines eternal life (17:3). It is for the Father and Son to dwell within the believer (John 14:23). It is abiding in God and knowing he abides in us (1 John 4:12-13). It is Christ, "coming in to him and eating with him" (Rev. 3:20).

CHAPTER FOUR

THE SPIRIT AND
THE SACRAMENTS

How did the community which stands behind the Fourth Gospel experience the reality of God? Its awareness of a vitality and freshness in spiritual experience is clearly evident from passages such as John 3:5-8; 4:10-14; 6:63; 1 John 2:20, 27; 3:24; 4:13; and 5:6-10. J. D. G. Dunn points to this evidence and remarks: "If these words, particularly the vigorous metaphors, mean anything at all, they denote a living religious experience which the Johannine community could attribute only to the Spirit."[1]

As we discovered above in our study of eschatology, Johannine Christianity had come to equate the experiential presence of the Spirit with the presence of Jesus. No historical distance separated the post-resurrection church from Jesus of Nazareth: there was direct and immediate continuity through the Paraclete. The substance of spiritual experience was thus to be found in Jesus experience. The Spirit which Jesus imparted in turn glorified him and mediated to the believer an acute sense of the Lord's presence. Thus 1 John 4:13 remarks, "by this we know that we abide in him and he in us, because he has given us of his own spirit [ἐκ τοῦ πνεύματος αὐτοῦ]."

Our questions in this chapter are practical. How did the believer first enter into this experience? How was the freshness of this experience maintained within the community? Acts points to conversion-initiation in which baptism and repentance played a major role in the believer's encounter with the Spirit. Oscar Cullmann's study of *Early Christian Worship* points out that the earliest eucharistic meals continued the communal sense of the Lord's presence: these feasts looked back not only to the Passover meal and its so-

---

1. J. D. G. Dunn, *Jesus and the Spirit*, 350; see also R. Schnackenburg, "Die johanneische Gemeinde und Ihre Geisterfahrung," in *Die Kirche des Anfangs*, 277-306.

briety but also to the resurrection meals of inexpressible joy (see Luke 24:30, 36-43; John 21:12ff.; Acts 1:4; 10:40-41).[2] For these reasons, it should come as no surprise to find both baptism and the eucharist playing some role in Johannine church life.

Of course, the question of sacraments in John has suffered a long and often confusing history. But our quest for the Johannine community's experience of the Spirit must necessarily intersect this problem: two key Spirit texts lie directly in the path of the passages generally paraded by the sacramentalist, John 3:5 and 6:63. If the relation of Spirit and sacrament is important for this Evangelist it will be necessary to identify its implications within the ongoing life of the community. Moreover, if John is concerned with topics that have a liturgical or cultic import, the dialogue of Jesus about "worship in Spirit and truth" (4:23ff.) must come into view. C. K. Barrett has underscored the importance and unity of the Spirit passages in these three chapters. "In three passages only (apart from places where the Spirit is spoken of as abiding upon or as given to Jesus himself, and the moment when the glorified Jesus bestows the Spirit upon the apostles) is the Spirit referred to in the present tense; that is, in chapters 3, 4, and 6."[3] These passages, Barrett adds, point to the context of Christian worship.

A. THE TRADITIONAL PROBLEM OF THE SACRAMENTS IN JOHN

Most exegetical studies of the sacramental material in John have been primarily concerned to establish the general orientation of the Evangelist to the sacraments. While some scholars stress serious sacramental interest here, others deny it completely. For example, C. T. Craig once remarked that John "breathes the intimacy of the cult group" and was not written for outsiders.[4] The rites of the sacraments abound in enigmatic references. Dodd suggests that the absence of straightforward sacramental references proves that John writes for a non-Christian public and will not directly divulge the "Christian mysteries." Thus he claims that nowhere in the Fourth Gospel will there be found "the slightest trace of any eucharistic idea."[5]

Various scholars have fully discussed the options open to us in viewing the sacraments in John (esp. Herbert Klos and Robert Kysar).[6] Our survey can

---

2. O. Cullmann, *Early Christian Worship*, 15-16.

3. Barrett, "The Holy Spirit in the Fourth Gospel," *JTS* 1 (1950) 5.

4. C. T. Craig, "Sacramental Interest in the Fourth Gospel," *JBL* 58 (1939) 31-41, quotation, p. 32; so Culpepper, *The Johannine School*, 262.

5. C. H. Dodd, *Interpretation*, 342n.3; quotation, "Eucharistic Symbolism in the Fourth Gospel," *Exp* 2 (1911) 537; see also W. L. Knox, as cited by E. K. Lee, *The Religious Thought of St. John*, 185; cf. Jeremias, *The Eucharistic Words of Jesus*, 125: "The Fourth Evangelist consciously omitted the account of the Lord's Supper because he did not want to reveal the sacred formula to the general public."

6. H. Klos, *Die Sakramente im Johannesevangelium* (Stuttgart: Katholisches Bibelwerk, 1970); R. Kysar, *The Fourth Evangelist and His Gospel*, 249-59. More generally see the bibliography of E. Malatesta, *St. John's Gospel*, 137-39; and H. Thyen, "Aus der Literatur zum Johan-

afford to be selective and will show only the major contours of interpretation. We shall argue for John's critical acceptance of baptism and the eucharist and then draw general guidelines for the sacramental interpretation of the Gospel. If this hypothesis is correct, we can go on to suggest a possible *Sitz im Leben* of the Gospel in terms of the Johannine community's awareness of the Spirit. We shall see that the vitality of spiritual experience in the Johannine community was of marked significance, and that it was defined in contrast to traditional forms of liturgical worship with which the community or the Evangelist was in debate.

1. SACRAMENTALISM

In recent discussion there has been broad agreement among both Catholics and Protestants that John is seriously concerned to present the sacraments of Christian worship throughout his Gospel.[7] For example, Paul Niewalda takes pains to show how the early Fathers and early Christian art found in John an array of sacramental symbols (cf. the commentary of Hoskyns as well). These observations consist of two types. On the one hand, seemingly direct references to baptism and the eucharist which develop elements of the rites in a liturgical/cultic setting can be found in John 2, 3, 6, and possibly 19. In 19:34 Cullmann argues typically that the blood and water are used by the Evangelist to connect both sacraments with the death of Christ.[8] On the other hand, vague, enigmatic allusions to these elements in the Gospel have been suggested in Jesus' baptism (1:29ff.), the Samaritan dialogue (4:1-30), the healing of the lame man (5:1-19) and the blind man (9:1-39), as well as the footwashing (13:1-20). The interpretation of these passages and others is very problematic and generally fails to call up any scholarly consensus. The extreme possibilities in this regard are illustrated by Bruce Vawter, who claims that sacramental anointing (John 12) and marriage (John 2) are sacramentally instituted in the Fourth Gospel.

It would be altogether unfair to say that the uncovering of symbolism in John is an unjustified attempt to read into the Gospel what is not there. John is

---

nesevangelium," *TRu* 44 (1979) 97-134; cf. W. Michaelis, *Die Sakramente im Johannesevangelium* (Bern: BEG-Verlag, 1946); W. F. Howard, *The Fourth Gospel in Recent Criticism and Interpretation*, 4th ed. (rev. C. K. Barrett) (London: Epworth, 1955) 195-212; Bernard, *John*, 1: clxii-clxxvi; Bultmann, *Theology*, 2: 3-14; R. Schnackenburg, "Die Sakramente im Johannesevangelium," *Sac-Pag* 2 (1959) 235-54; and R. E. Brown, "The Johannine Sacramentary," in *New Testament Essays*, 51-76.

7. Catholic scholars include B. Vawter, "The Johannine Sacramentary," *TS* 17 (1956) 151-66; P. Niewalda, *Sakramentssymbolik im Johannesevangelium* (Limburg: Lahn Verlag, 1958). R. Kysar (*The Fourth Evangelist*, 257-58) would include R. E. Brown in this group, but this is not entirely correct in that Brown is somewhat moderate in his assessment of sacramental interest in John. Brown believes, however, that John does have a serious commitment to the sacraments. Similar moderation is expressed by B. Lindars, "Word and Sacrament in the Fourth Gospel," *SJT* 29 (1976) 49-63. Protestant scholars include O. Cullmann, *Early Christian Worship*, 37-119; A. Corell, *Consummatum Est*, esp. 44-78. See Klos, *Die Sakramente*, 24-32; and the commentaries of R. H. Lightfoot and E. Hoskyns.

8. Cullmann, *Early Christian Worship*, 114-16.

very aware of symbolism, as even a cursory study of the "I am" sayings reveals. Indicators throughout his Gospel show that he is conscious of using symbols and willing to interpret them.[9] Therefore, although we may be rightly critical of some of these conclusions, the methodology employed is not as unwarranted as some would suppose.

The most celebrated example of a thoroughgoing attempt to find in John excessive sacramental imagery is Cullmann's *Early Christian Worship*. The chief strength of the work is not its exegetical arguments (which not a few have subjected to critique point by point),[10] but Cullmann's attempt to give a historical framework to this sacramental setting. He believes that "the Gospel of John regards it as one of its chief concerns to set forth the connexion between the contemporary Christian worship and the historical life of Jesus."[11] A type of transparency is therefore evident in the Gospel. Methodologically similar to J. L. Martyn's "two-level" interpretation of the conflicts in the Gospel is Cullmann's working principle that if a passage can be understood sacramentally, it should. The barest allusion to baptism or the eucharist unveils a contemporary comment on Johannine liturgics.[12]

The chief problem with this view of John is hermeneutical control. Here we may identify two specific difficulties. First, Niewalda, Brown, and Hoskyns rightly find patristic interpretation (in comment and art) instructive, yet this method has serious dangers. Once the sacraments were institutionalized in the second century, early interpreters sought to fit these rites into scripture (no doubt in illustrative preaching) and wholly overlooked the original intent of the text. It is thus incorrect to project the literary technique of the second century onto John. The interpretation of the Cana miracle (2:1-20) illustrates this point well. Various Fathers (Clement of Alexandria, Cyril of Jerusalem, Cyprian) and an Alexandrian catacomb fresco interpret this miracle in terms of the eucharist. While it is true that "wine" had become a fixed symbol in later

9. Here we might point to Peter's crucifixion in 21:18; the temple as the body of Jesus in 2:21; Spirit and water in 7:39; the brazen serpent in 3:14; and the loaves/manna analogy in 6:1ff. A sensitive interpretation along these lines is provided by V. Ruland, "Sign and Sacrament—John's Bread of Life Discourse (Chap. 6)," *Int* 18 (1964) 450-62.

10. See W. Michaelis, *Die Sakramente*, who criticizes Cullmann's 1st edition of 1944; also, see S. Smalley, "Liturgy and Sacrament in the Fourth Gospel," *EvQ* 29 (1957) 159-70; G. R. Beasley-Murray, *Baptism in the New Testament* (Exeter: Paternoster, 1962; repr. Grand Rapids: Eerdmans, 1973) 217-26; E. Lohse, "Wort und Sakrament im Johannesevangelium," *NTS* 7 (1960-61) 110-25, esp. 110-14; and J. G. M. Ladd, "The Sacramental Teaching of the Fourth Gospel with Special Reference to the Views of Oscar Cullmann," unpub. diss., University College of North Wales (Bangor), 1966.

11. *Early Christian Worship*, 37.

12. We must be clear that when scholars argue for sacramentality in John, they are not necessarily suggesting that John supports a view of instrumentality of sacramental grace. Rather, they are claiming that the Gospel intentionally evokes images of baptism and the Lord's Supper and gives them relevance and credibility through their connection with the historical Jesus. The material rite is not to be denied, but it is not the sole means through which God works. Thus Cullmann's summary of John 3 (*Early Christian Worship*, 118): "Both [sacraments] have this in common, that Christ employs material realities, which point to the Christ *event*, to disclose his presence in the Spirit (water, bread and wine). . . . These elements are not in themselves efficacious."

centuries, it is not so clear that the Fourth Evangelist limited his imagery thus.[13] A better method would be to start by establishing the sacramentality of the Evangelist's symbols, rather than projecting backward the later emphases.

Second, a methodology which stresses what John's audience "could have understood"—and then concludes about John's intentions—is exceedingly problematic (contra Cullmann). As Brown puts it, "that is a very delicate instrument of exegesis, or rather an instrument that is used with much more ease in eisegesis."[14] Above all, some clear internal indication needs to be present which reveals that the author himself intended a sacramental allusion. Turning once again to John 2, Corell is happy to see in the reference to "best wine" and "the hour" the church's sacramental wine made potent through Christ's death on the cross.[15] A more sober exegesis would follow Bultmann and Lindars, stressing that the new wine has a christological meaning. Purification waters now miraculously changed might refer to the work of Christ in the cult of Judaism (and not the liturgy of the church).

2. NON-SACRAMENTALISM

Sacramental interpreters find one abrupt difficulty in their view, however: there are no direct references to the sacraments in the Fourth Gospel. The baptismal commission of Matt. 28 is absent. Although John knows of the upper room meal (13:2), he does not maintain the words of institution. Even at Jesus' baptism John provides only an allusion and no direct reference. To be sure, any explanation of Johannine sacramentalism must account for these glaring omissions.

A growing group of scholars has found its answer to this problem in John's lack of interest in the sacraments. Others go a step further and posit a Johannine disdain for baptism and the eucharist. Thus Bultmann typically remarks that "while the evangelist came to terms with ecclesiastical practice in regard to baptism and the Lord's Supper, it remained suspect to him because of its misuse, and this is why he has made no mention of it."[16] While many scholars in general agreement with this statement would not bother to refute Cullmann's more speculative sacramental texts, most modern debate has focused on three passages: John 3:5; 6:51c-58; and 19:34. Linked to these texts are two interdependent hypotheses.

First, a redactional correction of the texts has been suggested. Here Bultmann pointed to his ecclesiastical editor, who conformed John's more esoteric doctrine of union with Christ to the traditional use of the sacraments.

---

13. This is the criticism of Schnackenburg, "Die Sakramente," 235ff.

14. *New Testament Essays*, 61; cf. D. W. B. Robinson, "Born of Water and Spirit. Does John 3:5 refer to Baptism?" *RTR* 25 (1966) 15-16.

15. *Consummatum Est*, 57; also Cullmann, *Early Christian Worship*, 66-71.

16. Bultmann, *John*, 472; idem, *Theology*, 2: 58-59; see also Klos, *Die Sakramente*, 11-21, who adds the following to this general view: E. Lohse, "Wort und Sakrament"; G. Bornkamm, "Die eucharistische Rede im Johannesevangelium," *ZNW* 47 (1956) 161-69; H. Köster, "Geschichte und Kultus im Johannesevangelium und bei Ignatius von Antiochien," *ZTK* 54 (1957) 56-69; and E. Schweizer, "Das Johanneische Zeugnis vom Herrenmahl," *EvT* 12 (1953) 341-63.

Thus ὕδατος καί in 3:5, the explicitly eucharistic section of the John 6 discourse, and the mention of blood and water in 19:34 were all foreign additions to the original text.[17]

A corollary of this hypothesis is that the eucharistic additions are also a part of an anti-docetic polemic.[18] Here scholars have also summoned 1 John 5:6, 8 to join 19:34 in order to demonstrate that docetism was a problem, and that while bearing witness to the genuine importance of the liturgical sacrament, the Johannine editor is also at work defending a genuine incarnation and death of Christ.

Although at first glance this approach may seem to solve the Evangelist's enigmatic use of baptismal and eucharistic themes, a non-sacramental position has significant problems. First, the argument that John altogether ignores the sacraments is not entirely true. In 1:32ff. it is quite clear that the traditional account of Jesus' baptism is present (although John has shifted the stress). In 3:26 and 4:1 baptism is affirmed as being a part of Jesus' ministry (although 4:2 reduces Jesus' role). The silence of John concerning a baptismal commission is not surprising in view of similar silences in Mark and Luke. Furthermore, Brown argues that the language of 6:51 betrays a Semitic original with a strong claim for antiquity (see below for more detail).[19]

Second, although we have argued above for the authenticity and non-eucharistic interpretation of 19:34 (though a baptismal theme may be secondary), John 3 and 6 are extremely suggestive passages which imply that John wants to remind the reader of the sacraments. The hypothesis that these chapters contain redactional additions is purely hypothetical, and, as we hope to show, it does not serve the original intentions of John. The idea of water fits the context of the Nicodemus dialogue well, and the authenticity of 6:61ff. has been repeatedly substantiated. Even with the removal of these texts, some scholars have argued that there are still cultic and sacramental elements in John 3 and 6.[20]

Third, more basic is the general interpretation of John presented by this view. As we have seen, John has a serious appreciation for the symbolic and the sacramental. In this sense, the general orientation of Cullmann is nearer the mark (although his specific exegesis is often farfetched). But Bultmann's stress on esoteric union with Christ untied to material elements seems wide of the mark. John stresses the importance of a mystic union with Christ in the Spirit Paraclete, yet this emphasis does not exclude his appreciation for material expressions of this union: namely, baptism and the Lord's Supper.

---

17. See esp. Lohse, "Wort und Sakrament"; this is the same solution accepted by R. Kysar in *The Fourth Evangelist*, 259: "The fourth gospel represents a maverick form of Christianity, to be sure, in which the sacraments, at first at least, were not known or practiced."

18. See esp. E. Schweizer, "Das Johanneische Zeugnis."

19. *New Testament Essays*, 60-61; also H. Schürmann, "Joh 6:51c—ein Schlüssel zur grossen johanneischen Brotrede," *BZ* 2 (1958) 244-62. Bultmann, *Theology*, 2: 59, suggests that the meal of fish and bread in John 21 evokes eucharistic imagery. So also Brown, *John*, 2: 1098-1100; B. Lindars, *John*, 628: "quasi-eucharistic"; cf. Cullmann, *Early Christian Worship*, 15-17.

20. Brown, *New Testament Essays*, 53, citing H. Köster, "Geschichte und Kultus"; cf. Kümmel, *Theology*, 311.

3. CRITICAL/CORRECTIVE

Once we have determined that the Fourth Gospel is not merely a foil for sacramental worship and that the "sacramental" allusions in John 3 and 6 are not redactional additions to the Gospel, the way is open to discover a secondary interest in sacraments. Some scholars have indicated that John may be responding to an imbalanced view of baptism and the eucharist. Barrett points to Paul's discussion of sacramental abuse in 1 Cor. 10 and 11 and aligns John with the same corrective tendency.[21] In his discussion of the eucharistic section of John 6, Dunn has given this view full expression. For him the community has reacted to docetism by adhering to a literalistic view of the eucharist. John deals forcefully with docetism but does not fail to correct the community at the same time. As viewed through 6:63, the eucharist overtones are then negative and corrective in import.[22]

As we have implied above, however, John's interest in the sacraments is not merely disparaging. He may point away from sacramental abuse, but he still points positively to the sacramental context. It is far better to follow the avenue suggested by C. F. D. Moule: "The Fourth Gospel is consciously and deliberately interpreting the sacraments themselves in terms of other categories, rather than interpreting other categories in terms of the sacraments."[23] In other words, the experience of the believer in the sacramental context must include more dimensions than simply the material. Herbert Klos ends his study on just this note. He points to the exclusive importance of John 3:5ff. and 6:51ff. in John's theology while arguing that in both passages the author is criticizing a misunderstanding of the sacraments as mechanistic. For him, the "other category" (to return to Moule's thought) is faith: "Therefore according to the Fourth Gospel, the sacrament is correctly understood when it is viewed as a concrete expression of faith in Jesus Christ—as a manifestation and fulfillment of faith."[24]

But Klos admits that faith is not a static religious experience for John. It is not the achievement of the believer alone. The reception of the sacraments in faith also means the reception of the Spirit in the sacramental context (3:5; 6:63). Klos thus concludes his study with a provocative look forward. The sacraments in John are a representation and application of Jesus' saving work on the cross. Yet from this cross stems the Spirit which draws believers and incorporates them into the historical event of salvation (19:34; 20:22). Therefore participation in this event—indeed, the application of this event in the believer's life—must involve the Spirit if it occurs in the sacramental context. The sacramental act is not humanity's movement into God but God bringing humanity into the movement he has begun through Christ and the Spirit.

---

21. Barrett, *John*, 84-85; compare the posture of G. H. C. MacGregor, *John*, 162, who argues that John did not ignore the eucharist, "but shows his desire to interpret and spiritualize these conceptions and thus save the church from superstitious materialism." See his similiar treatment of baptism, 72-73.

22. J. D. G. Dunn, "John VI: A Eucharistic Discourse?" *NTS* 17 (1970-71) 328-38, esp. 337.

23. C. F. D. Moule, "The Individualism of the Fourth Gospel," *NovT* 5 (1962) 185.

24. *Die Sakramente*, 99.

B. SACRAMENTAL INTEREST IN JOHN 3 AND 6

The enormous amount of exegetical energy spent on John 3 and 6 should come as no surprise when we consider the importance of their content and the complexities of their problems. But we must avoid simply reworking well-trod ground. Our aim will be to show a theological orientation shared by both passages. If sacramental interest is at all evident in the Fourth Gospel, we are convinced that it makes its appearance in the Nicodemus dialogue and in the conclusion to the Bread of Life discourse.[25] But such interest is strictly specialized. Both John 3 and 6 exhibit a parallel use of and critical appreciation for sacramental language.[26] If the two texts are used as portals into John's corrective view of baptism and the eucharist, important parallels become evident.

In both texts John employs what might be termed a cryptic or esoteric use of sacramental language. The references to "water" in 3:5 in the context of rebirth (v. 3), to the Spirit (v. 5), and to the demand for faith (vv. 15-16) are often considered baptismal allusions. Rebirth and baptism are possibly even analogous theological themes in the NT. Baptism is the starting point for and initiation into Christian experience. To be sure, rebirth functions for Johannine theology in this very way.[27] In a similar fashion, an even stronger case can be made for eucharistic language in John 6:51c-58. The consumption of the flesh and blood of the Son of Man points, at least on a secondary level, to eucharistic motifs. As in John 3, however, the Fourth Evangelist has alluded to the terminology while leaving the sacramental application vague.

In each passage the discussion moves (quite deliberately) away from the sacramental imagery. The images themselves take on a metaphorical value in the light of a more prominent Johannine theme. Thus a type of false sacramentalism is created. In John 3:5ff. the term *water* is summarily dismissed and the focus of attention turns to *Spirit*. Indeed, water is completely overshadowed by Spirit before the discourse concludes. Then again, following the so-called "eucharistic section" of John 6, the Evangelist records the offense that ensues among the disciples (6:60ff.). Jesus' answer does not include a repetition of the demand found in 6:53; instead he interprets it. Flesh and blood are symbols pointing to a dynamic, pneumatic union between Jesus and his disciples.

The sacraments are not replaced, as it were, by a mystic union with Christ. On the contrary, each passage emphasizes the need for faith in Christ in

---

25. Similarly, MacGregor, *John*, xxi-xxxii; Bernard, *John*, clxii-clxxvi; Lee, *The Religious Thought of St. John*, 184-90; Morris, *John*, 217-18, 337; Ladd, *Theology*, 248; Beasley-Murray, *Baptism*, 226-32.

26. Note the methodology of Dunn, *Baptism*, 183ff., 193, in which a discussion of John 6 forms an important part of his argument for John 3. Similarly see Klos, *Die Sakramente*, 59-74, 99; Schnackenburg, *John*, 1: 369; Howard, *Christianity According to St. John*, 148-49; Barrett, "The Holy Spirit in the Fourth Gospel," 6-7; idem, *John*, 89, 209; and on a nontechnical level, M. Green, *I Believe in the Holy Spirit* (Grand Rapids: Eerdmans, 1975) 78-79.

27. See the study of T. W. Manson, "Entry into Membership of the Early Church," *JTS* 48 (1947) 25-33; cf. R. H. Lightfoot, *John*, 116. Tit. 3:5 possibly aligns the concepts λουτρὸν παλιγγενεσίας; cf. Justin *Apol.* 1:66, ἀναγέννησιν λουτρόν. Various other references are provided by Bultmann, *John*, 138-139n.3; and Bernard, *John*, 1: 103-105.

the context of the salvation-historical events in his life. Thus both passages repeatedly underscore the demand for faith (3:12, 15, 16, 18, 36; 6:29, 35, 36, 40, 47, 64, 69) as well as the resultant eternal life (3:15, 16, 36; 6:27, 33, 51, 53, 54, 63, etc.). John 3:14-15 specifically points to the death/glorification of the Son of Man as the object of saving faith. Similarly, the life-creating consumption of the Son of Man's flesh is given definition in 6:51c. The giving of this flesh is to be found in Jesus' death.

Finally, John draws into this "sacramental redefinition" the centrality of the Spirit. Both passages direct our attention to the same experiential level. Faith may be generated by human beings, but the union with Christ held out by John is strictly a work of the Spirit. Thus rebirth cannot be acquired by Nicodemus—it can only be given to him. It is the unilateral movement of God in Spirit (3:6, 8).[28] Likewise, the flesh required in 6:53 is later depreciated in 6:63. The Spirit gives life, and the flesh (the same flesh as in 6:53) is of no avail. Both texts use σάρξ in their critical evaluation of their respective sacraments (3:6; 6:63a). Both also refer to the ascension of the Son of Man (3:13; 6:62) which will finally bring the Spirit who is able to create this rebirth and spiritual union (20:22).

In sum, John 3 and 6 are set in a historical drama, yet they employ sacramental language which evokes images relevant to the church. From here John moves forward to faith and the Spirit. To repeat Klos's phrase, the sacrament must be seen as a concrete expression of faith in Jesus Christ.[29] But this faith must be viewed as coordinate with an experience of the Spirit. Contrary to scholars who would simply identify the work of the Spirit as the believer's saving expression of faith (Vellanickal, Schweizer),[30] John insists on the mystical, nonquantifiable dimension of Spirit experience (3:8). Faith serves as a response to what God has already accomplished in the death of Christ (3:14ff.)—out of which has come the Spirit. John's stress on πνεῦμα thus underscores the priority of God's movement into humanity.

John urges that the Spirit is the starting point of Christian experience (3:3, 5) and the sustenance of it (6:63). Far from being restricted to the material sacraments, the Spirit is spontaneous and free and necessary if the birth depicted in baptism and the union depicted in the eucharist are to have any genuine reality.

C. JOHN 3: SPIRIT AND REBIRTH

The importance of John 3 in our reconstruction of Johannine religious experience must not be missed.[31] The reader is introduced to John's first characteris-

---

28. Schweizer, TDNT 6: 440.

29. Klos, Die Sakramente, 98.

30. Schweizer, TDNT 6: 439-41; M. Vellanickal, The Divine Sonship of Christians in the Johannine Writings (Rome: Biblical Institute Press, 1977) 185ff.; Vellanickal wrongly cites Smalley, "Liturgy and Sacrament," 165, as in agreement. Cf. F. Porsch, Anwalt der Glaubenden (Stuttgart: Katholisches Bibelwerk, 1978) 142-46.

31. In addition to the theological interests of the chapter, John 3 also presents critical problems. The structure of the passage has received much attention and found little consensus.

tic discourse wherein the person of Jesus, his work, and his call upon the convert's life are fully explicated. To follow Hoskyns, this discourse may be "The Discourse" whose themes are simply echoed in all the subsequent discourses.[32]

Beyond elucidating the theological message of this Spirit text and its connection with baptism, one must also note that the subject of rebirth is evidenced elsewhere in the Johannine corpus. In the Gospel's prologue, all those who receive the Logos become children of God; they are born of God (1:12-13). That this language was characteristic in the community's self-identity is further seen in 1 John. 1 John 2:20, 27, 29; 3:9; 4:7; 5:1, 4, and 18 all reveal an acute awareness of spiritual anointing and, more importantly, of present possession of the Spirit as a community distinctive. But how did this experience begin? Does John 3:5 point to baptism as the initiatory step in Johannine Christianity?

1. BAPTISMAL INTEREST IN JOHN 3

To be sure, the possibility that Nicodemus was presented with a call to full Christian baptism would be anachronistic if we allow the Evangelist any historical perspective whatsoever. But still, if a baptismal motif of any kind lies behind John's use of "water" in 3:5, something close to Christian baptism is approached when "water" is aligned with "Spirit" as the medium of rebirth. Therefore it is fair to say that baptismal interest really stands or falls with 3:5.[33] James Dunn outlines the main arguments for a baptismal reference as follows: (a) the so-called "sacramentalism" of the Gospel itself; (b) the symbolic use of water in the Gospel; and (c) the obviousness of the allusion. While Dunn rightly rejects (a) as a misnomer, the other two points are less easily overcome. It is clearly unsafe to speculate as to what would be "obvious" to a first-century Christian. But the force of this argument in 3:5 is powerful and not without some cogency.[34] Of more importance is the use of ὕδωρ and its meaning. This text does not join the other water texts in John as either a symbol

---

Redactional activity seems evident in that discourse material (vv. 16-21, 31-36) has been woven into a narrative sequence (vv. 1-15, 22-30). As we have suggested earlier, the final editor no doubt viewed vv. 16-21 as the conclusion or full development of the Nicodemus dialogue. Similarly, vv. 31-36 are the climax of the Baptist passage (vv. 22-30), or better, the summary of the entire chapter (Dodd). Above all, critics are right in arguing that vv. 31-36 must be viewed in close connection with vv. 1-21. See further Dodd, *Interpretation*, 308-11; S. Mendner, "Nicodemus," *JBL* 77 (1958) 293-323; R. Schnackenburg, *John*, 1: 360-63; idem, "Die 'situationsgelösten' Redestücke in Joh 3," *ZNW* 49 (1958) 88-94; Dodd, *Historical Tradition*, 279-87; Brown, *John*, 1: 136-37, 153ff.; L. J. Topel, "A Note on the Methodology of Structural Analysis in John 2:23-3:21," *CBQ* 33 (1971) 211-20; I. de la Potterie, "Naître de l'eau et naître de l'Esprit. Le texte baptismal de Jn 3,5," in *La Vie selon l'Esprit, Condition du chrétien*, ed. I. de la Potterie and S. Lyonnet, Unam Sanctum 55 (Paris: Cerf, 1965) 41-48; and Porsch, *Pneuma*, 83-89.

32. Hoskyns, *John*, 203.

33. So Dunn, *Baptism*, 183. For an overview of the history of exegesis, see M. Vellanickal, *The Divine Sonship of Christians*, 197ff.; cf. de la Potterie, "Naître de l'eau," 32-39.

34. Contra Dunn, ibid., 189-90; on the other hand, see Brown, *John*, 1: 141-42; Lindars, *John*, 152; Schnackenburg, *John*, 1:369; Beasley-Murray, *Baptism*, 228. Both Bultmann (*John*, 138n.3) and Vellanickal (ibid., 170-71, 186-90) agree but take ὕδωρ καί as inauthentic.

of the old dispensation and its limitations (1:26, 31, 33; 2:7, 9; 3:23; 5:7) or as a symbol for the Spirit (4:7, 10, 11, 13, 14, 15; 7:38; 19:34).[35] Ὕδωρ stands apart in its connection with πνεῦμα. The latter takes the former and makes it a part of Jesus' call for rebirth. So again we are forced back on the authenticity and meaning of "water." But its function in the Nicodemus dialogue must be seen not only in the exegesis of the details of the dialogue itself but in the broader context of the chapter.

a. Textual Considerations

Scholars have often challenged the authenticity of ὕδατος καί in 3:5.[36] These words are said to go back either to the Gospel's later ecclesiastical redactor (so Bultmann, Lohse, Braun) or to the Evangelist himself (so Bernard, de la Potterie, Vellanickal),[37] but not to Jesus. The reasons for this view are as follows: (1) ὕδωρ is present only in 3:5 and is absent in the remainder of the dialogue, notably vv. 6-8. (2) To accept the reference would be to admit a divergence of theological emphasis in John. Nowhere else does John entertain a connection between baptism/water and rebirth or anointing. (3) It is possible that the passage already shows signs of redactional activity, and scholars such as Porsch have suggested that this addition may have accompanied the redaction of 3:22-30.[38] (4) A reference to water almost certainly must be a reference to Christian baptism, which is surely an anachronism. The call to baptize is a post-resurrection commission and can hardly be admitted to this setting.[39]

While the force of some of these arguments may seem compelling, they are not entirely unassailable. (1) John 3:6, 8 can be viewed in terms of development, which would obviate the need for a repeated reference to ὕδωρ. The question of rebirth is framed in v. 6 in terms of the antitheses of Johannine dualism while in v. 8 a mystic/ecstatic motif is central. (2) The second point is equally implausible. Elsewhere we have noted the possible baptismal motifs in 19:34 and 1 John 5:6ff. But most importantly, this point overlooks the broader context of baptismal emphasis found in the contrast between Jesus and John the Baptist (so Hoskyns).[40] (3) It is true that John 3 may show signs of conflation of sources, but it is another matter to say that the content of the sources

---

35. Dunn, ibid., 186-88; ὕδωρ occurs in John twenty-one times.

36. We will not address the question of the authenticity of the entire dialogue itself, although recently B. Lindars has shown that John 3:3ff. probably stems from an independent version of the same Aramaic saying as we have it in Matt. 18:3. See "John and the Synoptic Gospels: A Test Case," *NTS* 27 (1981) 287-94.

37. On the former view see Bultmann, *John*, 138n.3; Lohse, "Wort und Sakrament," 110-25, as in *NTA* 5 (1961) 282-83; F.-M. Braun, "Le Don de Dieu et L'Initiation Chrétienne," *NRT* 86 (1964) 1025-48, as cited in Kysar, *The Fourth Evangelist*, 251. On the latter view see Bernard, *John*, 1: 104-105; de la Potterie, "Naître de l'eau," 41-53; Vellanickal, *Divine Sonship*, 170-71. The original suggestion stems from H. H. Wendt and was developed by Kirsopp Lake (so Johnston, *Spirit-Paraclete*, 40).

38. Porsch, *Pneuma*, 92n.55; Bultmann, *John*, 138n.3, believes this text was added along with 6:51-58; see above, p. 158n.31.

39. Bernard, *John*, 1:104; Vellanickal, *Divine Sonship*, 170.

40. Hoskyns, *John*, 214; see further below.

has been altered or editorially expanded. Such a correction is evident in 4:2 (cf. 3:24), but this text in no way compares with 3:5. In fact, the editor who had a hand in 4:2 was anti-baptismal if anything. (4) The primary reference in ὕδωρ need not be to Christian baptism. But at the same time, we hope to show that a secondary reference to (Christian) baptism in the context of the ministrations of John the Baptist would not necessarily be anachronistic. The fact that the commission to baptize is post-resurrection hardly invalidates its appearance in Jesus' earlier ministry (cf. 3:22ff.).[41] (5) One final objection must certainly be the absence of any significant variants in the text itself.[42]

We conclude therefore that the reliability of the present text can be maintained. The inclusion of "water" anchors the setting in the context provided by 1:26, 31, 33; 2:7ff.; and 3:22ff. and must be viewed as an integral part of the message about rebirth.

b. The Background and Meaning of Ὕδωρ

To accept the authenticity of ὕδατος καί is to introduce the problem of the word's meaning in the setting presented by the Evangelist. What could Nicodemus have understood as a first-century Jew?

(1) A Symbolic Interpretation

Following the lead of H. Odeberg, some scholars have found a symbol that points not to the Spirit or purification but to procreation (either physical or spiritual).[43] If ὕδωρ is related to Rabbinic Hebrew טיפה, "drop" could refer to male semen (cf. Mish. *Abot* 3:1). On the one hand, ἐκ ὕδατος καὶ πνεύματος could refer to physical birth followed by spiritual birth (thus making use of Nicodemus's confusion in v. 4). But this view is doubtful. It not only misses the unity of water and spirit, but if such were John's point, ἐξ αἵματος would have been more appropriate (cf. John 1:13).[44] On the other hand, water and spirit can be taken together to refer to birth through "spiritual semen."[45] Entry into Christ's kingdom was often thought of in terms of divine begetting. Terms like "father," "son," and "child" affirmed this metaphor. The crude realism of this imagery appears in 1 John 3:9, where God's seed (σπέρμα) abides in the

41. Many would argue that the concept of conversion/rebirth as a theological complex must also be later. But the obvious parallels in Mark 10:13-16 and Matt. 18:1-4 exclude this suggestion. Note the parallels: become like children/being begotten; entering the kingdom of heaven/kingdom of God. Compare Bernard, *John*, 1: 102; and Dodd, *Historical Tradition*, 358-59.

42. Schnackenburg, *John*, 1: 369n.70, notes that the words are absent only in the Vulgate codex Harleian 1023 (probably through inadvertence). Although Justin refers to John 3 (*Apol.* 1:61, ἀναγεννάω) without reference to water, his citation is typically inexact and could refer to John 3:3. The Sinaitic Syriac insignificantly reverses the word order (spirit and water); and finally, ὕδατος καί is added in v. 8 by ℵ (but this is due to assimilation to v. 5).

43. Odeberg, *The Fourth Gospel*, 48-71; cf. Strachan, *John*, 134-35; R. Fowler, "Born of Water and Spirit (John 3:5)," *ExpTim* 82 (1970) 159; and D. G. Spriggs, "The Meaning of 'Water' in John 3:5," *ExpTim* 85 (1973) 149.

44. Lindars, *John*, 152; cf. Schnackenburg, *John*, 1: 369n.70; and Z. Hodges, "John 3:5," *BSac* 135 (1978) 212.

45. Morris, *John*, 218, favors this interpretation.

believer (see the similar 1 Pet. 1:23 and Tit. 3:5). Similarly, such an interpretation would fit the common Hellenistic notion of primal heavenly waters through which human beings are re-created.[46]

(2) Ὕδωρ and Ritual Purification

A far more likely background is found in OT and Jewish antecedents. Ritual cleansings used from the earliest period were soon given metaphorical meaning for a cleaning of the human soul (see Ps. 51:7; Isa. 4:4; Jer. 33:8; cf. Philo Vit. Mos. 2:138).[47] In eschatological expectation, God himself will cleanse his people with a sprinkling of water—often described as the Spirit: "I will sprinkle clean water upon you and you shall be clean . . . a new Spirit I will put within you" (Ezek. 36:25-26).[48] As is well known, Judaism developed the importance of ritual washings in which the external rite pointed to the not yet fulfilled future and the symbolic present. Qumran's ritual cleansings are celebrated examples of this symbolism in their regular repetition (1QS 3:1-12; Josephus BJ 2:129, 149) and in their eschatological perspective (1QS 4:21).[49] Pharisaic Judaism likewise developed liturgical washings, foremost among these being proselyte baptism.[50]

This all too brief sketch shows that some form of spiritual transformation (incipient rebirth) in either symbolic or genuine form was conjoined with water and spirit in an identifiable Jewish background. Baptismal cleansings were required of the Qumran initiate, and in apocalyptic Judaism this cleansing and transformation were prerequisites for entry into the coming kingdom.[51]

Nevertheless, it is evident that the most significant contemporary usage of lustrations for the Johannine setting (and we might add, the most relevant one for the Evangelist) is the work of John the Baptist. The Baptist stands at the end of the Palestinian Jewish development outlined above. Therefore it does not seem extraordinary to conclude that the initial point of reference for ὕδωρ

---

46. Barrett, John, 209, refers to Gen. 1:2; Corpus Hermeticum 1:17; Acts of Thomas 52. Cf. Goppelt, TDNT 8: 315-17; Dodd, Interpretation, 138; C. Kaplan, "Some New Testament Problems in Light of Rabbinics and the Pseudepigrapha. The Cosmological Similies in John 3,5,"JSOR 15 (1931) 64-66.

47. See the references in Goppelt, TDNT 8: 320-21.

48. See further Isa. 32:15; 44:3; Jer. 2:13; 17:13; Joel 2:28-29; Ezek. 47:9. The use of water and spirit was employed esp. at Tabernacles (Ezek. 47:1-12; Zech. 13:1; 14:8; T.B. Sukka 55a; Midr. Rab. Gen. 29:2-3. This view of 3:5 in which water is parallel to spirit in OT prophecy—esp. Ezek. 36—has been recently argued by Linda L. Belleville, "Born of Water and Spirit: John 3:5," Trinity Journal 1 (1980) 125-40.

49. See 1QS 4:19-20; 3:17; 1QH 3:21; 7:21ff.; 9:32; 11:10-14.

50. Cf. the Mishna tractates Tohoroth, Mikwaoth, Niddah; O. Böcher, NIDNTT 3: 989. For primary evidence, see Oepke, TDNT 1: 545-46; Beasley-Murray, Baptism, 18-31 (sources: 18n.2). W. F. Howard cites the relevant Rabbinic saying (Rabbi Jose ben Halafta): "A proselyte who embraces Judaism is like a new-born child," (The Fourth Gospel in Recent Criticism, 204).

51. So Schnackenburg, John, 1: 370; cf. the synthesis of new creation through the Spirit and cleansings in Jub. 1:23-25; cf. 5:12; Ps. Sol. 18:6; 1 En. 92:3ff.; 10:16-17; As. Mos. 18; T. Levi 18:11; T. Jud. 24:3. This evidence rightly leads Schnackenburg to reject Hellenistic sources and the mysteries as the background of John 3:5.

in John 3:5 is John's baptism.[52] Other references to water in John 1–3 bear this out: all refer to the water of Jewish purification rites (καθαρισμός, 2:6; 3:25). Therefore for Jesus to refer to rebirth through water as well as Spirit must imply that Nicodemus has to submit to a feature of John's baptism as well as his own (a suggestion not readily acceptable to a Pharisee, Luke 7:30).

c. Ὕδωρ and John's Baptism

If it is correct that the most likely background to 3:5 is to be found in the baptismal waters and cultic lustrations of Palestinian Judaism (expressed esp. in Ezek. 36 and 1QS 4:19ff.), then the antecedent baptism of John the Baptist comes in view. But this argument does not rest only on Jesus' baptism in John 1 (which is problematic). Baptismal motifs are also evident in 3:22-30. As in John 1, where the Baptist is included as a witness to the transition from the old order to Christ, so too the identity of Christ in relation to John and the transition of leadership is again a prominent motif in 3:22ff. But here the discussion focuses on baptism—Jesus' baptism of his followers— and how Christ's work is superior.

(1) John 3:22-30

This passage itself is curious in that it provides the only NT record of Jesus and his followers baptizing. For this and other reasons Dodd labeled it "an itinerary fragment" comparable to the sections of Mark and thus having high historical value.[53] Another curiosity is its placement in chap. 3. Suggestions are often launched to find its original setting in chap. 1 or to rearrange the chapter in order to bring it up into the narrative sequence of 3:1-15 (or v. 12, following Schnackenburg).[54] The latter suggestion is convincing in view of the many parallels between vv. 31-36 and vv. 13-21 which urge that we have Johannine kerygmatic material woven into a traditional narrative. This conclusion is all the more important for our interest because it effectively connects the subjects here (vv. 22-30) with the Nicodemus dialogue.

The message of the pericope is summed up with "epigrammatic conciseness" (Lindars) in v. 30: "He [Jesus] must increase, but I [John] must de-

---

52. So Dunn, *Baptism*, 190; Marsh, *John*, 178; J. A. T. Robinson, "Elijah, John and Jesus. An Essay in Detection," *NTS* 4 (1957-58) 273.

53. "*Prima facie* there is here as strong a case as anywhere in the gospel for considering the view that the evangelist is composing out of pre-existing materials," *Historical Tradition*, 279; cf. the uncommon use of μετὰ ταῦτα (elsewhere only in 5:14; 13:7; 19:38), found also in Luke (5:27; 10:1; 16:12) but not in Matthew or Mark. In addition, there are the references of detail, the theological problem of Jesus' baptizing, and the chronological problem of the simultaneous ministry with the Baptist. Dodd, *Historical Tradition*, 281, found in vv. 26-30 a type of pronouncement story; but see the critical remarks of J. G. M. Ladd, "The Sacramental Teaching of the Fourth Gospel," 37-42, that the pericope is unhistorical.

54. For the former view see M. E. Boismard, "Les traditions johanniques concernant le Baptiste," *RB* 70 (1963) 5-42, esp. 25-30; also Brown, *John*, 1: 154-55; Lindars, *John*, 162. For the latter view see Schnackenburg, *John*, 1: 361-63, which summarizes his article, "Die 'situationsgelösten' Redestücke in Joh 3," *ZNW* 49 (1958) 88-99; unfortunately the organization of his commentary does not illustrate his connection of the narrative passages.

crease." The entire debate is therefore christological and framed around the superiority of Jesus (3:28-29) and his ministry of baptism (3:26-27). The Evangelist intentionally employs imperfect verbs throughout (ἐβάπτιζεν, δι-έτριβεν) to emphasize that Jesus' work is continuous and now takes up the mantle of the fading Baptist. Thus there is a stress on continuity as well as a witness to the transition: Jesus is the fulfillment of Jewish requirements for purification (3:25; cf. 2:6) which John had inaugurated. But the hallmark of this transition was Jesus' baptism, in which a transition of allegiance from the Baptist to Christ occurred: "here he is baptizing and all are going to him" (v. 26; cf. μαθητάς in 4:1). John prophetically affirms that this new work is of divine origin (3:27) and not to be refused (cf. 1:35-42).

If the christological context in 3:22-30 is built around the newness of Christ and the new priority of the baptism, and if the structure of the passage shows that this narrative is related to the earlier Nicodemus section, the reference to water in 3:5 must be informed by the baptismal motif in 3:22ff. Indeed, if this fragment was conflated from another setting, it was localized here to draw out the baptismal motif in 3:1-15.[55] We can thus cite Dodd's conclusion with full approval: "the passage 3:22-36 is intended (among other things) to explicate the meaning of regeneration ἐξ ὕδατος καὶ πνεύματος in relation to the work of Christ, and in particular to link the ideas of ὕδωρ and πνεῦμα through the idea of baptism—the church's baptism, that is to say, in contrast to that of John, which was ἐξ ὕδατος alone."[56]

(2) John 4:1-3

This brief text is interesting on several counts. While the grammar of v. 1 is tortuous though manageable, the clearly secondary nature of v. 2 shows another hand at work.[57] Again the subject of Jesus' baptizing is raised as a transition to the Samaritan episode. But John the Baptist has slipped entirely from view, and Jesus with his now successful baptizing ministry is the sole focus of the Pharisees' suspicion. Even if 4:2 is omitted, it is clear that the subject of Jesus' baptizing is the theme that the Evangelist has chosen to link together chaps. 3 and 4.[58]

In chap. 4, of course, we have another well-known use of ὕδωρ (4:7, 10, etc.). Although Cullmann argued that this is a direct reference to baptism

---

55. MacGregor, *John*, 88-89; Dodd, *Historical Tradition*, 286; E. K. Lee, *Religious Thought of St. John*, 188ff.; Lindars, "Word and Sacrament," 53; Brown, *John*, 1: 155; Barrett, *John*, 219. Westcott, *John*, 58, writes on 3:25-30: "We cannot but believe that Christ, when he administered a baptism through his disciples, explained to those who offered themselves the new birth which John's baptism and this preparatory baptism typified. At the same time He may have indicated, as to Nicodemus, the future establishment of Christian baptism, the sacrament of the new birth."

56. Dodd, *Historical Tradition*, 286.

57. Bernard, *John*, 134; Schnackenburg, *John*, 1: 422n.6; and Brown, *John*, 1:164, consider καίτοι γε as unjohannine (it is a hapax legomenon). This parenthesis no doubt stems from a later editor who was concerned to clear up any confusion with 3:22 which says that Jesus ἐβάπτιζεν (note the singular verb). The standard solution for 4:2 and 3:22, which is fully plausible, is that Jesus baptized only by virtue of his disciples' work. It is interesting that this editor did not make his insertion after 3:22, change the verb in 3:22 to a plural, or alter the earlier text altogether.

58. Dodd, *Interpretation*, 311-13; Westcott, *John*, 66; Lindars, *John*, 172.

THE SPIRIT AND THE SACRAMENTS

(that the living water is baptismal water),[59] the metaphor elsewhere in John (7:37ff.; cf. 19:34) most likely shows that John here is referring to the Spirit (see our discussion above). But the wider question of whether John intended his Christian readers to think of baptism is admirably set forth by Brown.[60] The Nicodemus and Samaritan incidents appear to be set in tandem[61] and are joined by the Gospel's most explicit references to baptism (3:22ff.; 4:1-2). Although here the image is drinking water (as opposed to rebirth through water), this metaphor is found in 1 Cor. 12:13 in the context of baptism: "For by one Spirit we were all baptized into one body . . . and all were made to drink of one Spirit."[62]

Therefore the added allusion to baptism in John 4 (on a very secondary level), when joined to the references in 3:22ff. and 4:1-2, strengthens the case for a baptismal reference in John 3:5. But in John 4 itself the theological orientation we are about to discover in John 3 is evident: baptism introduces the Samaritan pericope but is soon neglected, and Jesus' reference to water quickly becomes a metaphor for the Spirit. The same Jesus who was baptizing in water now offers water in a new context and symbolically portrays the Spirit through it. Therefore in both John 3 and 4 the surface meaning of "water" is transcended by the higher gift that Christ himself will give: the Spirit.[63]

2. THE MEANING AND SIGNIFICANCE OF REBIRTH

Thus far we have concluded: (a) ὕδωρ in 3:5 should refer to baptism as far as Nicodemus could understand it. This text probably then refers to the lustrations of John the Baptist in the context of the christological discussion evidenced in 3:22-30. (b) Jesus' own baptizing was a subject of debate, and its appearance in 3:22ff. reflects the message of 3:1-15 (and again, 3:5). Yet it is clear that Jesus' baptizing at this point was not entirely different from that of John. Granted, it called for a radical change in allegiance (3:26; 4:1; cf. 1:37ff.)—even discipleship—and this change was possibly a matter of division (3:26b), but essentially Jesus' baptism was Jewish, not Christian. "It was the addition of 'Spirit' which transformed John's into Christian baptism (cf. Acts 19:1-7)."[64] Since the Fourth Evangelist has presented the synthesis of Jewish baptism and the divine Spirit in 3:5, he no doubt intends his readers to draw

---

59. Cullmann, *Early Christian Worship*, 80-84; against this view see Beasley-Murray, *Baptism*, 219-20; Smalley, "Liturgy and Sacrament," 164.

60. Brown, *John*, 1: 179-80.

61. The radical differences between the two people make them almost caricatures of the extremes of Palestinian life: man/woman; Jew/Samaritan; Pharisee/harlot; teacher of the law/offender of the law. Both come (3:2; 4:7, 30, 39) to the location where Jesus confronts them.

62. Baptismal imagery is found in the Samaritan episode by Justin *Dial. Trypho* 14:1; Irenaeus *Adv. Haer.* 3.17.1. Did. 17:1-2 stipulates that baptism should be done in running water (ἐν ὕδατι ζῶντι). Brown, *John*, 1:180, notes how early catacomb art used the well scene for baptism; on this point see Niewalda, *Sakramentssymbolik*, 126.

63. Similarly, Barrett, *John*, 228; MacGregor, *John*, 92, 94; Lindars, *John*, 172; Smalley, "Liturgy and Sacrament," 164; Porsch, *Pneuma*, 87-89; P. L. Hammer, "Baptism with Water and Spirit," *Theology and Life* 8 (1965) 35-43.

64. Barrett, *John*, 209; cf. Tasker, *John*, 70-71.

the connection with their own experience of rebirth, Christian baptism, and the Spirit.[65]

Therefore, to understand the meaning of this experience of "birth from above" (γεννᾶν ἄνωθεν), it will be necessary to identify the relation between πνεῦμα and ὕδωρ and thus, by implication, the Johannine understanding of the relation between the Spirit and Christian baptism.

a. The Relation between Πνεῦμα and Ὕδωρ in Rebirth

The history of exegesis shows that almost every sacramental interpretation of the Gospel has claimed some support from John 3:5.[66] The problem is that of coordinating the event of baptism with the reception of the Spirit. Since both elements appear in 3:5, diverse exegetical traditions have evolved: the Spirit can be subordinate to the water (the water functioning as the instrumental means of anointing in this case); or the Spirit can be dissociated from the water, either as a second experience or as an expression of "faith" which works in conjunction with the sacrament.[67]

Since both nouns are anarthrous and are governed by a single preposition, what we most likely have is a hendiadys in which both terms should be coordinated in order to give a single concept. This means that 3:5 reflects the typical Johannine idiom of "pairs in tension."[68] The significance of the one spills over into the other; and as often is the case, the accent falls on the second noun. In commenting on 3:5, Barth effectively explains, "In this irreversible

---

65. In this limited sense, it would not be anachronistic for Jesus to refer to the later Christian rite. The materials for this synthesis were already present: baptismal lustrations in John, and the life-transforming eschatological Spirit which John himself had already predicted (1:33). Its full use in the later church was limited by chronological necessity: the Spirit had not yet come (7:39). Thus full development of this rite in the church only comes with the resurrection (Matt. 28:19; etc.) and Pentecost (Acts 2:38). See J. K. Parratt, "The Holy Spirit and Baptism. Part 1. The Gospels and the Acts of the Apostles," *ExpTim* 82 (1970-71) 231-35.

66. For the history of exegesis see Vellanickal, *Divine Sonship*, 181-86; and as cited by Vellanickal, I. de la Potterie, "Naître," 32-39; cf. Porsch, *Pneuma*, 125-30.

67. The first tradition runs through Chrysostom, Theodore of Mopsuestia, Catholic writers at the Reformation, and currently Schnackenburg. See Vellanickal, ibid., 181-83; and E. K. Lee, *The Religious Thought of St. John*, 189-90. For the second tradition see Hoskyns, *John*, 215, and much Pentecostal theology. The third tradition is reflected in writers such as Clement of Rome, Justin, Bede, Luther and the Reformers, and currently Schweizer and Grundmann. Cf. Vellanickal, ibid., 183-86. A careful look at some of these authors raises doubts as to whether they fit the category indicated by Vellanickal. To indicate that baptism has two elements, one visible and one invisible (Bede), is not to say that the latter is faith in the visible sacrament. Πνεῦμα indicates invisibility, but not necessarily faith. This thesis (that πνεῦμα in 3:5 stands for faith) is most thoroughly presented by Vellanickal himself, 186ff., and his mentor, de la Potterie, "Naître"; Vellanickal writes: "By putting Baptism and Faith (Spirit) as the two basic conditions of divine begetting, John shows that, while the initiative in the divine begetting lies with God, the realization of it is always inextricably connected with human conditions and response" (p. 244).

68. See the excellent exegesis of K. Barth, *Church Dogmatics*, tr. G. W. Bromiley, ed. G. W. Bromiley and T. F. Torrance (Edinburgh: T. & T. Clark, 1969) IV/4: 121, wherein he points to such pairs in 17:3; 1:17; 4:23; 19:34; 11:25; 6:45; 5:24; 6:30, 53, 69; cf. J. D. G. Dunn, *Baptism*, 192; Dodd, *Interpretation*, 314; and C. C. Tarelli, "Johannine Synonyms," *JTS* 47 (1946) 175-77.

order a step is taken, a critical synthesis made, in which the second member totally explains the first, absorbs it, and thus completely replaces it."[69]

Therefore, if we are correct in our conclusion that "water" points to baptism, rebirth ἐξ ὕδατος καὶ πνεύματος can point in one of two directions. It can mean water baptism, which is viewed in close connection to Spirit baptism—so close, in fact, as to be inseparable. Or it can mean water baptism in which the material element is either being depreciated or used simply as a symbol of spiritual cleansing. To be sure, these options do not have to be mutually exclusive. But through them all John's concern is to present rebirth ἐκ πνεύματος— ἐκ ἄνωθεν. John does not begin with baptism and seek a way to relate the Spirit to it. For him, the role of water in rebirth is wholly and exclusively defined in terms of Spirit. When this definition expands, water slips from view as if almost dispensable in the process. As with the earlier contrast between John the Baptist's baptism and that of Jesus, ὕδωρ is not the distinguishing element. The person reborn in Christ has experienced the Spirit, and this alone is the prerequisite for Nicodemus's entry into the kingdom. This exclusive emphasis on the Spirit can be seen in the following texts.

(1) John 3:3

The numerous parallels between 3:3 and 3:5 show that the latter is simply an expansion of the former.[70]

3:3 ἀμὴν ἀμὴν λέγω σοι, ἐὰν μή τις γεννηθῇ ἄνωθεν,
    οὐ δύναται ἰδεῖν
        τὴν βασιλείαν τοῦ θεοῦ.

3:5 ἀμὴν ἀμὴν λέγω σοι, ἐὰν μή τις γεννηθῇ ἐξ ὕδατος καὶ πνεύματος,
    οὐ δύναται εἰσελθεῖν
        εἰς τὴν βασιλείαν τοῦ θεοῦ.

Thus birth ἐξ ὕδατος καὶ πνεύματος is equivalent to birth ἄνωθεν. Although opinion is divided whether ἄνωθεν is meant to be temporal or local, no doubt this usage reflects the Johannine literary technique of double entendre.[71] But John's usage elsewhere indicates that his meaning is essentially

---

69. Barth, ibid., IV/4:121.

70. Lindars, John, 151; Porsch, Pneuma, 98; the change of ἰδεῖν to εἰσελθεῖν εἰς is simply stylistic (contra Vellanickal, Divine Sonship, 207); on the relation of Spirit and kingdom, see J. D. G. Dunn, "Spirit and Kingdom," ExpTim 82 (1970-71) 36-40.

71. Birth "from above" is supported by Braun, Schnackenburg, Büchsel, Brown, Porsch, Hoskyns, Str-B, Abbott, Lindars, and Corell. Birth "anew" or "again" is seen by Zahn, Bultmann, and has been argued at length by W. Mounce, "The Origin of the New Testament Metaphor of Rebirth," unpub. diss., Aberdeen University (1981), esp. chap. 3, "Johannine Rebirth." Both meanings are suggested to Cullmann, Dodd, Barrett, Tasker, and Hunter. Both translations had strong support in antiquity: see Vellanickal, Divine Sonship, 172-74; Hoskyns, John, 211-12; Büchsel, TDNT 1: 378. On the double entendre in John see Cullmann, "Der johanneische Gebrauch doppeldeutiger Ausdrücke als Schlüssel zum Verstandnis des vierten Evangeliums," TZ 4 (1948) 360-72; idem, Early Christian Worship, 50ff.; D. W. Wead, "Johannine Double Meaning," RestQ 2 (1970) 106-20; M. deJonge, "Nicodemus and Jesus: Some Observations on Misunderstanding and Under-

local (3:31; 19:11, 23). Nicodemus addresses Jesus as a teacher come from God (ἀπο θεοῦ). This is a statement of origin which suggests that in 3:3 Nicodemus must share this divine origin (through begetting) in order to join Jesus' kingdom. Nicodemus stumbles on γεννᾶν (be born) as well as the double meaning of ἄνωθεν and reduces the definition of this birth to the earthly sphere (v. 4). But this is a feature of the Johannine discourse: the misunderstood answer is used to transport the subject to a higher level.[72] The repeated use of ἄνωθεν in 3:31 (see our redactional study above) again points to the question of divine origins for Jesus and how this is determinative for the spiritual birth of the believer. John the Baptist is of the earth (ἐκ τῆς γῆς), but Jesus is from above— from heaven (ὁ ἄνωθεν—ἐκ τοῦ οὐρανοῦ ἐρχόμενος, v. 31b). Furthermore, Jesus has the distinctive endowment of the Spirit (3:34). Hence to join Jesus, Nicodemus must experience the ἄνω through birth ἐκ πνεύματος.

John 3:3 thus shows that the christological contrast worked out in vv. 31-36 is indicative for the believer.[73] The contrast turns on Jesus being from above and anointed with Spirit. This is the ground of the decisive precedence of Jesus over the Baptist. Thus the Baptist's baptism was of water only because he was of the earth. Jesus' distinctiveness stems from the addition of Spirit: the birth will come from above.

(2) John 3:6-8

As the dialogue develops, birth from water and Spirit is now viewed simply as birth through the Spirit (v. 6). The incipient dualism of v. 3 now comes to full expression: ἄνωθεν is the realm which is to be distinguished from σάρξ.[74] This birth, therefore, must be otherworldly and completely derived from the above (τὰ ἄνω) in contrast to the below (τὰ κάτω). It comes mysteriously (v. 8) and can neither be contained in anything of the earth (ὕδωρ, 3:5, or baptism) nor be predicated by any human expectation.[75] A human being cannot even comprehend the teaching of it (3:12). The stress in the demand for birth from water and Spirit falls entirely on the Spirit. The contributing features of the "water" are now dismissed: in its synthesis with Spirit, its role has been rendered superfluous.[76]

---

standing in the Fourth Gospel," *BJRL* 53 (1971) 337-59; and R. Shedd, "Multiple Meanings in the Gospel of John," in *Current Issues in Biblical and Patristic Interpretation: Studies in Honor of Merrill C. Tenney*, ed. G. F. Hawthorne (Grand Rapids: Eerdmans, 1975) 247-58. Other Greek wordplays include ἀνίστημι, 11:24; βαστάζω, 12:6; εἰς τέλος, 13:1; ἠγάπησεν, 13:1; τετέλεσται, 19:30; ἔθνος, 11:50; τὰ ἐρχόμενα, 16:13; μοναί, 14:2.

72. Brown, *John*, 1:138; Cullmann, "Der johanneische Gebrauch," 364-65.

73. Note the contrast between the believer and Jesus in 1 John 5:18.

74. In Johannine dualism, however, σάρξ does not have the negative connotation of sin as in Paul nor the distrust of the flesh as in Gnosticism. The Johannine notion contrasts the mortal and the immortal. "The flesh is to the spirit what the earthly is to the heavenly," so Vellanickal, *Divine Sonship*, 198; also Porsch, *Pneuma*, 92-96; E. Schweizer, *TDNT* 7: 124-44; and Barrett, *John*, 67-70.

75. Brown points out the christological parallel once again. Just as human beings are unable to know the Spirit (3:8), so too Jesus remains unknown in his person and movements (7:35). "The Spirit is the Spirit of Jesus; both the Spirit and Jesus are from above, and therefore they are mysterious to men from below" (*John*, 1: 141).

76. Barth, *Church Dogmatics*, IV/4: 121.

* * *

In sum, while water does play a role in the divine birth, John exhibits a cautious reserve. In the christological contrasts of the ensuing dialogue, water belongs to John the Baptist, the κάτω, and σάρξ. The believer must join Christ in being from above (ἄνωθεν) and anointed. Thus water (or Christian baptism) is only theologically meaningful if it is accompanied by the experiential presence of the Spirit. These verses militate against any view that would see water as instrumental. They also contradict the interpretation of Spirit as the activity of a person in faith. Divine birth is a mystical, dynamic experience begun by divine initiative. Jesus' message is not so much concerned with baptism or faith as with the new creation by the Spirit of God.[77]

b. The Objective Basis of Rebirth: The Cross and Faith

The final dialogue of the discourse is set forth following Nicodemus's incredulous question, "How can this be?" (v. 9). Nicodemus drops from sight and Jesus begins a lengthy explanation (3:10ff.). The answer is not found in a further examination of the mystery of birth (as vv. 5-8 develop v. 4). The birth finds its basis in the Christ event of death and ascension. Therefore, John's earlier emphasis on πνεῦμα is not left free to inspire an unbounded enthusiasm or mysticism. It has an objective basis at the cross.[78]

But the preeminent value of this basis is found in John's theological complex of cross, glorification, and the gift of the Spirit (see chapter 3 above). The answer to Nicodemus's question is found in Christ's death (3:14, 16) because this is the event for which the Spirit must wait (7:37ff.; cf. 19:30, 34). But, more importantly, the reference to ascension (v. 13) again points forward—perhaps to 20:22, which shares many parallels with this discourse (esp. v. 8)—and locks the gift of the Spirit into the glorification/departure of Christ.[79]

But Jesus' answer to Nicodemus's final question has an equally important subjective basis. The revelation of who Jesus is (3:18, 32) and what God has accomplished through his death (3:14-15, 16) must be met with a response of faith.[80] Thus in 7:39 it is those who believe who will receive the Spirit. Earlier, the result of divine birth was entry into God's kingdom (a phrase appearing in

---

77. Schnackenburg, *John*, 1: 370; Barrett, *John*, 209; contra Schweitzer, *Mysticism*, 352ff.

78. Beasley-Murray, *Baptism*, 230-31; Cullmann, *Early Christian Worship*, 76-77; M. de-Jonge, "Nicodemus and Jesus," 349; Barrett, *John*, 83.

79. Dunn, *Baptism*, 193; contra Bultmann, *John*, 150-51, who interprets this verse entirely in terms of the descending Gnostic redeemer.

80. Klos, *Die Sakramente*, 72ff.; cf. 3:12, 15, 16, 18, 36. Remarkably πιστεύειν is the most repeated term in the discourse (8 times) surpassing even πνεῦμα (6 times). It is well known that πιστεύειν is an important Johannine term. Out of 241 NT uses, 98 are in John and 9 in the Johannine Epistles (34 in the Synoptics; 54 in Paul). John 20:31 shows this faith to be the aim of the book. In addition, John's sole preference for the verbal form (omitting πίστις, which occurs 142 times in Paul) is clearly intentional and designed to show the dynamism expected of this faith. See Brown, *John*, 1: 512-15 (and his bibliography, p. 515); Bultmann, *TDNT* 6: 222-28; and E. K. Lee, *The Religious Thought of St. John*, 220-37.

John only in 3:3, 5), but now this traditional Jewish language is placed in typically Johannine idiom: faith in the Son of Man results in eternal life (3:15, 16, 36).[81] If we are correct that John 3 is working with a baptismal motif, the demand for faith in the context of baptism anchors this passage in the earliest traditional kerygma. Faith in Christ is the prerequisite of spiritual rebirth (which should be reflected in baptism).[82] That this requirement was normative in the Johannine community is seen especially in John 1:12-13. The power to become children of God—to be born of God (ἐκ θεοῦ ἐγεννήθησαν, v. 13)— stems from the reception of the Logos (cf. 3:22) and belief in his name.[83] Although John does not indicate the precise relation between Spirit and faith, it is clear that the new birth, while divinely originated and mystical, is not found in the person without faith. But the synthesis of the human endeavor and the divine initiative is unexplained and left in tension (as in Paul, Phil. 2:12-13). To gain eternal life one must be born from above and one must believe. But in the text before us the accent is on the former. Simple cognition of the facts of salvation and the confession of faith must be joined with a life-changing encounter with the Spirit. This feature was undoubtedly one of the hallmarks of Johannine Christianity.

* * *

To sum up, the use of baptismal language in John 3 suggests that the Evangelist is addressing a situation in which sacramental abuse may have been close at hand. This situation may have stemmed from the increasing institutionalizing of the church and the rigidity of sacramental use, from the changing climate brought on by the mystery cults, or even from the despair engendered by the delay of the parousia.[84] John reveals a concern that baptism not be elevated above either Jesus or the Spirit in Christian experience. This conclusion agrees with our earlier finding regarding the baptism/anointing of Jesus in John 1:29-32. There the water rite was removed altogether in order to underscore the descent and indwelling of the Spirit. Again in John 4, the baptizing ministry which leads to Samaria ultimately finds expression in the offer of living water, namely, the Spirit (see below).

While some have used this evidence to argue that John is anti-sacramental, it may be nearer the mark to say that John is more concerned to emphasize the significance which the Christian rite is meant to symbolize. John thus

---

81. This alteration from kingdom of God to eternal life suggests the very Johannine nature of the latter part of the discourse (3:12, 16ff.) and the possible use of traditional Jewish (or Synoptic-like) materials in the earlier section (3:1-12, 15).

82. Cf. Beasley-Murray, *Baptism*, 230; Lindars, "Word and Sacrament," 55.

83. The connection between John 3 and 1:12-13 is further seen in the use of πιστεύειν εἰς τὸ ὄνομα, which apears only in 1:12; 2:23; and 3:18.

84. For the first interpretation see Dunn, *Unity and Diversity*, 198-99. For the second see Howard, *Christianity According to St. John*, 149; MacGregor, "The Eucharist in the Fourth Gospel," *NTS* 9 (1962-63) 118; cf. A. J. B. Higgins, *The Lord's Supper in the New Testament*, SBT 1/6 (London: SCM; Naperville: Allenson, 1952) 84. For the third see Brown, "The Paraclete," 130-32. F. Mussner argues that the *Sitz im Leben* is the cessation of the physical presence of Jesus among his followers and the death of the apostolic eyewitnesses; see *The Historical Jesus in the Gospel of St. John*, tr. W. J. O'Hara (London: Burns and Oates; New York: Herder, 1967).

warns against a sacramental literalism. Yet John does not deny that baptism plays a role in Christian conversion/initiation. The positive references to baptism in 3:22ff. and 4:1-2 indicate that baptism was normative in the Johannine community. But for membership in this community this act was not the distinctive mark of conversion/initiation. Divine birth through the Spirit marked the Johannine Christian, and this was the event which the baptismal waters were expected to symbolize. To be sure, this begetting incorporated faith (3:15; 7:39), but it primarily denoted the dramatic reception of the Holy Spirit.[85] It remains to be shown only that divine birth and spiritual anointing appear elsewhere in the Johannine literature as the distinguishing feature of community life.

3. Spirit and Identity in 1 John

Any community which holds John 3:1-15 as its charter of discipleship is bound to exhibit a profound spiritual vitality. That "divine birth" was programmatic for the community is seen by a glance at 1 John.[86] The formulaic expression of the Gospel's prologue (ἐκ θεοῦ γεννᾶν, 1:13) is given full expression in the Epistle. Here Johannine Christians are said to be "born of God" (γεννᾶν ἐκ θεοῦ, 3:9; 4:7; 5:1, 4, 18) and "born of him" (γεννᾶν ἐξ αὐτοῦ, 2:29; 5:1).[87] Similarly πνεῦμα appears 12 times: 5 times as the distinguishing feature of the true community (3:24; 4:13; 5:7, 7, 8) and 7 times as the litmus test of fidelity to the orthodox faith (4:1-6). Therefore the immediacy of the divine presence retained its validity in the community. Christian identity is first found in birth through the Spirit.

---

85. Brown, *John*, 1: 140; Barth, *Church Dogmatics*, IV/4: 121. Barrett, *John*, 209, remarks, "John neither ignores nor repudiates the Christian rite, but sees it as a rite that is separable from its meaning, an outward that is separable from its inward, and thus issues the warning against a sacramental misapprehension of baptism." McPolin, "The Holy Spirit in Luke and John," 121; and Schweizer, *TDNT* 6: 438, unnecessarily reduce the dynamic and ecstatic features of the Spirit in John.

86. On the relation between 1 John and the Fourth Gospel, see Kümmel, *Introduction*, 435-52; Schnackenburg, *Johannesbriefe*, 34-39; C. H. Dodd, "The First Epistle of John and the Fourth Gospel," *BJRL* 21 (1937) 129-56; W. F. Howard, "The Common Authorship of the Johannine Gospel and Epistles," *JTS* 48 (1947) 12-25; W. G. Wilson, "An Examination of the Linguistic Evidence Adduced Against the Unity of Authorship of the First Epistle of John and the Fourth Gospel," *JTS* 49 (1948) 147-56; G. Johnston, *Spirit-Paraclete*, 75-79. We accept the conclusion that the Epistles (esp. 1 John) stem from the same milieu as the Fourth Gospel (contra Dodd, Howard), were written subsequent to it (contra Johnston), and are responding to distortions which have come from a misinterpretation of the Gospel itself. On this issue see J. A. T. Robinson, "The Destination and Purpose of the Johannine Epistles," *NTS* 7 (1960-61) 56-65; R. E. Brown, "The Relationship to the Fourth Gospel Shared by the Author of 1 John and by His Opponents," in *Text and Interpretation: Studies in the New Testament Presented to Matthew Black*, ed. E. Best and R. McL. Wilson (Cambridge: University Press, 1979) 57-68. R. Schnackenburg has argued that pneumatology is a decisive link between the two writings; see "Die johanneische Gemeinde und Ihre Geisterfahrung," 282-87.

87. Γεννᾶν appears 10 times and each usage employs the theological metaphor of divine birth. In 5:1 God is labeled the "parent" or begetter (τὸν γεννήσαντα), and in 5:18b Jesus, as the believer's paradigm, is described as γεννηθεὶς ἐκ τοῦ θεοῦ; see Büchsel, *TDNT* 1: 671-72. Marshall, *First John*, 252n.37, gives persuasive evidence for viewing Jesus as the subject in 5:18b.

The most exhaustive recent study of this aspect of the Epistle belongs to E. Malatesta (*Interiority and Covenant*, 1978). Malatesta traces the interiority language of the OT covenant through a study of εἶναι ἐν and μένειν ἐν. In 1 John he concludes that interiority of spiritual experience was characteristic of the community and was focused on the Spirit: "It would seem correct to say tht personal communion with the Holy Spirit is a touchstone of Christian interiority."[88] Ἐῖναι ἐν and μένειν ἐν commonly appear in the Fourth Gospel and are predictably concentrated in the Farewell Discourses.[89] This expectation of spiritual union with Christ is exemplified in the Epistle's description of Johannine believers "being in" God, Christ, truth, the light, etc. (19 times).[90] Similarly μένειν ἐν is coined as expressive of the identity and fidelity of the believers 25 times.[91] These statistics alone are surprising when one considers the length of the Epistle.

Every feature of 1 John, however, including this intense spirituality, must be seen in the light of the severe polemics in which the community is engaged.[92] Brook is right in arguing that the chief aim of the Epistle is not the refutation of the heterodox beliefs of the opponents.[93] It is rather the edification, or better, the affirmation of the authentic spiritual identity of the Johannine Christians. Thus we can agree with Brown that pneumatology played an important role in this dispute.[94] If the heresy stemmed from a distortion of the Fourth Gospel (which we find convincing), the authority for the secessionists' interpretation may have come from the Spirit. Thus heterodox Johannine Christians (cf. 2:19, 26) have taken the inspiration of the Paraclete seriously (John 14:26; 16:13). But this is also the case with the orthodox. The Paraclete who would teach all (14:26) has done so (1 John 2:27), and this capacity no doubt became a weapon taken up by the opponents.

Therefore the authenticity of spiritual experience has become a para-

---

88. Malatesta, *Interiority and Covenant*, 279.

89. In the Fourth Gospel, εἶναι ἐν appears 13 times, the personal uses of which are all in chaps. 14 and 17 (except 10:38); see 1:4, 10; 8:44; 9:5; 11:10; 12:35; 14:10, 17; 15:11; 17:11 (bis), 21, 26. The Paraclete is in the disciples (14:17), the Son is in the disciples (14:20), the disciples are in the Father and the Son (17:21). The prayer of Jesus in chap. 17 ends significantly with κἀγὼ ἐν αὐτοῖς. Μένειν ἐν occurs 16 times (5:38; 6:56; 8:31, 35; 12:46; 14:10; 15:4 [tris], 5, 6, 7 [bis], 9, 10 [bis]). The most important are in John 15, which might be termed "a hymn to Johannine mysticism." See S. Mary, *Pauline and Johannine Mysticism* (London: Darton, Longman, and Todd, 1964) 73-88.

90. 1 John 1:5, 7, 8, 10; 2:4, 5, 8 (bis), 9 (bis), 10, 11, 15; 3:5; 4:3, 17, 18; 5:10, 11.

91. 1 John 2:6, 10, 14, 24 (tris), 27 (bis), 28; 3:6, 9, 14, 15, 17, 24 (bis); 4:12, 13, 15, 16 (tris); 2 John 2, 9 (bis). In the Apocalypse, εἶναι ἐν appears 4 times and μένειν ἐν appears once (without theological meaning).

92. K. Weiss, "Orthodoxie und Heterodoxie im 1. Johannesbriefe," *ZNW* 58 (1967) 247-55; F. V. Filson, "First John: Purpose and Message," *Int* 23 (1969) 256-76; esp. K. Wengst, *Häresie und Orthodoxie im Spiegel des ersten Johannesbriefes* (Gütersloh: Mohn, 1976); R. E. Brown, *Community*, 93-144; Culpepper, *Johannine School*, 279-86; S. Smalley, "What About 1 John?" in *Studia Biblica III 1978. Papers on Paul and Other New Testament Authors*, JSNTSup 3 (Sheffield: JSNT Press, 1980) 337-43.

93. A. E. Brooke, *First John*, xxxviii-lii; cf. Houlden, *The Johannine Epistles*, Harper's New Testament Commentaries (New York: Harper & Row, 1973) 105.

94. Brown, "The Relationship to the Fourth Gospel," 68; esp. idem, *Community*, 138-44; similarly, Schnackenburg, "Die johanneische Gemeinde," 282-83; and J. Painter, *John*, 121-23.

THE SPIRIT AND THE SACRAMENTS

mount concern in the community schism. The author consistently affirms the pneumatic authority of the orthodox believers (1 John 2:20, 26-27) and hopes to uncover the inauthenticity of his opponents' experience through his well-known "tests of life." But note what John does not say. He cannot deny the spiritual activity in the opposite camp (they would simply return the tactic), but he can test the spirits to see if they have the wrong spirit. Their wrong christology (4:2ff.) and ethics (4:7ff.) prove that they are not born of God and do not have his Spirit (4:6). He does not simply confront their wrong beliefs, but rather he uses those beliefs as items which discredit the veracity of the spirit they claim to possess.

In this same situation one would have expected Paul to respond with an authoritative "I" (e.g., Galatians). But in the Johannine church the prominence of the Paraclete has relativized the authority of any single teacher.[95] Although John works to point back to an authoritative tradition (1:1-3; 2:7; ἀλήθεια 20 times), the tradition is to a certain degree fluid: the Paraclete will open up new truths (John 16:12-13). The Johannine schism is thus typical of a charismatic/enthusiastic schism: both sides are claiming authority through the authenticity of their own spiritual experiences.[96]

We can sum up by saying that the Johannine believer identified himself foremost as living in the Spirit. The Spirit provided discernment in the midst of false teaching (1 John 2:26-27; 4:1-2) and the power which binds together the community in love (4:7ff.; 5:1-5). Various texts confirm this pneumatic identification, including the following.

a. 1 John 3:24; 4:13

These two Spirit texts stand out in that here the Spirit is ascribed to believers as their assurance that Christ dwells within. As the parallels show, they are no doubt repetitions of the same thought, perhaps from a common didactic tradition.[97]

3:24   and in this we know that he abides in us,
         by the Spirit which he gave to us.

4:13   in this we know that we abide in him and he in us,
         by his own Spirit which he has given us.

3:24   καὶ ἐν τούτῳ γινώσκομεν ὅτι μένει ἐν ἡμῖν,
         ἐκ τοῦ πνεύματος οὗ ἡμῖν ἔδωκεν

4:13   ἐν τούτῳ γινώσκομεν ὅτι ἐν αὐτῷ μένομεν καὶ αὐτὸς ἐν ἡμῖν,
         ὅτι ἐκ τοῦ πνεύματος αὐτοῦ δέδωκεν ἡμῖν.

---

95. Brown, *Community*, 141; also, Grundmann, *TDNT* 9: 572; R. Schnackenburg, ibid., 287, 295-96; on a popular level, see Green, *I Believe in the Holy Spirit*, 93-94. Less convincingly, Culpepper (*Johannine School*, 282-83) has argued that the false teachers were claiming the Beloved Disciple's authority (since his death).

96. The relation between Spirit and word (or revelation) is an important one in this Epistle, and we shall turn to it in our final chapter.

97. Schnackenburg, "Die johanneische Gemeinde," 284, suggests that this may be community formula; compare Bultmann, *The Johannine Epistles*, Hermeneia, tr. R. P. O'Hara et al. (Philadelphia: Fortress, 1973) 59; and Malatesta, *Interiority and Covenant*, 303-304.

The important nuances of these texts emerge when we note their differences. While both verses establish their concern for the Spirit in the context of abiding or interiority, 4:13 enhances the theme of reciprocal indwelling. The Spirit is the means through which God enters the life of the Christian. But it is the Spirit that also confirms in believers their sense of confidence that they are identified as being in Christ. 1 John 4:13 also enhances the personal nature of this indwelling: God has given his own Spirit. No doubt this gift also accords with the needs of the letter's recipients in the midst of the polemic: they should successfully pass the test of spirits in the foregoing section (4:1ff.).

Finally, it is instructive to note that the tense of δίδωμι has changed. Although it is true that in Hellenistic Greek the line distinguishing the aorist and the perfect is sometimes difficult to draw, it is not apparent here that John intends the two verbs to be synonymous.[98] In fact, it might be accurate to see in John's frequent use of the perfect a theological meaning pointing to the present significance of Christ.[99] At the outset we should note that in John δίδωμι itself generally conveys a "special meaning referring to the heavenly gifts of God."[100] In 3:24 the author is concerned to confirm in his readers their identity on the orthodox side: "by this we know we are of the truth" (2:19). Thus the aorist stresses the confirmation of the believer in Christ and the Spirit. It establishes assurance for "when our hearts condemn us" (2:20-21). On the other hand, 4:13 stresses the continuity of the believer in the Spirit. The tests of orthodoxy and ethics question whether the ongoing life of the believer is consistent with the Spirit. The Spirit once given now finds tangible expression in love. This "present-ness" of the Spirit is anchored in 4:17, καθὼς ἐκεῖνός ἐστιν καὶ ἡμεῖς ἐσμεν. This present reality thus leads to perfection (4:17a) and perseverance until the last day (4:17b).

b. Χρῖσμα in 1 John 2:20, 27

The importance of the relation between Spirit and word in this Johannine "anointing" (χρῖσμα) will concern us in our final chapter. Here we need to determine the working concept employed by John in this Epistle. As we have said, the latter's aim is to confirm the believer's identity and authority in the Spirit in the midst of the schism. Here, however, John has chosen a relatively infrequent term and applied it to Christians (χρῖσμα appears only 3 times in the NT, 1 John 2:20, 27a, 27b).

Χρῖσμα is the nominal form of χρίω and was used in the LXX for

---

98. The narrow limits of this grammatical distinction when applied to the NT are shown by Moulton, *Grammar*, 1: 140-48; and Burton, *Moods and Tenses*, 37-44. Arguing for the distinction here is Malatesta, *Interiority and Covenant*, 275; pace Marshall, *First John*, 219n. 2; and Schnackenburg, *Johannesbriefe*, 241n.6. Note that the major grammars do not list 1 John 4:13 as an aoristic perfect.

99. See M. S. Enslin, "The Perfect Tense in the Fourth Gospel," *JBL* 55 (1936) 121-31, who counts 195 perfects in the Fourth Gospel (Matthew 49; Mark 45; Luke 104) and concludes that John's fondness for the perfect "is due neither to the breakdown of the distinction between the perfect and aorist nor to an attempt to give extra vividness to his narrative, but to his conviction of the eternal significance and abiding reality of the work and words of the One whom God has sent. Thus, for want of a better name, this usage of the perfect may well be styled 'theological'" (p. 131).

100. Vellanickal, *Divine Sonship*, 314; see his examples and those of Büchsel, *TDNT* 2: 166.

consecration into office and ultimately in eschatological use depicted the anointing of the future Messiah (ὁ χριστός).[101] Luke uses χρίω in Acts 10:38 to show the Lord's anointing in the Spirit which took place at baptism (cf. Luke 4:18; Acts 4:27; Heb. 1:9). As we noted above, the Fourth Evangelist gave special attention to this concept particularly in his account of Jesus' baptism as well as in 3:34 and 6:27. Even in the entire discourse of John 3, the Spirit endowment of Christ serves as the paradigm set before Nicodemus as he looks to his own experience. In effect, the Spirit is the mark of Christ and thus should be the mark of the Christian as well.[102]

In the present texts this anointing forms a part of the overall picture of possession of the Spirit (3:24; 4:13) and divine birth (2:29; 3:9; etc.), and it certainly refers to the messianic anointing promised in the Gospel. In John 14:26 it is promised that the Paraclete "will teach you all things" (διδάξει ὑμᾶς πάντα), and this promise is fulfilled in the anointing described in 1 John 2:27 (τὸ αὐτοῦ χρῖσμα διδάσκει ὑμᾶς περὶ πάντων).[103] One of the chief arguments against the interpretation that sees this anointing as only the word of God or the orthodox kerygma[104] is that this anointing dwells within the believer (τὸ χρῖσμα μένει ἐν ὑμῖν, 2:27). Therefore the anointing stands apart from the word as independent but finds its primary function in confirming the word and applying it in the present schism.

Does John refer this anointing to baptism? Dunn denies this possibility categorically, and we are inclined to agree.[105] To be sure, baptism is conspicuous by its absence. Interpreters may well be right that this χρῖσμα was in fact gained in baptism[106] or experienced in conjunction with baptismal initiation (John's use of the aorist ἐλάβετε may confirm this view), but nowhere does the author himself draw out this conclusion. As in John 3, the stress in these texts points to the believer's identification in the Spirit, not in baptism. In the Johannine controversy it is this charismatic authority that is being tapped in order to counter the secessionists.

c. Σπέρμα in 1 John 3:9

Dodd's attempt to interpret the interiority expressions of this Epistle solely in terms of the implanted word of God is least convincing here. Neither the

---

101. Note the verb's use for the consecration of priests (Exod. 29:7; Num. 35:25), kings (1 Sam. 9:16; 1 Kgs. 19:15-16), and prophets (1 Kgs. 18:16; Isa. 61:1). These in turn were regarded as being anointed with the Holy Spirit (1 Sam. 16:13; Isa. 61:1). See Brooke, *Johannine Epistles*, 55-56; and Grundmann, *TDNT* 9: 527-73.

102. Paul employs χρίω in 2 Cor. 1:21-22 thus: "But it is God who establishes us with you in Christ and has anointed us; he has put his seal on us and put the earnest of the Spirit in our hearts." See the further discussion of Lampe, *The Seal of the Spirit*, 61.

103. Schnackenburg, *Johannesbriefe*, 151-52; Dunn, *Baptism*, 197; Grundmann, *TDNT* 9: 572; cf. John 14:17; 15:26; 16:13.

104. C. H. Dodd, *First John*, 58-64; Beasley-Murray, *Baptism*, 233-36.

105. Dunn, *Baptism*, 198; cf. Bultmann, *First John*, 37; 1 John's stress on the Spirit and its suggestive silence regarding baptism has led W. Nauck to suggest that it is a tract for baptismal catechesis. See W. Nauck, *Die Tradition und Charakter der ersten Johannesbriefes* (Tübingen: Mohr, 1957).

106. Houlden, *First John*, 79; and those cited by Dunn, *Baptism*, 195n.2.

teaching function of the Spirit nor the kerygma comes into view. In addition, the alleged parallels found in Jas. 1:18 and 1 Pet. 1:23 are not convincing. To resort to a parallel with the parable of the sower is simply exegesis in desperation.[107]

On the other hand, the immediate context suggests that σπέρμα (NIV "seed") is simply a part of John's now familiar divine birth terminology: γεννᾶν ἐκ θεοῦ (2 times in 3:9). Divine birth employing God's σπέρμα echoes John 3:3ff., where such birth is also discussed in terms of the Spirit. Therefore σπέρμα in 1 John 3:9 is a symbol of the Spirit in a crude though legitimate application of the regeneration metaphor.[108]

But just as γεννᾶν in Johannine theology refers to the point of origin (here: children of God or of the devil),[109] σπέρμα conveys this same sense. Its three uses in the Fourth Gospel indicate the messianic credentials of Jesus (John 7:42) and the dubious blood lineage of the Jews (8:33, 37). 1 John 3:9 follows this pattern in identifying the origin of the Christian in the Spirit of God: through God's seed or Spirit the newly generated creature is truly "of God" (ἐκ τοῦ θεοῦ, 3:10) because this is the origin of his life (3:14).

d. Revelation 3:19-22

The pneumatology of the Apocalypse stands as one of the typically difficult items which complicate this book's relation to the remainder of the Johannine literature.[110] Chiefly lacking are any personal ascriptions to the Spirit in chaps. 1– 3. In addition, the book never specifies the relation among Father, Son, and Spirit.[111] Rev. 22:17 comes closest to providing us with what we need, but even here the image is cryptic and unclear. In spite of this problem, certain allusions do suggest a "Johannine" background: the Spirit is closely identified with Christ and the reader is offered the "water of life" (cf. John 4:7ff. and 7:37ff.).

W. M. Ramsay considered Rev. 3:19-22 to be the epilogue to the entire sequence of letters.[112] This view underscores this text's importance in closing a major unit of the work. Yet within its message two remarkable similarities with other Johannine texts we have been examining stand out. First, eschatological imagery is used to convey a sense of urgency in Christ's present relation to the church. While the passage may be only eschatologically future

---

107. Dodd, *First John*, 77; cf. Schulz, *TDNT* 7: 545; Dunn, ibid., 197, argues that in 1 Pet. 1:23 σπορά is distinct from the λόγος and represents the Spirit.

108. Brooke, *Johannine Epistles*, 89; Büchsel, *TDNT* 1: 671; Schnackenburg, *Johannesbriefe*, 190-91. Other scholars see here a synthesis of Spirit and word as in 2:20, 27; see Dunn, *Baptism*, 195-200; and Marshall, *First John*, 186-87.

109. Büchsel, *TDNT* 1: 671.

110. See Kümmel, *Introduction*, 426-74; and the older work of J. E. Carpenter, *The Johannine Writings. A Study of the Apocalypse and the Fourth Gospel* (London: Constable, 1927). On the pneumatology of the Apocalypse, see F. F. Bruce, "The Spirit in the Apocalypse," in *Christ and Spirit in the New Testament*, 333-44; E. Schweizer, *TDNT* 6: 449-51; and J. Massyngberde Ford, *Revelation*, AB (New York: Doubleday, 1975) 19-20.

111. Ford, ibid., 19.

112. Noted in R. Mounce, *Revelation*, NICNT (Grand Rapids: Eerdmans, 1977) 127.

or purely realized in orientation,[113] it may also be that a synthesis is in view. In much the same way as in the Fourth Gospel's Farewell Discourses, futurist language is employed for the present. In each letter but one, Jesus promises that he "will come," just as in the Farewell Discourses (Rev. 2:5, 16, 25; 3:3, 11, 20). Second, Rev. 3:20 may be a type of interiority expression. Note that throughout the letters it is the Spirit who addresses the churches (2:7, 11, 17, 29; 3:6, 13, 22). But this Spirit—and this is the decisive point—is none other than Jesus himself (2:1/7, 8/11, 12/17, 18/29, etc.).[114] The image of Christ "coming to him" and eating with him is an oriental expression of personal intimacy and directly echoes John 14:23, "And we [Jesus and the Father via the Spirit] will come to him and make our home with him."[115] Therefore in this admonition the Spirit is the extension of Jesus into the church. The result of repentance will be a personal encounter of Christ in Spirit.

4. CONCLUSION

Our study of John 3 in conjunction with other Johannine Spirit texts has shown the exuberant spiritual (or pneumatic) vitality known within the community. The hallmark of conversion/initiation was experience of the Spirit joined with faith in the saving work of Christ. As the believer grew in the faith, this identity of being "born of God" and abiding "in the Spirit" persevered as the central distinctive of Johannine discipleship.

We also discovered a confirmation of our hypothesis that baptism was relegated to a secondary position in the Johannine community (although it was not completely denied). John's cautious use of baptismal terminology in John 3 shows a corrective or even admonitory attitude. Moreover, the conspicuous absence of baptism in the remainder of the Johannine corpus suggests the same. John knew well that the symbol of conversion could become detached from its meaning. He admonishes the community that the waters of Christian baptism pale into insignificance when compared with the Spirit. Indeed, it is not baptism but the Spirit and faith that gain eternal life for the believer (John 3:5, 15).

Therefore it would be fair to label this community a "pneumatic community" in that each true believer was recognized as marked with the Spirit of God (1 John 2:20, 27). Although individualized gifts and ministries of the Spirit as they appear in Paul fail to enter this Johannine framework, the Spirit is identified clearly in the way he transforms and empowers the believer, creates community and inspires love, and finally preserves the church's orthodox confession through personal instruction and revelation.

---

113. For the former view see M. Rist, *Interpreter's Bible*, 12 vols. (Nashville: Abingdon, 1957) 12: 398; G. Vos, *The Synoptic Traditions in the Apocalypse* (Kampen: Kok, 1965) 95-100. For the latter see R. H. Charles, *Revelation*, ICC, 2 vols. (Edinburgh: T. & T. Clark, 1920) 1: 99-101; G. Ladd, *Revelation* (Grand Rapids: Eerdmans, 1972) 67-68.

114. Schweizer, *TDNT* 6: 449.

115. So Ladd, *Revelation*, 68; Charles, *Revelation*, 1:101. I. H. Marshall, *Last Supper and Lord's Supper* (Exeter: Paternoster; Grand Rapids: Eerdmans, 1980) 138-39, wants to view this meal as "an indication of what the Lord's Supper is meant to be."

But just as we have viewed John's corrective tendency in baptism, so too the same attitude is evident when we locate the eucharist in his theology. It is this concern with the danger of eucharistic worship as opposed to the real presence of Jesus in Spirit to which we must now turn.

D. JOHN 6: SPIRIT AND EUCHARIST

It seems highly unlikely that any Christian community in the NT period would be unaware of the institutions of baptism and the Lord's Supper. Thus Robert Kysar's suggestion that "the johannine community did not know the. institution narratives in any form" is improbable.[116] It is striking that Paul's most direct use of a saying of Jesus refers to the eucharist (1 Cor. 11). That John knew of the Lord's Supper itself is evidenced in the upper room discourse (13:2). The meal is at Passover (13:1), it coordinates well with the evening of the Synoptic supper, and it is climaxed by the betrayal of Judas (13:2, 21-30). But John is silent concerning the words of institution (for reasons we hope to show). Yet does this silence mean that he possessed no such tradition? Most scholars answer this question by referring to John 6.

1. A EUCHARISTIC ALLUSION IN 6:1-15, 35-50?

Sacramentalist interpreters have found an emphasis on the eucharist throughout John 6. At the outset, however, the case for seeing a primary reference to the eucharist in 6:1-15 is tenuous at best.[117] The arguments for this position generally run as follows: (a) John's reference to the Passover (6:4) shows that for him "the Lord's Supper is destined to supplant" the Jewish festival (MacGregor). (b) The use of εὐχαριστεῖν (v. 11) is unlike the parallel feedings in the Synoptics (which use εὐλογεῖν) and echoes the words of institution in Paul and Luke (1 Cor. 11:24; Luke 22:19). (c) John's unique reference to satisfaction (v. 12) and the gathering of the fragments (v. 12b) parallels Did. 9:4 and 10:1, which apply these phrases to the eucharist (cf. κλάσμα, συνάγειν).[118] John also emphasizes that none of the fragments should be lost, and according to MacGregor this emphasis points to the "sacredness of the eucharistic bread."[119] (d) Finally, Brown notes that Jesus himself distributes the loaves just as he did at the Last Supper instead of giving them to the disciples (Mark 6:41; 8:6).

But this case can hardly be sustained.[120] Initially Jesus makes no mention

---

116. Kysar, *The Fourth Evangelist*, 259; Kysar's comment presupposes a redactional correction of both John 3 and 6.

117. A eucharistic reference is supported by Cullmann, *Early Christian Worship*, 93-102; Corell, *Consummatum Est*, 63-67; A. Schweitzer, *Mysticism*, 362-63; G. H. C. MacGregor, "The Eucharist in the Fourth Gospel," 114-16; A. Guilding, *The Fourth Gospel and Jewish Worship*, 58ff.; R. H. Lightfoot, *John*, 155-56; Brown, *John*, 1: 246-49. Cf. P. Borgen, *Bread from Heaven*, 188-92; and Barrett, *John*, 84, 273, 276, who are favorable to this view.

118. See esp. C. F. D. Moule, "A Note on Didache ix., 4," *JTS* 6 (1955) 240-43; Brown, *John*, 1:248.

119. MacGregor, *John*, 131.

120. For criticism, see Dunn, "John VI: A Eucharistic Discourse?" 332-33; Strachan, *John*, 184-85; Bultmann, *John*, 213n.2; Morris, *John*, 343-47; Sanders and Mastin, *John*, 178-79.

of the breaking of bread. This element is common to all accounts of the supper in the NT and even in Ignatius (Ign. *Eph.* 20:2). In addition, each of the above points can be faulted. (a) John's mention of Passover probably refers to the manna metaphor in the subsequent discourse. Jesus' provision is certainly meant to contrast and supersede the Jewish festival, but this fulfillment is not found in the eucharistic bread but in Jesus himself (6:35, 48). (b) Although it is clear that εὐχαριστεῖν became a technical term in the postapostolic age,[121] similar certainty does not surround the NT period. Matthew and Mark use it in their account of the feeding of the 4,000 (Matt. 15:36; Mark 8:6) and not in the opening of their supper accounts (εὐλογεῖν: Mark 14:22; Matt. 26:26; but cf. εὐχαριστεῖν: Matt. 26:37; Mark 14:23). This usage suggests that εὐχαριστεῖν and εὐλογεῖν may well have been synonyms.[122] It is likely that in this case Jesus is simply conforming to Jewish custom in giving thanks at table, for which εὐχαριστεῖν was the usual term in Greek (Mark 8:6; Matt. 15:36; John 6:23; Acts 27:35).[123] (c) Although John 6 and Did. 9 exhibit numerous parallels, it may be that the latter has come under John's influence, in which case it adds no independent evidence.[124] In this case the fragments that should not be lost could metaphorically refer to the preservation of disciples similarly mentioned in 6:39. (d) Finally, that Jesus distributes the bread need not be a eucharistic allusion if it is understood that Jesus as the Jewish host would naturally be credited with this honor even if his disciples assisted as in the Synoptics.[125]

The chief problem in this debate about the interpretation of 6:1-15 probably stems from the exhaustive sacramental use of the scene among the Apostolic Fathers.[126] For example, barley bread was apparently used in the early church on the basis of John 6:9, 13 (κρίθινος).[127] The result has been that scholars have presupposed for John 6:1-15 what was later concluded from it. Therefore we find no compelling evidence for a strictly eucharistic interpretation of this section.

In 6:35-50 the place of eucharistic themes has considerably less support and can be held only if such a stress is presupposed for the feeding miracle. Thus Brown (wrongly in our opinion) uses his evidence from 6:1-15 to argue for a eucharistic motif in the subsequent discourse.[128] But when studied on its

---

121. Conzelmann, *TDNT* 9: 414-15; cf. Did. 9:1ff.; 10:1-4; Justin *Apol.* 65:5; 66:2; 67:5; Ign. *Eph.* 13:1; Ign. *Phil.* 4:1.

122. Ibid., 411; note esp. the use of both in Mark 6:22-23; Beyer, *TDNT* 2: 761-63; Brown, *New Testament Essays*, 83n.14; Lindars, *John*, 242.

123. Str-B, 1: 685-86; Conzelmann, *TDNT* 9: 409-11; Bultmann, *John*, 213n.2; Barrett, *John*, 276. In 6:23 (cf. v. 26) εὐχαριστεῖν τὸν ἄρτον occurs, and some have argued that the singular (ἄρτος) confirms a eucharistic allusion. This evidence is not conclusive, however, and probably should be viewed as an echo of 6:11, 13. It is also important that vv. 22-24 are highly problematic in terms of content and style (note the unjohannine ὁ κύριος) and that εὐχαριστήσαντος τοῦ κυρίου is omitted by D, the Old Latin, and the Syriac. Barrett, *John*, 285, comments that it is hard to know why these words might have been left out if they were original, and further, that omissions in the Western text are always noteworthy.

124. Dunn, "John VI," 333; contra Dodd, "Eucharistic Symbolism in the Fourth Gospel," *Exp* 2 (1911) 534-35.

125. Str-B, 4: 621.

126. See Bernard, *John*, 1: clxvii-clxix; Brown, *New Testament Essays*, 83-84.

127. Brown, *John*, 1:232, cites J. McHugh, *VD* 39 (1961) 222-39.

128. Brown, *John*, 1: 274; cf. MacGregor, "The Eucharist in the Fourth Gospel," 115.

own, 6:35-50 cannot sustain such an interpretation. In the NT the manna analogy moves in two directions. Christologically (as Jesus uses it) it looks back to the feeding miracle as a prophetic fulfillment. Sacramentally it was later applied in Christian usage (e.g., Paul, 1 Cor. 10:1-4). In the present discourse, however, John's stress is entirely on Jesus and the identification of him as the descended bread. The accent throughout the discourse is on Jesus and believing on him (6:29, 35, 36, 40, 47, 64).[129] Brown points out that in 6:35 the inclusion of drink and thirst fails to make sense in a discourse devoted to bread unless we resort to a eucharistic interpretation.[130] On this point we can note two things. First, the wisdom background which the discourse employs made use of this dual metaphor to convey the singular thought of spiritual need and desire (Sir. 24:21; Isa. 44:10). Second, eating and drinking are contrasted with coming to and believing in Jesus. Therefore just as the bread is metaphorical for Jesus himself, the consumption of this bread might also be spiritualized: it is "simply a vivid metaphor for coming to and believing in Jesus."[131]

To be sure, the wisdom background of 6:35-50 is important.[132] The notion of "bread from heaven" as divine instruction (wisdom, Torah) is well rooted in OT and Jewish thought. Philo in particular makes the connection complete.[133] In the verses before us the eating/drinking motif suggests wisdom (Amos 8:11-13; Sir. 15:3; Prov. 9:5), as does the citation of what precedes belief, "they shall all be taught by God" (John 6:45; cf. Isa. 54:13). But once again revelation is nowhere mentioned as if it were independent of Jesus. Thus the bread in vv. 35-51 does not refer to wisdom apart from Jesus nor does the bread in vv. 52-58 refer to a bread other than the Lord: Jesus himself is central throughout. To assimilate this true bread is to acquire Jesus—and not another commodity.

In 6:27 it does appear that Jesus points forward to a subsequent food which he will give.[134] But this reference must be seen in how the believer will ultimately acquire this true bread. Just as the seal (σφραγίς) of Jesus suggests his own Spirit anointing,[135] so too the Spirit will facilitate the climax of the anticipated union of Christ and believer. Thus the food that will endure to eternal life (6:27c) will be the Spirit (14:16; cf. 4:14).[136] It is noteworthy that the climax at the end of the so-called "eucharistic section" parallels this thought: it

---

129. Dunn, "John VI," 333; Dodd, *Interpretation*, 338; Hoskyns, *John*, 288: "The theme of the discourse is therefore unbelief and faith."

130. Brown, *John*, 1: 274.

131. Dunn, "John VI," 333; cf. Swete, *The Holy Spirit*, 140-42; MacGregor, *John*, 145; Bultmann, *John*, 225-27.

132. See Brown, *New Testament Essays*, 84-85; idem, John, 1: 266-67; Lindars, *John*, 251; Barrett, *John*, 293; see Odeberg, *Fourth Gospel*, 235-69, for exhaustive references.

133. So Dodd, *Interpretation*, 336; cf. Str-B, 2: 481; and Schnackenburg, *John*, 2: 65.

134. The future (p^{75} A B f^{13} and majority; cf. 6:51) is to be preferred over δίδωσιν (א D), which probably derived from 6:32. The future points to a time after Jesus' glorification (7:39) when his gifts would be given (see Barrett, *John*, 287). Note the parallel use in 4:14 (τὸ ὕδωρ ὃ δώσω αὐτῷ), where the metaphor most likely refers to the Spirit, and the result of this giving is also eternal life (4:14 par. 6:27).

135. See above, pp. 84-85.

136. Dunn, *Baptism*, 184; cf. Bultmann, *John*, 224-25; Barrett, *John*, 287.

is the Spirit alone that gives life (v. 63). A literalistic application of either the manna metaphor (6:26-27) or the eucharistic bread (6:60-63) will be of no avail for eternal life.

2. THE "EUCHARISTIC SECTION," 6:51/52-58

While we cannot be assured of eucharistic references in 6:1-15 or 35-50/51, the general scholarly consensus is that eucharistic language is employed in some form in vv. 52-58. The earlier exhortation of coming to and believing in Jesus adopts a fresh metaphor in "eating the flesh and drinking the blood" of the Son of Man. The inclusion of these concepts (esp. blood) "is inescapably reminiscent of the Lord's Supper."[137]

a. Eucharistic Realism

An immediate objection to viewing 6:52-58 as eucharistic is John's use of σάρξ (flesh) as a part of his "words of institution."[138] While it is true that σῶμα is the customary term for the bread of the eucharist in the NT and most of the Apostolic Fathers (except Ign. *Rom.* 7:3; *Phil.* 4; and Justin *Apol.* 1:66, who employ σάρξ), Jeremias has set forth an impressive case for viewing John's use of σάρξ as independent and possibly older.[139] It seems incontestable that one Hebrew or Aramaic word stood behind both Greek terms, namely, בשׂר. The LXX translates בשׂר by σῶμα 23 times and by σάρξ 145 times.[140] Paul appears to use the words interchangeably in Rom. 8:13, and the Syriac translates σῶμα in Heb. 13:11 using *bisra*. This evidence suggests that Jesus' original words may have been the Aramaic דן בשׂרי and דן אדמי, and John provides the nearest translation. Schweizer adds support to this argument with the point that for what Jesus wanted to convey, σῶμα καὶ αἷμα was a highly unlikely phrase: σῶμα was rarely used to designate sacrifice.[141] But once this objection to σάρξ is removed, the parallel of 6:51c with other texts at once becomes evident.[142]

John 6:51c	1 Cor. 11:24 (Luke 22:19)
ὁ ἄρτος δὲ ὃν ἐγὼ δώσω	τοῦτό (= ἄρτον, 11:23)
ἡ σάρξ μού ἐστιν	μού ἐστιν τὸ σῶμα
ὑπὲρ τῆς τοῦ κόσμου ζωῆς	τὸ ὑπὲρ ὑμῶν (Luke, διδόμενον)

---

137. Marshall, *Last Supper*, 136; cf. C. T. Craig, "Sacramental Interest in the Fourth Gospel," 36; and Barrett, *John*, 299, "This unmistakenly points to the eucharist."

138. So Morris, *John*, 374-75.

139. J. Jeremias, *Eucharistic Words*, 198-201; followed by Brown, *John*, 1: 285; and Lindars, *John*, 267; cf. Bernard, *John*, clxvii, for a study of the references in Ignatius and Justin; also, W. F. Howard, *The Fourth Gospel in Recent Criticism*, Appendix E, 304-305.

140. Schweizer, *TDNT* 7: 108; cf. Bernard, *John*, clxx-clxxi.

141. *TDNT* 7: 1059.

142. See Jeremias, *Eucharistic Words*, 199. Cf. Borgen, *Bread from Heaven*, 91-98. The eucharistic identification was early at any rate. The Old Syriac translates 6:51c using *pagar* (body), while the Old Latin enlists *corpus*.

On the one hand, John may have a theological motive for his use of σάρξ. This is an important term in his incarnational theology. This Jesus who became "flesh" will offer this flesh in sacrifice, and union with Christ demands acceptance of this fact (1 John 4:2). In terms of a debate with a docetic error (which is evident in 1 John), this would be effective language to heighten the offense of the incarnation and thereby broaden the significance of eucharistic participation (a tactic employed by Ignatius).[143] If τρώγειν still carried in the first century the cruder notion of "gnaw" or "chew," this too could have served these purposes.[144]

John's introduction of αἷμα (blood) in the discourse makes the eucharistic application inescapable. In Judaism the literal drinking of animal blood— much less human blood—was prohibited (Gen. 9:4; Lev. 17:10, 12, 14). In a transferred sense it could take on the meaning of slaughter or carnage (Jer. 46:10; Ezek. 39:17). Therefore Brown is right in saying that to give these verses "a favorable meaning, they must refer to the eucharist."[145] The impossibility of Odeberg's attempt to view the entire discourse (vv. 35-58) in terms of the appropriation of wisdom lies here: while wisdom may refer to hunger and thirst or even eating, no wisdom text mentions drinking blood.

A final, less definitive allusion to the eucharist is suggested by the reference to Judas's betrayal. The necessity of belief is found in 6:64ff. and contrasted with those who fail to believe (v. 64), those who are not called (v. 65), and the withdrawal of some disciples (v. 66). But the supreme example of abortive discipleship is Judas Iscariot (6:70-71). Hint of this betrayal appears in the Synoptics only in the upper room and takes the disciples by surprise. Similarly, in John the Judas motif receives marked attention as an important element in the arrest sequence (13:2, 21ff.; 18:2-6). Its explicit appearance here is surprising, however, especially in view of the later astonishment of the apostolic company (13:22). If this evidence does not suggest Brown's hypothesis of a transposed Johannine pericope (see below), it at least points to a theme which was only associated with the upper room meal.[146]

---

143. So Cullmann, *Early Christian Worship*, 99-100; O. S. Brooks, "The Johannine Eucharist," *JBL* 82 (1963) 297; Higgins, *The Lord's Supper in the New Testament*, 82; Borgen, *Bread from Heaven*, 184-92. Fenton, *John*, 86-87, argues for a parallel setting in 1 John and John 6:52-58, as does MacGregor, "The Eucharist in the Fourth Gospel," 116-17.

144. Scholars are divided on this point, however; see below, n. 150. For a positive appraisal, see Cullmann, *Early Christian Worship*, 99; Bultmann, *John*, 236 n. 3; Brown, *John*, 1: 283; Hoskyns, *John*, 298-99; Bernard, *John*, 1:210-11; Ruland, "Sign and Sacrament," 450-51. John's only other use is in 13:18 where he cites Ps. 41:9 in which the LXX reads ἐσθίω.

145. Brown, *John*, 1: 284-85; cf. Bultmann, *John*, 235; C. H. Dodd, "Eucharistic Symbolism in the Fourth Gospel," 533 n.2.

146. Cullmann, *Early Christian Worship*, 101; cf. 112-13; Schnackenburg, *John*, 2: 78; Howard, *The Fourth Gospel in Recent Criticism*, 209; and M.-E. Boismard (as cited by Brown, *John*, 1: 303, who provides no reference). Important connectives between 6:70-71 and chap. 13 include: παραδίδωμι, 6:71/13:21; reference to Ἰούδας Σίμωνος, 6:71/13:26 (the only reference in the NT); stress on election, ἐκλέγομαι, 6:70/13:18. It is also interesting to note that outside of John 6, the only use of τρώγειν appears in 13:18, where it refers to Judas, "he who eats [ὁ τρώγων] my bread lifted up his heel against me."

b. Authenticity and Coherence

If we conclude that John expects his reader to think of the eucharist in 6:52-58, then it is clear that the Bread of Life discourse moves to a new theological plane (or at least adopts new metaphors). Thus it comes as no surprise to find that scholars who see this shift as important have argued that the section exhibits the strains of redactional activity.[147] A shift is certainly evident in that eucharistic terminology comes to the fore, but there is no radical break in thought as Bultmann or Lohse would suggest. Dunn has successfully shown that their efforts to exaggerate the distinctiveness of the pericope are ungrounded.[148] Literary studies which have attempted to set apart this passage (along with trying to identify a uniform "Johannine style") have run aground, while the authentic character of 6:52-58 has all but been confirmed.[149] The only significant changes from the context are the introduction of σάρξ, αἷμα, and τρώγειν (which, again, may be an irregular present of ἔφαγον).[150] Brown has impressively shown the particular conformity of vv. 52-58 with its context. Following Ruckstuhl and Jeremias,[151] Brown believes that 6:51-58 is a Johannine interpolation taken from a eucharistic setting and fully integrated into the present discourse. The latent eucharistic themes in vv. 35-50 are elevated in this "second Bread of Life discourse."[152] For example, both sections are introduced with "I am the bread of life" (vv. 35, 51) and jointly mention origins in heaven (vv. 38, 51), eternal life (vv. 40, 47, 53), manna as a contrasting motif (vv. 30ff., 49-51, 58), etc.[153] Even if we disagree with Brown as to the origin of the section, it is clear that the author (either John or a redactor) has either created a doublet or so fully adopted "Johannine language" as to make linguistic analyses perilously subjective. Of note is the inclusion of σάρξ in 6:51c

---

147. See Bultmann, *John*, 234-37; G. Bornkamm, "Die Eucharistische Rede im Johannesevangelium," *ZNW* 47 (1956) 161-69; G. Richter, "Zur Formgeschichte und literarischen Einheit von Joh 6:31-58," *ZNW* 60 (1969) 21-55; Jeremias, *Eucharistic Words*, 106-108; E. Lohse, "Wort und Sakrament im Johannesevangelium," *NTS* 7 (1960-61) 110-25; C. Dekker, "Grundschrift und redaktion im Johannesevangelium," *NTS* 13 (1966-67) 77-78; cf. those listed by Borgen, *Bread from Heaven*, 25n.1; and more recently, Schnackenburg, *John*, 2: 435n.156.

148. Dunn, "John VI," 329.

149. E. Ruckstuhl, *Die literarische Einheit*, 220-21; cf. G. Richter, "Zur Formgeschichte"; and Klos, *Die Sakramente*, 59-69.

150. Τρώγειν does not appear in the LXX, Philo, or Josephus. It appears 6 times in the NT: Matt. 24:38; John 6:54, 56, 57, 58; 13:18. If it was "a popular substitution for ἐσθίω" (BDF, § 51), it is curious that John, who does not use ἐσθίω at all (but employs ἔφαγον 15 times), does not distribute the present tense throughout his Gospel. Compare the ratio of presents to aorists in the following: Matthew, 11 to 13; Mark, 11 to 17; Luke 12 to 21 (all of which exhibit equal distribution).

151. Ruckstuhl, *Die literarische Einheit*; J. Jeremias, "Joh 6:51c-58, redaktionell?" *ZNW* 44 (1952-53) 256-57; idem, *Eucharistic Words*, 107-108; cf. the criticisms of J. E. L. Oulton, *Holy Communion and Holy Spirit* (London: SPCK, 1951) 76-77.

152. Brown, *John*, 1:287-88; cf. idem, *New Testament Essays*, 85-92. Lindars argues similarly that vv. 51c-58 are necessary to complete latent themes in vv. 35-50, i.e., that Jesus who is the bread of life must die. "The object of these verses is thus, not to relate the discourse to the eucharist, but to exploit the eucharistic words for the needs of the discourse"; see "Word and Sacrament," 60.

153. See further, Dunn, "John VI," 329; and Brown, *John*, 1: 288-89.

before the clear Johannine literary divider of the Jews' dispute and Jesus' answer (vv. 52-53).

The unity and disunity of the discourse have been argued by methods other than linguistic studies. Peder Borgen has convincingly shown that John may have employed Jewish homiletic forms in the discourse.[154] In this case John 6 is an extended synagogue midrash on Ps. 78:24 (cf. Exod. 16:4, 15) that necessarily includes the "eucharistic section." In Borgen's view, 6:52-58 is an explanation of "to eat" which leads naturally to the eucharist, and 6:58 is a concise homiletic summary. This analysis gives impressive weight to the coherence of the entire discourse and reduces the likelihood of the final unit being an insertion.

Bornkamm believes that while linguistic study may not conclusively eliminate the passage, neither can it substantiate its authenticity.[155] But his claim that the offense recorded in v. 60 connects up with 6:50 (καταβαίνω, ἀναβαίνω, υἱὸς τοῦ ἀνθρώπου, v. 27) and thus reveals vv. 51c-58 as an intrusion fails to convince. While it is clear that 6:60ff. follows on the earlier problem of "descent," it is not so clear that these final verses have nothing to do with vv. 52-58. The frailty of Bornkamm's case has been identified by various critics, among them Klos.[156] The descent motif as well as the Son of Man is central to the eucharistic section as well as to the others (6:27, 53, 58, 62).[157] Thus the discourse was surely intended to be viewed as a whole.[158] Even if a critical re-editing is assumed, one such as Bultmann must admit that to this editor the σκληρὸς λόγος of 6:60 "consisted in the fact that the historical Jesus, while he was still alive, had referred to his flesh and blood as food."[159]

Dunn rightly points out that the really scandalous thing is this very talk of eating the Son of Man who has descended. Such a thought was abhorrent to Jewish ears.[160] If this is the case, it is both the christological notion of Jesus' descent as the true bread (6:41, 50) and the identification of this bread as his flesh which must be consumed that brings about the ultimate offense. His listeners do stumble on the former, but also their growing fears (ἐμάχοντο οὖν πρὸς ἀλλήλους, v. 52) are turned to horror when the discourse is com-

---

154. P. Borgen, "The Unity of the Discourse in John 6," *ZNW* 50 (1959) 277-78; idem, "Observations on the Midrashic Character of John 6," *ZNW* 54 (1963) 232-40; idem, *Bread from Heaven*, 28-58, and on John 6, pp. 59-98. Cf. R. Schnackenburg, "Zur Rede vom Brot aus dem Himmel: Eine Beobachtung zur Joh 6, 52," *BZ* 12 (1968) 248-52, who supports Borgen's thesis. But see the general criticisms of Borgen by G. Richter, "Zur Formgeschichte," passim, and his explicit critique of Schnackenburg, 54-55. Borgen is also reviewed by Johnston, *Spirit-Paraclete*, 131-35. Cf. the alternative earlier studies of B. Gärtner, *John 6 and the Jewish Passover* (Lund: Gleerup, 1959); and A. Guilding, *The Fourth Gospel and Jewish Worship*.

155. G. Bornkamm, "Die Eucharistische Rede," 161-69; also Brown, *John*, 1: 299-300.

156. Klos, *Die Sakramente*, 60-63; also, Dunn, "John VI," 330-31.

157. So C. K. Barrett, "Das Fleisch des Menschensohnes," 342-54.

158. Klos admits (p. 61) that a redactor could have absorbed the vocabulary of the context, but if this is admitted the exclusion of the section is then forced to rest on wholly unobjective criteria. Cf. Bultmann, *John*, 235n.4: "The editor clearly models himself on the evangelist's technique. . . ." Bultmann then goes on to reject the text.

159. Bultmann, *John*, 237.

160. Dunn, "John VI," 330; Dodd, *Interpretation*, 341.

pleted in 6:58. Therefore Jesus' dialogue with his disconcerted disciples must point to this entire picture.[161]

c. John 6:60-63 and the Antecedent of Σάρξ

Thus the σάρξ of 6:63 has to point back to the σάρξ of 6:52, 53, etc., in the context of the dual scandal mentioned above.[162] One of the major problems in the thesis supported by Bornkamm is that σάρξ does not appear in vv. 35-50. It appears only in 6:51c-56. Moreover, Barrett perceptively notes that in these verses Jesus offers "my flesh," or "the flesh of the Son of Man." But the crowd is confused about how Jesus can give simply "flesh" to eat.[163] "Flesh as such will do men no more good than quails in the desert, but the flesh of the Son of Man is the vehicle of the Spirit."[164] In this manner, it may be important that in 6:63 Jesus does not say "my flesh" is useless, but that "flesh" (unqualified) is of no avail.

Thus the dual scandal points to the notion of incarnation and the thought of the personal appropriation of this incarnate life. To interpret the σάρξ of v. 63 by means of the general usage in, for example, 3:6, does not exclude this interpretation. In both cases, σάρξ is the world of humanity which the Logos must enter in order to bring life. One of the chief aims of John's christology is to present the full offense of a literal incarnation (1:14; 1 John 4:2). But the Logos in flesh cannot be appropriated: it *is* of no avail. Just as in any human being it is not the σάρξ but the πνεῦμα that is the life principle, so it is in Jesus. It is the Logos crucified— σάρξ as sacrifice (6:51c)— which can give eternal life.[165] The believer must look to Jesus' glorification in which his flesh is sacrificed and the Spirit is given (7:39). Likewise a material appreciation of the eucharist (flesh and blood, 6:53ff.) must be refused. Just as the crowds wrongly focused on the loaves (v. 26) and missed their spiritual

---

161. Dodd, *Interpretation*, 340-41; Strachan, *John*, 196; Bernard, *John*, 1: 216; Borgen, *Bread from Heaven*, 190-92; Schnackenburg, *John*, 2:69; Guilding, *The Fourth Gospel and Jewish Worship*, 59; Barrett, *John*, 284, 302.

162. Contra Bornkamm, "Die Eucharistische Rede," 167; Brown, *John*, 1: 299-300; Johnston, *Spirit-Paraclete*, 22-25, 28; Borgen, *Bread from Heaven*, 191.

163. Τὴν σάρκα αὐτοῦ is read by p⁶⁶ B T, while αὐτοῦ is omitted by p⁷⁵ ℵ C D K f¹ f¹³. Even though external evidence is well balanced (see Metzger, *Textual Commentary*, 214; Brown, *John*, 1: 282), the shorter reading seems best: (1) the addition may reflect a scribal accommodation to the context for clarity; (2) the original reading better represents Johannine irony in the use of incredulous misunderstanding (so Barrett, *John*, 298).

164. Barrett, *John*, 302; cf. idem, "Das Fleisch des Menschensohnes," 348-49. Citing the support of Jeremias, Sidebottom, *Christology*, 133, translates: "The Spirit makes alive, the flesh only is of no avail." Cf. Corell, *Consummatum Est*, 85; Schnackenburg, *John*, 2:71; and J. Pascher, "Der Glaube als Mitteilung des Pneumas nach Joh 6,61-65," *TThQ* 117 (1936) 315ff.

165. Higgins, *The Lord's Supper*, 83. H. Schürmann, "Joh 6:51c—ein Schlüssel zur johanneischen Brotrede," *BZ* 2 (1958) 244-62, shows that σάρξ in 6:51c points not to eucharistic flesh but to sacrifice and death. That δώσω . . . ὑπέρ points to Jesus' death is indicated from John's frequent use of ὑπέρ (Matthew 5 times; Mark 2 times; Luke 5 times; John 13 times), which in all but four instances points to death (cf. John 10:11, 15; 11:50, 51-52; 15:13; 17:19; 18:14). See Bultmann, *John*, 235n.1, for parallel uses in the NT. Similarly, the notion of sacrifice is inherent in the thought of "flesh and blood"; so Dunn, "John VI," 331n.1.

significance, the eucharistic elements must be viewed as bearing a deeper spiritual reality. This σάρξ also is of no avail.

This redirection away from "flesh" finds its complete answer in 6:62, 63, in terms of the Spirit and the ascension. Dodd remarks that "this is the clue that the reader must hold fast in attempting to understand the discourse."[166] We are thus drawn once again into the Johannine complex of death-resurrection-ascension-Spirit that will give to the believer the very power of eternal life suggested throughout the discourse. This thought parallels John 3:13-15, where we learned that through the death of the Son of Man and his ascension, the believer gains new birth and its resultant eternal life.[167] In the Bread of Life discourse, the lasting food of the Son of Man provides eternal life (v. 27), and the descended manna—the true bread of God—will also give eternal life (vv. 32-33). The consumption of the Son of Man's flesh and blood will give eternal life as well (v. 54). The climactic answer to all these metaphors is finally realized in 6:63, "it is the Spirit that gives life." Therefore the death of Jesus (6:51c) and his ascent (6:63) will bring the Spirit, which will achieve the life-bearing union between Christ and disciple (20:22). To consume the Son of Man thus means union with Christ, and this union is brought about through receiving the Spirit.

3. John's Theology of the Eucharist

We have found that the discourse should be viewed as a unified whole, that the eucharist motif surfaces only in 6:52-58, and that σάρξ in the final dialogue of vv. 60-65 refers back not only to the wisdom section (vv. 35-51) but equally to the offensiveness of the realistic language in 6:52-58. We have thereby also ruled out the objection of Bultmann and Bornkamm that 6:52ff. is a departure from Johannine theology by virtue of its supposed stress on sacramental grace.[168] On the contrary, to argue that the discourse is unified is alone a cogent plea against this view: 6:60-65 then forms a corrective to the very sacramental error these scholars seem to have located in the text.

a. The Nature of the Corrective

The displacement of the eucharistic theme from its traditional mooring to the present context supports our point. John intends to integrate the meaning of the eucharist into the broader work and words of Jesus and thereby give it a

---

166. Dodd, *Interpretation*, 341; also cited by Dunn, ibid., 336; cf. Barrett, *John*, 301: "All that has been said about the bread of life must be viewed in light of two facts: the ascension and the gift of the Spirit." See also R. H. Lightfoot, *John*, 169; and Schnackenburg, *John*, 2: 71-72.

167. Dodd, *Interpretation*, 342; Lindars, *John*, 267; cf. Pascher, "Der Glaube als Mitteilung des Pneumas," 316-17; and MacGregor, "The Eucharist in the Fourth Gospel," 118.

168. Bultmann, *John*, 218-20; Bornkamm, "Die Eucharistische Rede," 168-69.

169. Barrett, *John*, 297; cf. Oulton, *Holy Communion*, 78-79; Lee, *The Religious Thought of St. John*, 185. See Howard, *The Fourth Gospel in Recent Criticism*, 212: "The upper room was no room for doctrinal polemic."

strictly personal interpretation.[169] J. Jeremias has suggested a different solution to this problem. But his attempt to show that John has concealed the mystery of the supper and protected it from profanation accords ill with his belief that the upper room discourses were themselves secret material.[170] If one of the purposes of the Fourth Gospel was concealment, why were these discourses revealed? It is indisputable that an arcane discipline existed (Jeremias's evidence is conclusive), but it is unclear how the Fourth Gospel fits this general picture.

It is best to conclude that John is avoiding the undue stress on the sacramental elements that is later evident in Ignatius ("medicine of immortality," φάρμακον ἀθανασίας, Ign. *Eph.* 20:2), and that the realism of his language springs from his consistent christological polemic against docetism. That the Johannine community had responded to this docetism with sacramental literalism—and the Evangelist is correcting both groups, according to Dunn—remains uncertain.[171] But at least the contours of the critique are clear.

First, the sacramental elements in themselves do not contain what they promise but are metaphors for that spiritual union with Jesus anticipated throughout the discourse. Those who place undue stress on the physical exhibit the same error as that rebuffed in John 3 and 4. Spiritual rebirth and living water are likewise metaphors for a deeper reality in the Spirit that in each case these people confuse (3:4; 4:11, 15). Thus it is best to say that John provides eucharistic teaching indirectly. His aim is to point readers away from an apparently traditional use and interpretation and lead them to true union with Christ in Spirit.[172] It is interesting that in John 13 the only mention of "eucharistic bread" being given refers to Judas. In the very act of receiving it (13:27) the devil enters into him. Thus for Judas, the only literal communicant in this Gospel, this eating became a communion not with Jesus but with Satan.[173]

Second, an important element in this corrective is faith. As in 6:35, eating and drinking should refer to belief in Jesus. The eucharist retains no magical properties, but through it faith is called forward and the believer may encounter Christ in Spirit.[174] It is no accident that after Jesus points his disciples to the Spirit and the ascension, he adds the rebuke: "but there are some of you that do not believe" (v. 64). Indeed, faith indicates the division between those who fall back (v. 66) and those who, with Peter, press on to eternal life (vv. 68ff.). Yet

---

170. *Eucharistic Words*, 125-37; also W. L. Knox, *Some Hellenistic Elements in Primitive Christianity* (1946), as cited by Lee, *The Religious Thought of St. John*, 185. Cullmann is criticized by Higgins, *The Lord's Supper*, 74; Bultmann, *John*, 472n.5, 485; and Lindars, "Word and Sacrament," 61. But Lindars believes that John omitted the words in chap. 13 in order to give primacy to the theme of discipleship and the betrayal of Judas.

171. "John VI," 337-38.

172. Pascher, "Der Glaube als Mitteilung des Pneumas," 320; Ladd, *Theology*, 285; cf. Odeberg, *Fourth Gospel*, 237-39; and Barrett, "Das Fleisch des Menschensohnes," 349.

173. MacGregor, "The Eucharist in the Fourth Gospel," 113. On the other hand, too much should not be made of this. Schweizer, for example, uses these verses to refer to "a sort of 'Satanic sacrament'"; see "The Conception of the Church in St. John," 238; also, Bultmann, *John*, 482.

174. MacGregor, ibid., 116; Klos, *Die Sakramente*, 67, 73.

this faith is fully confessional: it is filled with content about who Jesus is (the Holy One of God) and the reality of his complete incarnation. Those who fail to believe (in the Johannine community setting) might also be termed those who fail to possess the Spirit.

b. *Praesentia Realis* and the Spirit

If we attempt to draw together the divergent threads of John's theology of the eucharist, it becomes evident that two themes emerge. John is concerned that Jesus and his vicarious death remain the center of the church's eucharistic worship. Equally important, through the Spirit the believer is united with Christ in his work in the context of eucharistic participation.

The centrality of Jesus was a theme we heard throughout the entire discourse. Thus eucharistic symbols are only of use when they point the Christian to the full humanity and sacrificial death of Jesus. John's literal synchronizing of the death of Christ with the Jewish Passover stresses his interest in viewing this new Christian Passover meal sacrificially.[175] Thus the object of faith is always Jesus—Jesus crucified. The elements should lead the believer beyond themselves to the Jesus who stands behind them: fully present through the presence of the Spirit.

Union with Christ in Spirit is John's second theme. To consume the elements is to be one with the eucharist host (Jesus). Some have argued that John has heightened this thought of mystical union at the expense of any notion of sacrifice. Thus Dodd remarks that "John is preoccupied, not with sacrificial theory, but with his doctrine of mystical communion."[176] But this interpretation puts undue stress on John 13 and 15 and fails to draw out the sacrificial undertone of 6:51-58.[177] Thus union in death is vital (cf. Paul in 1 Cor. 10:16-17). But it is also through this death that the Spirit is given, and this gift fulfills the eucharistic promises. Thus once again the elements point to Jesus, union with Jesus, and finally to Jesus in Spirit. T. F. Torrance has clearly seen this stress on union, death, and Spirit in the Fourth Gospel: "The mystery of the eucharist is not to be understood in terms of external causal relations between Christ and the eucharist or between the eucharist and ourselves, but in terms of our participation through the Spirit in what the whole Christ, the incarnate, crucified, risen, and ascended Son, is in respect both of his activity from the Father towards mankind and of his activity from mankind towards the Father.

---

175. Stauffer, *Theology*, 164. Higgins, *The Lord's Supper*, 77-78, contends that John's alignment of cross and Passover and the displacement of the supper theme to chap. 6 is primarily to align the eucharist with the incarnation.

176. Dodd, "Eucharist Symbolism," 545-46; cf. MacGregor, "The Eucharist in the Fourth Gospel," 112.

177. Even John 15:13, in this regard, might conceal the notion of sacrifice, though not the full concept of vicarious suffering. But note how John employs here a ὑπέρ clause (see above, p. 185n.165) which parallels Synoptic eucharistic formulas (Mark 14:24; Luke 20:22) and evokes the image of sacrificial death. See Barrett, *John*, 476-77; and Brown, *John*, 2: 673.

It is Christ himself, in his paschal mystery, who constitutes the living content, reality, and power of the eucharist."[178]

In that the Spirit draws the believer into union with Christ, who was truly incarnate and who died, eucharistic participation serves to usher the believer toward eternal life (6:53, 54). As in baptismal water, bread and wine are simply our Godward expression of faith. But within this worship, the movement of God toward us involves the Spirit, who accomplishes both the rebirth and the union through his transforming of our worship and material expressions. It is what we might term pneumatic worship (χρῖσμα, 1 John 2:20; etc.) that John hopes for in the eucharist as the Spirit actively leads us to Christ.

4. Does John 15:1-17 Refer to the Eucharist?

In view of the popularity of the vine image in the OT, in Judaism, and even in Hellenistic religions,[179] it seems difficult to agree with those who would claim to have identified a direct reference to the eucharist here.[180] For example, this vine motif does not mention the believer drinking, and as Bultmann points out, there is no mention of wine. Having said this, however, John's use of ἄμπελος parallels what appears to be a NT usage almost limited to the eucharistic setting (τὸ γένημα τοῦ ἀμπελοῦ, Mark 14:25; Matt. 26:29; Luke 22:18).[181] But MacGregor clearly strains the evidence when he says that "the vine was a recognized eucharistic symbol at the time the gospel was written."[182] To be sure, fine examples of a eucharistic interpretation of John 15 can be found in the postapostolic church—the vine emerging from a chalice in early church apse painting being especially noteworthy.[183] But one has to use parallels like Did. 9:2 as if they antedate the Fourth Gospel (as Dodd seems to) in order to give such arguments cogency.

On the other hand, could John have intended a secondary eucharistic meaning? In this case he may be doing much the same as he did in John 6 in that more or less remote images of the eucharist have been employed to give a veiled allusion. Four items suggest this interpretation. (a) The setting of the discourse is concurrent with the eucharistic meal. The problem of 14:31 in the Farewell Discourses is well known, but as Barrett points out, if John 14 is

---

178. T. F. Torrance, "The Paschal Mystery of Christ and the Eucharist," in *Theology in Reconstruction* (London: SCM; Grand Rapids: Eerdmans, 1975) 109.

179. On OT and Jewish parallels, see Bernard, *John*, 2: 477-78; and Brown, *John*, 2: 669-72; for non-Jewish usage, see Bultmann, *John*, 530-32; and Behm, *TDNT* 1: 342-43.

180. Cullmann, *Early Christian Worship*, 111-13; Marsh, *John*, 516; Corell, *Consummatum Est*, 73-74; MacGregor, *John*, 286ff.; D. M. Stanley, "I Am the Genuine Vine (John 15:1)," *BiTod* 1 (1963) 484-91; and esp. B. Sandvik, "Joh 15 als Abendmahlstext," *TZ* 23 (1967) 323-28.

181. Ἄμπελος occurs 3 times in John 15 and outside of the Synoptic eucharist setting only in Jas. 3:12 and Rev. 14:18, 19. In 1 Cor. 10 and 11, Paul employs τὸ ποτήριον.

182. MacGregor, "The Eucharist in the Fourth Gospel," 112; similarly, Dodd, "Eucharistic Symbolism," 539.

183. See Niewalda, *Sakramentssymbolik*, 76-79; Dodd, "Eucharistic Symbolism," 540-41. See the excellent examples of art in J. Wilpert, *Malereien der Katakomben Roms* (Freiburg: Herder, 1903).

viewed as an alternate version of the last discourse, the opening verses of John 15 might well follow the supper of John 13.[184] This point adds strength to the sacramental allusion hidden in the vine metaphor.

(b) There are also numerous thematic parallels with 6:51-58.[185] In both, mutual indwelling is stressed (μένειν, 15:5; 6:56);[186] wisdom may supply the background for some of the imagery; mutual indwelling comes through Jesus' death (15:13; 6:51); the sections are introduced with an "I am" saying (15:1; 6:51); and finally concern is shown for the fate of unbelievers (15:2, 6; 6:60ff.).

(c) The word plays a part in the sustenance of the believer. In John 6 it is a medium of life and the Spirit (6:63), while in John 15 this same word cleanses (15:3) and becomes a feature of Christ's indwelling (15:7).[187]

(d) Finally, the theological emphasis of John 15, when viewed together with a secondary eucharistic allusion, stands in concert with the sacramental corrective shown above for John 6. The primary aim of the vine discourse is to express the fruit-bearing union of Christ and disciple (μένειν, 11 times). Because this portrayed union is immediate, John 15 clearly excludes any view of sacramental grace, but this hardly invalidates any allusion to the Lord's Supper.[188] The immediate interiorization of Christ in Spirit is the desired emphasis of John in both chaps. 6 and 15. Eucharistic elements are secondary; Jesus is central. Yet even in John 15 it is the Spirit that prevails. MacGregor rightly sees the broader importance of the Farewell Discourses setting. Union with Christ the Vine must come about through the Spirit Paraclete. The most obvious fact is the most basic: the traditional (Synoptic) climax of the evening in the upper room was the institution of the eucharist. John's emphasis throughout is the personal indwelling of Jesus through the Paraclete. This is also his message about eucharistic worship.[189]

E. WORSHIP IN SPIRIT AND TRUTH: JOHN 4:20-24

The conclusion of Jesus' dialogue with the Samaritan woman serves not only as a fitting summary of the likely life setting of John 3 and 6, but also makes its own contribution to the nature of the Johannine concern for authentic spirituality. C. K. Barrett observes that John 4 offers general reflections on worship

---

184. Barrett, *John*, 470; Sanders and Mastin, *John*, 336; Marsh, *John*, 516; MacGregor, *John*, 112; Johnston, *Spirit Paraclete*, 162-71; J. M. Reese, "The Literary Structure of John 13:31–14:31; 16:5-6, 16-33," *CBQ* 34 (1972) 321-31. Cullmann's attempt to see the betrayal of Judas in John 15 is farfetched (*Early Christian Worship*, 112-13; see 13:10 par. 15:2).

185. Higgins, *The Lord's Supper*, 86, comments that "the fifteenth chapter is, in fact, a very close counterpart to the sixth." Cf. Cullmann, *Early Christian Worship*, 111-12; Brown, *New Testament Essays*, 72-73; idem, *John* 2: 673.

186. Malatesta notes that in John, with the exception of 14:10, all of the personal indwelling texts are concentrated in two chapters, John 6 and 15. He concludes: "The communion between the disciples and Christ expressed by μένειν ἐν is understood primarily in relationship to Christ as the living bread (John 6) and as the true vine (John 15), that is, in relationship to the eucharist" (*Interiority and Covenant*, 31).

187. R. H. Lightfoot, *John*, 163; Dunn, "John VI," 335.

188. Dunn, ibid.

189. See esp. Brown, *John*, 2: 674; Barrett, *John*, 84, 470-71; and Lindars, "Word and Sacrament," 62-63.

while chaps. 3 and 6 are specific.[190] This exchange in 4:20-24 does not focus simply on the rejection of ritualism and ceremony—although this element must be considered. Nor does it merely deliberate the values of inner spiritual experience as opposed to outward ceremonies. For John, the decisive new factor in this new worship is the introduction of Jesus—the facilitator of true worship. John 4:20-24 presupposes in the reader's mind a knowledge of the Spirit, clearly anticipated through the living water image (4:7-15; see above), which is given to effect this worship. Thus Jesus will not become embroiled in a controversy over Gerizim and Jerusalem (vv. 20-21): he shifts the question from the place of worship to the manner of worship.[191]

1. THE CRITERIA OF TRUE WORSHIP

In both John 3 and 6 the Evangelist employs a historical perspective in which later, post-resurrection events are proleptically offered in the life of Jesus. Thus we found in 6:52ff. eucharistic language describing real union with Christ which would only come through the Spirit. In John 3 the same could be argued for rebirth. The surprising use of plurals in 3:11-12 (cf. the difficult 3:13) may confirm this view and suggest that the Evangelist is fully aware of the contemporary relevance of these passages in his own life setting. In John 4 we find parallel phenomena. John 4:22 echoes 3:11 in what might be termed a "community perspective": "you worship what you do not know, we worship what we know" (ὑμεῖς προσκυνεῖτε ὃ οὐκ οἴδατε. ἡμεῖς προσκυνοῦμεν ὃ οἴδαμεν).[192]

This "co-projection" (i.e., having two temporal references)[193] becomes evident in 4:23, "the hour is coming and now is" (ἔρχεται ὥρα, καὶ νῦν ἐστιν; cf. 5:25). While one is tempted to refer the former phrase to Jesus' perspective and the latter to John's, another solution may be at hand. Linked to this phrase is John's specialized use of "the hour." Ὥρα occurs 26 times in John and frequently refers to "the hour" of glorification. As Brown has shown, however, this specialized meaning follows John's use of ὥρα with the definite article.[194]

---

190. Barrett, "The Holy Spirit in the Fourth Gospel," 6.

191. The question of the place of worship recedes even more once it is remembered that John Hyrcanus destroyed the Samaritan temple on Gerizim in 128 B.C. Cf. Josephus *Ant.* 13:255-56; 18:85-87 (Str-B, 1: 549ff.; Lindars, *John*, 188). If a post-70 perspective is presupposed for John these verses could also be pregnant with meaning for Judaism. See A. E. J. Rawlinson, "In Spirit and in Truth: an Exposition of St. John 4:16-24," *ExpTim* 44 (1932-33) 14.

192. There are seven plurals in 4:21-22. The suggestion that all of these reflect a later dispute of Christians against Samaritans is not demanded if the plurals in the second person refer generally to the Samaritans who will later appear. (Note that the singular οἶδα in v. 25 [p⁶⁶* p⁷⁵ ℵ* A B C D] is to be preferred over the later οἴδαμεν.) G. Johnston, *Spirit-Paraclete*, 135-36, argues for this perspective in John 3. Cf. F. Mussner, "The We-Formula," in *The Historical Jesus in the Gospel of John*, 70ff. Mussner refers on p. 70n.12 to the early study of A. von Harnack (1923). This perspective may also be reflected in the plurals of 1:14, 16.

193. B. Olsson, *Structure and Meaning*, 196; cf. Porsch, *Pneuma*, 147ff.; and N. A. Dahl, "The Johannine Church and History," in *Jesus in the Memory of the Early Church* (Minneapolis: Augsburg, 1976) 99-119.

194. This excludes clearly temporal phrases (19:14, 27; etc.). See 2:4; 4:52; 7:30; 8:30; 12:23, 27 (bis); 13:1; 16:4; 17:1; Brown, *John*, 1: 517-18.

When it is without the article, the reference is generally to the effects of the hour of death present even before this point.[195] In three of these instances "an hour" is referred to as coming and yet already present: in 5:25 eternal life is available to those already dead; in 16:32 persecution and scattering are mentioned; and in 4:23 true worship is described in terms of the Spirit to come (7:39). Yet even in these references, their true fulfillment comes only after the cross and resurrection. Therefore we probably should say that this fluid chronological perspective means that chiefly later experiences are present in an incipient and anticipated way before the cross. This view parallels the Synoptic tension between present and future in the kingdom sayings. In Jesus' person the kingdom of God is present in power, and subsequent to his death, this power continues in the Spirit. But it is not until the eschaton that the kingdom will be finally fulfilled. For John's own readers in the present context, this "now" (νῦν) speaks directly to their experience in which the Spirit has come. Worship in Spirit and truth was certainly an essential experience in the Johannine community.

a. God Is Spirit

Although the announcement of worship appears twice, it is centered on a more basic statement about the nature of God (4:24). Commentators agree that πνεῦμα ὁ θεός is not so much a Greek philosophical definition of who God is as it is a description of his dynamic attributes in relation to human beings.[196] He is the God who gives the Spirit (14:16), and the Spirit in turn becomes the medium of his relation to human beings. Two similar descriptions in 1 John bear this sense: God is light (1:5) and God is love (4:8). This is how God acts in respect to the world. God gives the world light through his Son (3:19; 8:12; 9:5) as a tangible sign of his love (3:16). To say to a human being that God is Spirit is to say that their relationship must be a spiritual relationship. Because God is Spirit, human beings must possess the Spirit.[197]

This basic definition therefore puts constraints on the worshiper. He must experience the medium inherent to God when God chooses to join himself to humanity. Schnackenburg therefore points out that what we have is a thought complementary to John 3. One must be joined with "the above"—be born of the Spirit—in order to share in the discipleship of Jesus, who has descended from this place.[198] The entire orientation of worship in Spirit and truth should point away from personal efforts and ambitions and focus on the power of God at work.

b. Worship in Spirit

This kind of worship must therefore be eminently spiritual by virtue of the object of its adoration. But when Jesus twice stresses human activity in this

---

195. See 4:21, 23; 5:25, 28; 16:2, 25, 32.

196. Porsch, *Pneuma*, 150; Brown, *John*, 1: 172; Odeberg, *The Fourth Gospel*, 172; Schweizer, *TDNT* 6: 439; contra Johnston, *Spirit-Paraclete*, 15-16.

197. Lindars, *John*, 190.

198. See the commentaries of Schnackenburg, 1: 439; Lindars, 190; Barrett, 239; Bultmann, 190; Brown, 1: 181. Cf. Odeberg, *The Fourth Gospel*, 170ff.

endeavor (4:23, 24b), is his emphasis on the inner emotional experience of the believer? Scholars have suggested various possibilities for viewing this meaning. On the one hand, πνεῦμα here could refer to the inner spiritual recesses of the believer in which he should contemplate God.[199] Dodd similarly spoke of an abstract or generalized worship as opposed to corporeal objects and a fixed cult.[200] On the other hand, Schnackenburg, Brown, and Porsch argue compellingly that πνεῦμα is an exterior power from God mediated by Christ.[201] Therefore, as Hoskyns has so famously observed, the worshiper must look outward "towards the flesh and blood of Jesus."[202] This Spirit is the very Spirit that descended upon and remained with Jesus.[203]

Even though Jesus is not mentioned explicitly, it is inherent in these words that he will supply the Spirit which will empower this worship. It is here that the living water metaphor becomes vital. Once the woman recognizes the identity of Jesus, the significance of this water (the Spirit) becomes clear: Jacob's well is excluded just as are Jerusalem and Gerizim.[204] Hence "spiritual worship is not a privilege for the spiritually minded, but is a possibility of all who receive the Spirit from Jesus, who himself is the true means of worship, the place where God and man are united."[205] The inner experience of the believer is therefore important only by virtue of the Spirit he has received. Worship in Spirit affirms spiritual activity which incorporates the union of worshiper with Christ through the Spirit that Christ himself has provided. To this extent, in John 4:20ff. we have drawn close to the Pauline notion: worship ἐν πνεύματι is also worship ἐν Χριστῷ.[206]

c. Worship in Truth

The addition of ἀλήθεια may confirm either of the two possibilities described above.[207] It can mean worship that is genuine and grounded in reality (ἀληθῶς), or it can draw in the christological stress as with πνεῦμα. The latter choice is the best alternative. John's frequent use of "truth" indicates his interest in a

---

199. Bernard, *John*, 1: 149. J. Bligh, "Jesus in Samaria," *HeyJ* 3 (1962) 338, refers to the "spiritual condition of the worshipper." This view has been also supported by Zahn, Westcott, Bauer, Loisy, and others; cf. Porsch, *Pneuma*, 152n.72.

200. Dodd, *Interpretation*, 170, 223, 314; cf. Porsch, *Pneuma*, 152n.73; πνεῦμα might thus be understood adverbially, προσκυνεῖν ἐν πνεύματι = προσκυνεῖν πνευματικῶς.

201. Schnackenburg, *John*, 1:436-37; Brown, *John*, 1: 180; Porsch, *Pneuma*, 152-54; contra E. D. Freed, "The Manner of Worship in John 4:23f.," in *Search the Scriptures: NT Studies in Honor of R. T. Stamm*, ed. J. M. Meyers et al., Gettysburgh Theological Studies 3 (Leiden: Brill, 1969) 37-38.

202. Hoskyns, *John*, 245, cited frequently. The full quotation runs as follows: "Inadequate worship is worship that rests purely upon the hope of some future action of God. True worship is directed towards the flesh and blood of Jesus because there ye shall see heaven open, and the angels of God ascending and descending upon the Son of Man (1:51)."

203. Marsh, *John*, 218; cf. Bultmann, *TDNT* 1: 246-47.

204. Dodd, *Interpretation*, 314; R. H. Lightfoot, *John*, 124.

205. Barrett, "The Holy Spirit in the Fourth Gospel," 6; Bultmann, *John*, 191.

206. Schweizer, *TDNT* 6: 439; Schnackenburg, *John*, 1: 438; Porsch, *Pneuma*, 160.

207. Bernard, *John*, 1: 150, notes that the only variant is in ℵ*, which reads ἐν πνεύματι ἀληθείας (cf. 14:17).

specialized meaning.[208] Rather than following the Greek usage meaning non-concealment (as argued by Dodd and Bultmann), Brown is right in finding a Jewish background here that stresses the personal and moral features of God's revelation, and possibly even wisdom.[209] In fact, John's notion of truth is intertwined with his presentation of Jesus (for which wisdom categories are important): Jesus is the truth (14:6) in that he reveals in his person the highest reality of God (8:45; 18:37). Moreover, the Spirit is the Spirit of Jesus and he is identified as the "Spirit of Truth" (14:17; 15:26; 16:13; cf. 1 John 4:6; 5:7). Therefore truth and Spirit must function as a unity especially in their dependence on Jesus.[210] John's use of a single preposition governing both substantives confirms this interpretation. The sphere of Christian worship is delineated by the power brought by the resurrected Christ ($\pi\nu\epsilon\tilde{\upsilon}\mu\alpha$) and the single basis of this supernatural life, Jesus Christ ($\dot{\alpha}\lambda\acute{\eta}\theta\epsilon\iota\alpha$).[211] Therefore worship in Spirit and truth is worship that is focused on and empowered by Jesus.

In recent discussion, two scholars have independently concluded that Qumran's parallel use of "Spirit and truth" should form the background for our present passage. Schnackenburg and more adamantly Freed have noted that "Spirit and truth" at Qumran denote ethical conduct as a means of proper worship.[212] Thus in 1QS 4:20 God will cleanse and purify the community both by his truth and by the Spirit of holiness, causing "the spirit of truth to gush forth" (4:21). Freed argues that John is unique in his stress on doing the truth ($\pi\text{oie}\tilde{\iota}\nu \tau\grave{\eta}\nu \dot{\alpha}\lambda\acute{\eta}\theta\epsilon\iota\alpha\nu$, John 3:21; 1 John 1:6), and while there is ample OT and Jewish background for this usage (see LXX Isa. 26:10; Tob. 4:6; 13:6; Sir. 27:9; T. Jud. 20:1, 5), the Qumran writings parallel the Fourth Evangelist most closely.[213] Freed wants to drive a wedge between the use of $\pi\nu\epsilon\tilde{\upsilon}\mu\alpha$ in the description of God (John 4:24a) and the application of $\pi\nu\epsilon\tilde{\upsilon}\mu\alpha$ with truth in the surrounding texts. For him, "spirit and truth" is a hendiadys describing the sole effort of righteous conduct.

This view seems extreme.[214] In the first instance, Freed interprets the Fourth Gospel as if it had been written within the Dead Sea Community along

---

208. Ἀλήθεια occurs in Matthew once; Mark 3 times; Luke 3 times; John 25 times; 1–3 John 20 times. See Bultmann, TDNT 1: 241-47; Dodd, Interpretation, 170ff.; J. Blank, "Der johanneische Wahrheits-Begriff," BZ 7 (1963) 164-73; Brown, John, 1: 499ff.; Porsch, Pneuma, 155-59.

209. Brown, John, 1: 500; cf. Porsch, Pneuma, 156.

210. Schweizer, TDNT 6: 439; cf. F. Hahn, "Das biblische Verständnis des Heiligen Geistes," in Erfarhung und Theologie des Heiligen Geistes, ed. C. Heitmann and H. Mühlen (Hamburg: Agentur des Rauen Hauses; München: Kösel, 1974) 144; and J. McPolin, "The Holy Spirit in Luke and John," 129.

211. Barrett, John, 239.

212. Schnackenburg, "Die 'Anbetung in Geist und Wahrheit' (Joh 4,23) im Lichte vom Qumran-Texten," BZ 3 (1959) 88-94; cf. idem, John, 1: 437-38; E. D. Freed, "The Manner of Worship," 33-48. Important texts include 1QS 3:6-7; 4:20-21; 8:5-6; 9:3-6. Freed includes CD 2:12 and T. Gad 3:1. Cf. R. E. Breck, "The Spirit of Truth. A Study of the Background and Development of Johannine Pneumatology," unpub. diss., Rupprecht-Karl Universität, Heidelberg, 1971.

213. See 1QS 1:12-15; 3:18-26; 4:23-26; 5:3-5, 10-11; 8:1-4. See also Freed, ibid., 36-40. Cf. R. E. Brown, "The Qumran Scrolls and the Johannine Gospel and Epistles," CBQ 17 (1955) 403-19, 559-74.

214. See the criticisms of Brown, John, 1: 180-81.

with 1QS. John's vocabulary must be allowed to stand on its own. Moreover, Freed makes the fatal mistake of arguing that "the Spirit of Jesus and the Spirit of Truth are not the same."[215] This is the one fact quickly gleaned from the Farewell Discourses (see chapter 3 above). Spirit and truth are indeed a hendiadys, but they denote the Spirit who will bring the Truth, that is, Jesus. This Spirit will convey the true revelation of Christ about God in that it will convey Christ himself.[216] To be sure, John would hardly exclude ethics in his appeal for this worship (cf. 3:18ff. and 1 John 4:1-6 and the context of love), but this does not exhaust his meaning. Schnackenburg sees clearly that John has moved beyond Qumran. Here is his balanced appraisal: "In true worship there is an encounter with God for which God must make man capable by his grace. . . . If a man is to adore God in 'Spirit and truth,' he must first be filled and penetrated by the Spirit of God. . . . True adoration demands the 'doing of the truth' (John 3:21; 1 John 1:6)."[217]

2. SAMARIA, STEPHEN, AND JOHN

If we are correct that John 4:20-24 may form the manifesto for the Johannine community's concern for worship and that it accurately describes the life setting of John's sacramental corrective in both John 3 and 6, two features begin to stand out. First, this worship is christocentric. It is Jesus who both sends the Spirit and reveals the truth of God. Therefore only union with him in Spirit will bring about this worship. To this extent, Christ becomes a new center in faith and expression. Second, if the latter point is true, this worship overturns every other cultus. Moreover, another Gerizim or Jerusalem will not come to the fore—this worship has an interior quality. It is worship generated by God's Spirit within believers themselves.

But why is this emphasis introduced in John 4? Three suggestions have been advanced which repay consideration. (a) John Bowman has suggested that John may have been attempting to build "a bridge between Samaritans and Jews in Christ."[218] This view has merit in that John has used theological categories favorable in Samaria (e.g., a Moses christology) and presented Jesus as a kind of Samaritan *Taheb:* teaching the law and establishing true worship.[219] (b) Raymond Brown believes that this episode should be seen as a page in Johannine church history wherein Samaritan converts, with their anti-

---

215. Freed, "Manner of Worship," 38.

216. Porsch, *Pneuma*, 159, comments: "In reality, therefore, it is not two elements or principles, but only one: the Truth received by believers through the Spirit or the 'pneumatic' revelation of Jesus." It is noteworthy that "Spirit of Truth" in 1 John 4:6 refers to right doctrine and belief although ethics are referred to in the surrounding context.

217. Schnackenburg, *John*, respectively, 1: 437, 38, 39; cf. also the sound remarks of Brown, *John*, 1: 180-81.

218. J. Bowman, "The Fourth Gospel and the Samaritans," *BJRL* 40 (1958) 302; also E. D. Freed, "Samaritan Influence in the Gospel of John," *CBQ* 30 (1968) 580-87; idem, "Did John Write His Gospel Partly to Win Samaritan Converts?" *NovT* 12 (1970) 241-56.

219. Brown, *John*, 1: 171-72; cf. J. D. Purvis, "The Fourth Gospel and the Samaritans," *NovT* 17 (1975) 161-98; W. Meeks, *The Prophet-King*, 216-57.

temple views, entered the Johannine community.[220] Although this suggestion may strain the evidence, it at least points to a place for Samaritan believers in early stages of community life (see further below). (c) Finally, according to J. Bligh the problem of worship only came to the fore with the introduction of Samaritans into early Christianity.[221] The evangelization of Samaria forced the church to deal with the place and manner of worship. The question became: could true Christians avoid temple worship? To be sure, the earliest and most decisive answer to this problem came from Stephen (Acts 6–8).

a. The Temple and Samaria

Oscar Cullmann has argued for a connection among Stephen, heterodox Judaism, and John, and Brown has recently defended a variation of his case.[222] The Hellenistic Christians represented by Stephen held views in extreme opposition to the temple. F. F. Bruce has commented that "we meet nothing quite so radical elsewhere in the New Testament."[223] Stephen's speech in Acts 7 spurned the cult of Judaism, rejected the sanctity of the temple, and aroused keen hostilities against the Hellenists (Acts 8:1). But the result of their dispersion is significant. After the stoning of Stephen, the first mission of the Hellenists, that of Philip, led the church to Samaria. It was Hellenistic Christianity formulated under the leadership of Stephen that had ultimately broken with Judaism and was now able to make the message of Christ acceptable in Samaria. The very issue that might have made Jewish Christianity intolerable in Samaria—the temple and cult—was the catalyst that brought the earlier division.[224]

Similar themes are presented in the Fourth Gospel. Various scholars have noted how John successfully presents Jesus as the replacement of the Jewish temple and its services. Among the many items suggested by McKelvey, the following are important:[225] Jesus is the new dwelling place of God's presence, 1:51; he inaugurates his ministry by cleansing the temple, 2:13-22; and he justifies this act with a prophecy concerning the building's destruction, 2:19ff. Further, specific ideas associated with the temple cult are transferred to Jesus: he is the lamb, 1:29, the perfect sacrifice, 19:36ff.; he is the source of living

---

220. Brown, *Community*, 36ff.; cf. J. L. Martyn, *The Gospel of John in Christian History* (New York: Paulist, 1979); and P. Parker, "The Kinship of John and Acts," in *Christianity, Judaism, and Other Greco-Roman Cults*, 4 vols., ed. J. Neusner (Leiden: Brill, 1975) 1: 196.

221. "Jesus in Samaria," *HeyJ* 3 (1962) 338; cf. McKelvey, *The New Temple*, 88; O. Cullmann, "Samaria and the Origins of Christian Mission," in *The Early Church*, 185-92; A. Spiro, "Stephen's Samaritan Background," Appendix V in J. Munck, *Acts*, AB (New York: Doubleday, 1967) 287-88; and C. H. H. Scobie, "The Origin and Development of Samaritan Christianity," *NTS* 19 (1972-73) 390-414.

222. Cullmann, *The Johannine Circle*, 39-56; Brown, *Community*, 36-40.

223. F. F. Bruce, *Peter, Stephen, James, and John: Studies in Non-Pauline Christianity* (Grand Rapids: Eerdmans, 1979) 55; cf. McKelvey, *The New Temple*, 85-88.

224. Other possible documents reflecting this attitude of the Hellenistic Christians may be Hebrews and the Epistle of Barnabas (which parallels Acts 7:49-50 in its citation of Isa. 66).

225. McKelvey, *The New Temple*, 76ff.

water at Tabernacles, 7:37ff.; he replaces the major feasts; and he converts items of ritual for his own use, 2:1ff.

When this evidence is viewed together with Jesus' remarks in John 4:20-24, one far-reaching conclusion becomes evident: the Johannine community had combined a theology of worship much like Stephen's with mission in Samaria, and this combination of factors now forms the setting of our present passage. John hardly embraces the Samaritan cult in turn. Instead, in Christ God had announced the dissolution of all religious divisions.[226] The new worship inaugurated by Christ deprived both Jerusalem and Gerizim of their functions. Once again, it is Christ who is the new religious center.

b. The Johannine Expression

Considering the serious hostilities with the Jews in the Fourth Gospel and this evidence of a formal break with the temple, one might think it likely that Johannine Christianity viewed itself as untied to any Jewish form of religious expression. But does this mean that the community had likewise despaired of the material and cultic expressions quickly developing in early Christianity? Brown rejects this thought and believes that eucharistic gatherings, baptismal services, hymn singing, etc., must have played a central part in the community.[227] At best, we can only be sure that cultic expressions, in particular baptism and the eucharist, were viewed critically and with reserve. Did they lead the worshiper to faith? Did they glorify Jesus? Did they deepen the believer's experience and knowledge of the Spirit? Did they instill in the community a sense of unity and love? These are Johannine questions. The expression of this community focused on the worship of God through the Spirit of Christ which they confidently possessed.

Therefore the Johannine expression of spirituality held two foci: it was *christocentric* in that Christ was present in grace, truth, and love, and it was *pneumatic* in that the Spirit was present in reality and power.[228] But in experience there was actually a single focus. It was Christ in power—Christ in Spirit—that the community knew. If we can be certain about anything in the Johannine community, we can be assured that it stirred with spiritual vitality and strength. Above all, these were Christians who knew they had been transformed by the Spirit (John 3:3-4; 1 John 2:29; 4:7), united with Christ in Spirit (John 6:53, 63; 15:4ff.), and fully enabled to worship in power (4:24). They had been anointed with the Spirit (1 John 2:20, 27), and this mark had become their strength and distinctive.

---

226. Painter, *John*, 13-14; Bligh, "Jesus in Samaria," 337-38.

227. Brown, *John*, 1: 180.

228. Porsch, *Pneuma*, 160, emphasizes the former focus; the latter focus is contra Johnston, *Spirit-Paraclete*, 147. See Schnackenburg, "Die johanneische Gemeinde und Ihre Geisterfahrung," 304, who concludes: "The picture that we have acquired of the experience and understanding of the Spirit within the Johannine community contains unique features when we compare it with other early Christian communities and theologians. Chief among these is the strict connection made between the Spirit and the acute awareness of his presence and effects."

CHAPTER FIVE

SPIRIT, MISSION, AND ANAMNESIS

In the NT the experience of the Spirit is never insular. It pushes the Christian community out into the world. Therefore an important corollary of NT pneumatology is mission and witness. While the Johannine writings affirm this emphasis, the Johannine community also held an acute sense of its rejection and persecution. This was explained in terms of the rejection of Jesus. "He was in the world . . . yet the world did not know him. He came to his own people, but they did not receive him" (John 1:10-11). If the world rejected Jesus and if the Paraclete was Jesus in Spirit in his continuing mission and trial within the community, then rejection and conflict would necessarily accompany discipleship. This is the tacit conclusion of John 15:18ff.: "If they persecuted me, they will persecute you; if they kept my word, they will also keep yours." Therefore an unrelenting division existed between the Johannine church and the world, and it was focused on the person and presence of Jesus.

The Synoptic Gospels give equal testimony to this expectation of persecution. They add, however, that in this struggle it will be the Spirit that provides the church with its witness during trial. This is also the conclusion of John 15. The Johannine power for success amid persecution is the Paraclete (15:26-27). But the Fourth Evangelist gives exceptional emphasis to one feature of this aid. In the Johannine writings, one more factor converges with the twin themes of mission and rejection: namely, revelation. The Paraclete would recall the words of Jesus in the testimony of the church, lead the community into previously unrecognized truths, convince the world of its error, and through these ministries vindicate the message of Christ in the church's mission.

Thus in its mission the Johannine community was eminently aware of the revelatory power of the Spirit, especially in that its mission led to conflict with the world. "If the Johannine eagle soared above the earth, it did so with talons bared for the fight."[1] Raymond Brown here gives poignant expression to the fact that while we find profound spiritual insight in this community, its deepest truths about Christ, the strengthening role of the Spirit, and the Spirit's interpretative, revealing work were all honed by struggle. The community did not merely enjoy tranquil reflection or the satisfaction of spiritual enthusiasm; its life was intimately involved with history. Its word of testimony became flesh and actively engaged the surrounding world.

A. SPIRIT AND MISSION: JOHN 20:21

While all the Gospels record some commission of Jesus' disciples to witness,[2] Luke and John draw particular attention to the Spirit in this process. In Luke 24:48-49 witness and Spirit are specifically aligned, and in the beginning of Acts it is the awaited anointing that will empower the disciples' mission: "You shall receive power when the Holy Spirit has come upon you; and you shall be my witnesses" (Acts 1:8).[3] Various passages allude to the witness of the Spirit (Acts 5:32; 15:8; 20:23) and confirm that for Luke there was an inseparable connection between the divine anointing and the church's mission.

The Fourth Evangelist makes this same point by attaching to the account of the Spirit insufflation (20:22) a type of apostolic commissioning reminiscent of the Synoptics yet characteristically framed in Johannine idiom (v. 21).[4] It is this idiom that must be grasped in its theological context in order to bring out the unique character of Jesus' mission, the church's mission, and the mission of the Paraclete. In John, the construction καθώς . . . κἀγώ is a favorite device to indicate that Jesus conveys to his disciples a relationship similar to that enjoyed by himself with the Father.[5] Just as he has been loved or sent by the Father, so too Jesus loves and sends the disciples (15:9; 17:18). In 20:21 the mission of the church is set in this framework. In this *locus classicus* of Johannine mission, the sending of Jesus is the paradigm for the sending of the church.[6] In this way, the Christ-centered mission of the Paraclete is already anticipated: while the Paraclete sustains the presence of Christ in the church, the disciples are commissioned in the very pattern belonging to Jesus.

---

1. Brown, *Community*, 24.

2. Various nuances accompany each account. Matthew stresses baptism and discipleship (28:19), while the Markan appendix introduces condemnation for those who refuse the call (16:16). Luke 24:47 parallels John 20:23 in its reference to forgiveness.

3. For a comparison of Luke and John, see J. McPolin, "The Holy Spirit in Luke and John," *ITQ* 45 (1978) 117-31, esp. 123ff. Cf. A. A. Trites, *Concept of Witness*, 66-77, 78ff.; J. Boice, *Witness and Revelation*, 29ff.; and J. H. E. Hull, *The Holy Spirit in Acts*, 125ff.

4. Dodd has argued (*Historical Tradition*, 142-51) that in John 20:21ff. v. 21 has the highest claim to historical credibility in view of the Synoptic parallels. Cf. Lindars, *John*, 611; Bultmann, *John*, 692n.3.

5. Καθώς appears 31 times in John (Matthew 3 times; Mark 8 times; Luke 17 times) and 13 times in the Johannine Epistles. See esp. John 6:57; 15:19; 17:18, 21. Cf. Bernard, *John*, 1:212.

6. Although in v. 21 two different verbs are employed (ἀπέσταλκεν, πέμπω), they should be seen as virtually synonymous in John. So Bernard, *John*, 1: 118-19; Sanders and Mastin, *John*, 433; Brown, *John*, 2: 1022; Barrett, *John*, 569. Cf. Dodd, *Historical Tradition*, 344.

1. JESUS: GOD'S APOSTLE

The introductory clause of 20:21 points to a fundamental element in Johannine christology: Jesus has been sent or commissioned by God.[7] This element is indicated by John's interest in the verbs ἀποστέλλειν and especially πέμπειν. The first verb is applied 18 times to Jesus and is the constant witness to Jesus' authority as a messenger sent from God to humanity.[8] Thus in 3:17 this authority is the basis of the salvation from God which only Jesus can accomplish. In 6:57 the flesh which is to be consumed—Jesus' life—is only vivifying by virtue of its origins in God. John 17 is especially important in that now Jesus is about to finish his mission, and as he gives a résumé of his works, he commissions the disciples using the same vocabulary (17:18; see below).

This special interest is brought out even further in the use of πέμπειν, which John has no doubt elevated to the level of formula. Of 32 instances of this term in John (Matthew 4 times; Mark once; Luke 10 times), 25 refer to Jesus being sent by God.[9] This term usually conveys the notion of a divine commission, and it is applied not only to Jesus but also to John the Baptist (1:33), the disciples (13:20; 20:21; cf. 13:16), and the Paraclete (14:26; 15:26; 16:7).

The category of christology that explains this phenomenon most accurately in the Fourth Gospel is *agency*. Jesus is God's agent. While it cannot be denied that this concept was at home in a Hellenistic milieu, impressive arguments have shown the suitability of a Jewish background of wisdom and prophetism as well.[10] Possibly a Jewish Hellenism nurtured this concept, and

---

7. Lightfoot, *John*, 150, claims that this notion of Jesus' sending appears 42 times in John. That the concept is simply a highly developed Synoptic motif is evident from Mark 9:37; Matt. 10:40; 18:5; Luke 9:48; 10:16. Cf. Dodd, *Historical Tradition*, 344. On the sending of Jesus in John (and its role in christology) see W. F. Howard, *Christianity According to St. John*, 25-26; J. E. Davey, *The Jesus of St. John*, 100-102; Rengstorf, *TDNT* 1: 404-406; Bultmann, *New Testament Theology*, 2: 33-40; E. Haenchen, "Der Vater, der mich gesandt hat," *NTS* 9 (1963) 208-16; and J. Kuhl, *Die Sendung Jesu und der Kirche nach dem Johannesevangelium* (St. Augustin: Steyler, 1967). See the discussion of Haenchen and Kuhl in R. Kysar, *The Fourth Evangelist*, 196ff.

8. Ἀποστέλλειν receives equal attention among the four Gospels (Matthew 22 times; Mark 20 times; Luke 25 times; John 28 times), but in John it is used esp. for Jesus: 3:17, 34; 5:36, 38; 6:29, 57; 7:29; 8:42; 10:36; 11:42; 17:3, 8, 18, 21, 23, 25; (18:24); 20:21. Cf. 1 John 4:9, 10, 14.

9. See John 4:34; 5:23, 24, 30, 37*; 6:38, 39, 44*; 7:16, (18*), 28*, 33; 8:16*, 18*, 26*, 29*; 9:4; 12:44, 45, 49*; 13:(16), 20; 14:24; 15:21; 16:5. Nine of these (marked with an asterisk *) employ the characteristic Johannine phrase ὁ πέμψας με.

10. Adherents to the Hellenistic background include Bultmann, *John*, passim; Cf. the discussion of Barrett, *John*, 570, who cites E. Percy, *Untersuchungen über den Ursprung der johanneischen Theologie* (Lund: Gleerup, 1939) 199-200; and S. Schulz, *Das Evangelium*, 63-64, as reviewed by Kysar, *The Fourth Evangelist*, 115. For criticisms of this view, see Schnackenburg, *John*, 1: 543-47; and Rengstorf, *TDNT* 1: 443-45. Adherents to the Jewish background are T. Preiss, *Life in Christ*, 9-31; Dodd, *Interpretation*, 254ff.; P. Borgen, "God's Agent in the Fourth Gospel," in *Religions in Antiquity*, ed. J. Neusner (Leiden: Brill, 1968) 137-48, who finds impressive Rabbinic parallels; cf. Rengstorf, *TDNT* 1: 414-16. P. Miranda, *Der Vater, der Mich Gesandt Hat* (Frankfurt: Lang Bern, 1972), argues for an OT prophetic background; and E. Schweizer, "Zum religionsgeschichtlichen Hintergrund der 'Sendungsformel,'" *ZNW* 57 (1966) 199-210, seeks a background in Hellenistic-Jewish wisdom. J. D. M. Derrett, *Law in the New Testament* (London: Darton, Longman, and Todd, 1970) 53-55, gives a general description of Jewish agency.

the Fourth Evangelist, addressing such an audience, has capitalized on this particular thought. This description of Jesus is clearly important to John's presentation of Jesus' sonship. In meeting the "Sent One," persons in the Gospel necessarily encounter the "Sender." Thus to receive (13:20), honor (5:23), see (12:45; 14:9), or hate (15:23) Jesus is to do likewise with the Father. This thought of agency might even stand behind the "unity" passages of the Gospel: Jesus and the Father are one (10:30) in view of the way that God is "in Jesus" in all that Jesus does (10:36-38; 14:10-11; 17:21-23). In 5:16-18, when Jesus is called upon to explain his working on the Sabbath, he does so in terms of agency—this is not his work but that of God. Therefore his opponents are really dealing with God (the one for whom this agent stands). For the Evangelist, the consequence of this assertion is clear: Jesus has made himself equal (ἴσος) with God (5:18).

An important aspect of agency is that the agent speaks words which originate not with himself but with his sender.[11] To be sure, John has heightened this aspect in that Jesus is no mere mortal messenger, but in him the word of God itself is incarnate. The prologue as well as the "I am" sayings affirm this point. The Gospel points as well to this form for the authority of Jesus' words: the Father supplies his words and teachings (8:42ff.; 12:49; 7:16), and this is the nucleus of his authority. "The word which you hear is not mine, but the Father's who sent me" (14:24).[12] In this respect we would do well to note 3:34 in which agency, revelation, and the Spirit are united. "For he whom God has sent speaks the words of God, for it is not by measure that he [God] gives the Spirit."[13] This text implies—and this point will be of central importance shortly—that in the divine mission of Jesus, one role of the Spirit will be to convey the words of God with authority as this "sending" or agency indicates a transferral of authority from God to Jesus in the Spirit.

To sum up, the agency terminology of the Fourth Gospel gives the impression that for John there is primarily one agent and one mission in God's design. This is Jesus' mission. With Bernard, we might say that in this respect Jesus is "pre-eminently ὁ ἀπόστολος" (cf. Heb. 3:1).[14] Along with the Evangelist's possible interest in decentralizing the place of the Twelve, his avoidance of ἀπόστολος generally may also point to the primacy of Jesus and his mission. Any other mission that results from 20:21 is achieved only to the extent that the disciple carries on Jesus' mission in the Paraclete.

2. AGENCY AND APOSTOLIC MISSION

Peder Borgen has shown that one feature of Jewish agency is that the agent can himself appoint another agent to carry on his task.[15] This is the key to the

11. Borgen, "God's Agent," 142ff.; Derrett, ibid., 53.
12. For texts, see J. E. Davey, *The Jesus of St. John*, 100-101.
13. See our discussion of 3:34 above, pp. 81-84.
14. Bernard, *John*, 2:676. It may be that the absence of any sending of the Twelve—or the 70—serves to heighten the emphasis on Jesus' sole mission and the final commission of 20:21. Cf. Dodd, *Historical Tradition*, 403-405.
15. Borgen, "God's Agent," 143; cf. A. E. Harvey, *Jesus on Trial*, 106.

unique Johannine view of the church's mission: agency language is employed for both the disciples and the Paraclete. This mission of Christ will thus be carried on despite his absence through the Spirit-led witness of the church.

a. The Disciples

The first hint of this agency is found in 13:16, 20 (cf. the similar 4:38). In 13:16 the criteria of agency are identified: the sender is always superior and this leads to a requisite obedience and dependence on the part of the agent.[16] In 13:20 the exact parallel between Jesus and the disciple is to be noted. Both are commissioned with an absolute authority. In both, the world is confronted by God. Although ἀπόστολος appears only at 13:16 in this Gospel, it is clearly not a technical term. As Barrett remarks, it is "simply a passive verbal noun" intended to convey the notion of commission without the thought of office.[17]

In John 17 the thought of Jesus' mission is central. Ἀποστέλλειν occurs 6 times with the reference to Jesus' successful work as an agent and his imminent return to the Father (17:3, 8, 18, 21, 23, 25). John 17:4 confirms this image of agency: "I glorified thee on earth, having accomplished the work you gave me to do." But while Jesus is looking to the completion of his work, he is also anticipating the continuation of this task of revealing the Father. Here we find our closest parallel with 20:21 in 17:18: "Just as you sent me into the world, so too I have sent them into the world" (καθὼς ἐμὲ ἀπέστειλας εἰς τὸν κόσμον, κἀγὼ ἀπέστειλα αὐτοὺς εἰς τὸν κόσμον). The mission of the disciples is therefore the resumption of the mission of Jesus. They are now his agents. Just as Jesus had been consecrated by the Father (10:36, ἁγιάζειν), so here Jesus prays that the disciples might be similarly consecrated (17:17, ἁγιάζειν). As agents, both have been set aside for their tasks.[18] Of special interest to commentators is this phrase in 17:17, ἁγίασον αὐτοὺς ἐν τῇ ἀληθείᾳ. This consecration certainly involves God's word, which is truth (17:17b) and which the disciples now bear (17:6, 14). But it is equally important to recall that Jesus is both the Word and the Truth in John (1:1ff.; 14:6).[19] Therefore, as Brown remarks, this may simply be an aspect of belonging to Jesus. But as v. 19 makes certain, this belonging will only come about through Jesus' sacrificial death.[20]

Another aspect of this consecration involves the Spirit.[21] The Paraclete is the Spirit of Truth (14:17; etc.) and through his revealing functions (14:26; 16:12-13; see below) he will preserve and vivify the "word" which Jesus has entrusted to them. Similarly, holiness is an aspect of the consecration, and in 14:26 the Paraclete is termed the *Holy* Spirit. Finally, Jesus remarks that a result

---

16. Note the use of πέμπειν in both verses. Cf. the discussions of Barrett, *John*, 443-45; and Harvey, *Jesus on Trial*, 117-18.

17. Barrett, *John*, 444; so too Sanders and Mastin, *John*, 310; Bernard, *John*, 2:466-67; Rengstorf, *TDNT* 1: 421. Cf. Lindars, *John*, 453.

18. Cf. Barrett, *John*, 510; and Lindars, *John*, 528. Ἁγιάζειν appears only 3 times in John: twice for Jesus (10:36; 17:19) and once for the disciples (17:17).

19. Brown, *John*, 2: 765.

20. Hoskyns, *John*, 502.

21. Brown, *John*, 2: 766; Bernard, *John*, 2: 574. Cf. Barrett, *John*, 510.

of the glory he has passed on to his disciples is unity: both with one another and with him (v. 22). In Johannine thought, all these effects come through the Spirit.

Therefore, as Jesus looks forward to the future of his mission through his disciples, he commissions and prepares them just as he was commissioned and prepared. They will be agents serving him as he served God. They are sent into the world (17:18) as they receive the equipping of the Spirit (20:21-22). Within the world they function as revealers: bearing God's word (17:14) and glorifying Jesus through the Paraclete, who will do the same (14:26; 16:14). Finally, in the world they will suffer persecution and rejection (17:14)—on the model of Christ (15:18)—but the Paraclete will be their aid (15:26).

b. The Paraclete

Our second observation concerns John's view of the Paraclete in this framework of agency. Πέμπειν is used, as we have seen, for the sending of both Jesus and the disciples. Jesus also refers to the coming Paraclete in the same fashion. In 14:26 the Father will send the Paraclete. In 16:7 Jesus will send him. John 15:26 places these two views in direct tension: Jesus will send the Paraclete who proceeds (ἐκπορεύεται) from the Father. As Brown comments, there is no theological tension here. Jesus and the Father are one (10:30), and John's point is the divine agency of the Paraclete.[22] No doubt we should draw attention here once again to the numerous parallels between Jesus and the Paraclete. In parallel to Christ, the Paraclete is given by the Father, is sent into the world, provides divine testimony, and finally is rejected by the world.

Therefore the Paraclete is sent as an agent of God as Jesus was sent. This notion may even stand behind the phrase in 14:16, where the Spirit is introduced as ἄλλος παράκλητος. In the forensic metaphor (see below) the Spirit and Jesus play parallel roles.

One important feature of Jesus' agency was subordination in word. As Jesus reveals only what he has seen and heard, in the Farewell Discourses the Paraclete will be strictly subordinate to Jesus. His revelation is restricted to recalling Jesus' words (14:26) and speaking only what he hears from Jesus (16:13). This revelatory relationship between Jesus and the Paraclete is discussed in 16:13, which expresses this relationship both negatively and positively.[23] On the one hand, the Paraclete lacks any authority to speak on his own—to speak creatively. On the other hand, he can speak with authority when he is relaying that which he has heard from Christ. This christocentric feature secures the glory of Jesus (16:14) in that the Paraclete will function faithfully as an agent: "he will take what is mine and declare it to you."

If both the disciples and the Paraclete are commissioned and sent into the world, is their work separate or is it to be seen together? A. A. Trites

---

22. Brown, *John*, 2: 689, who cites Loisy: "They are variant formulas, not variant ideas."
23. The formula in 16:13 (οὐ γὰρ λαλήσει ἀφ' ἑαυτοῦ, ἀλλ' ὅσα ἀκούσει λαλήσει) parallels many similar passages of the source of Jesus' revelatory knowledge. Cf. 7:17; 8:26, 40; 12:49; 14:10, 20. See Porsch, *Pneuma*, 300; Kothgasser, "Die Lehr-," 594ff.

comments: "The witness of the apostles is linked with the witness of the Holy Spirit (15:27; 20:21). 'It is as anointed with His Spirit that they are bearers of his commission, and in no other way . . . Indeed, the Holy Spirit is Himself the primary and essential witness, and it is only his presence in the disciples which makes it possible for them truly to witness to Him.' "[24]

Therefore, as 15:26-27 points out, the witnessing tasks of the Paraclete and the disciples coalesce in the mission of the church. John 14:17 likewise affirms this relation. The Paraclete will be both in them (indwelling) and with them (accompanying their work). Church and Spirit function as a unit. 1 John 4:13-14 stresses this similarly: "He has given us of his own Spirit . . . and we witness . . ." (cf. 2 John 12). This unity of witness is a frequent NT theme.[25] In addition, the chief Synoptic promise of the Spirit envisions a context in which the Spirit speaks through the disciples (Matt. 10:20). Therefore we can say that the function of revelation between the Paraclete and the disciples is similar to that between Jesus and the Father. The Father speaks through Jesus and there is thus one testimony (12:49). In a similar fashion, the Paraclete speaks through the disciples (echoing Jesus' revelation) and thus creates a single voice of witness.[26]

* * *

We may summarize by affirming that Johannine Christianity viewed its mission as strictly christocentric. It was carrying on the mission of Christ. To be sure, the Spirit Paraclete was viewed as the continued presence of Jesus in the community (see chapter 4 above), and this continuity certainly molded the community's view of mission. But in addition, the mission of the church was meant to be patterned after the mission of Jesus (17:18; 20:21). As the Father commissioned Jesus—and anointed him with the Spirit (1:33; 3:34)—so too Jesus commissioned his disciples (20:21), anointing them with the Spirit (20:22). Indeed, the Paraclete is also commissioned as an agent because he sustains the presence of Jesus, and he joins with the church in effectively enabling it to complete the revealing work of Christ. Thus Christ was ὁ ἀπόστολος and the Johannine church regarded itself as continuing his "apostolic" mission by virtue of its commission and anointing by him to do so.

B. TRIAL AND REVELATION

One of the assured results of Johannine scholarship in recent years has been the conclusion that the underlying pattern of the Fourth Evangelist's presentation

---

24. A. A. Trites, *Concept of Witness*, 116-17, citing L. Newbigin, *The Household of God* (London: SCM, 1953) 95; cf. J. McNaugher, "The Witnessing Spirit and the Witnessed Christ," *BSac* 88 (1931) 207-19; A. E. Harvey, *Jesus on Trial*, 112-13; Brown, *John*, 2: 700, who cites the discussion of M.-F. Berrouard, "Le Paraclète, défenseur du Christ devant la conscience du croyant (Jn 16, 8-11)," *RSPT* 33 (1949) 361-89.

25. Johnston, *Spirit-Paraclete*, 64-65. Cf. Acts 5:32; 6:10; 15:28. J. Giblet, "Les Promesses de l'Esprit et le Mission des Apôtres dans les Evangiles," *Irenikon* 30 (1957) 17-43.

26. Brown, *John*, 2: 700, who cites Augustine: "Because he [the Spirit] will speak, you will also speak—he in your hearts, you in words—he by inspiration, you by sounds." In this context, Martyn (*History and Theology*, 143-51) shows that parallels can be drawn not only between Christ and the Paraclete, but also among Christ/Paraclete/and Christian witnesses.

of Christ is his unique "trial motif." John's careful attention to the theme of "witness" has long been recognized;[27] but he has skillfully placed this witness in a juridical framework. Jesus and the question of his messiahship—even his agency[28]—is on trial as witnesses appear and disappear giving their contributions throughout chaps. 1–12. Jesus and his revelations are offered with the specific aim of "presenting evidence for a verdict."[29] Initially this lawsuit is presented on a historical level as Jesus debates with the Jews, but in addition, readers are forced to adjudge the case for themselves and assess the validity of the Evangelist's verdict (20:31).[30]

This feature of the Gospel seems certain. A less developed theme, indeed a more nuanced message, concerns the Spirit. This context of juridical trial and persecution presents us with the most likely catalyst for John's introduction of the term ὁ παράκλητος. In fact, it is the comprehensive activity of the Spirit as a forensic witness that best explains the varied tasks of the Paraclete in the Farewell Discourses. Christ was still on trial before the world, and the Johannine church regarded its existence vicariously: it was on trial for Christ. Hence the Paraclete as an advocate implored and persuaded the opposition concerning the truth; and as a witness the Paraclete brought forward evidence establishing the case for Christ (and his church).[31]

1. THE ORIGIN OF THE PARACLETE SAYINGS: JOHN 15:18–16:4A

Following the earlier work of C. H. Dodd, Raymond Brown has argued that the Synoptic predictions of the Spirit form the traditional context from which the Paraclete passages were born.[32] The threat of persecution plays a significant part in the Synoptic eschatological discourses (Mark 13; Matt. 24–25; Luke 21). In the eschatological material which Matthew has moved forward into 10:17-25, this threat is joined with the notion of witness. According to Matthew, the mission of the Twelve will be met with rejection and persecution

---

27. Strathmann, *TDNT* 4: 497-99; J. C. Hindley, "Witness in the Fourth Gospel," *SJT* 18 (1965) 319-37; J. M. Boice, *Witness and Revelation*; M. C. Tenney, "The Meaning of Witness in John," *BSac* 132 (1975) 229-41; N. A. Dahl, "The Johannine Church and History," 106-12; Trites, *Concept of Witness*, 78ff. For example, μαρτυρεῖν occurs in Matthew once; Luke once; John 33 times; Acts 11 times; Paul 8 times; not at all in Mark. Μαρτυρία occurs in Mark 3 times; Luke once; John 14 times; Acts once; Paul twice; not at all in Matthew. Trites claims that witness terminology occurs 83 times in John (p. 66).

28. Borgen, "God's Agent," 140-41, comments, "The Johannine idea of the mission of Christ as God's agent is seen within the context of a lawsuit." Also cited in Trites, ibid., 86.

29. Hindley, "Witness in the Fourth Gospel," 321.

30. The trial motif in John has found wide attention (see the general survey in chap. 1 above). Most recently, see Preiss, *Life in Christ*, 9-31; Trites, *Concept of Witness*; Betz, *Der Paraklet*, 120-26; Harvey, *Jesus on Trial*; Brown, *John*, 1: 145; Porsch, *Pneuma*, 222-27 (and references).

31. I am chiefly dependent on Trites *(Concept of Witness)* for the division of tasks in oriental advocacy (although other scholars have identified the same). According to Trites the dual functions of witness and advocate are found in the OT (p. 22) and are exemplified by Isa. 40–55 (pp. 35-47). This model, esp. the Isaianic forensic model, is applied directly to the Fourth Gospel (pp. 79, 84).

32. Brown, *John*, 2: 696-95, 698-701, 1141-42; idem, "The Paraclete," 126ff.; Dodd, *Historical Tradition*, 407-13; Porsch, *Pneuma*, 268-69; and the recent valuable study of J. Kremer, "Jesu Verheissung des Geistes," 262-67. See our discussion above, pp. 31ff.

(10:14ff.) by virtue of their bearing the name of Christ (v. 18). In Matt. 10 as well as in the other major discourses mentioned above (Mark 13; etc.), the context is strictly forensic. Persecution will come through trial, and in each instance the Spirit will assist the disciple in his testimony (Matt. 10:20; Mark 13:11; Luke 21:12).

The numerous parallels between John 15:18–16:4a and this Synoptic tradition (esp. Matt. 10; see above) indicate that the Fourth Evangelist is in touch with reliable historical tradition.[33] This is not to say that John has copied the Synoptic tradition directly, but that all the Evangelists were indebted to a parallel account which especially the Fourth Evangelist has shaped in the present discourse. This evidence levels serious questions against all those who would completely deny the historical credibility of the Spirit texts in John 15 and 16.[34] Hostility accompanied Jesus' ministry, and as Jesus makes pertinent observations about the imminent fate of his followers in all the accounts, he predicts hostility for them as well. But in each case it is the Spirit that will make bold their witness.

The peculiarly Johannine title for the Spirit, ὁ παράκλητος, fits this forensic Synoptic context well.[35] John's authority for applying this term to the Spirit in his Farewell Discourses thus stemmed from the tradition (hence possibly from Jesus): the Spirit was known in the acutely juridical context of persecution, and John's employment of the title "the Paraclete" gave this thought precision. Brown sums up: "There is a possibility that when the traditional material about persecution now found in 15:18–16:4a was introduced into the context of the Last Discourse, the forensic description of the Spirit in that material was a catalyst to the formation of the Johannine picture of the Paraclete that found its way into the other divisions and subdivisions of the Last Discourse."[36]

Therefore we can conclude that John 15:18ff. is a key passage which anchors the Paraclete in a traditional context of persecution and witness. The traditional context also affirms our earlier conclusion about the unity of witness in 15:26-27. The church carries on its mission in concert with the Spirit and confronts the world through the power of the Spirit. As we have indicated, the Johannine church viewed itself as a church on trial. The juridical features of the Spirit were elevated through intense struggle with the world. In the first instance, the juridical metaphor is directly applied in 16:8-11 as the Paraclete

---

33. This passage provides Dodd with a classic example of "historical tradition in the Fourth Gospel." But John has narrowed the setting to refer to persecution from the synagogue (Dodd, ibid., 412-13) in contrast to secular persecution (Matt. 10:17-18; etc.). Dodd describes a "Jewish-Christian community, absorbed in the task of witness before their fellow-Jews, and dreading, next to martyrdom, the exclusion from the commonwealth of Israel." In his analysis of the Synoptic Spirit promises in these passages, Barrett concludes that Luke 21:14 is the oldest form and ultimately rejects the historicity of the Synoptic record. See his *The Holy Spirit and the Synoptic Tradition*, 130-32.

34. U. B. Müller, "Die Parakletenvorstellung," 66ff.; J. Becker, "Die Abschiedsreden Jesu im Johannesevangelium," *ZNW* 61 (1971) 215-46.

35. Dodd, *Historical Tradition*, 411. Cf. Trites, *Concept of Witness*, 117.

36. Brown, *John*, 2: 700.

FIGURE 8. PARALLELS BETWEEN JOHN 15:18–16:4A AND THE SYNOPTIC ESCHATOLOGICAL DISCOURSE*

John 15:18-16:4a	Matt. 10:17-25, 24:9-10	Mark 13:9-13; Luke 21:12-17
15:18: "The world hates you . . . has hated me before you"	10:22: "You will be hated by all because of my name"; also 24:9	Mark 13:13; Luke 21:17: same as Matthew
20: "No servant is more important than his master"	10:24: "No servant is above his master"	
20: "They will persecute you"	10:23: "When they persecute you"; cf. also 23:34	Luke 21:12: "They will persecute"
21: "They will do all these things to you because of my name"	See first parallel above	See first parallel above
26: "The Paraclete . . . will bear witness on my behalf"	10:20: "The Spirit of your Father speaking through you"	Mark 13:11: "The Holy Spirit (speaking)"; cf. Luke 12:12
27: "You too should bear witness"	10:18: "You will be dragged before governors and kings . . . to bear witness"	Mark 13:9: Luke 21:12-13: almost the same as Matthew
16:1: "To prevent your faith from being shaken"	24:10: "The faith of many will be shaken"	
2: "They are going to put you out of the Synagogue"	10:17 "They will flog you in their synagogues"	Mark 13:9: "You will be beaten in synagogues"; Luke 21:12: "Delivering you up to the synagogues"; cf. also Luke 6:22
2: "The man who puts you to death"	24:9: "They will put you to death"	Mark 13:12: "Children will rise against parents and will put them to death" (= Matt. 10:21); Luke 21:6: "Some of you they will put to death"

*Slightly modified from p. 694 of *The Gospel according to John XIII-XXI* (Anchor Bible), translated and edited by Raymond Brown. Copyright © 1970 by Doubleday & Company, Inc. (for the USA and Canada) and Geoffrey Chapman, a division of Cassell Publications Ltd (for the rest of the world). Reprinted by permission of the publishers.

functions as an aggressive advocate before a hostile world. Then in 14:26 and 16:12-15 the Paraclete is identified as substantiating the church's case through witness and revelation. Both these forensic attributes spawned important developments in Johannine Christianity. On the one hand, the Spirit led the community into active witness before the world much like Paul's bold defense before Felix in Acts 24. On the other hand, at the same time this witness sparked an avid interest in the material case for Christ. This forensic setting led to a heightened revelatory role for the Spirit, and as the community grew (ultimately finding its conflict with secessionists) this pneumatic development posed nearly irresolvable difficulties.

2. THE PARACLETE AS ADVOCATE: JOHN 16:8-11

In our introductory chapter we explored the background of John's use of ὁ παράκλητος and concluded that it should be seen chiefly as a forensic term evolving out of the Jewish juridical sphere. While John's use of this term in 14:16, 26, and 15:26 exhibits a departure from (or better, a development of) this background, the present verses reflect it well. The Evangelist has clearly in view a forensic scene.[37] But rather than supplying the disciples with a personal testimony (as in the Synoptic promise), Jesus says that this advocate will "pass to the attack."[38] He becomes a prosecuting counsel. This transition is similar to that found in John 9:35ff., where Jesus comes forward to the aid of his disciple directly. The Johannine community did not envisage a passive role in the trial resulting from its mission. Like Jesus, it too would expose the world in its sin and disbelief. As 15:26-27 suggests, this activity would transpire in the community's witness and preaching.

While this much can be affirmed with confidence, the way in which this activity is perceived in 16:8-11 has brought little scholarly unanimity. In view of the numerous studies already available on these verses, especially D. A. Carson's exhaustive discussion,[39] we shall review only the major contours of the debate.

---

37. Bernard, *John*, 2: 505; Sanders and Mastin, *John*, 351. Cf. the recent work (to the contrary) by K. Grayston, "The Meaning of PARAKLĒTOS," *JSNT* 13 (1981) 67-82 (as in *NTA* 26 [1982] 137). According to Bultmann, the Evangelist's original source connected 15:18-26 with the present texts, 16:4-11b.

38. A. E. Harvey, *Jesus on Trial*, 118.

39. D. A. Carson, "The Function of the Paraclete in John 16:7-11," *JBL* 98 (1979) 547-66. In the following I am chiefly indebted to Carson and the concise outline of Barrett (*John*, 487-88). See also W. Hatch, "The Meaning of John 16:8-11," *HTR* 14 (1921) 103-105; A. H. Stanton, "Convince or Convict (John 16:8)," *ExpTim* 33 (1921-22) 278-79; L. J. Lutkemeyer, "The Role of the Paraclete (John 16:7-15)," *CBQ* 8 (1946) 220-29; M. F. Berrouard, "Le Paraclète, défenseur du Christ devant la conscience du croyant (Jn 16, 8-11)," *RSPT* 33 (1949) 361-89; D. Holwerda, *The Holy Spirit*, 53-59; M. Zerwick, "Vom Wirken des Heiligen Geistes in uns. Meditationsgedanken zu Jo 16,5-15," *GeistLeb* 38 (1965) 224-30; G. Johnston, *Spirit-Paraclete*, 34-36; B. Lindars, "Δικαιοσύνη in John 16:8 and 10," in *Mélanges Bibliques en hommage au R. P. Béda Rigaux*, ed. A. Descamps and A. Halleux (Gembloux: Duculot, 1970) 275-85; E. Bammel, "Jesus und der Paraklet in Johannes 16," in *Christ and Spirit in the New Testament*, 199-217; Porsch, *Pneuma*, 275-89; de la Potterie, *La Verité*, 1: 399-421.

While Carson surveys various exegetical problems (five in all), two chief questions dominate the others. On the one hand, how do we understand ἐλέγχειν περί in 16:8? Does the Paraclete convince, convict, or prove the world wrong? In whom does this work transpire: in the disciples or among their opponents? On the other hand, how do we translate the three ὅτι clauses? Are they explicative, explaining the nature of sin, righteousness, and judgment? Or are they causal, providing the basis of this conviction and hence modifying the verb ἐλέγχειν?

Initially, the semantic range of ἐλέγχειν securely places it in a forensic sphere and urges that we translate "to convict" or better, "to convince."[40] In the juridical image, this idiom conveys the thought of an advocate eliciting the surrender of his legal adversary. It evokes thoughts of persuasion and compulsion. If this is true, one of two interpretations may be chosen. First, the Spirit may convict the world with regard to its wrong ideas of sin, righteousness, and judgment. This interpretation has the advantage of treating the three ὅτι clauses identically (e.g., the wrong notion of sin, etc., belonging to the world) and retaining the symmetry of the passage.[41] But as Barrett points out, John's use of ἐλέγχειν περί in 8:46 poses a stiff objection to this translation.[42] Ἐλέγχειν περί should refer to a genuine object and not simply to wrong ideas (contra Bultmann).

The second interpretation still translates ἐλέγχειν "to convict/convince," but then takes the three clauses either as explicative of the sin or causally related to the main verb. Harvey and others have argued for the former understanding, asserting that in these verses we are not told why the Paraclete carries on this work, but rather we are informed as to the content of these accusations.[43] While this alternative must not be ruled out, Carson, Barrett, and Hoskyns give convincing reasons that interpreting these as causal clauses seems best. Carson parts company with the others, however, by demanding that all three nouns (sin, righteousness, judgment) must refer to the world. His greatest hurdle is δικαιοσύνη, and here he explains that the Spirit convicts the world of its (ironic) sense of righteousness. This interpretation gives δικαιοσύνη a negative meaning and preserves a perfect symmetry.[44]

But is it necessary to insist that "maintenance of the symmetry is a necessary condition of a reasonable interpretation"?[45] If not, Carson's only

---

40. Trites, *Concept of Witness*, 118-19; BAG, 249; Barrett, *John*, 487-88; Carson, ibid., 558.

41. Carson, ibid., 549-50, refers to Bauer, Loisy, Westcott, Strathmann, Blank, and esp. Schnackenburg, among others who support this view. Cf. Bultmann, *John*, 562-63; Brown, *John*, 2: 704-705; and Berrouard, "Le Paraclète," 361-69, who defend a modified version of this position, claiming that the proof is provided for the disciples. Carson, ibid., 551-54, gives close attention to de la Potterie's similar view.

42. Barrett, *John*, 487; Carson, ibid., 550. The verb occurs only 3 times in John (3:20; 8:46; 16:8).

43. Harvey, *Jesus on Trial*, 113; cf. Brown, *John*, 2: 711-14. Büchsel, *TDNT* 2: 474, insists that "to take ὅτι causally in 16:9-11 is artificial."

44. Carson, "Function," 558-66. Cf. Lindars's unique interpretation of ἁμαρτία (as guilt) and δικαιοσύνη (as innocence), in "Δικαιοσύνη," and in his commentary, 502-503. See the cogent remarks of Carson, ibid., 555-56, concerning this view.

45. Pace Carson, ibid., 553; cf. 554, 560.

criticism of Barrett and Hoskyns falls away. The sense would then be that John is giving the fundamental bases of the Spirit's work of conviction.[46] This point is especially clear in the first clause. Unbelief is the cause of sin throughout the Fourth Gospel, and it will be a part of the witness of the church. The Spirit will also convince the world concerning Christ's righteousness (not its own!) because in his departure the Father has vindicated and glorified him. In his absence (v. 10b) the disciples will receive the Spirit. Finally, this Spirit will convince the world concerning its judgment because through Christ's death and resurrection the world's ruler has been judged.

Far more important than the syntactical explanation of these elements is the general promise that one major role of the Spirit Paraclete will be the confrontation of the world—indeed, the persuasion of the world. Thus Brown's use of 14:17 to argue that the Paraclete does not convince the world and that "the forum is internal" does not seem compelling.[47] In this first Paraclete saying, the question is the reception and possession of the Spirit, not his initial convicting role. As Trites concludes, "the *testimonium Spiritus sancti internum* is [thus] a *sine qua non* in John's concept of witness."[48] According to 16:8-11 the Spirit will work through the testimony of the community, convincing the world of the evidence it holds about Christ. As the community stands on trial for Christ, the Spirit will turn the tables (as in reality Christ had already done in his "trial") and address the world through the church with the veracity of its own Christ-centered message. As Schnackenburg suggests, this more or less confrontational function may even be seen at work in the polemics that ultimately swept the community when the courtroom shifted from the world to the community itself.[49]

Therefore in its trial the Johannine community experienced the Spirit as an advocate as it addressed its own opponents. But Trites explains that in the juridical setting one other function stands alongside the advocate model, namely, that of the "witness."[50] Here the focus is less on the opponent and more on the evidence. In the Johannine community, who was the chief witness? What was the source of the community's testimony about Christ?

3. THE PARACLETE AS WITNESS

To be a witness for Christ is to bring forward evidence that substantiates his case. Those scholars who have found a parallel between the Paraclete and the Beloved Disciple are correct on at least one count: in the Johannine community the Beloved Disciple was the witness par excellence. For example, John 19:34-35 offers a witness to the crucifixion that is obviously intended to have evidential value. Similarly, 21:24 seems to offer the credentials of this disciple almost as if to authenticate the Gospel itself (cf. 1 John 1:1-3). On the other

---

46. See Barrett, *John*, 488; Hoskyns, *John*, 484-85; Tasker, *John*, 179-80.
47. Brown, *John*, 2: 711-12.
48. Trites, *Concept of Witness*, 119.
49. Schnackenburg, "Johanneische Gemeinde," 291.
50. Trites, *Concept of Witness*, 22, 46, 84, 114-22.

hand, the face-value identification of the Paraclete as the Beloved Disciple (initially at any rate) by Sasse, Culpepper, and others does not seem convincing.[51] One catalyst that inspired interest in the revealing, witnessing work of the Spirit may have been the Beloved Disciple's death (John 21:20-23). But it is certainly incorrect to say that the other Paraclete was created to assuage the grief of the "orphaned" disciples after this leader's death.[52] The former "Paraclete" was Jesus (not the Beloved Disciple), and the "other Paraclete" is a post-Jesus figure, not a post-Beloved Disciple figure. It is probably correct to say that while the Beloved Disciple was a historical person, he was also an ideal disciple, especially to the extent that he modeled the Paraclete's presence within the community.[53] Through him the Paraclete bore witness to (15:26) and glorified Christ (16:4), but this activity was also to continue throughout the life of the church.

One of the greatest crises in the early church was certainly the gradual death of the apostolic eyewitnesses and the growing awareness of distance from the historical Jesus.[54] Johannine Christianity had bridged this gap by finding in the Spirit the present reality of Christ. But in the church's mission what authority would continue to forge the kerygma as the church confronted the world? Certainly the apostolic circle originally played this role. While there are parallels to the Spirit's teaching function in the rest of the NT (cf. Luke 12:12), only the Fourth Evangelist develops the "recalling" function of the Spirit.[55] As the Johannine church engaged the world in this divine lawsuit, the evidence it carried substantiating its case for Christ stemmed from the Spirit Paraclete.

a. Anamnesis: John 14:25-26

Pointing to the Pauline evidence for the recollection of tradition, Nils Dahl has joined Birger Gerhardsson in commenting that the "church's memory grew spontaneously out of its missionary experience."[56] But while Gerhardsson

---

51. S. H. Sasse, "Der Paraklet im Johannesevangelium," *ZNW* 24 (1925) 273-77; A. Culpepper, *The Johannine School*, 267ff.; and esp. A. Kragerud, *Der Lieblingsjunger*, passim.

52. Culpepper, ibid., 269. Culpepper's use of form criticism here leads him to reconstruct the community as follows: The Beloved Disciple (= BD) was the first Paraclete for the community. The Paraclete sayings can thus be "used as further evidence concerning the role of the BD in the community." After the BD died, the community formulated its concept of the Spirit Paraclete around the image of the BD's activity and was thus assured of this continued personal aid.

53. Brown, "The Paraclete," 130.

54. Brown, *John*, 2: 1141-42, indicates these points to be the major features of the *Sitz im Leben* of the Paraclete sayings.

55. U. B. Müller, "Die Parakletenvorstellung," 44.

56. N. A. Dahl, "Anamnesis—Memory and Commemoration in Early Christianity," in *Jesus in the Memory of the Early Church* (Minneapolis: Augsburg, 1976) 15; B. Gerhardsson, *Memory and Manuscript: Oral Tradition and Written Transmission in Rabbinic Judaism and Early Christianity* (Uppsala: Gleerup, 1961) 280-88. Martin Hengel gives a brief though valuable discussion of "memory" among Hellenistic writers and applies this to the Gospels and Acts in *Acts and the History of Earliest Christianity*, tr. J. Bowden (London: SCM, 1979; Philadelphia: Fortress, 1980) 27-29.

focused attention on the NT evidence for this recollection in Luke and Paul, Dahl has correctly observed that the Fourth Evangelist has made explicit what the other NT writers only imply. In John 14:25-26 it is claimed that the Spirit will recall to memory all that Jesus has spoken: ἐκεῖνος ὑμᾶς διδάξει πάντα καὶ ὑπομνήσει ὑμᾶς πάντα ἃ εἶπον ὑμῖν ἐγώ. "These words," remarks Dahl, "are like a key to the Gospel of John."[57]

The terminology for "recalling" appears under three verbs in the Fourth Gospel. Μιμνήσκομαι occurs three times (2:17, 22; 12:16), ὑπομιμνήσκω once (14:26), and μνημονεύω three times (15:20; 16:4, 21). It is evident, however, that this concept of "remembering" is bound to the misunderstanding of the disciples in John.[58] Their post-Easter enlightenment through the Spirit has corrected their once-distorted, earlier discipleship. This points to the pivotal nature of 7:39, not just as a road sign indicating the coming life in the Spirit, but that in this Spirit a new hermeneutical perspective will be born. Thus in 12:16 the Evangelist frankly admits, "his disciples did not understand these things at first" (ταῦτα οὐκ ἔγνωσαν αὐτοῦ οἱ μαθηταὶ τὸ πρῶτον). The text makes clear that only after the glorification of Jesus (cf. 7:39) was the proper explanation of Zech. 9:9 known. Only through the Spirit was this anamnesis possible. In John 2:22 a similar perspective prevails. The saying about resurrection was mysterious until the post-resurrection context enlightened the disciples' minds.[59] As Franz Mussner has remarked on this verse, in remembrance Jesus' words "are not only reproduced by memory but at the same time are unfolded for faith."[60] The Spirit works not simply mechanically but interpretatively as well. The historical sayings of Jesus are transposed into the living kerygma of the church.

John 16:4 and 20:8 illustrate this perspective.[61] In 16:4 Jesus warns his disciples of the coming tribulation and claims that the future anamnesis of this warning will bring understanding and comfort (cf. 14:29). Therefore the perspective is forward-looking and anticipates a period of later, reflective, inspired contemplation. In 16:12 Jesus again adopts this perspective, but this time he remains silent while leaving the work of revelation entirely in the hands of the coming Paraclete (16:13ff.). In 20:8-9 the Evangelist makes an editorial comment. Here the projection is retrospective: he now knows the scripture about resurrection (20:9) and has experienced the Spirit, but in the period before his anointing (20:22) he was unenlightened. This phenomenon of recollection may have centered on the OT as well as on Jesus' words, and thus, as Trites believes, may account for the numerous fulfillment texts in John.[62]

The primary importance of 14:26 is that it affirms a definite historicizing

---

57. Dahl, ibid., 28; Cullmann, *Early Christian Worship*, 48.

58. The perspective may also be disguised in the many other misunderstandings and double meanings in John. See above, pp. 167-68.

59. For similar ideas in Luke, cf. Luke 24:13-43, esp. vv. 27, 31; cf. Acts 11:16.

60. Mussner, *The Historical Jesus*, 41.

61. Porsch, *Pneuma*, 264.

62. Trites, *Concept of Witness*, 120, refers to John 2:17/Ps. 69:9; John 12:13-16/Ps. 118:26 and Zech. 9:9. Cf. Painter, *John, Witness*, 67; and Cullmann, *Early Christian Worship*, 48ff.

work of the Spirit. He calls forward the OT and what Jesus has said, but brings no spontaneous revelation of his own. As Barrett puts it, "There is no *independent revelation* through the Paraclete, but only an application of the revelation in Jesus."[63] Hence the Paraclete is a conservative, preserving force in revelation.[64] In this respect we would do well to read 14:26 in conjunction with 16:13-14. The revealing work of the Paraclete is entirely dependent on Jesus: it is christocentric in that there can be no departure from what Jesus has already revealed. Thus in 16:13-14 we learn that the Paraclete will not speak on his own authority (οὐ γὰρ λαλήσει ἀφ' ἑαυτοῦ), but he will declare only that which he hears from Jesus. This is the standard that must always be used for comparison in any discussion of the revelatory work of the Spirit in John.[65] As Kothgasser has made plain, the Paraclete must follow the revelatory pattern set down by Jesus: he will not speak of himself (5:19; 8:28; 7:16-18; 12:49; 14:10; etc.). The revelatory Spirit finds its analogy in Jesus: he is subordinate to the One who has sent him.[66]

This, of course, is a far cry from scholars such as Michel who claim that "in no circumstances should we misunderstand this Biblical μιμνήσκομαι along historicizing or intellectualistic lines."[67] But surely this is John's whole point: in the Johannine community's witness before the world, it could present historical evidence for the claims of Christ. Even the Fourth Gospel itself no doubt served as an anchor in history and became a vehicle of remembrance for those who were not eyewitnesses.

To be sure, the historical critic will quickly point out that what the Gospel may contain is only the disciples' memory of Jesus and not the life of Jesus.[68] But this is another matter. What is plain is that John has a clear sense of historical perspective and has not allowed the present horizon to engulf completely the distant one. The present revelation is anchored in the past: the Spirit brings forward the material facts and words of Christ and interprets them in the life of the church. Thus in John μιμνήσκομαι points to a material recollection.

While we can be sure that John appreciates this historical perspective, for him the Spirit also plays an interpretative role. In 14:26, Windisch for one wishes to separate the teaching of the Paraclete from his recalling.[69] That is,

---

63. Barrett, *John*, 467, emphasis mine; cf. Kothgasser, "Die Lehr-" (1972) 29ff.

64. Thus the variant of D (ἄν εἴπω for εἶπον) is excluded on theological grounds.

65. This is particularly stressed in the study of Kothgasser, "Die Lehr-" (1971) esp. 595ff. He writes, "With few exceptions the author never tires of saying repeatedly that the Holy Spirit brings nothing basically new, has not 'supplemented' the revelation, nor ever shall substitute through something new and better a rival to this revelation. Rather the author stresses far more that the Spirit enables the revelation of Christ to be recalled, interpreted, and experienced ever anew. Christ is *the* Revealer and the Holy Spirit is the teacher, not alongside Christ, but after Christ and subordinate to him" (pp. 596-97, emphasis mine). Cf. his 1972 article, 29-36.

66. Kothgasser, "Die Lehr-" (1972) 36-39.

67. O. Michel, *TDNT* 4: 678. Michel interprets such remembrance as a personal evangelistic call to embrace the gospel. Similarly, Bultmann (*John*, 626-27) rejects this anamnesis as a "historical reconstruction" and finds a reference only to "eschatological decision."

68. Dahl, "Anamnesis," 28-29.

69. Windisch, *The Spirit Paraclete*, 6-7; but cf. Porsch, *Pneuma*, 257ff.

the Spirit completes the revelation of Christ by helping the church formulate the apostolic kerygma which arose after Easter. While this exegesis of 14:26 may be dubious, it observes correctly that the revelatory work of the Paraclete is not simply mechanistic. The Paraclete advances the knowledge of the believer in the historical data and applies it to the present situation of the church. This is the "Johannine mode of vision," as Mussner calls it. It is anamnesis directed to the historical event—as well as interpretation directed toward the hidden meaning within this history.[70] Cullmann expresses it thus: "This 'remembering' is not merely a remembering of the material facts, it includes alongside of this that understanding of the facts which is first granted through the Holy Spirit."[71]

Therefore we should examine this Johannine "mode of vision"—this unique hermeneutical outlook—especially as it involves interpretation and possibly supplementary revelation.

b. The Johannine Hermeneutic: John 16:12-15

When we turn to the fifth Paraclete saying, we find that scholars are quick to note that the Johannine perspective is not simply historical. While 14:26 stressed anamnesis, 16:12-15 implies that in the mission of the church the Paraclete will provide supplementary revelations. What kind of testimony is this and how does it determine the Johannine hermeneutical perspective?

John 16:12-13a have often been used to justify either novel later revelations or authoritative ecclesiastical dogmas.[72] Jesus claims that he has many things to say (πολλὰ λέγειν), but in view of the disciples' inability to bear them, it will be the task of the Paraclete to reveal these things later. But this passage seems to contradict 15:15, where Jesus tells his followers that he has already made known to them everything (πάντα) he has heard. Porsch finds a helpful solution in the perspective found in 16:25. There Jesus refers to two epochs of revelation: one former period when Jesus spoke figuratively (ἐν παροιμίαις), and another time when he will speak openly ([ἐν] παρρησίᾳ). This transition turns on Jesus' glorification; according to Porsch, "this speaking of Jesus ἐν παρρησίᾳ is identical with the Spirit's future revelatory work."[73] Therefore the Spirit will have an interpretative relationship to the first, parabolic epoch. He will have a retrospective view in which he takes the former things of Christ and perfectly clarifies them for the church.

This two-epoch perspective is also apparent in 16:12. By his word order John has emphasized ἄρτι[74] and contrasted it with a future time (ὅταν δέ). Once again, this differentiation points to the activity of the Spirit. But in these verses, despite the suggestion of Porsch, John is not talking about a clarifica-

---

70. Mussner, *Historical Jesus*, 44. "The Johannine mode of vision and the work of the Paraclete belong inseparably together" (p. 67).

71. Cullmann, *Early Christian Worship*, 49.

72. Brown, *John*, 2: 714; cf. Kothgasser, "Die Lehr-" (1972) 15ff.

73. Porsch, *Pneuma*, 291. Contra Hauck, *TDNT* 5: 856, who refers to the parousia as the time of unconcealed revelation.

74. Bernard, *John*, 2: 509. Cf. ἄρτι in 13:7; 9:19. Cf. Kothgasser, "Die Lehr-" (1972) 18-19.

tion of the former epoch. That the disciples cannot bear to hear these revelations indicates that they have *not* heard them. Jesus may be relying on the Paraclete to take the disciples into new revelatory experiences, not merely recitative exercises.[75] This is certainly the meaning of 16:13a. Guidance into "all truth"[76] must in the first instance mean fidelity to Jesus Christ (who is the Truth). But then this guidance also implies a degree of freedom. Like the LXX use of ὁδηγέω (e.g., Ps. 25:5; 77:20; 78:72; 143:10), this guidance will be divine direction which involves moving forward.[77]

This new revelatory work is not without limitations, however, and the Evangelist quickly adds that the Spirit is strictly dependent on Jesus for all that he says. The Spirit will speak only what he will hear (ἀκούσει). But notice the tense of this verb. John does not say that the Spirit will only reiterate what Jesus has said (anamnesis): there may be future, progressive revelation. The revelation of Jesus will still continue in the community, and the Spirit Paraclete will be his authoritative channel. But these revelations must not depart from the original revelation of the historical Christ. The Spirit will recall these, interpret them, and continue their presence in the life of the community.

On the one hand, τὰ ἐρχόμενα in John 16:13b could refer to the historical setting of the Gospel and mean the coming passion and resurrection.[78] But this view has been challenged by various scholars who find here a prophetic gift functioning within the Evangelist's own perspective. For example, Bernard remarks that "this is the only place in John where any of the Pauline χαρίσματα of the Spirit are mentioned (cf. 1 Cor. 12:29, 30)."[79] If this is true, a direct link with the Apocalypse may be at hand.[80]

Brown attempts to counter this view in his study of ἀναγγέλλειν. He claims that in John the prefix (ἀνα) preserves its force of reiterative announcement (as in classical and LXX Greek).[81] The Spirit will reannounce the things to come. This means that the Spirit is once again dependent on the prior historical revelation of Jesus in these verses (cf. vv. 14, 15).

But is this argument compelling? It may be that John 16:13b introduces a

---

75. So Lindars, *John*, 504; Bernard, *John*, 2: 509; cf. F. Relton, "The Unfinished Teaching of Christ (John 16:12)," *ExpTim* 4 (1892-93) 446-50; and the exposition of D. A. Carson, *The Farewell Discourse and the Final Prayer of Jesus* (Grand Rapids: Baker, 1980) 149-50, who sees the climax of this revelation in the canon.

76. The textual "improvement" of εἰς + accusative (A B K Δ Π Ψ f[13]) is probably secondary to ἐν + dative (ℵ D L W Θ f[1] et al.). Cf. Metzger, *Textual Commentary*, 247. It is best not to see any theological significance in the change. So Brown, *John*, 2: 707; Barrett, *John*, 489. Cf. BDF, § 218.

77. J. Kremer, "Jesu Verheissung," 255.

78. Marsh, *John*, 538; cf. Kremer, ibid., 256-57; and Barrett, *John*, 490.

79. Bernard, *John*, 2: 511. Cf. Lindars, *John*, 505; Betz, *Der Paraklet*, 191-92; Windisch, *Spirit Paraclete*, 12; Boring, "The Influence of Christian Prophecy," 119; Bultmann, *John*, 575. Barrett, *John*, 490, seems to overtax John's realized eschatology when he argues that the only final eschatological event is the judgment, which for John is already operative (as in 16:8-11). Cf. Dodd, *Interpretation*, 414.

80. Bultmann, *John*, 575n.3; D. Hill, *New Testament Prophecy*, 151. Against this view, see R. Schnackenburg, "Johanneische Gemeinde," 303.

81. Brown, *John*, 2: 708, cites P. Joüon, *RSR* 28 (1938) 234-35. Cf. Schniewind, *TDNT* 1: 64. Ἀναγγέλλειν appears 5 times (4:25; 5:15 var.; 16:13, 14, 15). Cf. ἀπαγγέλλειν in 16:25 and ἀγγελία in 1 John 1:5; 3:11. See the critical remarks of Kremer, "Jesu Verheissung," 257.

broader problem. When John says that the Paraclete will speak only what he hears—that he will only give what he takes from Jesus—does this refer to the prior words of Jesus given in the historical ministry? Or does this mean that since the Paraclete is the Spirit from Christ (*Christus praesens*), no matter what he announces must exhibit fidelity to the historical Christ? Kremer successfully argues that in the christocentric nature of the Paraclete's revelation, it may also be *Christus praesens* that is meant.[82] Of course, the Evangelist was assured that this revelation reflected the *ipsissima vox Jesu*, but at the same time there is latitude in how the Spirit may work. He may reveal the future prophetically; and this, John would claim, is from Christ. The Paraclete may not, however, deviate from the prior revelation, from the anamnesis. Therefore there is control. Thus in 1 John the argument with the secessionists centers on what was "in the beginning." The Spirit they claimed to possess had brought revelations which had left the traditional moorings (1 John 4:2-3; see further below).

* * *

We can sum up by saying that the revelatory work of the Paraclete found in John 14 and 16 exhibits a dialectical relationship between tradition (anamnesis) and inspiration. The Paraclete preserved the words of Christ in the memory of the church. Furthermore, the Paraclete led the Evangelist and his community into "all truth." This was the Spirit of Truth. The historical words and events of Christ were given their right meaning and interpreted relevantly in the proclamation of the church. But in addition the Paraclete was ready to aid the church prophetically in any new context. To be sure, there is a tension here. Hoskyns rightly sees that in these verses "the power of the Spirit does not consist in secret and mystical revelation . . . in new truths."[83] Rather, it means declaring the word of Jesus afresh and not departing from the historic anchor. This then excludes Marcion's strained employment of these verses to justify his own fantastic agenda. There may be prophetic movement only when it does not abandon the traditional moorings of Christ.

Johannine scholarship is indebted to Mussner for his careful attention to this dialectic and its relation to the Spirit Paraclete in John. He concludes that as the Evangelist looks back to the tradition (anamnesis) and experiences the present revelation of Christ, "the time horizons merge, but this of course must not be misunderstood. In this merging the past is not annulled; in its actualization for the present and in the present, it entirely preserves its importance, supplying the material by which the act of vision can perpetually enkindle anew."[84]

In the Johannine hermeneutic, therefore, there is freedom *and* control. The two horizons are separable in the Evangelist's view of history, and as

---

82. Kremer, ibid., 260-61; cf. W. E. Bowen, "The Inspiration of the Church," *ExpTim* 10 (1898-99) 26-33.

83. Hoskyns, *John*, 486.

84. Mussner, *The Historical Jesus*, 46. Note Mussner's use of the "we formulas" in John to illustrate the coming together of the two horizons (pp. 70-72).

Schnackenburg firmly asserts, there must always be a return to the tradition and to Jesus.[85] The revelatory work of the Paraclete is entirely christocentric—it is centered on the foundation of what Jesus historically said and did—but it also builds (interpreting and supplementing through deeper insights) while never exceeding the perimeters laid out by its former work of anamnesis.

One is tempted to apply these results to the nature of the Fourth Gospel itself. D. M. Smith, for example, refers to the words of Jesus in John as the product of a Spirit-inspired community and a "fulfillment of the promise of the Paraclete."[86] Kothgasser speaks of the Gospel as a "spirit-directed recollection, a new insight, understanding, and experience of the entire reality of Christ."[87] Some have found in the Paraclete a type of "self-legitimization" which the Evangelist is consciously tapping to bring greater authority to his presentation of Christ.[88] This may be particularly true in the discourses where, as Cullmann observes, John has used this conviction to lead the reader deeper into the historic *ipsissima vox Jesu*.[89] Again, there is freedom and control: there is a balance between the apostolic and the prophetic offices as the Evangelist, under the inspiration of the Paraclete, presents Jesus ἐν τῇ ἀληθείᾳ πάσῃ. In addition, there is sensitivity to development. If the Evangelist's community was in debate with docetic Christians or hostile Judaism, the Gospel properly presents those aspects of Christ that suit the current crisis.

Yet in all this we must be clear that John has a definite sense of history. The perimeters of the historical anamnesis must be held intact at all costs. John's hermeneutic places historicity at its very center. J. A. T. Robinson expresses it thus: "Nor is to 'remember,' however creatively, to invent. Rather, it is, in the power and truth and freedom of the Spirit, to take the things of Jesus and hold them up to the light, so that the light can transfigure them and show them in their true glory. It is not to make up things about Jesus in order to illustrate timeless truths. For John has a profound reverence for history, for happenedness. As the locus of incarnation, it cannot be treated lightly or wantonly: it is holy ground."[90]

4. PROPHECY AND HETERODOXY

We noted in chapter 1 those scholars who suspect that behind the Paraclete sayings we can find traces of early Christian prophetism. For example, both David Hill and M. E. Boring, make the cogent observation that the Spirit in

---

85. Schnackenburg, *John*, 3: 151; cf. idem, "Johanneische Gemeinde," 287-88.

86. Smith, "Johannine Christianity," 232-33; cf. Mussner, "Historical Jesus," 82ff.; R. E. Brown, "Kerygma," 395-96; Schnackenburg, "Johanneische Gemeinde," 289; and J. R. Michaels, "The Johannine Words of Jesus and Christian Prophecy," in *SBL Seminar Papers*, vol. 2 (Missoula: Scholar's Press, 1975).

87. Kothgasser, "Die Lehr-" (1971) 593.

88. Müller, "Die Parakletenvorstellung," 51, 77; Cullmann, *Early Christian Worship*, 48.

89. Cullmann, *Johannine Circle*, 18. Cf. Brown, "Kerygma," 396.

90. J. A. T. Robinson, "The Use of the Fourth Gospel for Christology," in *Christ and Spirit in the New Testament*, 67.

John 14–16 describes a "pneumatic Christian speech charism."[91] Verbs such as διδάσκειν (14:26), ὑπομιμνῄσκειν (14:26), μαρτυρεῖν (15:26), ἐλέγχειν (16:8), ἀναγγέλλειν (16:13), ὁδηγεῖν (16:13), and δοξάζειν (16:14) lead to the conclusion that the Johannine community was not unaware of a prophetic charism. Although Boring's attempt to see in the Johannine Christ the model of an early Christian prophet is unsatisfactory,[92] his identification of a "revelatory chain-of-command" in John and in the Apocalypse is intriguing. The angel and prophet in the Apocalypse are forged into the one figure of the Paraclete in John. Therefore, if there is a connection between the two writings, the prophet of Rev. 1 may exemplify the activity of a prophet within the Johannine community.

As we saw above, the raw materials for this prophetic charism were latent in the figure of the Paraclete (esp. 16:13). To be sure, Rev. 1–3 may provide evidence of prophetic activity of this very kind. Here the glorified Christ speaks to the churches through the prophet who is "in the Spirit" (Rev. 1:10). Various scholars have noted the importance of these chapters, and Bultmann and numerous others have pressed Rev. 1–3 to extract the conclusion that prophetic λόγια 'Ιησοῦ were indistinguishable from the traditional words of Jesus (the anamnesis).[93] Hill's criticisms of the latter suggestion are certainly penetrating: in the Apocalypse the genre of literature (prophecy) is clearly defined for what it is (not so in the Gospels).[94] Where parallels between these prophetic utterances and the tradition are possible (e.g., Rev. 16:15 par. Luke 12:39; Matt. 24:43), it may be the case that genuine logia of Jesus were taken up by the prophets and reapplied in the church. This reapplication is precisely one of the interpretative functions of the Paraclete.

Another promising avenue of evidence for Johannine prophetism may come to us from 1 John. The author writes that "you have no need for anyone to teach you" (2:27), while simultaneously warning that "many false prophets have gone out into the world" (4:1; cf. ἀντίχριστος, 1:18; 4:3). It is uncertain whether the problem that confronted the Johannine community at this stage was the appearance of spirit-inspired prophets advocating new words of the risen Lord.[95] Certainly this possibility cannot be dismissed. But it may be that these heterodox teachers/prophets had justified their gnosticizing christology on the very basis of the Paraclete's revelatory activity that the community knew so well.[96] If this heresy stemmed from the Fourth Gospel itself and its inter-

---

91. M. E. Boring, "The Influence of Christian Prophecy," 113; Cf. David Hill, *New Testament Prophecy*, 149ff.; see above, pp. 38-41.

92. See above, pp. 39-40.

93. D. M. Smith, "Johannine Christianity," 233; Johnston, *Spirit-Paraclete*, 139-40; D. Hill, "Prophecy and Prophets in the Revelation of St. John," *NTS* 18 (1971-72) 401-18; Bultmann, *History of the Synoptic Tradition*, tr. J. Marsh (Oxford: Blackwell; New York: Harper & Row, 1963) 127-28. Cf. Hill, *New Testament Prophecy*, 160-85.

94. Hill, ibid., 168; idem, "On the Evidence for the Creative Role of Christian Prophets," *NTS* 20 (1973-74) 262-74.

95. Smith, "Johannine Christianity," 233; Brown, *Community*, 138ff.; Büchsel, *Die Johannesbriefe*, Theologischer Handkommentar zum Neuen Testament (Leipzig: Deichert, 1933) 4-5, as cited by Marshall, *First John*, 16. Cf. Kümmel, *Introduction*, 440-41; and Woll, "Departure," 235-39.

96. Brown, *Community*, 139; Culpepper, *Johannine School*, 283; cf. above, pp. 171ff.

pretation, then the Johannine hermeneutic and all its tensions may have been pressed into service, and in its misuse, broken.

It is not in our interest to identify the nature of the heresy nor the identity of its bearers. We have already stressed that the debate was pneumatic and turned on the spiritual authority of the secessionists to validate their case.[97] What is now important is to note the response of the Epistle's author. If the Paraclete's revelatory work created a dialectic between anamnesis and inspiration, how does the author resolve what is obviously a problem of revelation? Has this prophetic abuse—departure from the anamnesis—caused a reassessment of the Johannine hermeneutic?

a. The Johannine Adjustment

Windisch argued that the absence of characteristic Paraclete motifs from 1 John indicated that the community's awareness of the Spirit "had nothing to do with the Paraclete."[98] While this evidence is important, it led Windisch to the wrong conclusion. Here the author is addressing a problem that stemmed directly from the Paraclete, and now in his rebuttal the last thing to which he wishes to allude is the same tradition which the secessionists may have employed. He eschews those very attributes of the Spirit Paraclete that forced the error.

This perspective is evident first from the stress on tradition in the Epistle. Ἀπ' ἀρχῆς occurs with marked frequency to point the readers back to their traditional basis (1:1; 2:7, 13, 14, 24; 3:8, 11; 2 John 5, 6).[99] Thus in 2:24 he exhorts, "Let what was in the beginning abide in you." Again in 3:11, "This is the message which you heard from the beginning." We might say that the author's perspective is entirely retrospective: he points back to experiences and knowledge from an earlier authoritative time (cf. 1:1-5) and reasserts what to him are "old commandments" (2:7).

This perspective is also found in the Epistle's notion of truth. No longer is it a dynamic idea to be explored by the Spirit as described in the Farewell Discourses. Here it is static. Ἀλήθεια occurs frequently in 1 John and often denotes something possessed or adhered to, such as a dogma. Thus in 1 John 3:9 the author affirms that his community is "of the truth." 2 John 8 speaks of "workers in the truth," and v. 12 personifies the concept still further.[100] No longer is there any notion of "going forward." There is only a desperate attempt to grasp at the past.

Finally, one datum of spiritual authenticity in 1 John is found in its stress on being in or remaining in "the word" (1:10; 2:14; cf. 1:1; 2:5, 7; 3:18).[101] Indeed, word and Spirit function closely in this Epistle in the personal identity of the believer. Thus in 2:26-27 this anointing which undoubtedly refers to the

---

97. See above, pp. 171-78.

98. Windisch, *Spirit Paraclete*, 23.

99. H. Conzelmann, "Was von Anfang War," in *Neutestamentliche Studien für R. Bultmann*, NovTSup 21 (Berlin: Töpelmann, 1954) 194-201.

100. Bultmann, *First John*, 102; Marshall, *First John*, 93.

101. Dunn, *Baptism*, 196-97; Grundmann, *TDNT* 9: 572.

Spirit[102] exhibits itself chiefly in teaching and securing sound orthodoxy. The role of the Spirit then is to give the believer clarity of thought and instruction concerning belief. Moreover, to receive and accept the orthodox faith (or word) is paramount to knowing with certainty that one holds the true Spirit.[103]

These aspects of 1 John, when joined with the author's suspicion of outright prophetic activity, lead us to conclude that in the Johannine hermeneutic the conservative, preserving emphasis had won out. Anamnesis had overtaken inspiration and no longer worked along with it. Indeed, 1 John 2:27 directly echoes John 14:26 in its stress on teaching and the fidelity to tradition.[104] Because of the schism which strained the revelatory work of the Spirit, the Johannine community ultimately disparaged the office of prophet but retained the revelatory function of the Spirit in personal confirmation and testimony.[105]

b. Early Catholicism?

This evidence has led some to believe that what we have in 1 John is the earliest signs of incipient catholicism. In this fashion, Conzelmann named this Epistle "a Johannine pastoral epistle."[106] That is, in the question of entrenchment or expansion, the community ultimately chose the security of the former. Käsemann and Bornkamm find this catholicism budding in the "elder" of 2 John and in the recipient of 3 John, Gaius.[107]

We would suggest that rather than locating conflicting models of church and ministry in the Johannine writings, the community should be viewed in terms of its historical evolution. Brown correctly observes that the Johannine community was forced to adjust itself following its crisis in pneumatology and revelation.[108] The dialectic between tradition and prophecy—anamnesis and inspiration—did not survive as it was set out in the Fourth Gospel. This Gospel provided not only the doctrinal materials but the hermeneutical methods which finally led to the secession in the community and the Evangelist's counterbalancing response. In some respects, *Christus praesens* had been silenced in the community. But this evidence should not be taken too far. Charism is not set entirely in opposition to tradition. Pneumatic vitality still persists in the Epistle. To claim that 2 John and 3 John are full movements away from the more decentralized charismatic model is to find more evidence in these texts than is warranted.

Despite the conservative drift that the Johannine literature exhibits, it is likely that when the Johannine writings were fully accepted into the church,

---

102. See our discussion in chapter 4, pp. 174-75.

103. Dunn, *Baptism*, 198-99; Houlden, *First John*, 83; and Dodd's commentary on the Epistle.

104. Schnackenburg, *Johannesbriefe*, 161.

105. Schnackenburg, "Johanneische Gemeinde," 303.

106. Conzelmann, "Was von Angang War," 201; cf. M. E. Boring, "Christian Prophecy," 119.

107. Bornkamm, *TDNT* 6: 670-72; Käsemann, *The Testament of Jesus*. Cf. the discussion of Culpepper, *Johannine School*, 283ff.

108. Brown, *Community*, 138-44.

catholicism was already well underway. When considered from this vantage, one can appreciate how uncatholic the Epistles really are and especially how powerful the message of the Spirit must have seemed. The Spirit was not simply confined to the tradition: at the community's lowest ebb (1 John 2:20, 26-27) the Spirit was still actively alive in all believers assessing the validity of any new teaching and leading the church deeper into the truth of Christ.

C. CONCLUSION

We have argued that the christocentric life of the Johannine community is evidenced both in its view of mission and in its experience of revelation. We have suggested that the Johannine interest in the Spirit in the Farewell Discourses evolved from the traditional Synoptic setting of persecution and spiritual aid. The Fourth Evangelist and his community experienced intense conflict with the Jews and the world, and this conflict led them to elevate the traditional "persecution" context to the level of a literary motif: Jesus was presented as if on trial and the church was commissioned as his agents to carry on his lawsuit. Thus in the church's witness, the term *Paraclete* was employed to serve this juridical backdrop. The Spirit offered forensic evidence to establish the case of Christ (and thus of the church).

The demand for evidence in the community for teaching and preaching further inspired the acute interest of John 14 and 16 in the revelatory work of the Spirit. The Spirit would primarily recall the words of Jesus and thus sustain his case before the world. But in addition the Spirit would lead the community into the depth of these truths, inspiring reflection and development. This created a dialectic in the community's understanding of revelation and finally led to the tensions evidenced in the later Epistles. In the end, the revelatory, witnessing work of the Paraclete remained conservative: preserving the tradition and inhibiting development. But this conservatism did not daunt the spiritual vitality of the community for which the ultimate evolution of office and tradition could reside in harmony with enthusiasm and spiritual vigor.

Epilogue

In this study we have endeavored to show that pneumatology was a central concern in the thought and experience of the Johannine community. Beginning with the notorious problem of the background of ὁ παράκλητος, we concluded that recent research has eliminated the possibility of any Gnostic or Hellenistic antecedents and pointed to a Jewish background, particularly intertestamental Judaism and its interest in advocacy. But the Paraclete is a very nuanced figure. The most important feature of the Paraclete is the community's complete reshaping of his image to conform to early Christian experience of the Spirit. Stemming from an experience of rejection and persecution, the community knew the Spirit as its advocate, aid, and revealer (advancing the material evidence in the case for Christ).

But this interest in the Spirit could likewise contribute to christology. Christ also experienced persecution and rejection (cf. the "trial motif") and was the supreme revealer of God. Indeed, his experience of the Spirit could become paradigmatic for the community. While the early church could unite the Spirit with the presence of the resurrected Christ, Johannine thought carried this comparison back into Jesus' earthly career. The Spirit anointed Jesus and was resident within him (as it would anoint and be resident in the believer). It remained on him powerfully. Thus in Jesus' death/glorification, we find the notion that here the Spirit is released (7:37ff.; 19:30, 34). In fact, it is within the process of glorification that the disciples are anointed (20:22). This relation explains the full adjustment of Johannine eschatology. If Spirit and Christ were one, to experience the eschatological Spirit was to experience the eschaton and Christ. Therefore 20:22 serves not only as a fulfillment of the Paraclete promises but as the climax of the Gospel itself: Christ brings himself to his followers in a coalescing of images from the resurrection, Pentecost, and the parousia.

If discipleship in this community was seen especially in terms of the Spirit, what were its features of initiation and worship? In the Fourth Gospel important Spirit texts are aligned with the two most direct allusions to the sacraments. John warns against sacramental abuse in his interest in finding within baptism and the eucharist a genuine experience of Christ in Spirit. In this sense, the Johannine community was a pneumatic community. As 1 John demonstrates, spiritual birth/anointing was the hallmark of Christian identity.

But again, the most pressing concern in this community was its awareness of persecution and rejection. Once more, Christ became a model. That his model was pressed into service in other areas is seen in the language of mission and witness. Just as a feature of the Johannine christology was the "agency" of Christ, so too the disciples were agents fulfilling similar tasks. In the heat of debate, the Spirit was known as a revelatory aid (cf. Synoptic parallels) recalling the words of Christ (anamnesis) and leading into new frontiers of truth. While this work of revelation brought success to the community in its witness before the world, it also opened up an array of problems. The community ultimately found itself sharply divided on issues which clearly stemmed from an abuse of the revelatory work of the Paraclete. In brief, the final crisis of the Johannine community was essentially pneumatic. The spiritual inspiration and experiential focus of the community were pressed into use without serious controls and, in the process, severely strained. 1 John counters this situation with a new dialectic between tradition and experience. The former sayings of Jesus (in the Gospel) must serve as an anchor and limit to unbounded prophetic enthusiasm.

Bibliography

Aalen, S., "'Truth,' A Key Word in St. John's Gospel," in *SE 2 = TU* 87, ed. F. L. Cross (Berlin: Akademie Verlag, 1964) 3-24.

Abbott, E. A., *Johannine Grammar* (London: A. & C. Black, 1906).

———, *Johannine Vocabulary* (London: A. & C. Black, 1905).

Aland, K., Black, M., Martini, C. M., Metzger, B., Wikgren, A., *The Greek New Testament*, 3rd ed. (New York: United Bible Society, 1975).

Albright, W., "Recent Discoveries in Palestine and the Gospel of St. John," in *The Background of the New Testament and Its Eschatology*, ed. W. D. Davies and D. Daube (Cambridge: University Press, 1956) 153-71.

Allen, E. L., "Jesus and Moses in the New Testament," *ExpTim* 67 (1955-56) 104-106.

Anderson, A. A., "The Use of 'Ruah' in 1QS, 1QH, and 1QM," *JSS* 7 (1962) 293-303.

Anderson, B. W., "Hosts, Host of Heaven," *IDB* 2:654-56.

Appold, M. L., *The Oneness Motif in the Fourth Gospel* (Tübingen: Mohr, 1976).

Aune, D. E., *The Cultic Setting of Realized Eschatology in Early Christianity*, NovTSup 28 (Leiden: Brill, 1972).

Bacon, B. W., "The 'Other' Comforter," *Exp* viii, 14 (1917) 274-82.

Bailey, J. A., *The Traditions Common to the Gospels of Luke and John*, NovTSup 7 (Leiden: Brill, 1963).

Bammel, E. "Jesus und der Paraklet in Johannes 16," in *Christ and Spirit in the New Testament*, ed. B. Lindars and S. Smalley (Cambridge: University Press, 1973) 198-217.

Bampfylde, G., "John 19:28—A Case for a Different Translation," *NovT* 11 (1969) 245-60.

Barker, C. J., "Repentance and the New Birth," in *Studies in the Fourth Gospel*, ed. F. L. Cross (London: Mowbray, 1957) 45-51.

Barrett, C. K., "Christocentric or Theocentric? Observations on the Theological Method of the Fourth Gospel," in *La Notion biblique de Dieu*, Bibliotheca ephemeridum theologicarum lovaniensium 41 (1976) 361-76.

———, "The Dialectical Theology of St. John," in *New Testament Essays* (London: SPCK, 1972) 49-69.

———, " 'The Father is Greater Than I' (John 14:28): Subordinationist Christology in the New Testament," in *Neues Testament und Kirche*, ed. J. Gnilka (Freiburg: Herder, 1974) 160-71.

———, "Das Fleisch des Menschensohnes (Joh 6, 53)," in *Jesus und der Menschensohn. Für Anton Vögtle*, ed. R. Pesch and R. Schnackenburg (Freiburg: Herder, 1975) 342-54.

———, *The Gospel According to St. John*, 2nd ed. (London: SPCK; Philadelphia: Westminster, 1978).

———, *The Gospel of John and Judaism* (London: SPCK; Philadelphia: Fortress, 1975).

———, *The Holy Spirit and the Gospel Tradition* (London: SPCK, 1966).

———, "The Holy Spirit in the Fourth Gospel," *JTS* 1 (1950) 1-15.

———, "Important Hypotheses Reconsidered: The Holy Spirit and the Gospel Tradition," *ExpTim* 67 (1955-56) 142-45.

———, "The Lamb of God," *NTS* 1 (1954-55) 210-18.

———, "The Old Testament in the Fourth Gospel," *JTS* 48 (1947) 155-69.

———, "The Place of Eschatology in the Fourth Gospel," *ExpTim* 59 (1947-48) 302-305.

———, *The Prologue of St. John's Gospel*, The Ethel M. Wood Lecture, University of London, 19 February 1970 (London: Athlone Press, 1971; repr. in *New Testament Essays* [London: SPCK, 1972] 27-48).

———, "The Theological Vocabulary of the Fourth Gospel and of the Gospel of Truth," in *Current Issues in New Testament Interpretation: Essays in Honor of Otto A. Piper*, ed. W. Klassen and G. F. Snyder (London: SCM; New York: Harper and Brothers, 1962) 210-23.

Barry, W. A., "The Spirit of Truth and of Life in John's Gospel," *BiTod* 1 (1963) 601-608.

Bartlett, W., "The Coming of the Holy Ghost According to the Fourth Gospel," *ExpTim* 37 (1925-26) 72-75.

Bates, H. W., "Born of Water (John 3:5)," *BSac* 85 (1928) 230-36.

Bauckham, R. J., "The Role of the Spirit in the Apocalypse," *EvQ* 52 (1980) 66-83.

Bauer, W., *A Greek-English Lexicon of the Greek New Testament*, 2nd ed. revised by F. W. Gingrich and F. W. Danker (Chicago: University Press, 1979)

———, *Das Johannesevangelium*, Handbuch zum Neuen Testament, 3rd ed. (Tübingen: Mohr-Siebeck, 1933).

Beare, F., "The Risen Lord Bestows the Spirit [John 20:19-23]," *CJT* 4 (1958) 95-100.

Beasley-Murray, G. R., *Baptism in the New Testament* (Exeter: Paternoster, 1962; repr. Grand Rapids: Eerdmans, 1981).

———, "The Eschatology of the Fourth Gospel," *EvQ* 18 (1946) 97-108.

———, "Jesus and the Spirit," in *Mélanges Bibliques en hommage au R. P. Béda Rigaux*, ed. A. Descamps and A. de Halleux (Gembloux: Duculot, 1970) 463-78.

Becker, H., *Die Reden des Johannesevangeliums und der Stil der gnostischen Offenbarungsreden*, Forsuchungen zur Religion und Literatur des Alten und Neuen Testaments 50 (Gottingen: Vandenhoeck & Ruprecht, 1956).

Becker, J., "Die Abschiedsreden Jesu im Johannesevangelium," *ZNW* 61 (1971) 215-46.

———, "Joh 3, 1-21 als Reflex johanneischer Schuldiskussion," in *Das Wort und die Wörter. Festschrift für Gerhard Friedrich zum 65. Geburtstag*, ed. H. Balz and S. Schulz (Stuttgart-Mainz: Kohlhammer, 1973) 85-95.

Behm, J., "Παράκλητος," *TDNT* 5:800-814.

Benjamin, H. S., "Pneuma in John and Paul: A Comparative Study of the Term with Particular Reference to the Holy Spirit," *BTB* 6 (1976) 27-48.

Benoit, P., "L'Ascension," *RB* 56 (1949) 161-203 [cf. *TToday* 8 (1960) 105-10].

Berchmans, J., "Anointed With Holy Spirit and Power," *Jeevadhara* [Kottayam, Kerala, India] 8 (1978) 201-17.

Bernard, J. H., *The Gospel of John*, 2 vols., ICC (Edinburgh: T. & T. Clark, 1928).

Bernas, C., "The Activity of the Spirit Paraclete," *BiTod* 72 (1974) 1589-94.

Berrouard, M. F., "Le Paraclète, défenseur du Christ devant la conscience du croyant (Jean 16, 8-11)," *RSPT* 33 (1949) 361-89.

Best, E., "Spirit Baptism," *NovT* 4 (1960) 236-43.

Betz, O., "Dead Sea Scrolls," *IDB* 1:790-802.

———, *Der Paraklet* (Leiden: Brill, 1963).

Billings, J. S., "The Ascension in the Fourth Gospel," *ExpTim* 50 (1939) 285.

Black, M., *An Aramaic Approach to the Gospels and Acts* (Oxford: University Press, 1954; 3rd ed. 1967).

Blank, J., "Bindung und Freiheit. Das Verhältnis der nachapostolische Kirche zu Jesus von Nazaret," *BK* 33 (1978) 19-22.

———, *Krisis: Untersuchungen zur johanneischen Christologie und Eschatologie* (Freiburg: Lambertus, 1964).

Blass, F., and Debrunner, A., *A Greek Grammar of the New Testament*, tr. and ed. R. W. Funk (Chicago: University Press, 1961).

Blenkinsopp, J., "John vii, 37-39. Another Note on a Notorious Crux," *NTS* 6 (1959-60) 95-98.

Bligh, J., "Jesus in Samaria," *HeyJ* 3 (1962) 329-46.

Böcher, O., *Der Johanneische Dualismus im Zusammenhang des nachbiblischen Judentums* (Gütersloh: Mohn, 1965).

———, "Wasser und Geist," *Verborum Veritas. Festschrift für Gustav Stählin zum 70. Geburtstag*, ed. O. Böcher and K. Haacker (Wuppertal: Brockhaus, 1970) 197-209.

Bogart, J., *Orthodox and Heretical Perfectionism in the Johannine Community as Evident in the First Epistle of John* (Missoula: Scholars Press, 1977).

———, "Review Article: Recent Johannine Studies," *ATR* 60 (1978) 80-87.

Boice, J. M., *Witness and Revelation in the Gospel of John* (Exeter: Paternoster; Grand Rapids: Zondervan, 1970).

Boismard, M.-E., "L'evolution du thème eschatologique dans les traditions johanniques," *RB* 68 (1961) 507-24.

———, "The First Epistle of John and the Writings of Qumran," in *John and Qumran*, ed. J. H. Charlesworth (London: Chapman, 1972) 156-65.

———, "Jésus, le prophète par excellence, d'après Jean 10, 24-39," in *Neues Testament und Kirche. Für Rudolph Schnackenburg*, ed. J. Gnilka (Freiburg: Herder, 1974) 160-71.

———, "La révélation de l'Esprit Saint," *RevThom* 55 (1955) 5-21.

———, "Les traditions johanniques concernant le Baptiste," *RB* 70 (1963) 5-42.

Borgen, P., *Bread from Heaven. An Exegetical Study in the Concept of Manna in the Gospel of John and the Writings of Philo*, NovTSup 10 (Leiden: Brill, 1965).

———, "God's Agent in the Fourth Gospel," in *Religions in Antiquity. Essays in Memory of E. R. Goodenough*, ed. J. Neusner (Leiden: Brill, 1968) 137-48.

———, "Observations on the Midrashic Character of John 6," *ZNW* 54 (1963) 232-40.

———, "The Unity Discourse in John 6," *ZNW* 50 (1959) 277-78.

Boring, M. E., "How May We Identify Oracles of Christian Prophets in the Synoptic Tradition? Mark 3:28-29 as a Test Case," *JBL* 91 (1972) 501-21.

———, "The Influence of Christian Prophecy on the Johannine Portrayal of the Paraclete and Jesus," *NTS* 25 (1978) 113-23.

Bornkamm, G., "Der Paraklet im Johannesevangelium," in *Geschichte und Glaube, Gesammelte Aufsätze*, 3 vols. (München: Kaiser, 1968) 3:68-89 (completely updated from "Der Paraklet im Johannes-Evangelium," in *Festschrift für Rudolf Bultmann* [Stuttgart: Kohlhammer, 1949] 12-35).

———, "Die Zeit des Geistes," *Geschichte und Glaube, Gesammelte Aufsätze*, 3 vols. (München: Kaiser, 1968) 3:90-103.

Bouman, H. J. A., "The Baptism of Christ with Special Reference to the Gift of the Spirit," *CTM* 28 (1957) 1-15.

Bourke, J., "The Wonderful Counsellor," *CBQ* 22 (1960) 123-43.

Bousset, W., *Kyrios Christos*, tr. J. E. Steely (Nashville: Abingdon, 1970).

Bowen, W. E., "The Inspiration of the Church (John 16:13)," *ExpTim* 10 (1898-99) 26-33.

Bowman, J., "The Fourth Gospel and the Samaritans," *BJRL* 40 (1958) 298-308.

Boyd, W. J. P., "The Ascension According to St. John," *Theol* 70 (1967) 207-11.

Braumann, G., "Advocate," *NIDNTT* 1:88-91.

Braun, F. M., "Le baptême d'après le quatrième Evangile," *RevThom* 48 (1948) 347-93.

———, "L'eau et l'Esprit," *RevThom* 49 (1949) 5-30.

———, *Jean le théologien*, 4 vols. (Paris: Gabalda, 1959, 1964, 1966, 1972).

Breck, R. E., "The Spirit of Truth. A Study of the Background and Development of Johannine Pneumatology," unpub. diss., Ruprecht-Karl Universität (Heidelberg), 1971.

Brooke, A. E., *The Johannine Epistles*, ICC (Edinburgh: T. & T. Clark, 1912).

Brooks, O. S., "The Johannine Eucharist—Another Interpretation," *JBL* 82 (1963) 293-300.

Brown, B. S., "The Paraclete Sayings," *TheolRev* 3 (1966) 1-10.

Brown, R. E., *The Community of the Beloved Disciple* (London: Chapman; New York: Paulist, 1979).

―――, *The Gospel According to John*, 2 vols., AB (New York: Doubleday, 1966, 1970).

―――, "The Gospel of Thomas and St. John's Gospel," *NTS* 9 (1962-1963) 155-77.

―――, "Johannine Ecclesiology―The Community's Origins," *Int* 31 (1977) 179-93.

―――, "The Johannine Sacramentary Reconsidered," in *New Testament Essays* (Milwaukee: Bruce, 1965; London: Chapman, 1967) 51-76.

―――, "The Kerygma of the Gospel According to John," *Int* 21 (1967) 387-400.

―――, "Other Sheep Not of this Fold―The Johannine Perspective on Christian Diversity in the Late First Century," *JBL* 97 (1978) 5-22.

―――, "The Paraclete in Light of Modern Research," *SE* 4 (1968) 158-65.

―――, "The Paraclete in the Fourth Gospel," *NTS* 13 (1966-67) 113-32.

―――, "The Passion According to John," *Worship* 49 (1975) 126-34.

―――, "The Problem of Historicity in John," in *New Testament Essays* (Milwaukee: Bruce, 1965; London: Chapman, 1967) 143-167.

―――, "The Qumran Scrolls and the Johannine Gospels and Epistles," *CBQ* 17 (1955) 403-19, 559-74.

―――, "The Relationship to the Fourth Gospel Shared by the Author of 1 John and by his Opponents," in *Text and Interpretation: Studies in the New Testament Presented to Matthew Black*, ed. E. Best and R. McL. Wilson (Cambridge: University Press, 1979) 57-68.

―――, "Three Quotations from John the Baptist in the Gospel of John," *CBQ* 22 (1960) 292-98.

Bruce, F. F., "The Ascension in the Fourth Gospel," *ExpTim* 50 (1938-39) 478.

―――, "Christ and Spirit in Paul," *BJRL* 59 (1977) 259-85.

―――, "Holy Spirit in the Qumran Texts," *Annual of Leeds University Oriental Society* 6 (1966-68) 292-309.

―――, *Peter, Stephen, James, and John: Studies in Non-Pauline Christianity* (Grand Rapids: Eerdmans, 1979) (= *Men and Movements in the Primitive Church. Studies in Early Non-Pauline Christianity* [Exeter: Paternoster, 1979]).

―――, "The Spirit in the Apocalypse," in *Christ and Spirit in the New Testament, Studies in Honour of C. F. D. Moule*, ed. B. Lindars and S. Smalley (Cambridge: University Press, 1973) 333-44.

Bruns, J., "The Fourth Gospel: Present Trends of Analysis," *BiTod* 59 (1972) 699-703.

Büchsel, F., *Der Geist Gottes im Neuen Testament* (Gütersloh: Mohn, 1928).

Bultmann, R., "Ἀλήθεια," *TDNT* 1:232-51.

―――, "Die Bedeutung der neuerschlossenen mandäischen und manichäischen Quellen für das Verständnis des Johannesevangeliums," *ZNW* 24 (1925) 100-146.

―――, "Die Eschatologie des Johannesevangeliums," in *Glauben und Verstehen, Gesammelte Aufsätze*, 2 vols. (Tübingen: Mohr, 1952, 1954) 1:134-52 (= *Faith and Understanding I*, tr. L. P. Smith, ed. R. W. Funk [London: SCM, 1969] 165-183).

―――, *The Gospel of John*, tr. G. R. Beasley-Murray (Oxford: Blackwell; Philadelphia: Westminster, 1971).

————, *The History of the Synoptic Tradition*, tr. J. Marsh (Oxford: Blackwell; New York: Harper & Row, 1963).

————, "Johannesevangelium," *RGG* 3:840-49.

————, *The Johannine Epistles*, Hermeneia, tr. R. P. O'Hara et al. (Philadelphia: Fortress, 1973).

————, *The Theology of the New Testament*, 2 vols., tr. K. Grobel (London: SCM; New York: Scribner's, 1952, 1955).

Burkitt, F. C., "The Baptism of Jesus," *ExpTim* 38 (1926-27) 198-202.

Burney, C. F., *Aramaic Origin of the Fourth Gospel* (Oxford: Clarendon Press, 1922).

————, *The Poetry of Our Lord* (Oxford: Clarendon Press, 1925).

Burton, E., *Syntax of Moods and Tenses in New Testament Greek* (Edinburgh: T. & T. Clark, 1898; repr. Grand Rapids: Kregel, 1976).

Butler, B. C., "Spirit and Institution in the New Testament," *TU* 88 (1964) 138-65.

Cadman, W. H., *The Open Heaven: The Revelation of God in the Johannine Sayings of Jesus*, ed. G. B. Caird (Oxford: University Press; New York: Herder, 1969).

Caird, G. B., "The Glory of God in the Fourth Gospel," *NTS* 15 (1968-69) 265-277.

————, "John, Letters of," *IDB* 2:946-52.

Carpenter, J. E., *The Johannine Writings. A Study of the Apocalypse and the Fourth Gospel* (London: Constable; New York: Houghton & Mifflin, 1927).

Carpenter, J. W., "Water Baptism in John 3:3-5; Acts 2:38; 22:15-16," *RevExp* 54 (1957) 59-66.

Carson, D. A., *The Farewell Discourse and the Final Prayer of Jesus. An Exposition of John 14-17* (Grand Rapids: Baker, 1980).

————, "The Function of the Paraclete in John 16:7-11," *JBL* 98 (1979) 547-66.

————, "Spirit and Eschatology in the Gospel of John," Tyndale Fellowship Paper, Cambridge, England (Autumn, 1975).

Cassien, A., *Le Pentecôte johannique* (Paris: Editeurs Réunis, 1939).

Charles, R. H., *The Apocrypha and Pseudepigrapha of the Old Testament*, 2 vols. (Oxford: University Press, 1913).

Charlesworth, J. H., "A Critical Comparison of the Dualism in 1QS 3:13–4:26 and the 'Dualism' Contained in the Gospel of John," in *John and Qumran*, ed. J. H. Charlesworth (London: Chapman, 1972) 76-106.

Charlesworth, J. H., ed., *John and Qumran* (London: Chapman, 1972).

Charlier, C., "L'amour en Esprit (I Jean 4, 7-13)," *BVC* 10 (1955) 57-72.

Chavasse, C., "Jesus Christ and Moses," *Theol* 54 (1951) 244-50, 289-96.

Chevallier, M. A., *L'Esprit et le Messie dans le Bas-Judaisme et le Nouveau Testament* (Paris: Presses Universitaires, 1958).

————, *Souffle de Dieu. Le Saint-Esprit dans le Nouveau Testament* (Paris: Editions Beauchesne, 1978).

Clark, N., *An Approach to the Theology of the Sacraments* (London: SCM, 1956).

Clifton, J. P., "The Holy Spirit as Paraclete," *BiTod* 72 (1974) 1582-88.

Cock, J. de, "Het symbolisme van de duif bij het doopsel van Christus" (= "The Symbolic Meaning of the Dove at Christ's Baptism"), *Bijdragen* (Nijmegen) 21 (1960) 363-76.

Cody, Z. T., "The Work of the Paraclete," *RevExp* 16 (1919) 164-80.

Colwell, E. C., and Titus, E. L., *The Gospel of the Spirit: A Study in the Fourth Gospel* (New York: Harper & Row, 1953).

Congar, Y. M. J., "Le St-Esprit et le corps apostolique réalisateurs de l'oeuvre du Christ," *RSPT* 36 (1952) 613-25; 37 (1953) 24-48.

Conybeare, F. C., "The Holy Spirit as Dove," *Exp* iv, 9 (1884) 451-58.

Conzelmann, H., *An Outline of the Theology of the New Testament*, tr. J. Bowden (London: SCM; New York: Harper & Row, 1969).

_____, "Was von Anfang War," in *Neutestamentliche Studien für R. Bultmann*, supplement to *ZNW* 21 (Berlin: Töpelmann, 1954) 194-201.

Cook, J. I., "John 20:19-23. An Exegesis," *RTR* 21 (1967) 2-10.

Cook, R. W., *The Theology of John* (Chicago: Moody, 1979).

Coppens, J., "Le don de l'esprit d'après les textes de Qumran et le quatrième évangile," in *L'évangile de Jean* (Louvain: Recherches Bibliques, 1958) 209-23.

Corell, A., *Consummatum Est. Eschatology and Church in the Gospel of St. John* (London: SPCK, 1958; New York: Macmillan, 1959).

Cortez, J. B., "Yet Another Look at John 7:37-38," *CBQ* 29 (1967) 75-86.

Couture, P., "The Teaching Function in the Church of 1 John (1 John 2:20-27)," unpub. diss,. Pontificia Universitas Gregoriana (Rome), 1968.

Craig, C. T., "Sacramental Interest in the Fourth Gospel," *JBL* 58 (1939) 31-41.

Crehan, J., *The Theology of St. John* (London: Darton, Longman, and Todd, 1965).

Cribbs, F. L., "St. Luke and the Johannine Tradition," *JBL* 90 (1971) 422-50.

Cross, F. L., ed., *Studies in the Fourth Gospel* (London: Mowbray, 1957).

Cross, F. M., *The Ancient Library of Qumran* (London: Duckworth, 1958).

Crump, F. J., *Pneuma in the Gospels*, Studies in Sacred Theology, 2nd series, no. 82 (Washington: Catholic University of America Press, 1954).

Cullmann, O., *Baptism in the New Testament*, SBT 1/1, tr. J. K. S. Reid (London: SCM; Naperville: Allenson, 1950).

_____, *The Christology of the New Testament*, tr. S. C. Guthrie and C. A. M. Hall (London: SCM; Philadelphia: Westminster, 1959; 2nd ed. 1963).

_____, *Early Christian Worship*, SBT 1/10, tr. A. S. Todd and J. B. Torrance (London: SCM; Naperville: Allenson, 1953).

_____, "Der johanneische Gebrauch doppeldeutiger Ausdrücke als Schlüssel zum Verständnis des vierten Evangeliums," *TZ* 4 (1948) 360-72.

_____, *The Johannine Circle*, tr. J. Bowden (London: SCM; Philadelphia: Westminster, 1975).

_____, "A New Approach to the Interpretation of the Fourth Gospel," *ExpTim* 71 (1959-60) 8-12, 39-43.

_____, *Salvation in History*, tr. S. G. Sowers (London: SCM, 1967).

_____, "Samaria and the Origins of the Christian Mission," in *The Early Church*, tr.

A. J. B. Higgins and S. Godman, ed. A. J. B. Higgins (London: SCM; Philadelphia: Westminster, 1956) 185-92.

Dahl, N. A., "Anamnesis—Memory and Commemoration in Early Christianity," in *Jesus in the Memory of the Early Church*, tr. F. O. Francis et al. (Minneapolis: Augsburg, 1976) 11-29.

―――, "The Johannine Church and History," in *Jesus in the Memory of the Early Church* (Minneapolis: Augsburg, 1976) 99-119.

Dahms, J. V., "Isaiah 55:11 and the Gospel of John," *EvQ* 53 (1981) 78-88.

Danby, H., *The Mishnah* (Oxford: Clarendon Press, 1933).

Daniélou, J., "Joh 7, 37 et Ezéch 47, 1-11," *SE* 2 = *TU* 87 (Berlin: Akademie-Verlag, 1964) 158-63.

Davey, J. E., *The Jesus of St. John. Historical and Christological Studies in the Fourth Gospel* (London: Lutterworth, 1958).

Davies, J. G., "The Primary Meaning of Paracletos," *JTS* 4 (1953) 35-38.

―――, *The Spirit, the Church, and the Sacraments* (London: Faith Press, 1954).

Davies, W. D., *Paul and Rabbinic Judaism* (London: SCM, 1948; 2nd ed. 1955).

―――, "Paul and the Dead Sea Scrolls: Flesh and Spirit," in *The Scrolls and the New Testament*, ed. K. Stendahl (London: SCM; New York: Harper, 1958) 157-82.

deJonge, M., "The Beloved Disciple and the Date of the Gospel of John," in *Text and Interpretation: Studies in the New Testament Presented to Matthew Black*, ed. E. Best and R. McL. Wilson (Cambridge: University Press, 1979) 98-114.

―――, "Jesus as Prophet and King in the Fourth Gospel," *ETL* 49 (1973) 160-77.

―――, "Jewish Expectations about 'Messiah' According to the Fourth Gospel," *NTS* 19 (1973) 246-70.

―――, "Nicodemus and Jesus: Some Observations on Misunderstanding and Understanding in the Fourth Gospel," *BJRL* 53 (1971) 337-59.

deJonge, M., ed., *L'Evangile de Jean* (Louvain: University Press, 1977).

de Pinto, B., "Word and Wisdom in St. John," *Scripture* 19 (1967) 20-27 (repr. in *A Companion to John*, ed. M. J. Taylor [New York: Alba, 1977] 59-68).

Derrett, J. D. M., *Law in the New Testament* (London: Darton, Longmann, and Todd, 1970).

de Vries, E., "Johannes 4, 1-42. In geest en hoofdzaak" (John 4:1-42. In Spirit and Substance), *Gereformeerd Theologisch Tijdschrift* (Amsterdam) 78 (1978) 93-114.

Dilschneider, O. A., "Die Notwendigkeit neuerer Antworten auf neue Fragen," in *Erfahrung und Theologie des heiligen Geistes*, ed. C. Heitmann and H. Mühlen (Hamburg: Agentur des Rauen Hauses; München: Kösel, 1974) 151-61.

Dion, H. M., "L'origine du titre de 'Paraclet,'" *ScEc* 17 (1965) 143-49.

Dobbin, E. J., "Towards a Theology of the Holy Spirit," *HeyJ* 17 (1976) 5-19, 129-49.

Dodd, C. H., *The Apostolic Preaching and Its Developments* (London: Hodder and Stoughton, 1936, 3rd ed. 1963).

―――, "Eternal Life," in *New Testament Studies* (Manchester: University Press, 1953) 160-73.

―――, "Eucharistic Symbolism in the Fourth Gospel," *Exp* viii, 2 (1911) 530-46.

―――, "The First Epistle of John and the Fourth Gospel," *BJRL* 21 (1937) 129-56.

_____, *Historical Tradition in the Fourth Gospel* (Cambridge: University Press, 1963).

_____, *The Interpretation of the Fourth Gospel* (Cambridge: University Press, 1953).

_____, "Jesus as Teacher and Prophet," in *Mysterium Christi, Christological Studies by British and German Theologians*, ed. G. K. A. Bell and A. Deissmann (London: Longmans, 1930) 53-66.

_____, *The Johannine Epistles* (London: Hodder and Stoughton, 1946).

_____, "Some Johannine 'Herrnworte' with Parallels in the Synoptic Gospels (John 13:16; 12:25; 13:20; 20:23)," *NTS* 2 (1955) 75-86.

_____, "The Portrait of Jesus in John and in the Synoptics," in *Christian History and Interpretation: Studies Presented to John Knox*, ed. W. R. Farmer et al. (Cambridge: University Press, 1968).

_____, "The Prologue to the Fourth Gospel and Christian Worship," in *Studies in the Fourth Gospel*, ed. F. L. Cross (London: Mowbray, 1957) 9-22.

Dods, M., "The Gospel of John," in *The Expositor's Greek Testament*, 5 vols., ed. W. R. Nicoll (repr. Grand Rapids: Eerdmans, 1976) 1:655-872.

Donfried, K. P., "Ecclesiastical Authority in 2-3 John," in *L'Evangile de Jean*, ed. M. de-Jonge (Louvain: University Press, 1977) 325-34.

Donn, T. M., "The Voice of the Spirit (John 3:8)," *ExpTim* 66 (1954-55) 32.

Dunn, J. D. G., "1 Corinthians 15:45—Last Adam, Life-Giving Spirit," in *Christ and Spirit in the New Testament*, ed. B. Lindars and S. Smalley (Cambridge: University Press, 1973) 127-41.

_____, "2 Cor. 3:17—'The Lord is the Spirit,'" *JTS* 21 (1970) 309-20.

_____, "The Birth of Metaphor, Baptized in Spirit," *ExpTim* 89 (1978) 134-38, 173-75.

_____, *Christology in the Making* (London: SCM; Philadelphia: Westminster, 1980).

_____, *Jesus and the Spirit* (London: SCM; Philadelphia: Westminster, 1975).

_____, "John VI: A Eucharistic Discourse?" *NTS* 17 (1970-71) 328-38.

_____, "A Note on *dōrea*," *ExpTim* 81 (1970) 349-51.

_____, "Prophetic 'I' Sayings and the Jesus Tradition. The Importance of Testing Prophetic Utterances within Early Christianity," *NTS* 24 (1977-78) 175-98.

_____, "Spirit and Fire Baptism," *NovT* 14 (1972) 81-92.

_____, "Spirit and Kingdom," *ExpTim* 82 (1971) 36-40.

_____, "Spirit, Holy Spirit," *NIDNTT* 3:693-707.

_____, *Unity and Diversity in the New Testament* (London: SCM; Philadelphia: Westminster, 1977).

_____, "The Washing of the Disciples' Feet in John 13:1-20," *ZNW* 61 (1970) 247-52.

Dupont-Sommer, A., *The Essene Writings from Qumran*, tr. G. Vermes (Oxford: Blackwell, 1961).

du Toit, A. B., ed., *The Christ of John. Essays on the Christology of the Fourth Gospel*, Neotestamentica 2 (Potchefstroom, S. Africa: Pro Rege Press, 1971).

Edwards, A. D., "Spirit and Eschatology in 1 John," Tyndale Fellowship Paper, Cambridge, England (Autumn, 1975).

Ellis, E. E., "Christ and Spirit in 1 Corinthians," in *Christ and Spirit in the New Testament*, ed. B. Lindars and S. Smalley (Cambridge: University Press, 1973) 269-78.

————, *The Gospel of Luke*, New Century Bible, rev. ed. (London: Oliphants, 1974; repr. Grand Rapids: Eerdmans, 1981).

————, "Prophecy in the New Testament Church and Today," in *Prophetic Vocation in the New Testament and Today*, ed. J. Panagopoulos (Leiden: Brill, 1977) 46-57.

————, *The World of St. John* (London: Lutterworth, 1965; repr. Grand Rapids: Eerdmans, 1984).

Emerton, T. A., "Binding and Loosing—Forgiving and Retaining," *JTS* 13 (1962) 325-33.

England, H. G., "The Christ and the Holy Spirit," *HeyJ* 39 (1940-41) 325-32.

Enz, J., "The Book of Exodus as a Literary Type for the Gospel of John," *JBL* 76 (1957) 208-15.

Evans, E., "The Verb ἀγαπᾶν in the Fourth Gospel," in *Studies in the Fourth Gospel*, ed. F. L. Cross (London: Mowbray, 1957) 64-71.

Fee, G., "Once More, John 7:37-39," *ExpTim* 89 (1978) 116-18.

Fenton, J. C., *The Gospel According to St. John* (Oxford: Clarendon Press, 1970).

Feuillet, A., *Johannine Studies*, tr. T. E. Crane (New York: Alba, 1964).

Filson, F., "First John: Purpose and Message," *Int* 23 (1969) 259-76.

————, "The Gospel of Life: The Study of the Gospel of John," in *Current Issues in New Testament Interpretation: Essays in Honor of Otto A. Piper*, ed. W. Klassen and G. F. Snyder (London: SCM; New York: Harper and Brothers, 1962) 111-123.

————, "Who Was the Beloved Disciple?" *JBL* 48 (1949) 83-88.

Findlay, G. G., "Christ's Name for the Holy Spirit," *ExpTim* 12 (1901) 445-49.

Fiorenza, E. S., "Quest for the Johannine School: The Apocalypse and the Fourth Gospel," *NTS* 23 (1977) 402-407.

Firor, W. M., "Fulfillment of the Promise: The Holy Spirit and the Christian Life," *Int* 7 (1953) 299-314.

Fitzmyer, J. A., *Essays on the Semitic Background of the New Testament* (London: Chapman, 1971; repr. Missoula: Society of Biblical Literature, 1974).

Floor, L., "The Lord and the Holy Spirit in the Fourth Gospel," in *The Christ of John: Essays on the Christology of the Fourth Gospel*, Neotestamentica 2 (Potchefstroom, S. Africa: Pro Rege Press, 1971) 122-30.

Foerster, W., "Der Heilige Geist im Spätjudentum," *NTS* 8 (1961-62) 117-34.

Fonck, L., "Duplex fructus Spiritus Sancti (Ioh 16:23-30)," *VD* 1 (1921) 115-20.

Ford, J. M., "'Mingled Blood' from the Side of Christ (John 19:34)," *NTS* 15 (1968-69) 337-38.

Forestell, J. T., "Jesus and the Paraclete in the Gospel of John," in *Word and Spirit, Essays in Honor of D. M. Stanley*, ed. J. Plevnik (Willowdale, Ontario: Regis College Press, 1975) 151-97.

————, *The Word of the Cross* (Rome: Biblical Institute Press, 1974).

Fortna, R., "Christology in the Fourth Gospel: Redaction-Critical Perspectives," *NTS* 21 (1975) 489-504.

————, "From Christology to Soteriology. A Redaction-Critical Study of Salvation in the Fourth Gospel," *Int* 27 (1973) 31-47.

————, *The Gospel of Signs. A Reconstruction of the Narrative Source Underlying the Fourth Gospel* (Cambridge: University Press, 1970).

Freed, E. D., "The Manner of Worship in John 4:23f.," in *Search the Scriptures: NT Studies in Honor of R. T. Stamm*, ed. J. M. Meyers et al., Gettysburgh Theological Studies 3 (Leiden: Brill, 1969) 33-48.

———, *Old Testament Quotations in the Gospel of John* (Leiden: Brill, 1965).

———, "Samaritan Influence in the Gospel of John," *CBQ* 30 (1968) 580-87.

———, "Variations in the Language and Thought of John," *ZNW* 55 (1964) 167-97.

———, "John 20:19-23," *Int* 32 (1978) 180-84.

Fuller, R. H., *The Foundations of New Testament Christology* (New York: Scribner's, 1965).

———, *Interpreting the Miracles* (London: SCM, 1963).

———, "John 20:19-23," *Int* 32 (1978) 180-84.

Gaffin, R. B., *Perspective on Pentecost: New Testament Teaching on the Gifts of the Spirit* (Grand Rapids: Baker, 1979).

Gärtner, B., *John 6 and the Jewish Passover* (Lund: Gleerup, 1959).

Gerhardsson, B., *Memory and Manuscript. Oral Tradition and Written Transmission in Rabbinic Judaism and Early Christianity* (Uppsala: Gleerup, 1961).

———, *The Origins of the Gospel Traditions* (London: SCM, 1979).

Giblet, J., "Les Promesses de l'Esprit et le Mission des Apôtres dans les Evangiles," *Irenikon* 30 (1957) 17-43.

Gillieron, B., *Le Saint-Esprit, Actualité du Christ* (Geneve: Labor et Fides, 1978).

Glassell, M. E., "The Use of Miracles in the Markan Gospel," in *Miracles*, ed. C. F. D. Moule (London: Mowbray, 1965) 149-62.

Glasson, T. F., "John the Baptist in the Fourth Gospel," *ExpTim* 67 (1955-56) 245-46.

———, *Moses in the Fourth Gospel*, SBT 1/40 (London: SCM; Naperville: Allenson, 1963).

Goguel, M., *La notion johannique de l'Esprit et ses antécédents historiques* (Paris: 1902).

———, "Paulinisme et Johannisme," *RHPR* 10 (1930) 504-26; 11 (1931) 1-19, 129-56.

———, "Pneumatisme et Eschatologie dans le Christianisme primitif," *RHR* 132 (1946) 124-69; 133 (1947) 103-61.

Goodenough, E. R., "John, a Primitive Gospel," *JBL* 64 (1945) 145-82.

Graf, J., "Nikodemus (Joh 3, 1-21)," *TThQ* 132 (1952) 62-86.

Grayston, K., "The Meaning of PARAKLETOS," *JSNT* 13 (1981) 67-82.

Grech, P., "2 Cor. 3:17 and the Pauline Doctrine of Conversion to the Holy Spirit," *CBQ* 17 (1955) 420-37.

Griffiths, D. R., "Deutero-Isaiah and the Fourth Gospel," *ExpTim* 65 (1953-54) 355-60.

Grigsby, B., "The Fourth Gospel's Understanding of the Death of Christ," unpub. diss., Aberdeen University (Scotland), 1979.

Grill, J., *Untersuchungen über die Entstehung des vierten Evangeliums*, 2 vols. (Tübingen: Mohr-Siebeck, 1902, 1923).

Grundmann, W., "Zur Rede Jesu vom Vater im Johannesevangelium; Eine redaktions- und bekenntnisgeschichtliche Untersuchung zu Joh 20, 17 und seiner Vor- bereitung," *ZNW* 52 (1961) 213-30.

Guilding, A., *The Fourth Gospel and Jewish Worship* (Oxford: Clarendon Press, 1960).

Gundry, R., "'In My Father's House are Many *Monai*' (John 14:2)," *ZNW* 58 (1967) 68-72.

Guthrie, D., *New Testament Theology* (Leicester/Downers Grove: IVP, 1981).

Haacker, K., *Die Stiftung des Heils: Untersuchungen zur Struktur der johanneischen Theologie* (Stuttgart: Calwer Verlag, 1972).

Haenchen, E., "Aus der Literatur zum Johannesevangelium 1929-1956," *TRu* 23 (1955) 295-355.

———, "Der Vater, der mich gesandt hat," *NTS* 9 (1963) 208-16.

———, "Vom Wandel des Jesusbildes in der frühen Gemeinde," in *Verborum Veritas. Festschrift für Gustav Stählin zum 70. Geburtstag*, ed. O. Böcher and K. Haacker (Wuppertal: Brockhaus, 1970) 3-14.

Hahn, F., "Das biblische Verstandnis des Heiligen Geistes. Soteriologische Funktion und 'Personalitat' des Heiligen Geistes," in *Erfahrung und Theologie des heiligen Geistes*, ed. C. Heitmann and H. Muhlen (Hamburg: Agentur des Rauen Hauses; München: Kösel, 1974) 131-50.

———, *The Titles of Jesus in Christology*, tr. H. Knight and G. Ogg (London: Lutterworth, 1969).

Hamilton, N. Q., *The Holy Spirit and Eschatology in Paul*, SJT Occasional Papers, No. 6 (Edinburgh: Oliver and Boyd, 1957).

Hammer, P. L., "Baptism with Water and the Spirit (John 3:5)," *Theology and Life* 8 (1965) 35-43.

Harries, R., "Sacraments and Eschatology in the Fourth Gospel and the Dead Sea Scrolls," unpub. diss., Manchester University (England), 1958.

Harter, J. L., "Spirit in the New Testament. A Reinterpretation in the Light of the Old Testament and Intertestamental Literature. A Study in Biblical Theology," unpub. diss., Cambridge University (England), 1966.

Hartmann, G., "Die Osterberichte im Joh 20 im Zusammenhang der Theologie des Johannesevangelium," unpub. diss., Kiel University (Germany), 1963.

———, "Die Vorlage der Osterberichte in Joh 20," *ZNW* 55 (1964) 197-220.

Harvey, A. E., *Jesus on Trial. A Study of the Fourth Gospel* (London: SPCK, 1976).

Hastings, J., "The Paraclete: A Bible Word Study," *ExpTim* 10 (1898-99) 169-71.

Hatch, E., and Redpath, H. A., *A Concordance to the Septuagint*, 3 vols. (Oxford: Clarendon Press, 1897-1906).

Hatch, W. H. P., "The Meaning of John 16:8-11," *HTR* 14 (1921) 103-105.

Haufe, G., "Form und Funktion des Pneuma-Motivs in der frühchristlichen Paränese," *TU* 103 (1968) 75-80.

Hauschild, W. D., *Gottes Geist und der Mensch, Studien zur frühchristlichen Pneumatologie* (München: Kaiser, 1972).

Hawthorne, G. F., "The Concept of Faith in the Fourth Gospel," *BSac* 116 (1959) 117-26.

Heise, J., *Bleiben, Menein in den johanneischen Schriften* (Tübingen: Mohr-Siebeck, 1967).

Hendriksen, W., *An Exposition of the Gospel of John* (London: Banner of Truth, 1959).

Hennecke, E., *New Testament Apocrypha*, 2 vols., tr. R. McL. Wilson et al. (London: Lutterworth; Philadelphia: Westminster, 1963, 1965).

Herrmann, I., *Kyrios und Pneuma* (München: Kösel Verlag, 1961).

Higgins, A. J. B., *The Historicity of the Fourth Gospel* (London: Lutterworth, 1960).

_____, *The Lord's Supper in the New Testament*, SBT 1/6 (London: SCM; Naperville: Allenson, 1952).

Hill, D., "Christian Prophets as Teachers or Instructors in the Church," in *Prophetic Vocation in the New Testament and Today*, ed. J. Panagopoulos (Leiden: Brill, 1977) 108-30.

_____, *Greek Words and Hebrew Meanings. Studies in the Semantics of Soteriological Terms* (Cambridge: University Press, 1967).

_____, *New Testament Prophecy* (London: Marshall, Morgan & Scott; Atlanta: John Knox, 1979).

_____, "On the Evidence for the Creative Role of Christian Prophets," *NTS* 20 (1973-74) 262-74.

_____, "Prophecy and Prophets in the Revelation of St. John," *NTS* 18 (1971-72) 401-18.

Hindley, J. C., "Witness in the Fourth Gospel," *SJT* 18 (1965) 319-37.

Hodge, T. W., "The Paraclete and the World," *ExpTim* 13 (1901-1902) 10-12.

Hodges, Z. C., "Problem Passages in the Gospel of John. Part 3: Water and Spirit, John 3:5," *BSac* 135 (1978) 206-20.

Hoeferkamp, R., "The Holy Spirit in the Fourth Gospel from the Viewpoint of Christ's Glorification," *CTM* 33 (1962) 517-29.

Hofrichter, P., *Nicht aus Blut sondern monogen aus Gott geboren, Joh 1, 13-14* (Würzburg: Echter Verlag, 1978).

Holdsworth, W. W., "The Life of Faith (John 16:1-15)," *ExpTim* 21 (1908-10) 310-12.

Holwerda, D. E., *The Holy Spirit and Eschatology in the Gospel of John. A Critique of Ruldolf Bultmann's Present Eschatology* (Kampen: Kok, 1959).

Holzmeister, U., "Paraclitus autem Spiritus sanctus (Ioh 14:26)," *VD* 12 (1932) 135-39.

Hooke, S. H., "The Spirit Was Not Yet," *NTS* 9 (1962-63) 372-80.

Hoskyns, E., *The Fourth Gospel*, ed. F. N. Davey, 2nd ed. (London: Faber and Faber, 1947).

_____, "Gen. 1–3 and St. John's Gospel," *JTS* 21 (1920) 210-18.

Houlden, J. L., *The Johannine Epistles*, Black's/Harper's New Testament Commentary (London: A. & C. Black; New York: Harper & Row, 1973).

Howard, D. M., *By the Power of the Holy Spirit* (Downers Grove: IVP, 1973).

Howard, W. F., *Christianity According to St. John* (London: Duckworth, 1943).

_____, "The Common Authorship of the Johannine Gospel and Epistles," *JTS* 48 (1947) 12-25.

_____, *The Fourth Gospel in Recent Criticism and Interpretation* (London: Epworth, 1931; 2nd ed. 1955 rev. C. K. Barrett).

_____, "The Gospel According to St. John," in *The Interpreter's Bible*, ed. G. A. Buttrick, 12 vols. (New York: Abingdon, 1952) 8:437-811.

_____, "'Son of God' in the Fourth Gospel," *NTS* 10 (1963-64) 227-37.

Hull, J. H. E., *The Holy Spirit in the Acts of the Apostles* (London: Lutterworth, 1967).

Hunt, W. B., "John's Doctrine of the Spirit," *SWJT* 8 (1965) 45-65.

Hunter, A. M., *The Gospel According to John* (Cambridge: University Press, 1965).

Hutton, W. R., "The Johannine Doctrine of the Holy Spirit," *CrozQ* 24 (1947) 334-44.

Iersel, B. M. F. van, "Tradition und Redaktion in Joh 1, 19-36," *NovT* 5 (1962) 245-68.

Imschoot, P. van, "Baptême d'eau et baptême d'Esprit Saint," *ETL* 13 (1936) 653-66.

Isaacs, M. E., *The Concept of Spirit. A Study of Pneuma in Hellenistic Judaism and Its Bearing on the New Testament*, Heythrop Monographs 1 (London: Heythrop College, 1976).

Jeremias, J., *The Eucharistic Words of Jesus*, tr. N. Perrin (Oxford: Blackwell, 1955, 2nd ed. 1966; Philadelphia: Fortress, 1977).

―――, *New Testament Theology 1. The Proclamation of Jesus*, tr. J. Bowden (New York: Scribner's, 1971).

Johansson, N., *Parakletoi. Vorstellungen von Fürsprechern für die Menschen vor Gott in der alttestamentlichen Religion, im Spätjudentum, und Urchristentum* (Lund: Gleerup, 1940).

Johnston, G., *The Doctrine of the Church in the New Testament* (Cambridge: University Press, 1943).

―――, "Spirit," in *A Theological Wordbook of the Bible*, ed. A. Richardson (New York: Macmillan, 1950) 233-47.

―――, "'Spirit' and 'Holy Spirit' in the Qumran Literature," in *New Testament Sidelights: Essays in Honor of A. C. Purdy*, ed. H. K. McArthur (Hartford: Hartford Seminary Foundation, 1960) 27-42.

―――, "The Spirit-Paraclete in the Gospel of John," *Perspective* 9 (1968) 29-38.

―――, *The Spirit-Paraclete in the Gospel of John*, NovTSup 12 (Cambridge: University Press, 1970).

Karotemprel, S., *The Promise of Living Water* (Bombey: Asian Trading Corp., 1977).

Käsemann, E., "Ketzer und Zeuge," *ZTK* 48 (1951) 292-311.

―――, *The Testament of Jesus According to John 17*, tr. G. Krodel (Philadelphia: Fortress, 1968).

Kasper, E., ed., *Gegenwart des Geistes. Aspekte der Pneumatologie* (Freiburg: Herder, 1979).

Kealy, S. P., *That You May Believe, The Gospel According to John* (Middlegreen, Slough: St. Paul, 1978).

Keck, L. E., "The Spirit and the Dove," *NTS* 17 (1970) 41-67.

Kilpatrick, G. D., "The Punctuation of John 7:37-38," *JTS* 11 (1960) 340-42.

―――, "The Religious Background of the Fourth Gospel," in *Studies in the Fourth Gospel*, ed. F. L. Cross (London: Mowbray, 1957) 36-44.

Kipp, J. L., "The Relationship between the Conceptions of the 'Holy Spirit' and 'Risen Christ' in the Fourth Gospel. A Study of John 1–20," unpub. diss., Princeton Seminary (New Jersey), 1964.

Klos, H., *Die Sakramente im Johannesevangelium* (Stuttgart: Katholisches Bibelwerk, 1970).

Köster, H., "Geschichte und Kultus im Johannesevangelium und bei Ignatius von Antiochien," *ZTK* 54 (1957) 56-69.

―――, "John xiv, 1–12. A Meditation," *ExpTim* 73 (1961) 88.

Kothgasser, A. M., "Die Lehr-, Erinnerungs-, Bezeugungs-, und Einfurhungs-funktion des Johanneischen Geist-Parakleten gegenüber der Christus-Offenbarung," *Salesianum* 33 (1971) 557-98; 34 (1972) 2-51.

Kragerud, A., *Der Lieblingsjünger im Johannesevangelium. Ein exegetischer Versuch* (Oslo: Universitätverlag, 1959).

Kremer, J., "Jesu Verheissung des Geistes. Zur Verankerung der Aussage von Joh 16:13 im Leben Jesu," in *Die Kirche des Anfangs, Festschrift für Heinz Schürmann zum 65. Geburtstag*, Erfurter Theologische Studien 38, ed. R. Schnackenburg, J. Ernst, and J. Wanke (Leipzig: St. Benno-Verlag, 1977) 247-76.

Kümmel, W. G., "Jesus und die Anfäng der Kirche," in *Heilsgeschehen und Geschichte, Gesammelte Aufsätze 1933-1964*, Marburger theologische Studien 3, ed. E. Grässer, O. Merk, and A. Fritz (Marburg: Elwert, 1965) 289-309.

———, *Introduction to the New Testament*, rev. ed., tr. H. C. Kee (London: SCM; New York: Abingdon, 1975).

———, *The Theology of the New Testament According to Its Major Witnesses: Jesus, Paul and John*, tr. J. E. Steely (New York: Abingdon, 1973).

Kundsin, K., "Die Wiederkunft Jesu in den Abschiedsreden des Johannesevangeliums," *ZNW* 33 (1934) 210-15.

Kysar, R., "Background of the Prologue of the Fourth Gospel: A Critique of Historical Methods," *CJT* 16 (1970) 250-55.

———, "Community and Gospel: Vectors in Fourth Gospel Criticism," *Int* 31 (1977) 355-66.

———, "The Eschatology of the Fourth Gospel. A Correction of Bultmann's Redactional Hypothesis," *Perspective* 13 (1972) 23-33.

———, *The Fourth Evangelist and His Gospel. An Examination of Contemporary Scholarship* (Minneapolis: Augsburg, 1975).

———, *John: The Maverick Gospel* (Atlanta: John Knox, 1976).

———, "The Source Analysis of the Fourth Gospel—A Growing Consensus?" *NovT* 15 (1973) 134-52.

Ladd, G. E., *A Theology of the New Testament* (Grand Rapids: Eerdmans, 1974).

Ladd, J. G. M., "The Sacramental Teaching of the Fourth Gospel with Special Reference to the Views of Oscar Cullmann," unpub. diss., University College of N. Wales (Bangor, Wales), 1966.

Lagrange, M.-J., *Evangile selon Saint Jean* (Paris: Gabalda, 1948).

Lamont, D., *Studies in the Johannine Writings* (London: James Clarke, 1956).

Lampe, G. W. H., "Baptisma in the New Testament," *SJT* 5 (1952) 163-74.

———, *God as Spirit* (Oxford: University Press, 1977).

———, "Holy Spirit," *IDB* 2:626-39.

———, "The Holy Spirit and the Person of Christ," in *Christ, Faith, and History: Cambridge Studies in Christology*, ed. S. W. Sykes and J. P. Clayton (Cambridge: University Press, 1972) 111-30.

———, "The Holy Spirit in the Writings of St. Luke," in *Studies in the Gospels, Essays in Memory of R. H. Lightfoot*, ed. D. E. Nineham (Oxford: Blackwell, 1955) 159-200.

———, "Paraclete," *IDB* 3:654-55.

———, *The Seal of the Spirit* (London: Longmans, 1951).

la Potterie, I. de, "Jesus et Nicodemus: de necessitate generationis ex Spiritu (Jo 3, 1-10)," *VD* 47 (1969) 193-214.

―――, "Naître de l'eau et naître de l'Esprit. Le texte baptismal de Jn 3, 5," in *La Vie selon l'Esprit, Condition du chrétien*, ed. I. de la Potterie and S. Lyonnet, Unam Sanctam 55 (Paris: Cerf, 1965) 31-63.

―――, "L'onction du Christ. Etude de théologie biblique," *NRT* 8 (1958) 225-52.

―――, "L'onction du chrétien par la foi," *Bib* 40 (1959) 12-69.

―――, "Le Paraclet," in *La Vie selon l'Esprit, Condition du Chrétien*, ed. I. de la Potterie and S. Lyonnet, Unam Sanctam 55 (Paris: Cerf, 1965) 85-105.

―――, "Parole et esprit dans S. Jean," in *L'Evangile de Jean*, ed. M. deJonge (Louvain: University Press, 1977) 177-202.

―――, "Studiorum Novi Testamenti Societas: Reports on Noordwijkerhout Seminars; 'L'Esprit Saint dans L'Evangile de Jean,'" *NTS* 18 (1971-72) 448-51.

―――, *La Verité dans St. Jean*, 2 vols. (Rome: Biblical Institute Press, 1977).

la Potterie, I. de, and Lyonnet, S., *The Christian Lives by the Spirit*, tr. J. Morriss (New York: Alba House, 1971)

Leal, J., "Spiritus et caro in Jo 6, 64," *VD* 30 (1952) 257-64.

Leaney, A. R. C., "The Historical Background and Theological Meaning of the Paraclete," *Duke Divinity School Review* 37 (1972) 146-59.

―――, "The Johannine Paraclete and the Qumran Scrolls," in *John and Qumran*, ed. J. H. Charlesworth (London: Chapman, 1972) 38-61.

―――, *The Rule of Qumran and Its Meaning* (Philadelphia: Westminster, 1966).

―――, "The Scrolls and the New Testament," in *A Guide to the Scrolls*, ed. A. R. C. Leaney (London: SCM, 1958) 79-121.

Lee, E. K., *The Religious Thought of St. John* (London: SPCK, 1950).

Lemonnyer, A., "L'Esprit-Saint Paraclet," *RSPT* 16 (1927) 293-307.

Lentzen-Deis, F., *Die Taufe Jesu nach den Synoptikern. Literarkritische und gattungsgeschichtliche Untersuchungen*, Frankfurter Theologische Studien 4 (Frankfurt: Knecht, 1970).

Levonian, L., "Insufflation (John 20:21)," *Exp* viii, 22 (1921-22) 149-54.

Lieb, F., "Der Heilige Geist als Geist Jesu Christi," *EvT* 23 (1963) 281-98.

Liese, H., "Spiritus Sanctus testimonium (Ioh 16:5-15)," *VD* 14 (1934) 101-107.

Lightfoot, J. B., *Biblical Essays* (London: MacMillan, 1893; repr. Grand Rapids: Baker, 1979).

Lightfoot, R. H., *St. John's Gospel* (Oxford: University Press, 1960).

Lindars, B., *Behind the Fourth Gospel* (London: SPCK, 1971).

―――, "The Composition of John 20," *NTS* 7 (1960-61) 142-47.

―――, "Δικαιοσύνη in John 16:8 and 10," in *Mélanges Bibliques en hommage au R. P. Béda Rigaux*, ed. A. Descamps and A. de Halleux (Gembloux: Duculot, 1970) 275-85.

―――, "The Fourth Gospel: An Act of Contemplation," in *Studies in the Fourth Gospel*, ed. F. L. Cross (London: Mowbray, 1957) 23-35.

―――, *The Gospel of John*, New Century Bible (London: Oliphants, 1972; repr. Grand Rapids: Eerdmans, 1981).

_____, "John and the Synoptic Gospels: A Test Case," *NTS* 27 (1980-81) 287-94.

_____, "Word and Sacrament in the Fourth Gospel," *SJT* 29 (1976) 49-63.

Lloyd, R. B., "The Word 'Glory' in the Fourth Gospel," *ExpTim* 43 (1931-32) 546-48.

Locher, G. W., "Der Geist als Paraklet," *EvT* 26 (1966) 565-79.

Lofthouse, W. F., *The Father and the Son: A Study in Johannine Thought* (London: SCM, 1934).

_____, "The Holy Spirit in the Acts and the Fourth Gospel," *ExpTim* 52 (1941) 334-36.

Lohse, E., "Miracles in the Fourth Gospel," in *What About the New Testament? Essays in Honor of Christopher Evans*, ed. M. Hooker and C. Hickling (London: SCM, 1975) 64-75.

_____, "Wort und Sakrament im Johannesevangelium," *NTS* 7 (1960-61) 110-25.

Longenecker, R., *The Christology of Early Jewish Christianity*, SBT 2/17 (London: SCM; Naperville: Allenson, 1970).

Lutkemeyer, L. J., "The Role of the Paraclete (John 16:7-15)," *CBQ* 8 (1946) 220-29.

McCool, F. J., "Living Water in John," in *The Bible in Current Catholic Thought*, ed. J. L. McKenzie (New York: Herder, 1962) 226-33.

MacDonald, A. J., *The Holy Spirit* (London: SPCK, 1927).

MacDonald, W. G., "Problems of Pneumatology in Christology: The Relationship of Christ and the Holy Spirit in Biblical Theology," unpub. diss., Southern Baptist Theological Seminary (USA), 1970.

MacGregor, G. H. C., "The Eucharist in the Fourth Gospel," *NTS* 9 (1962-63) 111-19.

_____, *The Gospel of John* (London: Hodder and Stoughton, 1928).

McKelvey, R. J., *The New Temple. The Church in the New Testament* (Oxford: University Press, 1968).

McNamara, M., "'To Prepare a Resting-Place for You.' Targumic Expression and John 14:2f.," *Milltown Studies* [Dublin] 3 (1979) 100-108.

McNaugher, J., "The Witnessing Spirit and the Witnessed Christ," [John 15:26] *BSac* 88 (1931) 207-19.

McPolin, J., "Holy Spirit in Luke and John," *ITQ* 45 (1978) 117-31.

_____, "Johannine Mysticism," *Way* [London] 18 (1978) 25-35.

_____, *John* (Dublin: Veritas, 1979).

_____, "Studies in the Fourth Gospel—Some Contemporary Trends," *IBS* 2 (1980) 3-26.

Malatesta, E., *Interiority and Covenant. A Study of* εἶναι ἐν *and* μένειν ἐν *in the First Letter of St. John* (Rome: Biblical Institute Press, 1978).

_____, "The Literary Structure of John 17," *Bib* 52 (1971) 190-214.

_____, *St. John's Gospel 1920-1965* (Rome: Biblical Institute Press, 1967).

Maloney, F. J., *The Johannine Son of Man* (Rome: LAS, 1976).

Mann, C. S. "Pentecost, the Spirit, and John," *Theol* 62 (1959) 188-90.

Manson, T. W., "Entry into Membership of the Early Church," *JTS* 48 (1947) 25-33.

_____, *On Paul and John* (London: SCM, 1963).

_____, *The Teaching of Jesus*, 2nd ed. (Cambridge: University Press, 1935).

Mansure, A. L., "The Relation of the Paraclete to the Spiritual Presence of Jesus in the Fourth Gospel," unpub. diss., Boston University (USA), 1950.

Margoliouth, D. S., "Baptising with Fire," *Exp* viii, 13 (1917) 446-51.

Marsh, J., *Saint John*, Pelican Gospel Commentaries (Middlesex/Baltimore: Penguin, 1968).

Marsh, T., "Holy Spirit in Early Christian Teaching," *ITQ* 45 (1978) 101-16.

Marshall, I. H., "To Baptize," *EvQ* 45 (1973) 130-40.

———, *The Epistles of John*, NICNT (Grand Rapids: Eerdmans, 1978).

———, *The Gospel of Luke. A Commentary on the Greek Text*, New International Greek Testament Commentary (Exeter: Paternoster; Grand Rapids: Eerdmans, 1978).

———, *The Origins of New Testament Christology* (Leicester: IVP, 1976).

———, "The Significance of Pentecost," *SJT* 30 (1977) 347-69.

———, "Son of God or Servant of Yahweh—A Reconsideration of Mark 1:11," *NTS* 15 (1968-69) 326-36.

Martin, A. G., "La Saint-Esprit et l'Evangile de Jean dans une perspective trinitaire," *Revue Réformée* [St. Germain-en-Laye] 29 (1978) 141-51.

Martin, J. P., "History and Eschatology in the Lazarus Narrative. John 11:1-44," *SJT* 17 (1964) 332-43.

Martyn, J. L., *History and Theology in the Fourth Gospel*, 2nd ed. (Nashville: Abingdon, 1979).

Mary, S., *Pauline and Johannine Mysticism* (London: Darton, Longman, and Todd, 1964).

Mealand, D. L., "The Christology of the Fourth Gospel," *SJT* 31 (1978) 449-67.

Meeks, W. A., "Am I a Jew? Johannine Christianity and Judaism," in *Christianity, Judaism, and Other Greco-Roman Cults: Studies for Morton Smith at 60*, 4 vols., ed. J. Neusner (Leiden: Brill, 1975) 1:163-86.

———, "The Man from Heaven in Johannine Sectarianism," *JBL* 91 (1972) 44-72.

———, *The Prophet-King. Moses Traditions and the Johannine Christology*, NovTSup 14 (Leiden: Brill, 1967).

Meijer, P. W., "The Eschatology of the Fourth Gospel. A Study in Early Christian Reinterpretation," unpub. diss., Union Theological Seminary, New York (USA), 1955.

Mendner, S., "Nikodemus," *JBL* 77 (1958) 293-323.

Metzger, B. M., *A Textual Commentary on the Greek New Testament* (London: United Bible Society, 1971).

Michaelis, W., *Die Sakramente im Johannesevangelium* (Bern: BEG Verlag, 1946).

———, "Zur Herkunft des Johanneischen Paraklet-Titels," in *Coniectanea Neotestamentica 11*, Festschrift A. Fridrichsen (Uppsala: Apud Seminarium Neotestamenticum, 1947) 147-62.

Michaels, J. R., "The Centurion's Confession and the Spear Thrust," *CBQ* 29 (1967) 102-109.

———, "The Temple Discourse in John," in *New Dimensions in New Testament Study*, ed. R. Longenecker and M. Tenney (Grand Rapids: Zondervan, 1974) 200-213.

Michel, O., "Ein johanneischer Osterbericht," in *Studien zum Neuen Testament und zur*

Patristik. Erich Klostermann zum 90. Geburtstag dargebracht = *TU* 77 (Berlin: Akademie, 1961) 35-42.

Michl, J., "Der Geist als Garant des rechten Glaubens," in *Vom Wort des Lebens. Festschrift für M. Meinertz*, ed. N. Adler (Münster: Aschendorff, 1951) 142-51.

Micklem, N., *Behold the Man. A Study in the Fourth Gospel* (London: Bles, 1969).

Miguens, M., "Nota exegetica: Juan 20:17," *SBFLA* 7 (1957) 221-31.

_____, *El Paraclito (Juan 14–16)*, Studii Biblici Franciscani Analecta 2 (Jerusalem: Franciscan Press, 1963).

_____, "Salio sangre y agua (Juan 19:34)," *SBFLA* 14 (1963) 5-31.

Miller, E. L., "The Logos was God," *EvQ* 53 (1981) 65-77.

Mollat, D., *Etudes johanniques* (Paris: Editions du Seuil, 1979).

Montague, G. T., *The Holy Spirit: Growth of a Biblical Tradition* (New York: Paulist, 1976).

_____, *The Spirit and His Gifts* (New York: Paulist, 1974).

Moody, D., *Spirit of the Living God* (Nashville: Broadman, 1968).

Morgenthaler, R., *Statistik des Neutestamentlichen Wortschatzes* (Zürich: Gotthelf, 1958).

Morris, L., *The Gospel According to John*, NICNT (Grand Rapids: Eerdmans, 1971).

_____, "The Jesus of Saint John," in *Unity and Diversity in New Testament Theology: Essays in Honor of George E. Ladd*, ed. R A. Guelich (Grand Rapids: Eerdmans, 1978) 37-53.

_____, *Studies in the Fourth Gospel* (Grand Rapids: Eerdmans, 1969).

Morton, A. Q., and McLeman, J., *The Genesis of John* (Edinburgh: St. Andrews Press, 1980).

Moule, C. F. D., "2 Cor. 3:18b, καθάπερ ἀπὸ κυρίου πνεύματος," in *Neues Testament und Geschichte. Oscar Cullmann zum 70. Geburtstag*, ed. H. Baltensweiler and B. Reicke (Zürich: Theologischer Verlag, 1972) 231-37.

_____, "Baptism with Water and with Holy Spirit," *Theol* 48 (1945) 246-49.

_____, "Fulfillment-Words in the New Testament: Use and Abuse," *NTS* 14 (1967-68) 293-320.

_____, *The Holy Spirit* (London: Mowbray, 1978).

_____, "The Holy Spirit in the Scriptures," *CQ* 3 (1971) 279-87.

_____, *An Idiom-Book of New Testament Greek* (Cambridge: University Press, 1959).

_____, "The Individualism of the Fourth Gospel," *NovT* 5 (1962) 171-90.

_____, "The Meaning of 'Life' in the Gospel and Epistles of John," *Theol* 78 (1975) 114-25.

_____, "A Neglected Factor in the Interpretation of Johannine Eschatology," in *Studies in John Presented to Professor J. N. Sevenster on the Occasion of His Seventieth Birthday*, NovTSup 24 (Leiden: Brill, 1970) 155-60.

_____, *The Origins of Christology* (Cambridge: University Press, 1977).

Moulton, J. H., *A Grammar of New Testament Greek*, vol. 1: *Prolegomena*; vol. 2: *Accidence and Word-Formation* [for vols. 3 and 4 of same series, see N. Turner below] (Edinburgh: T. & T. Clark, 1908, 1920).

Moulton, J. H., and Milligan, G., *The Vocabulary of the Greek New Testament* (Grand Rapids: Eerdmans, 1930).

Mowinckel, S., "The 'Spirit' and the 'Word' in the Pre-Exilic Reforming Prophets," *JBL* 53 (1934) 199-227.

————, "Die Vorstellung des Spätjudentums vom heiligen Geist als Fürsprecher und der johanneische Paraklet," *ZNW* 52 (1933) 97-130.

Mueller, J. T., "Notes on John 16:5-16," *CTM* 23 (1952) 16-23.

Müller, U. B., *Messias und Menschensohn in spätjüdischen Apokalypsen und in der Offenbarung des Johannes*, Studien zum Neuen Testament 6 (Gütersloh: Mohn, 1972).

————, "Die Parakletenvorstellung im Johannesevangelium" *ZTK* 71 (1974) 31-78.

————, *Prophetie und Predigt im Neuen Testament*, Studien zum Neuen Testament 10 (Gütersloh: Mohn, 1975).

Mussner, F., *The Historical Jesus in the Gospel of St. John*, tr. W. J. O'Hara (London: Burns and Oates; New York: Herder, 1967).

————, "Die johanneische Parakletsprüche und die apolstolische Tradition," *BZ* 5 (1961) 56-70.

Nauck, W., *Die Tradition und der Charakter des ersten Johannesbriefes* (Tübingen: Mohr, 1957).

Neill, S., *The Interpretation of the New Testament 1861-1961* (London: Oxford University Press, 1964).

Neugebauer, F., "Geistsprüche und Jesuslogien," *ZNW* 53 (1962) 218-28.

Neyrey, J. H., "John 3—A Debate over Johannine Epistemology and Christology," *NovT* 23 (1981) 115-27.

Nicol, W., "[Johannine Interpretation] During the Past Century," in *The Christ of John. Essays on the Christology of the Fourth Gospel* (Potchefstroom, S. Africa: Pro Rege Press, 1971) 8-18.

————, *The Sēmeia in the Fourth Gospel* (Leiden: Brill, 1972).

Nossol, A., "Der Geist als Gegenwart Jesu Christi," in *Gegenwart des Geistes*, ed. W. Kasper (Freiburg: Herder, 1979) 132-54.

Nötscher, F., "Geist und Geister in den Texten von Qumran," in *Mélanges Bibliques rédigés en l'honneur de André Robert* (Paris: Bloud et Gay, 1956) 305-15.

Nunn, H. P. V., *The Authorship of the Fourth Gospel* (Oxford: Blackwell, 1952).

Odeberg, H., *The Fourth Gospel Interpreted in its Relation to Contemporaneous Religious Currents in Palestine and the Hellenistic-Oriental World* (Uppsala/Stockholm: Almquist and Wicksell, 1929).

O'Grady, J. F., "Individualism and Johannine Ecclesiology," *BTB* 5 (1975) 227-61.

————, "Johannine Ecclesiology: A Critical Evaluation," *BTB* 7 (1977) 36-44.

Olsson, B., *Structure and Meaning in the Fourth Gospel. A Text-Linguistic Analysis of John 2:1-11 and 4:1-42*, Coniectanea Biblica 6 (Lund: Gleerup, 1974).

O'Rourke, J., "John's Fulfillment Texts," *ScEc* 19 (1967) 433-44.

Ousersluys, R. C., "Eschatology and the Holy Spirit," *RTR* 19 (1965) 3-12.

Pagels, E. H., *The Johannine Gospel in Gnostic Exegesis* (Nashville: Abingdon, 1973).

Painter, J., "The Church and Israel in the Gospel of John," *NTS* 25 (1978-79) 103-112.

———, "Eschatological Faith in the Gospel of John," in *Reconciliation and Hope: New Testament Essays on Atonement and Eschatology Presented to L. L. Morris on His Sixtieth Birthday*, ed. R. Banks (Exeter: Paternoster; Grand Rapids: Eerdmans, 1974) 36-52.

———, *John: Witness and Theologian* (London: SPCK, 1975).

Pancaro, S., *The Law in the Fourth Gospel: The Torah and the Gospel, Moses and Jesus, Judaism and Christianity According to John*, NovTSup 42 (Leiden: Brill, 1975).

———, "The People of God in St. John's Gospel," *NTS* 16 (1969-70) 114-29.

———, "The Relationship of the Church to Israel in the Gospel of John," *NTS* 21 (1974-75) 396-405.

Parker, P., "The Kinship of John and Acts," in *Christianity, Judaism, and Other Greco-Roman Cults: Studies for Morton Smith at 60*, 4 vols., ed. J. Neusner (Leiden: Brill, 1975) 1:187-205.

———, "Two Editions of John," *JBL* 75 (1956) 303-14.

Parratt, J. K., "The Holy Spirit and Baptism," *ExpTim* 82 (1971) 231-35.

Pascher, J., "Der Glauben als Mitteilung des Pneumas nach Jo 6, 61-65," *TThQ* 117 (1936) 301-21.

Patrick, J. G., "The Promise of the Paraclete," *BSac* 127 (1970) 333-45.

Pecorara, G., "De Berbo 'manere' [μένειν] apud Joannem," *DThom* 40 (1937) 159-71.

Pesch, R., "'Ihr müsst von oben geboren werden': Eine Auslegung von Joh 3, 1-12," *BibLeb* 7 (1966) 208-19.

Phillips, G. L., "Faith and Vision in the Fourth Gospel," in *Studies in the Fourth Gospel*, ed. F. L. Cross (London: Mowbray, 1957) 83-96.

Pillai, C. J., "Advocate: Christ's Name for the Holy Spirit," *BiTod* 30 (1967) 2078-81.

Pinnock, C. H., "The Concept of Spirit in the Epistles of Paul," unpub. diss., Manchester University (England), 1963.

Piper, O. A., "1 John and the Didache of the Primitive Church," *JBL* 66 (1947) 437-51.

Plummer, A., *The Gospel According to St. John* (Cambridge: University Press, 1889).

Pollard, T. E., *Johannine Christology and the Early Church* (Cambridge: University Press, 1970).

Porsch, F., *Anwalt der Glaubenden. Das wirken des Geistes nach dem Zeugnis Johannesevangelium* (Stuttgart: Katholisches Bibelwerk, 1978).

———, *Pneuma und Wort. Ein Exegetischer Beitrag zur Pneumatologie des Johannesevangeliums*, Frankfurter Theolgische Studien 16 (Frankfurt: Knecht, 1974).

Preiss, T., *Life in Christ* (London: SCM, 1954).

Price, J. L., "Light from Qumran upon Some Aspects of Johannine Theology," in *John and Qumran*, ed. J. H. Charlesworth (London: Chapman, 1972) 9-37.

Quispel, G., "Qumran, John, and Jewish Christianity," in *John and Qumran*, ed. J. H. Charlesworth (London: Chapman, 1972) 137-55.

Ramsey, A. M., *Holy Spirit* (London: SPCK, 1977).

———, "What Was the Ascension?" in *Historicity and Chronology in the New Testament*, ed. D. E. Nineham (London: SPCK, 1965) 135-44.

Rawlinson, A. E. J., "In Spirit and in Truth: An Exposition of St. John 4:16-24," *ExpTim* 44 (1932-33) 12-14.

Reese, J. M., "The Literary Structure of John 13:31–14:31; 16:5-6, 16-33," *CBQ* 34 (1972) 321-31.

Reiling, J., "Prophecy, the Spirit, and the Church," in *Prophetic Vocation in the New Testament and Today*, ed. J. Panagopoulos (Leiden: Brill, 1977) 58-76.

Reim, G., *Studien zum altestamentlichen Hintergrund des Johannesevangeliums* (Cambridge: University Press, 1974).

Relton, F., "The Unfinished Teaching of Christ (John 16:12)," *ExpTim* 4 (1892-93) 446-50.

Ricca, P., *Die Eschatologie des vierten Evangeliums* (Zürich: Gotthelf, 1966).

Richardson, A., *The Gospel According to St. John*, Torch Bible Commentary (London: SCM, 1959).

———, *An Introduction to the Theology of the New Testament* (New York: Harper and Row, 1958).

Richter, G., "Blut und Wasser aus der durchbohrten Seite Jesu (Joh 19, 34b)," *MTZ* 21 (1970) 1-21.

———, "Die Fleischwerdung des Logos im Johannesevangelium," *NovT* 13 (1971) 81-126; 14 (1972) 257-76.

———, "Zur formgeschichte und literarischen Einheit von Joh 6, 31-58," *ZNW* 60 (1969) 21-55.

Riesenfeld, H., "A Probable Background to the Johannine Paraclete," in *Ex Orbe Religionum: Studia Geo Widengren*, ed. C. J. Bleeker, S. G. F. Brandon, and M. Simon (Leiden: Brill, 1972) 266-74.

Ringgren, H., *The Faith of Qumran. Theology of the Dead Sea Scrolls*, tr. E. T. Sanders (Philadelphia: Fortress, 1963).

———, *Word and Wisdom. Studies in the Hypostatization of Divine Qualitites and Functions in the Ancient Near East* (Lund: Hakan Ohlssons, 1947).

Robertson, A. T., *A Grammar of the Greek New Testament in Light of Historical Research* (Nashville: Broadman, 1934).

Robinson, D. W. B., "Born of Water and Spirit: Does John 3:5 Refer to Baptism?" *RTR* 25 (1966) 15-23.

Robinson, H. W., *The Christian Experience of the Holy Spirit* (London: Nisbet, 1928).

Robinson, James, "The Johannine Trajectory," in *Trajectories Through Early Christianity*, ed. J. M. Robinson and H. Koester (Philadelphia: Fortress, 1971) 232-52.

Robinson, James, ed., *The Nag Hammadi Library* (New York: Harper and Row, 1977).

———, "Recent Research in the Fourth Gospel," *JBL* 78 (1959) 242-52.

Robinson, John A. T., "The Baptism of John and the Qumran Community," *HTR* 50 (1957) 175-91.

———, "The Destination and Purpose of St. John's Gospel," *NTS* 6 (1959-60) 117-31.

———, "The Destination and Purpose of the Johannine Epistles," *NTS* 7 (1960-61) 56-65.

———, *Jesus and His Coming* (London: SCM, 1957, 2nd ed. 1979).

———, "The New Look on the Fourth Gospel," *SE* 1 = *TU* 73 (1959) 338-50.

———, "The Use of the Fourth Gospel in Christology Today," in *Christ and Spirit in the New Testament: Studies in Honour of C. F. D. Moule*, ed. B. Lindars and S. Smalley (Cambridge: University Press, 1973) 61-78.

Ruckstuhl, E., *Die literarische Einheit des Johannesevangeliums* (Fribourg: Paulusverlag, 1951).

Rudolph, K., *Mandaeism* (Leiden: Brill, 1978).

Ruland, V., "Sign and Sacrament. John's Bread of Life Discourse," *Int* 18 (1964) 450-62.

Rusch, F., "Signs and Discourse: The Rich Theology of John 6," *Currents in Theology and Mission* [St. Louis, Mo] 5 (1978) 386-90.

Russell, E. A., "The Holy Spirit in the Fourth Gospel," *IBS* 2 (1980) 84-94.

Saake, H., *Pneumatologica. Untersuchungen zum Geistverständnis im Johannesevangelium, bei Origenes und Athanasios von Alexandria* (Frankfurt am Main: Diagonal Verlag, 1973).

Sanders, J. N., *The Fourth Gospel in the Early Church. Its Origin and Influence on Christian Theology up to Irenaeus* (Cambridge: University Press, 1943).

————, *The Gospel According to St. John*, ed. and completed by B. A. Mastin, Black's/Harper's New Testament Commentary (London: A. & C. Black; New York: Harper and Row, 1968).

————, "John, Gospel of," *IDB* 2:932-46.

————, "Who was the Disciple Whom Jesus Loved?" in *Studies in the Fourth Gospel*, ed. F. L. Cross (London: Mowbray, 1957) 72-82.

Sasse, H., "Der Paraklet im Johannesevangelium," *ZNW* 24 (1925) 260-77.

Sava, A. F., "The Wound in the Side of Christ," *CBQ* 19 (1957) 343-46.

Schaeffer, O., "Der Sinn der Rede Jesu von der vielen Wohnung in seines Vaters Haus," *ZNW* 32 (1933) 210-17.

Schäfer, P., *Die Vorstellung vom heiligen Geist in der rabbinischen Literatur* (München: Kösel, 1972).

Schlafer, F. G., "The Johannine Doctrine of Christian Sonship," unpub. diss., Southern Baptist Theological Seminary, Louisville, Kentucky (USA), 1948.

Schlatter, A., *Der Evangelist Johannes* (Stuttgart: Calwer, 1930).

————, *Die Geschichte des Christus* (Stuttgart: Calwer, 1921).

Schlier, H., "Der Heilige Geist als Interpret nach dem Johannesevangelium," *Internationale Katholische Zeitschrift "Communio"* 2 (1973) 97-108.

————, "Herkunft, Ankunft, und Wirkung des Heiligen Geistes im Neuen Testament," in *Erfahrung und Theologie des heiligen Geistes*, ed. C. Heitmann and H. Mühlen (Hamburg: Agentur des Rauen Hauses; München: Kösel, 1974) 118-30.

————, "Zum Begriff des Geistes nach dem Johannesevangelium," in *Besinnung auf das Neue Testament, Exegetische Aufsätze und Vortrage II* (Freiburg: Herder, 1964) 264-71.

Schmithals, W., "Geisterfahrung als Christuserfahrung," in *Erfahrung und Theologie des Heiligen Geistes*, ed. C. Heitmann and H. Mühlen (Hamburg: Agentur des Rauen Hauses; München: Kösel, 1974) 101-17.

Schnackenburg, R., "Das Anliegen der Abschiedsrede in Joh 14," in *Wort Gottes in der Zeit. Festschrift Karl Hermann Schelkle zum 65. Geburtstag*, ed. H. Feld and J. Nolte (Düsseldorf: Patmos, 1972) 95-110.

————, "Die 'anbetung in Geist und Wahrheit' (Joh 4, 23) im Licht von Qumran Texten," *BZ* 3 (1959) 88-94.

————, "Christus, Geist, und Gemeinde (Eph 4, 1-16)," in *Christ and Spirit in the New Testament: Studies in Honour of C. F. D. Moule*, ed. B. Lindars and S. Smalley (Cambridge: University Press, 1973) 279-96.

————, "Entwicklung und Stand der johanneischen Forschung seit 1955," in *L'Evangile de Jean*, ed. M. deJonge (Louvain: University Press, 1977) 19-44.

————, *God's Rule and Kingdom*, tr. J. Murray (New York: Herder, 1963).

————, *The Gospel According to St. John*, 3 vols., vols. 1-2 tr. K. Smith et al. (New York: Seabury, 1980; vol. 3 tr. D. Smith and G. A. Kon (New York: Crossroad, 1982).

————, "Die johanneische Gemeinde und Ihre Geisterfahrung," in *Die Kirche des Anfangs. Festschrift für Heinz Schürmann zum 65. Geburtstag*, Erfurter theologische Studien 38, ed. R. Schnackenburg, J. Ernst, and J. Wanke (Leipzig: St. Benno, 1977) 277-306.

————, *Die Johannesbriefe*, Herders theologischer Kommentar zum Neuen Testament, 3rd ed. (Freiburg: Herder, 1963).

————, "Paraklet," *Lexicon für Theologie und Kirche*, 10 vols., ed. J. Höfer and K. Rahner (Freiburg: Herder, 1957-1965) 8:77-78.

————, "Die 'situationsgelösten' Redestücke in Joh 3," *ZNW* 49 (1958) 88-89.

————, "The Theology of St. John," in *New Testament Theology Today*, tr. D. Askew (New York: Herder, 1963) 90-106.

————, "Tradition und Interpretation im Spruchgut des Johannesevangelium," in *Begegnung mit dem Wort. Festschrift für Heinrich Zimmermann*, ed. J. Zmijewski and E. Nellessen (Bonn: Hanstein, 1980) 141-59.

————, "Zur johanneischen Forschung," *BZ* 18 (1974) 272-87.

Schneider, J., "Zur Frage der Komposition von Joh 6, 27-58. Die Himmelsbrotrede," in *In Memoriam Ernst Lohmeyer*, ed. W. Schmauch (Stuttgart: Evangelisches Verlag, 1951) 132-42.

————, "Zur Komposition von Joh 7," *ZNW* 45 (1954) 108-19.

Schneiders, S. M., "History and Symbolism in the Fourth Gospel," in *L'Evangile de Jean*, ed. M. deJonge (Louvain: University Press, 1977) 371-76.

Scholte, F. E., "An Investigation and an Interpretation of John 20:22," unpub. diss., Dallas Theological Seminary (USA), 1953.

Schottroff, L., "Joh 4, 5-15 und die Konsequenzen des johanneischen Dualismus," *ZNW* 60 (1969) 199-214.

Schreiner, J., "Geistbegabung in der Gemeinde von Qumran," *BZ* 9 (1965) 161-80.

Schulz, S., *Das Evangelium nach Johannes*, Neue Testament Deutsch, 13th ed. (Göttingen: Vandenhoeck & Ruprecht, 1972).

————, *Komposition und Herkunft der johanneischen Reden* (Stuttgart: Kohlhammer, 1960).

————, *Untersuchungen zur Menschensohn-Christologie im Johannesevangelium* (Göttingen: Vandenhoeck & Ruprecht, 1957), esp. "Die Paraklet Thematradition," 142-58.

Schulze-Kadelbach, G., "Zur Pneumatologie des Johannesevangeliums," *ZNW* 46 (1955) 279-80.

Schürmann, H., "Joh 6, 51c—ein Schlüssel zur grossen johanneischen Brotrede," *BZ* 2 (1958) 244-62.

————, *Das Lukasevangelium*, Herders theologischer Kommentar zum Neuen Testament (Freiburg: Herder, 1969).

Schweitzer, A., *The Mysticism of Paul the Apostle*, tr. W. Montgomery (London: A. & C. Black; New York: Macmillan, 1953).

Schweizer, E., "Christus und Geist im Kolosserbrief," in *Christ and Spirit in the New Testament: Studies in Honour of C. F. D. Moule*, ed. B. Lindars and S. Smalley (Cambridge: University Press, 1973) 297-313.

————, "The Concept of the Church in the Gospel and Epistles of St. John," in *New Testament Essays: Studies in Memory of T. W. Manson*, ed. A. J. B. Higgins (Manchester: University Press, 1959) 230-45.

————, *Ego eimi. Die religiongeschichtliche Herkunft und theologische Bedeutung der johanneischen Bildreden, zugleich ein Beitrag zur Quellenfrage des vierten Evangeliums* (Göttingen: Vandenhoeck & Ruprecht, 1938) (= FRLANT 56 [1939; 2nd ed. 1965]).

————, "Gegenwart des Geistes und Eschatologische Hoffnung (bei Zarathustra, Spätjüdischen Gruppen, Gnostikern, und den Zeugen des Neuen Testaments," in *The Background of the New Testament and Its Eschatology: Studies in Honour of C. H. Dodd*, ed. W. D. Davies and D. Daube (Cambridge: University Press, 1965) 482-508.

————, *Geist und Gemeinde im Neuen Testament und Heute*, Theologische Existenz Heute 32 (München: Kaiser, 1952).

————, *The Holy Spirit*, tr. R. H. Fuller and I. Fuller (London: SCM; Philadelphia: Fortress, 1980).

————, "Orthodox Proclamation. The Reinterpretation of the Gospel by the Fourth Evangelist," *Int* 8 (1954) 387-96.

————, "Πνεῦμα, [NT]," *TDNT* 6:396-451.

————, "The Spirit of Power: The Uniformity and Diversity of the Concept of the Holy Spirit in the New Testament," *Int* 6 (1952) 259-78.

Sciberras, L., "Water in the Gospel of St. John According to the Greek Fathers and Writers of the Church," unpub. diss., Pontificia Universitas Antoniana, Jerusalem (Israel), 1975.

Scott, E. F., *The Fourth Gospel, Its Purpose and Theology* (Edinburgh: T. & T. Clark, 1906).

————, *The Spirit in the New Testament* (London: Hodder and Stoughton, 1923).

Scott, M. V., "The Eschatology of the Fourth Gospel and the Johannine Epistles," unpub. diss., Edinburgh University (Scotland), 1953.

Scroggs, R., "The Eschatology of the Spirit by Some Early Christians," *JBL* 84 (1965) 359-73.

Seitz, O. J. F., "Two Spirits in Man," *NTS* 6 (1959-60) 82-95.

Shafaat, A., "Geber of the Qumran Scrolls and the Spirit Paraclete of the Gospel of John," *NTS* 27 (1980-1981) 263-69.

Shorter, M., "The Position of Chapter 6 in the Fourth Gospel," *ExpTim* 84 (1973) 181-83.

Sidebottom, E. M., "The Ascent and Descent of the Son of Man in the Gospel of John," *ATR* 2 (1957) 115-22.

————, *The Christ of the Fourth Gospel* (London: SPCK, 1961).

Siebeneck, R., "The Dove as Epiphany," *Worship* 35 (1961) 97-102.

Simon, U. E., "Eternal Life in the Fourth Gospel," in *Studies in the Fourth Gospel*, ed. F. L. Cross (London: Mowbray, 1957) 97-110.

Simpson, I. G., "The Holy Spirit in the Fourth Gospel," *Exp* ix, 4 (1925) 292-99.

Sjöberg, E., "Wiedergeburt und Neuschöpfung im palästinensischen Judentum," *ST* 4 (1950) 44-85.

Smail, T. A., *Reflected Glory. The Spirit in Christ and Christians* (London: Hodder and Stoughton, 1975).

Smalley, S., "The Christ-Christian Relation in Paul and John," in *Pauline Studies: Essays Presented to F. F. Bruce on His Seventieth Birthday*, ed. D. A. Hagner and M. J. Harris (Exeter: Paternoster; Grand Rapids: Eerdmans, 1980) 95-105.

_____, "The Delay of the Parousia," *JBL* 83 (1964) 41-54.

_____, "Diversity and Development in John," *NTS* 17 (1970-71) 276-92.

_____, "Johannes 1:51 und die Einleitung zum vierten Evangelium," in *Jesus und der Menschensohn. Für Anton Vögtle*, ed. R. Pesch and R. Schnackenburg (Freiburg: Herder, 1975) 300-313.

_____, "The Johannine Son of Man Sayings," *NTS* 15 (1968-69) 278-301.

_____, *John, Evangelist and Interpreter* (Exeter: Paternoster, 1978; Nashville: Nelson, 1984).

_____, "Liturgy and Sacrament in the Fourth Gospel," *EvQ* 29 (1957) 159-70.

_____, "New Light on the Fourth Gospel," *TynBul* 17 (1966) 35-62.

_____, "The Sign in John xxi," *NTS* 20 (1973-74) 275-88.

_____, "The Treatment of Jesus: Another Look," *SE* 6 (1973) 495-501.

_____, "What about First John?" in *Studia Biblica III 1978. Papers on Paul and Other New Testament Authors*, Sixth International Congress on Biblical Studies, Oxford, April, 1978, JSNTSup 3, ed. E. A. Livingston (Sheffield: JSNT Press, 1980) 337-43.

Smith, D. M., *The Composition and Order of the Fourth Gospel—Bultmann's Literary Theory* (New Haven: Yale University Press, 1965).

_____, "Johannine Christianity: Some Reflections on Its Character and Delineation," *NTS* 21 (1974-75) 222-48.

_____, "John and the Synoptics: Some Dimensions of the Problem," *NTS* 26 (1979-80) 425-44.

_____, "The Presentation of Jesus in the Fourth Gospel," *Int* 31 (1977) 367-78.

Smith, T. C., "The Christology of the Fourth Gospel," *RevExp* 71 (1974) 19-30.

Snaith, H. H., "The Meaning of the Paraclete," *ExpTim* 57 (1945-46) 47-50.

_____, "The Spirit of God in Jewish Thought," in *The Doctrine of the Holy Spirit*, The Headingly Lectures, 1937 (London: Epworth Press, 1937) 9-38.

Solignac, A., "Le Saint-Esprit et la présence du Christ auprès de ses fideles," *NRT* 77 (1955) 478-90.

Sparks, H. F. D., *The Johannine Synopsis of the Gospels* (New York: Harper and Row, 1974).

Spitta, F., *Das Johannes-Evangelium als Quelle der Geschichte Jesu* (Göttingen: Vandenhoeck & Ruprecht, 1910).

Stagg, F., "Orthodoxy and Orthopraxy in the Johannine Epistles," *RevExp* 67 (1970) 423-32.

Stählin, G., "Τὸ πνεῦμα Ἰησοῦ (Apostelgeschichte 16:7)," in *Christ and Spirit in the New Testament: Studies in Honour of C. F. D. Moule*, ed. B. Lindars and S. Smalley (Cambridge: University Press, 1973) 229-52.

Stamm, R., "Luke-Acts and Three Cardinal Ideas in the Gospel of John," in *Biblical Studies in Honor of H. C. Alleman*, ed. J. M. Myers, O. Reinherr, and H. N. Bream (New York: J. J. Augustin, 1960) 170-204.

Stanley, D. M., "From his Heart Will Flow Rivers of Living Water (John 7:38)," *Cor Jesu I* [Commentationes in Litteras Encyclicas, "Haurietis Aguas"] (Roma: Herder, 1959) 509-42.

Stanton, A. H., "Convince or Convict (John 16:8)?" *ExpTim* 33 (1921-22) 278-79.

Stauffer, E., "Agnostos Christos: Joh 11, 24 und die Eschatologie des vierten Evangeliums," in *The Background of the New Testament and Its Eschatology: Essays in Honour of C. H. Dodd*, ed. W. D. Davies and D. Daube (Cambridge: University Press, 1956) 281-99.

_____, *New Testament Theology*, tr. J. Marsh (London: SCM; New York: Macmillan, 1955).

Stenger, W., "Δικαιοσύνη in Joh xvi.8, 10," *NovT* 21 (1979) 2-12.

_____, "Der Geist ist es, der lebendig macht, das Fleisch nützt nichts (Jo 6, 63)," *TTZ* 85 (1976) 116-22.

Stevens, G. B., *The Johannine Theology* (Edinburgh: T. & T. Clark, 1894).

Stirnimann, H., "Die Kirche und der Geist Christi," *DThom* 31 (1953) 3-17.

Stockton, E. D., "The Holy Spirit in the Writings of St. John," unpub. diss., The Theological Faculty of the University of Sydney (Australia), 1960.

_____, "The Paraclete," *The Australasian Catholic Record* 39 (1962) 255-63.

Strachan, R. H., *The Fourth Evangelist: Dramatist or Historian?* (London: Hodder and Stoughton, 1925).

_____, *The Fourth Gospel, Its Significance and Environment*, 3rd ed. (London: SCM, 1941).

Strathmann, H., *Das Evangelium nach Johannes*, Neue Testament Deutsch, 10th ed. (Göttingen: Vandenhoeck & Ruprecht, 1963).

Sundberg, A. C., "Christology in the Fourth Gospel," *Biblical Research* 21 (1976) 29-37.

Swain, L., *The Gospel According to John for Spiritual Reading* (London: Sheed and Ward, 1978).

Tasker, R. V. G., *The Gospel According to St. John*, Tyndale New Testament Commentaries (London: Tyndale; Grand Rapids: Eerdmans, 1960).

Taylor, J. V., *The Go-Between God* (London: SCM, 1972).

Taylor, V., "The Spirit in the New Testament," in *The Doctrine of the Holy Spirit*, The Headingly Lectures, 1937 (London: Epworth Press, 1937) 39-68.

Teeple, H. M., *The Mosaic Eschatological Prophet* (New York: Abingdon, 1957).

_____, "Qumran and the Origin of the Fourth Gospel," *NovT* 4 (1960) 6-25.

Temple, S., *The Core of the Fourth Gospel* (London: Mowbray, 1975).

Temple, W., *Readings in St. John's Gospel, 1st and 2nd Series* (London: MacMillan, 1955).

Tenney, M. C., "The Meaning of 'Witness' in John," *BSac* 132 (1975) 229-41.

Terry, B., "Baptized in One Spirit," *Restoration Quarterly* [Abilene, TX] 21 (1978) 193-200.

Terry, F., "Jesus and the Era of the Spirit," *HeyJ* 51 (1952-53) 10-15.

Thüsing, W., *Die Erhöhung und Verherrlichung Jesu im Johannesevangelium*, Neutestamentliche Abhandlungen xxi, 1-2 (Münster: Aschendorff, 1960).

Thyen, H., "Aus der Literatur zum Johannesevangelium," *TRu* 39 (1974-75) 1-69; 222-52; 289-330; 43 (1978) 328-59; 44 (1979) 97-134.

Töpel, L. J., "A Note on Methodology of Structural Analysis in John 2:23–3:21," *CBQ* 33 (1971) 211-20.

Torrey, C. C., "The Aramaic Origin of the Gospel of John," *HTR* 16 (1923) 305-34.

Tribble, H. W., "The Convicting Work of the Holy Spirit," *RevExp* 32 (1935) 269-80.

Trites, A. A., *The New Testament Concept of Witness* (Cambridge: University Press, 1977).

Turner, M. M. B., "The Concept of Receiving the Spirit in John's Gospel," *Vox Evangelica* 10 (1976) 24-42.

──────, "Luke and the Spirit. Studies in the Significance of Receiving the Spirit in Luke-Acts," unpub. diss., Cambridge University (England), 1980.

──────, "The Significance of Spirit Endowment for Paul," *Vox Evangelica* 9 (1975) 56-69.

Turner, N., *A Grammar of New Testament Greek: Style* (Edinburgh: T. & T. Clark, 1976) [vol. 4 of Moulton series].

──────, *A Grammar of New Testament Greek: Syntax* (Edinburgh: T. & T. Clark, 1963) [vol. 3 of Moulton series].

──────, *Grammatical Insights into the New Testament* (Edinburgh: T. & T. Clark, 1965).

Turner, W., "Believing and Everlasting Life; a Johannine Inquiry," *ExpTim* 64 (1952-53) 50-52.

Turrado, L., "El bautismo 'in Spiritu sancto et igni,'" *Estudios Eclesiasticos* [Madrid] 34 (1960) 807-17.

Ubbink, J. T., "καὶ ἔμεινεν ἐπ' αὐτόν (Ioh 1, 32)," *NThS* 5 (1922) 8-10.

Vanderlip, D. G., *Christianity According to John* (Philadelphia: Westminster, 1975).

──────, *John: the Gospel of Life* (Valley Forge, Pa: Judson, 1979).

Van Hartingsveld, L., *Die Eschatologie des Johannesevangeliums* (Assen: Van Gorcum, 1962).

Van Iersel, B. M. F., "Tradition und Redaktion in Joh 1:19-36," *NovT* 5 (1962) 245-67.

Van Unnik, W. C., "A Greek Characteristic of Prophecy in the Fourth Gospel," in *Text and Interpretation: Studies in the New Testament Presented to Matthew Black*, ed. E. Best and R. McL. Wilson (Cambridge: University Press, 1979) 211-29.

Vawter, B., "Ezekiel and John," *CBQ* 26 (1964) 450-58.

──────, "Johannine Theology," in *The Jerome Biblical Commentary*, ed. R. E. Brown, J. A. Fitzmyer, and R. E. Murphy, 2 vols. (London: Chapman, 1968) 2:828-39.

_____, "John's Doctrine of the Spirit: A Summary of His Eschatology," in *A Companion to John*, ed. M. J. Taylor (New York: Alba, 1977) 177-85.

_____, "Some Recent Developments in Johannine Theology," *BTB* 1 (1970) 30-58.

Vellanickal, M., "Blood and Water (John 19:34)," *Jeevadhara* [Kottayam, Kerala, India] 8 (1978) 218-30.

_____, "Christian: Born of the Spirit," *Biblebhashyam* 2 (1976) 153-74.

_____, *The Divine Sonship of Christians in the Johannine Writings* (Rome: Biblical Institute Press, 1977).

Vercruysse, D., "The Paraclete," *Clergy Monthly* 30 (1966) 137-44.

Violet, B., "Ein Versuch zu Joh 20:17," *ZNW* 24 (1925) 78-80.

Von Mirtow, P., "The Glory of Christ in the Fourth Gospel," *Theol* 49 (1946) 336-40; 359-65.

Walvoord, J. F., "The Holy Spirit in Relation to the Person and Work of Christ," *BSac* 98 (1941) 29-55.

Wead, D. W., "The Johannine Double Meaning," *RestQ* 2 (1970) 106-20.

_____, *The Literary Devices in John's Gospel* (Basel: F. Reinhardt Kommissionsverlag, 1970).

Weisengoff, J. P., "Light and Its Relation to Life in St. John," *CBQ* 8 (1946) 448-51.

Wellhausen, J., *Das Evangelium Johannes* (Berlin: Georg Reimer, 1908).

Wells, J., "The Two Paracletes and the Under-Paraclete," *ExpTim* 14 (1902-1903) 562-65.

Wengst, K., *Häresie und Orthodoxie im Spiegel des ersten Johannesbriefes* (Gütersloh: Mohn, 1976).

Wenham, D., "Spirit and Life: Some Reflections on Johannine Theology," *Themelios* 6 (1980) 4-8.

Wennemer, K., "Geist und Leben bei Johannes," *GeistLeb* 30 (1957) 185-98.

_____, "Theologie des 'Wortes' im Johannesevangelium," *Scholastik* 38 (1963) 1-17.

Wernberg-Møller, P., "A Reconsideration of the Two Spirits in the Rule of the Community," *RQ* 3 (1961) 413-41.

Westcott, B. F., *The Gospel According to John* (Cambridge, University Press, 1881; repr. Grand Rapids: Eerdmans, 1973).

White, R. E. O., *The Answer is the Spirit* (Edinburgh: St. Andrews Press, 1979).

Wikenhauser, A., *Das Evangelium nach Johannes*, Regensburger Neues Testament, 3rd ed. (Regensburg: Verlag Friedrich Pustet, 1961).

Wilckens, U., "Der eucharistische Abschnitt der johanneischen Rede vom Lebensbrot (Joh 6, 51c-58)," in *Neues Testament und Kirche. Für Rudolf Schnackenburg*, ed. J. Gnilka (Freiburg: Herder, 1974) 220-48.

Wiles, M. F., *The Spiritual Gospel. The interpretation of the Fourth Gospel in the Early Church* (Cambridge: University Press, 1960).

Wilkens, W., *Zeichen und Werke. Ein Beitrag zur Theologie des vierten Evangeliums in Erzählungs- und Redestoff* (Zürich: Zwingli Verlag, 1969).

Williams, F. E., "Fourth Gospel and Synoptic Tradition—Two Johannine Passages," *JBL* 86 (1967) 311-19.

253

Wilson, R. McL., "The Spirit in Gnostic Literature," in *Christ and Spirit in the New Testament: Studies in Honour of C. F. D. Moule,* ed. B. Lindars and S. Smalley (Cambridge: University Press, 1973) 345-55.

Windisch, H., "Jesus und der Geist nach synoptischer Überlieferung," in *Studies in Early Christianity,* ed. S. J. Case (New York: Century, 1928) 209-36.

————, *The Spirit-Paraclete in the Fourth Gospel,* tr. J. W. Cox (Philadelphia: Fortress, 1968).

Wink, W., *John the Baptist in the Gospel Tradition* (Cambridge: University Press, 1968).

Winstanley, E., *Spirit in the New Testament* (Cambridge: University Press, 1908).

Woll, D. B., "The Departure of 'the Way:' The First Farewell Discourse in the Gospel of John," *JBL* 99 (1980) 225-39.

Woodhouse, H. F., "The Paraclete as Interpreter," *BiTod* 18 (1968) 51-53.

————, "The Spirit Was Not Yet Given," *Theol* 67 (1965) 310-12.

Woods, M. W., "The Use of the Old Testament in the Fourth Gospel: The Hermeneutical Method Employed in the Semeia and Its Significance for Contemporary Biblical Interpretation," unpub. diss., Southwestern Baptist Seminary (USA), 1980.

Wotherspoon, A. W., "Concerning the Name Paraclete," *ExpTim* 34 (1922-23) 43-44.

————, "Note on St. John 16:10," *ExpTim* 33 (1921-22) 521-22.

Wurzinger, A., "Der Heilige Geist bei Johannes," *BLit* 36 (1962-63) 288-94.

Yates, J. E., *The Spirit and the Kingdom* (London: SPCK, 1963).

Young, F. W., "A Study of the Relation of Isaiah to the Fourth Gospel," *ZNW* 46 (1955) 215-33.

Zerwick, M., *Biblical Greek,* tr. J. Smith (Rome: Scripta Pontificii Instituti Biblici, 1963).

————, "Vom Wirken des Heiligen Geist in uns. Meditationsgedanken zu Jo 16, 5-15," *GeistLeb* 38 (1965) 224-30.

Zimmermann, H., "Struktur und Aussageabsicht der johanneischen Abschiedsreden (Jo 13–17)," *BibLeb* 8 (1967) 279-90.

INDEX OF AUTHORS

Abbott, E. A.   7, 52, 54, 57, 88, 89, 167
Achtemeier, P. J.   66
Allen, E. L.   70
Allen, W. C.   89
Alonso, V. E.   144
Anderson, B. W.   16
Appold, M. L.   75, 79
Aune, D. E.   144

Bailey, J. A.   118, 123, 130, 134
Balague, M.   88
Baltensweiler, H.   66
Bammel, E.   208
Barbour, R. S.   4
Barrett, C. K.   4, 9, 15, 23, 28, 29, **32–35**, 39, 41, 42, 51, 52, 54, 55, 56, 59, 62, 64, 65, 66, 67, 68, 69, 72, 81, 82, 83, 85, 87, 88, 90, 94, 106, 108, 114, 115, 116, 119, 123, 124, 125, 133, 134, 135, 138, 140, 142, 143, 151, 156, 157, 162, 164, 165, 167, 168, 169, 171, 178, 179, 180, 181, 184, 185, 186, 188, 190, 191, 192, 193, 194, 199, 200, 202, 206, 208, 209, 210, 213, 215
Barth, G.   51
Barth, K.   166, 167, 168, 171
Bauckham, R. J.   34, 143
Bauer, W.   6, 8, 10, 30, 82, 125, 138, 193, 209
Bauernfeind, O.   55
Beare, F.   120
Beasley-Murray, G. R.   33, 56, 114, 153, 157, 159, 162, 165, 169, 170
Becker, H.   12

Becker, J.   5, 25, 78, 206
Behm, J.   6, 7, 8, 10, 11, 14, 15, 16, 88, 91, 189
Benoit, P.   125, 136
Benjamin, H. S.   42
Bernard, J. H.   9, 58, 59, 75, 82, 83, 85, 88, 98, 134, 142, 152, 157, 160, 161, 164, 179, 181, 182, 185, 189, 193, 199, 201, 202, 207, 214, 215
Berrouard, M. F.   204, 208, 209
Bertram, G.   132
Betz, O.   5, 6, 7, 12, 14, 15, 16, **17–20**, 21, 24, 25, 30, 33, 37, 43, 52, 120, 121, 125, 142, 205, 215
Billerbeck, P.   97
Billings, J. S.   124
Black, M.   56, 81, 82, 83, 89, 103
Blank, J.   20, 115, 194, 209
Blenkinsopp, J.   89
Bligh, J.   193, 196, 197
Böcher, O.   162
Boice, J. M.   140, 141, 199, 205
Boismard, M.-E.   44, 59, 89, 90, 91, 94, 114, 144, 163, 182
Borgen, P.   105, 178, 181, 182, 183, 184, 185, 200, 201, 205
Boring, M. E.   4, **38–40**, 215, **217–18**, 220
Bornkamm, G.   3, 6, 11, 20, **23–25**, 26, 30, 33, 51, 140, 154, 183, 184, 185, 186, 220
Bouman, H. J. A.   52
Bousset, W.   10, 59, 85

Bowen, W. E.   216
Bowman, J.   99, 195
Braun, F. M.   59, 89, 95, 124, 134, 160, 167
Breck, R. E.   17, 194
Brooke, A. E.   172
Brooks, O. S.   182
Brown, B. S.   9
Brown, R. E.   4, 5, 6, 7, 8, 10, 12, 14, 17, 19, 20, 22, 23, 29, **30–35**, 40, 43, 44, 52, 53, 54, 58, 59, 61, 75, 78, 79, 81, 82, 83, 86, 89, 90, 94, 95, 105, 111, 112, 115, 119, 120, 123, 124, 125, 126, 132, 135, 136, 137, 138, 139, 140, 142, 144, 152, 153, 155, 159, 163, 164, 165, 167, 168, 169, 170, 171, 172, 173, 178, 179, 180, 181, 182, 183, 184, 185, 188, 189, 190, 191, 192, 193, 194, 195, 196, 197, 199, 202, 203, 204, **205–208,** 209, 210, 211, 214, 215, 217, 218, 220
Bruce, F. F.   36, 130, 176, 196
Büchsel, F.   97, 134, 167, 171, 174, 176, 209, 218
Bullinger, E. M.   89
Bultmann, R.   5, 6, 8, **10–12**, 24, 30, 33, 36, 43, 53, 59, 70, 78, 79, 82, 83, 84, 86, 88, 89, 90, 94, 96, 98, 101,'103, 105, 107, 114, 115, 116, 118, 125, 126, 132, 134, 137, 140, 142, 143, 144, 146, 152, **154–55,** 157, 159, 160, 167, 169, 173, 175, 178, 179, 180, 182, 183, 184, 185, 186, 187, 189, 192, 193, 194, 199, 200, 208, 209, 213, 215, 218, 219
Burkitt, F. C.   59
Burney, C. F.   61, 86, 88, 89, 91, 112, 144
Burton, E.   174

Cadman, W. H.   88, 113
Caird, G. B.   4, 22, 70
Carpenter, J. E.   176
Carson, D. A.   117, 118, 123, **208–10,** 215
Cassian, A.   124
Charles, R. H.   56, 102, 177
Charlesworth, J. H.   17, 58
Chavasse, C.   70
Chevallier, M.-A.   57
Collins, J. J.   89
Colpe, C.   64, 86
Colwell, E. C.   59, 80, 87
Congar, Y. M. J.   5
Conzelmann, H.   179, 219, 220
Corell, A.   60, 61, 79, 94, 105, 114, 123, 152, 154, 167, 178, 185, 189
Cortez, J. B.   88, **89–90**
Craig, C. T.   151, 181
Cross, F. M.   20
Cullmann, O.   23, 29, 37, 44, 51, 59, 61, 67, 68, 69, 70, 83, 91, 94, 96, 99, 105, 107, 108, 116, 150, 151, **152–54,** 155, 165, 167, 168, 169, 178, 182, 187, 189, 190, 196, 212, 214, 217
Culpepper, A.   44, 151, 172, 173, 211, 218, 220

Dahl, N. A.   191, 205, 211, 212
Dahms, J. V.   137
Danby, H.   92
D'Angelo, M. R.   70
Daniélou, J.   19
Davey, J. E.   9, 73, 78, 83, 100, 200, 201
Davies, J. G.   8, **28**
deJonge, M.   32, 56, 107, 110, 167, 169
Dekker, C.   183
Delafossa, H.   5
Delitzsch, F.   7
Delling, G.   118, 126
DePinto, B.   29
Derrett, J. D. M.   200, 201
Dibelius, M.   66
Dion, H.-M.   17
Dobbin, E. J.   142
Dodd, C. H.   10, 12, 13, 31, 35, 43, 52, 59, 68, 82, 83, 85, 86, 89, 90, 100, 105, 106, 107, 108, 109, 113, 115, 119, 122, 123, 125, 134, 138, 143, 144, 147, 151, 159, 161, 162, 163, 164, 166, 167, 171, 176, 179, 180, 182, 184, 185, 186, 188, 189, 193, 194, 199, 200, 201, 205, 206, 215, 220
Drower, E. S.   12
Dunn, J. D. G.   28, 34, 39, 49, 50, 55, 63, 64, 66, 68, 83, 85, 89, 90, 96, 97, 105, 106, 112, 118, 121, 122, 123, 124, 125, 126, 131, 132, 150, 156, 157, **159–60,** 163, 166, 167, 169, 170, 175, 176, 178, 179, 180, **183–84,** 185, 186, 190, 219, 220

Edwards, A. D.   146
Ellis, E. E.   51
Enslin, M. S.   174
Ernst, J.   7

Fenton, J. C.   182
Ferraro, G.   42
Feuillet, A.   57
Filson, F.   125, 172
Fiorenza, E. S.   146
Fitzer, G.   85
Fitzmyer, J. A.   60, 111
Floor, L.   80, 119
Foerster, W.   74
Ford, J. M.   94, 95, 135, 176
Forestell, J. T.   9
Fortna, R.   53, 78
Fowler, R.   161
France, R. T.   63
Freed, E. D.   23, 88, 90, **193–95**
Friedrich, G.   68, 69, 70, 108, 127
Fritsch, I.   86

Fuller, R. H. 58, 63, 66, 68, 69, 75, 111, 124

Galot, J. 112
Gärtner, B. 184
Gerhardsson, B. 211
Giblet, J. 204
Gilmour, S. M. 131
Ginzberg, L. 94
Glasson, T. F. 92, 93, 94, 107, 108, 109
Glasswell, M. E. 66, 75
Goguel, M. 42, 53
Goppelt, L. 102, 126, 162
Gourbillon, J. G. 82
Grayston, K. 208
Green, M. 157, 173
Greeven, H. 53, 57
Grelot, P. 92
Grill, J. 10
Grundmann, W. 61, 65, 66, 75, 85, 124, 173, 175, 219
Guilding, A. 89, 92, 178, 184, 185
Gundry, R. 59, 145
Guthrie, D. 117

Haenchen, E. 10, 79, 200
Hahn, F. 25, 68, 107, 111, 194
Hamerton-Kelly, R. G. 64
Hammer, P. L. 165
Hanson, J. S. 67
Hanson, R. P. C. 130
Harnack, A. 59, 191
Harris, J. R. 29, 89, 91
Harvey, A. E. 16, 31, 37, 108, 141, 201, 202, 204, 205, 208, 209
Hatch, W. H. P. 208
Hauck, F. 54, 55, 214
Haufe, G. 9
Heise, J. 54
Held, H. J. 51
Hendriksen, W. 117
Hengel, M. 211
Hennecke, E. 50, 58
Higgins, A. J. B. 170, 182, 185, 187, 188, 190
Hill, D. 53, 68, 69, 83, 108, 125, 146, 215, 217, 218
Hindley, J. C. 205
Hodges, Z. C. 88, 89, 161
Holwerda, D. E. 14, 16, 36, 119, 133, 138, 208
Hooke, S. H. 91, 124
Hooker, M. D. 59
Horsley, R. A. 67
Hort, F. J. A. 142
Hoskyns, E. C. 9, 83, 86, 88, 89, 94, 95, 118, 120, 122, 126, 134, 135, 138, 139, 152, 153, 159, 160, 166, 167, 180, 182, 193, 202, 210, 216

Houlden, J. L. 172, 175, 220
Howard, W. F. 42, 83, 114, 115, 152, 157, 162, 170, 171, 181, 182, 200
Howton, D. J. 59, 60
Hull, J. H. E. 62, 199
Hull, J. M. 65, 66
Humphries, A. L. 145
Hunt, W. B. 34
Hunter, A. M. 82, 83, 125, 126, 167
Hutton, W. R. 34, 112, 140, 143

Isaacs, M. E. **29**, 62, 71, 100, 125, 130

Jeremias, J. 25, 39, 53, 58, 59, 60, 61, 63, 64, 66, 67, 69, 70, 86, 89, 92, 108, 131, 151, 181, 183
Johansson, N. **14–16**, 30
Johnston, G. **4–6**, 14, 15, 17, 18, 20, **21–23**, 30, 35, 38, 41, 42, 52, 55, 57, 82, 83, 160, 171, 184, 185, 190, 191, 192, 197, 204, 208, 218
Joüon, P. 215

Kaplan, C. 162
Karotemprel, S. 135
Käsemann, E. 40, 44, 72, 95, 116, 123, 144, 220
Kealy, S. P. 125
Keck, L. E. 57, 58
Kilpatrick, G. D. 13, 89
Kittel, G. 81, 112
Klos, H. 151, 152, 154, 156, 158, 169, 184, 187
Knox, W. L. 103, 151, 187
Köster, H. 154, 155
Kothgasser, A. M. 37, 41, 140, 203, 213, 214, 217
Kragerud, A. 38, 211
Kremer, J. 4, 7, **31–32**, 205, 215, 216
Kretschmar, G. 133
Kuhl, J. 200
Kuhn, K. H. 89
Kümmel, W. G. 33, 60, 71, 115, 155, 171, 176, 218
Kysar, R. 24, 34, 36, 114, 115, 143, 151, 152, 155, 160, 178, 200

Ladd, G. E. 75, 115, 117, 157, 177, 187
Ladd, J. G. M. 153, 163
Lagrange, M.-J. 59, 82, 83
Lake, K. 160
Lampe, G. W. H. 51, 57, 58, 64, 66, 72, 73, 85, 147, 175
la Potterie, I. de 4, 7, 14, 30, **37–38**, 41, 59, 67, 103, 104, 134, 159, 160, 166, 208, 209
Leaney, A. R. C. 17, 20, 21, 28, 121, 125
Lee, E. K. 35, 103, 109, 132, 137, 139, 151, 157, 164, 166, 169, 187

Lemonnyer, A. 9
Léon-Dufour, X. 5, 89
Lightfoot, R. H. 59, 82, 83, 88, 115, 125, 134, 152, 157, 178, 186, 190, 193, 200
Liefeld, W. 70
Lindars, B. 4, 59, 74, 78, 83, 85, 88, 95, 105, 120, 126, 135, 138, 152, 155, 159, 160, 161, 163, 164, 165, 167, 170, 179, 180, 181, 186, 187, 190, 191, 192, 199, 202, 208, 209, 215
Lofthouse, W. F. 61
Lohse, E. 75, 153, 154, 155, 160, 183
Loisy, A. 59, 89, 134, 193, 209
Longenecker, R. 69, 107
Luther, M. 8
Lutkemeyer, L. J. 208

McCool, F. J. 98, **103–104**
MacDonald, A. J. 23, 69, 98, 99
MacGregor, G. H. C. 98, 105, 115, 124, 156, 157, 164, 165, 170, 178, 179, 180, 182, 186, 187, 188, 189, 190
McHugh, J. 179
McKelvey, R. J. 86, 89, 90, 93, 95, 196
McNamara, M. 145
McNaugher, J. 204
McPolin, J. 51, 171, 194, 199
MacRae, G. W. 92
Malatesta, E. 4, 54, 151, **172–73,** 174, 190
Mann, C. S. 117, 125
Manson, T. W. 59, 64, 69, 70, 112, 157
Mansure, A. L. 33
Marsh, J. 83, 120, 123, 124, 163, 189, 190, 193, 215
Marshall, I. H. 4, 51, 59, 61, 63, 95, 127, 130, 133, 136, 171, 174, 176, 177, 181, 218, 219
Martin, J. P. 34
Martyn, J. L. 35, 44, 108, 140, 146, 153, 196, 204
Mary, S. 172
Mastin, B. A. 178, 190, 199, 202, 208
Mattijs, F. D. 88
Mealand, D. L. 132, 143
Meeks, W. A. 4, 99, 107, 108, 109, 110, 195
Menard, J. E. 88
Mendner, S. 159
Menoud, P.-H. 120, 136
Metzger, B. M. 127, 185, 215
Meyer, P. W. 36
Meyer, R. 67
Michaelis, W. 6, 12, 86, 87, 88, 152, 153
Michaels, J. R. 217
Michel, O. 61, 213
Miguens, M. 94, 111
Miranda, P. 200
Moffat, J. 124

Mollat, D. 89
Morgan-White, J. E. 138
Morris, L. 7, 17, 29, 59, 82, 83, 85, 88, 92, 120, 123, 124, 139, 142, 157, 161, 178, 181
Moule, C. F. D. 64, 100, 115, 124, 156, 178
Moulton, J. H. 56, 88, 174
Mounce, R. 176
Mounce, W. 167
Mowinckel, S. 6, 10, **13–15,** 30
Müller, D. 120
Müller, T. 33
Müller, U. B. 4, 6, 14, 17, 20, 22, 24, **25–28,** 30, 206, 211, 217
Mussner, F. 6, 9, 38, 170, 191, 212, 214, 216, 217

Nauck, W. 96, 175
Nestle, E. 59, 88
Newbigin, L. 204
Nicol, W. 78, 79, 108
Niewalda, P. 152, 153, 165, 189
Nossol, A. 139
Nötscher, F. 29

Odeberg, H. 86, 88, 102, 103, 104, 105, **161,** 180, 182, 187, 192
Oepke, A. 61, 68, 162
Olsson, B. 37, 97, 103, 191
Oulton, E. J. 183

Painter, J. 89, 116, 117, 140, 172, 197, 212
Pancaro, S. 141
Pannenberg, W. 112
Parker, P. 130, 196
Parratt, J. K. 166
Pascher, J. 43, 185, 186, 187
Pecorara, G. 54
Percy, E. 200
Pesch, R. 86
Peterson, E. 11
Piper, O. A. 111
Plummer, A. 127
Popkes, W. 134
Porsch, F. **3–5,** 6, 7, 14, 20, 24, 25, 31, 32, 33, **37–38,** 41, **43–44,** 59, 83, 84, 89, 95, 97, 103, 118, **122–23,** 124, 125, 131, 133, 134, 135, 140, 158, 159, 160, 165, 166, 167, 168, 191, 192, 193, 194, 195, 197, 203, 205, 208, 212, 213, 214
Preiss, T. 37, 200, 205
Purvis, J. D. 195

Quispel, G. 19, 20, 86

Ramsay, W. M. 176
Ramsey, A. M. 125, 136

Rawlinson, A. E. J. — 191
Reese, J. M. — 190
Reim, G. — 28, 55, 59
Relton, F. — 215
Rengstorf, K. H. — 67, 78, 79, 80, 88, 120, 200, 202
Ricca, P. — 115
Richardson, A. — 9, **28,** 53, 57, 60, 65, 67, 69, 75, 85, 117
Richter, G. — 94, 105, 106, 135, 183, 184
Rieger, J. — 138
Riesenfeld, H. — 29, 63, 68
Rist, M. — 177
Robertson, A. T. — 83
Robinson, D. W. B. — 154
Robinson, H. W. — 16
Robinson, J. A. T. — 35, 95, 115, 163, 171, 217
Robinson, W. C. — 111
Rodd, C. S. — 64
Rowley, H. H. — 25
Ruckstuhl, E. — 78, 105, 183
Ruland, V. — 153, 182
Russell, E. A. — 126, 135

Sabourin, L. — 5
Satake, A. — 146
Sanders, J. N. — 125, 178, 190, 199, 202, 208
Sandvik, B. — 189
Sasse, H. — 38, 142, 211
Sava, A.F. — 94
Schlatter, A. — 88
Schlier, H. — 35, 36, 37, 38, 125, 137
Schlosser, J. — 5
Schmid, J. — 112
Schmithals, W. — 32
Schnackenburg, R. — 5, 7, 10, 11, 17, 20, 23, 24, 27, **40,** 44, 52, 54, 59, 60, 79, 80, 81, 82, 83, 85, 86, 87, 88, 92, 95, 96, 100, 101, 102, 105, 106, 114, 116, 119, 122, 126, 134, 152, 154, 159, 161, 162, 163, 164, 167, 169, 171, 172, 173, 174, 175, 180, 182, 183, 184, 186, 192, 193, 194, 195, 197, 200, 209, 210, 215, 217, 220
Schnider, F. — 68, 69, 70, 107, 108
Schniewind, J. — 127, 215
Scholte, F. E. — 125
Schrenk, G. — 60
Schubert, K. — 17
Schulz, S. — 24, 200
Schulze-Kadelbach, G. — 125
Schürmann, H. — 63, 105, 155, 185
Schwarz, E. — 78
Schweitzer, A. — 42, 169, 178
Schweizer, E. — 38, 39, 42, 43, 53, 54, 60, 61, 62, 65, 71, 72, 78, 88, 133, 140, 147, 154, 155, 158, 168, 171, 176, 177, 181, 192, 193, 194, 200
Scobie, C. H. H. — 196

Scott, E. F. — 3, 13, 33, 35, 42, 124, 137, 143, 146, 147
Scott, M. V. — 114, 147
Seesemann, H. — 62
Shafaat, A. — 21
Shedd, R. — 168
Sidebottom, E. M. — 29, 59, 60, 113, 185
Simpson, I. G. — 3, 33
Sjöberg, E. — 52, 56, 67
Smail, T. A. — 135
Smalley, S. — 4, 10, 34, 60, 72, 86, 153, 158, 165, 172
Smith, D. M. — 217, 218
Sowers, S. G. — 116
Spiro, A. — 196
Spitta, F. — 59, 142
Spriggs, D. G. — 161
Stanley, D. M. — 89, 189
Stanton, A. H. — 208
Starcky, J. — 60
Stauffer, E. — 56, 79, 114, 115, 125, 188
Stevens, G. B. — 35
Stockton, E. D. — 9, 98
Strachan, R. H. — 31, 83, 124, 161, 178, 185
Strack, H. L. — 97
Strathmann, H. — 205, 209
Swete, H. B. — 119, 126, 180

Tarelli, C. C. — 166
Tasker, R. V. G. — 59, 82, 83, 133, 165, 167, 210
Taylor, V. — 68
Teeple, H. M. — 17, 78, 107
Temple, S. — 119
Tenney, M. C. — 205
Thüsing, W. — 43, 83, 89, 115, 122
Thyen, H. — 119, 125, 151
Töpel, L. J. — 159
Torrance, T. F. — 136, 188, 189
Trites, A. A. — 37, 141, 199, 203, 204, 205, 206, 209, 210, 212
Turner, C. H. — 88
Turner, M. M. B. — 51, 88, **120–22,** 123, 126
Turner, N. — 50, 89

VanHartingsveld, L. — 114, 115
Van Unnik, W. C. — 103
Vawter, B. — **28–29,** 75, 123, 152
Vellanickal, M. — 89, 95, 158, 159, 160, 166, 167, 168, 174
Von Campenhausen, H. — 111
Von Dobschutz, E. — 131
Von Rad, G. — 81
Vos, G. — 177

Walvoord, J. F. — 75
Wead, D. W. — 167
Weiss, K. — 172

Wellhausen, J.   5, 78
Wendt, H. H.   160
Wengst, K.   172
Westcott, B. F.   59, 88, 118, 120, 121, 126, 142, 164, 193, 209
Wilkens, W.   78, 79
Wilpert, J.   189
Wilson, W. G.   171
Windisch, H.   5, 9, 10, 71, 83, 86, 112, 119, 142, 145, 213, 215, 219
Wink, W.   24

Wolff, H. W.   91
Woll, D. B.   144, 145
Wurzinger, A.   55, 98, 100

Yates, J. E.   37, 115
Young, F. W.   28

Zahn, T.   59, 83, 88, 98, 117, 167, 193
Zerwick, M.   89, 208
Zugibe, F. T.   94

INDEX OF SCRIPTURE

A. THE OLD TESTAMENT

Genesis
1–3	122
1:2	162
2:7	118, 122, 125, 130
7:22	130
8:8–9	57
9:4	182
18:23–33	13
28:12	86
29:2–3	92
35:9	93

Exodus
8:19	64
11:2	93
12:22	135
12:46	135
13:21	92
16:4	184
16:28–36	93
19:10	97
19:19	52
29:7	175
32:11–14	13
33:12–17	14
33:13	138
47:1–2	92

Leviticus
17:10	182
17:12	182
17:14	182

Numbers
9:12	135
11:17	26
11:25	26
11:26–29	55
14:13–19	14
16:15–16	14
17:1–2	57
20:8–9	91
20:11	94
27:18	26
35:25	176

Deuteronomy
5:5	109
8:3	105
8:11–12	93
9:1ff.	93
10:4	109
13:2–6	108
18:5	23, 70
18:15	23, 90
18:16	90
18:18	23, 71, 108, 109
18:18–23	108
34:9	23, 26

Joshua
5:13–14	16

Judges
14:6	97

14:19	97
15:14	97

1 Samuel
7:8–9	14
9:16	175
10:10	97
16:13	175

2 Samuel
22:16	130

1 Kings
8:1ff.	92
18:16	175
19:11	130
19:15–16	175
22:19	16

2 Kings
2:9–15	23

Nehemiah
9:12–15	93
9:20	91, 105

Job
1:1ff.	16
4:21	117, 125
16:19–22	15
16:32	7

Job (cont'd)					
33:21–28	15	6:1ff.	16	11:13	29
37:10	130	9:5–6	21	12:6–7	29
		11:1ff.	62	13:13	130
Psalms		11:1	57	21:11–12	29
1:3	97	11:2	55, 56, 58	21:31	117, 125
2:1ff.	59–60, 62	12:3	92	21:36	117
2:7	59, 61	14:24	55	22:20	125
9:7	55	26:10	194	22:30	117
22:16	135	32:1–2	90	36:1ff.	163
25:5	215	32:15	97, 162	36:25ff.	90, 97, 162
30:5	134	35:5–7	90	37:1–2	64
34:20	135	40:1	28	37:8–10	130
36:9–10	90	40:8	55	37:9	117, 125
40:8	103	41:18	90	39:17	182
46:5–6	90	42:1ff.	59–60, 61, 62	47:1–12	90, 91, 92, 135, 162
51:7	162	42:1	55, 59		
69:9	212	42:1–4	56	47:9	162
69:22	135	43:19–20	91		
77:20	215	43:19–21	90	**Daniel**	
78:15–30	91	43:20	93	2:4, 7, 9	14
78:20	94	44:3	91, 93, 162	6:26	55
78:24	184	44:10	180	10:1ff.	16
78:72	215	48:12	93	10:13	14
82:1ff.	16	48:16	55	12:1	16
92:12–13	97	48:21	91		
101:12	55	49:10	90	**Joel**	
105:32–45	91	51:12	28	2:28	51
105:39–41	93	53:7	61	2:28–29	32, 162
113–118	92	53:12	134	3:1	97
118:26	212	54:13	105, 180	3:18	90, 92
143:10	215	55:1	102		
		55:11	137	**Amos**	
Proverbs		58:11	90	7:2, 5–6	14
1:20	103	61:1	55, 63, 175	8:11–13	105, 180
1:28–29	103	66:1ff.	196		
5:15–16	90	66:10–19	28	**Micah**	
8:2–3	103	66:22	55	3:8	15
9:3	103				
9:5	105, 180	**Jeremiah**		**Nahum**	
13:14	102	2:13	90, 93, 98, 162	2:1	125
16:22	102	14:7–9	14	2:2	117
18:4	90, 102	14:19–22	14		
20:5	102	17:13	90, 98, 162	**Zephaniah**	
24:12	130	18:20–23	14	3:1	57
24:28	15	33:8	162		
		46:10	182	**Zechariah**	
Ecclesiastes		46:16	57	3:1–10	14
5:1	145			9:9	212
		Ezekiel		12:10	97
Isaiah		4:4–8	29	13:1	90, 92, 162
4:4	162	8:1–2	64	13:1–10	14
		9:8	24	14:8	91, 92, 93, 162

B. THE NEW TESTAMENT

Matthew		3:14	50	4:17	23
1:20	111	3:16	51, 53, 57, 86	5:3–4	63–64
2:11	80	3:17	53	5:4	28
3:2	23	4:3	63	5:17	69
3:13	50, 52	4:12	23	5:26	134

Matthew (cont'd)

8:11	64
8:31	74
10:7	64
10:14	206
10:17	31
10:17–25	205
10:18	206
10:19–20	29
10:20	8, 31, 204, 206
10:22	31
10:23	31, 34
10:32	14
10:40	69, 200
11:2–6	63–67
11:3	108
11:5–6	63
11:9	67
11:11–12	64
11:20–21	66
11:25–26	70
11:27	70
12:28	64
12:31–32	64
12:38–39	78
12:41	68
13:11	64
13:31	64
13:33	64
13:53–58	63
15:24	69
15:36	179
16:1–4	67–68
18:1–4	161
18:18	119, 120
18:25–26	134
19:24	64
21:11	69
24:3	78
24:9	31
24:10	31
24:19	31
24:24	78
24:30	78
24:38	183
24:42	43
25:31–32	115
26:26	179
26:29	189
26:37	179
26:64	87
27:40	60
27:50	134
27:66	84
28:16	120
28:16–20	136
28:19	199
28:20	118

Mark

1:1	89
1:4–8	51
1:8	51
1:9–11	51
1:10	53, 57
1:11	59, 111
1:12–13	51
1:22	63
1:24	63
1:27	63
1:40–45	66
2:8	68
2:17	69
3:10	66
3:14–15	63
3:22–23	64
3:23–24	74
3:28–29	64
4:11	70
5:30	66
6:1–6	63
6:4	68, 107
6:5	78
6:7	63
6:14	69
6:15	68
6:41	178
8:6	178, 179
8:28	68
8:31	132
9:7	70
9:14–15	63
9:31	132
9:37	69, 200
10:1–12	69
10:13–36	161
10:30	115
10:33–34	132
10:45	69
11:2	68
11:27–33	63, 69
11:32	67
13:11	29, 31, 206
13:13	31
13:26	87, 115, 188, 144
13:30	34
14:22	179
14:23	179
14:25	189
14:27–28	68
14:65	68
15:37	117
15:39	117
16:8	74
16:14	120
16:16	199
16:17–18	64
16:19	127

Luke

1:17	65
1:32	113
1:35	65, 111, 113
1:41,44	52
1:68	69
2:23	89
2:25	28
3:12	53
3:16	130
3:21	87
3:21–22	87
3:22	59
4:1	62
4:14	62, 65
4:17–21	28
4:18ff.	63, 85, 175
4:20	134
6:19	66
6:20	63
6:35	115
7:16	68, 69
7:18–23	63
7:26	67
7:30	163
7:39	68
7:42	134
9:8	68
9:19	68
9:31	70
9:35	60
9:42	134
9:48	200
10:16	200
10:18	18
10:22	70
11:2	51
11:13	51
11:20	64
12:8, 14	59, 134
12:10	64
12:11–12	29
12:12	211
12:39	218
12:59	134
13:33	68
19:44	69
21:12	31, 206
21:14–15	29
21:16	31
22:18	189
22:19	178
22:21–38	116
22:37	134
22:39	116
22:53	73
23:8	78
23:35	60
23:46	134
24:1ff.	121, 122
24:13–35	148
24:13–43	212
24:19	63, 80
24:30	151

Luke (cont'd)
24:33 — 120
24:36 — 118, 131
24:36–43 — 151
24:38 — 131
24:39 — 118
24:41 — 118, 131
24:44–45 — 37
24:45–46 — 28
24:46–49 — 118, 127
24:47 — 131, 199
24:48–49 — 199
24:49 — 65, 118, 131
24:51 — 127, 148

John
1:1 — 112, 113, 202
1:1–3 — 173
1:3 — 125
1:4 — 172
1:5 — 73
1:6 — 75
1:7–8 — 140
1:10 — 172
1:10–11 — 198
1:11 — 141
1:12 — 61, 88, 115
1:12–13 — 170
1:13 — 112, 161
1:14 — 58, 61, 80, 101, 106, 112, 113, 115, 185, 191
1:14, 18 — 52
1:16 — 191
1:17 — 103, 108, 109, 166
1:18 — 88, 109, 113
1:19–20 — 141
1:21 — 108
1:25 — 108
1:26 — 98, 160
1:29 — 61, 96, 152, 196
1:29–32 — 170
1:29–34 — 43, **50–62,** 61
1:31 — 160
1:32 — 40, 52, 53, 59, 155
1:32–33 — 56–57, 73, 84, 85, 87, 101
1:33 — 40, 42, 52, 53, 54–55, 57, 88, 96, 98, 99, 115, 126, 132, 142, 148, 160, 200, 204
1:34 — 52, 59, 60
1:35–42 — 164
1:35–51 — 73
1:36 — 61
1:37 — 165
1:39 — 54
1:41 — 60
1:42 — 108
1:45 — 109
1:45–46 — 86

1:45–48 — 108
1:49 — 87
1:50 — 86
1:51 — **86–87,** 196
2:1 — 197
2:1–2 — 93
2:4 — 132, 191
2:6 — 75, 163, 164
2:7 — 160, 173
2:9 — 160
2:11 — 75, 78, 80
2:13–22 — 196
2:17 — 38, 39, 212
2:18 — 78
2:18–19 — 93
2:21 — 153
2:22 — 25, 27, 34, 37, 212
2:23–35 — 79
3:1ff. — 28, **158–78**
3:1–12 — 170
3:1–15 — 121, 171
3:1–21 — 82
3:2 — 79
3:3 — 158, **167–68,** 170
3:3–4 — 197
3:4 — 187
3:5 — 40, 42, 83, 84, 86, 97, 112, 151, 154, 155, 156, 157, 158, 159, **160–63,** 165, 170, 177
3:5–8 — 150
3:6 — 42, 106, 158, 185
3:6–8 — **168–69**
3:8 — 42, 130, 158
3:10 — 169
3:11 — 25, 27
3:11–12 — 191
3:12 — 83, 102, 158, 169, 170
3:12–21 — 101
3:13 — 102, 132, 158
3:13–14 — 133, 186
3:14 — 108, 132, 153, 158, 169
3:15 — 169, 170, 171, 177
3:16 — 96, 141, 169, 170, 192
3:16–21 — 81
3:17 — 33, 98, 107, 200
3:18 — 120, 158, 169, 170, 195
3:18–19 — 115, 141
3:19 — 192
3:19–20 — 18
3:20 — 209
3:21 — 194, 195
3:22 — 115, 141, 161, 165, 170, 171
3:22–30 — 83, 83, **163–64**

3:23 — 160
3:24 — 42, 161
3:25 — 163, 164
3:25–26 — 24
3:26 — 88, 155, 164
3:27 — 164
3:31 — 60, 83, 168
3:31–32 — 84
3:31–36 — 81, 82, 101, 168
3:32 — 88, 169
3:33 — 83, 84, 85
3:34 — 5, 42, 43, 55, 73, **81–84,** 97, 98, 99, 101, 106, 107, 108, 132, 168, 175, 200, 201, 204
3:35 — 80, 83, 84
3:36 — 54, 158, 169, 170
4:1 — 24, 42, 115, 164
4:1–2 — 155, 171
4:1–3 — **164–65**
4:1–30 — 152
4:2 — 42, 161
4:3 — 42
4:6 — 42
4:7 — 164, 176
4:7–8 — 97, 103
4:7–15 — **96–99,** 135
4:9 — 97
4:10 — 88, 90, 97, 103, 164
4:10–14 — 150
4:11 — 187
4:13 — 42
4:13–15 — 135
4:14 — 88, 90, 91, 97, 103, 104, 107, 180
4:15 — 97, 187
4:16–17 — 97
4:19 — 97, 99, 107, 108
4:20–24 — **190–97**
4:21 — 192
4:22 — 191
4:23 — 42, 98, 115, 151, 166, 191, 192
4:23–24 — 97, 193
4:24 — 42, **192–95**
4:25 — 23, 98, 99, 109, 141, 215
4:26 — 99
4:29 — 103
4:32 — 38, 39
4:34 — 80, 107, 108, 134, 200
4:38 — 202
4:39 — 97
4:40 — 54, 97
4:41–42 — 97
4:42 — 99
4:44 — 39, 97, 99, 107

John (cont'd)

4:46–47	75	6:31	89	7:16	107, 108, 200, 201
4:48	78, 79	6:32	93, 108	7:16–18	213
4:50	75	6:33	158	7:17	141, 203
4:52	191	6:35	88, 89, 90, 91, 107,	7:18	107, 108, 200
4:54	78		135, 158	7:19	103, 108
5:1–19	152	6:35–50	106, **179–81**	7:20	39, 74
5:6	42	6:36	107	7:21	80
5:7	160	6:37	83	7:22	108
5:8	42	6:38	107, 112, 200	7:23	108
5:11	88	6:38–39	108	7:24	89
5:14	75	6:39	107, 200	7:28	38, 107, 200
5:15	215	6:39–40	115, 144	7:29	107, 200
5:16–18	201	6:40	107, 158	7:30	132, 191
5:17	78, 80, 81, 140	6:41	184	7:31	79
5:18	112	6:44	88, 107, 115, 144,	7:33	103, 107, 200
5:19	213		200	7:37	38, **88–93**, 92,
5:19–20	78, 140	6:45	88, 166, 180		93, 97, 118, 135, 165, 169,
5:19–25	146	6:46	60		176, 197
5:20	80	6:47	107, 158	7:37–38	90, 94, 95, 96,
5:22	27	6:50	184		103
5:23	107, 108, 200, 201	6:51	97, 155, 158	7:37–39	**88–93**, 91,
5:24	106, 107, 108, 115,	6:51–58	**105–106,**		135
	166, 200		154, 157, **181–85**, 188,	7:38	88, 92, 93, 97, 103
5:25	115, 191, 192		190	7:39	40, 42, 45, 50, 80,
5:26–30	146	6:53	166, 197		82, 90, **95**, 96, 97, 100,
5:27	78	6:53–54	158		117, 119, 121, 125, 126,
5:28	192	6:54	115, 144, 183		132, 133, 137, 142, 153,
5:28–29	115, 144	6:56	54, 172		171, 185, 212
5:30	27, 107, 108, 200	6:56–58	183	7:40	91, 93, 97, 108
5:31	141	6:57	33, 107, 199, 200	7:42	176
5:33–34	24	6:58–59	97	7:47	39
5:36	80, 98, 107, 200	6:60–63	**185–89**	7:49	103
5:37	107, 200	6:60–65	104	7:51	109
5:38	54, 98, 104, 107,	6:61	155	7:52	107
	172, 200	6:61–65	43	8:5	108
5:39	109	6:62	106, 158	8:6	83
5:39–47	109	6:62–63	133	8:8	83
5:40	88	6:63	5, 25, 42, 43, 79,	8:12	73, 93, 97, 192
5:43	33, 107, 141		83, 84, 85, 97, **104–107,**	8:13	141
5:45	108		121, 150, 151, 156, 158,	8:16	27, 107, 200
5:46	108, 109		**185–89,** 197	8:17	109
5:47	109	6:64	106, 107, 158, 182,	8:18	107, 200
5:51	106		187	8:19	80, 107, 108, 141
5:53	141	6:65	60, 88	8:20	132, 141
6:1ff.	153, **178–90**	6:66	106, 187	8:21–29	24
6:1–15	**178–79**	6:67	115, 120	8:23	89
6:2	79	6:68	104, 106, 187	8:26	24, 107, 108, 141,
6:14	91, 108	6:69	33, 60, 158, 166		200, 203
6:14–15	75, 78	6:70	60, 73, 120	8:28	109, 132, 140, 213
6:21	83	6:70–71	182	8:29	98, 107, 200
6:23	179	6:71	120	8:30	191
6:24	79	7:1–2	79	8:31	54, 104, 172
6:26	78, 79, 106	7:3	80	8:33	176
6:26–51	105	7:5	79	8:35	172
6:27	54, **84–85**, 158,	7:7	18, 141	8:37	176
	175	7:9	54	8:38	73, 112
6:29	107, 158, 200	7:12	39	8:40	203
6:29–30	80	7:14	92	8:42	73, 107, 200, 201
6:30	78, 106, 166	7:14–15	141	8:44	18, 73, 74, 172
		7:14–18	108	8:45	194

John (cont'd)

8:46	209
8:48	74
8:48–59	98
8:49	74
8:50	74
8:51	106
8:52	74, 107
8:53	74, 107
8:58	99, 112
9:1–39	152
9:3–4	80
9:4	107, 108, 200
9:5	172, 192
9:16	75, 78, 79
9:17	107, 108
9:19	214
9:28	108
9:29	108
9:33	78
9:35	60, 208
9:37	75
9:40	120
9:41	141
10:11	185
10:14	141
10:15	81, 185
10:18	78, 134
10:19–22	78
10:20	74
10:21	74
10:25	80
10:30	55, 81, 140, 147, 201, 203
10:31	74
10:32	80, 108
10:34	109
10:34–36	108
10:36	107, 200, 202
10:36–38	201
10:37	108
10:37–38	80, 99
10:38	172
10:40	54
10:41	78
10:53	74
11:4	80, 81, 107
11:10	172
11:11	108
11:14	108
11:24	114, 168
11:25	166
11:27	108
11:33	42, 133
11:37	78
11:40	80
11:42	107, 108, 200
11:45	75, 79
11:47	78
11:50	168

11:50–52	185
11:53	79
12:3	109
12:6	168
12:13	108
12:13–16	212
12:14	89
12:16	34, 37, 132, 212
12:18	79
12:20–33	11
12:23	132, 191
12:24	83
12:27	132, 134, 191
12:28	141
12:28–30	59
12:31	18, 27, 73
12:32	83, 132, 133
12:33	132
12:34	54, 132
12:35	172
12:38	109
12:44	38, 107, 200
12:44–45	103, 108
12:45	80, 107, 200, 201
12:46	54, 172
12:48	27, 33, 115, 141, 144
12:49	106, 107, 108, 200, 201, 203, 204, 213
13:1	132, 133, 168, 178, 191
13:1–20	152
13:2	73, 154, 178, 182
13:3	133, 138
13:7	214
13:16	120, 200, 202
13:18	60, 109, 183
13:19	87
13:20	107, 200, 201, 202
13:21	42, 134, 182
13:21–30	178
13:22	182
13:27	73, 187
13:31	81, 132, 140
13:31–32	80, 115
13:31–33	25
13:31–14:31	25, 26
13:33	133, 138, 141
13:36	133, 138
14:1–3	25, **143–46,** 147
14:1–10	144
14:1–11	25
14:2	133, 138, 168
14:3	36, 133, 138
14:4	133, 138
14:5	133, 138
14:6	33, 141, 194, 202
14:7	87, 126

14:9	81, 100, 101, 109, 140, 201
14:10	80, 99, 106, 108, 141, 172, 203, 213
14:10–11	54, 201
14:11	80
14:12	35, 64, 80, 90, 133, 138
14:12–26	25
14:13–14	18
14:13–17	104
14:15	26, 140
14:15–16	7
14:15–21	139
14:15–24	133, 138
14:16	6, 12, 24, 39, 90, 97, 180, 192, 203, 208
14:16–17	141
14:17	17, 29, 33, 34, 36, 42, 54, 85, 118, **138,** 145, 172, 193, 194, 202, 204, 210
14:18	9, 36, 100, 113, 138, 144, 147
14:19	141
14:19–20	80, 143
14:20	60, 138, 141, 172, 203
14:23	26, 36, 106, 138, 145, 147, 149
14:24	106, 107, 108, 200, 201
14:25	13, 36
14:25–26	7, **211–14**
14:26	5, 6, 24, 26, 27, 29, 36, 37, 38, 42, 84, 101, 104, 107, 118, 140, 141, 142, 143, 172, 175, 200, 202, 203, 208, **211–13,** 218, 220
14:27	25, 126, 138
14:28	36, 133, 137, 138, 147
14:29	212
14:30	18, 73, 74
14:31	189
15:1–17	**189–90**
15:4	197
15:4–5	54
15:4–7	172
15:6	54, 138
15:7	104
15:9	199
15:9–10	172
15:10	54
15:11	172
15:13	185, 188
15:15	214
15:16	18, 60, 133
15:18	35, 198, 203

John (*cont'd*)

15:18–27	141
15:18–16:4	**31–32, 205–208**
15:19	60, 199
15:20	31, 212
15:21	31, 107, 200
15:22	141
15:23	201
15:24	80
15:25	109
15:26	6, 17, 24, 33, 39, 42, 85, 138, 140, 141, 142, 143, 194, 200, 203, 208, 218
15:26–27	8, 9, 29, 120, 198
15:27	204
16:1	31
16:2	31, 192
16:3	141
16:4	191, 211, 212
16:5	107, 133, 138, 200
16:6	9
16:7	6, 8, 24, 33, 50, 122, 130, 133, 137, 138, 141, 142, 143, 147, 200, 203
16:7–11	7, 120
16:8	27, 138, 141, 142, 209
16:8–9	8
16:8–11	85, **208–10**
16:10	133, 138
16:11	18, 73
16:12	24, 32, 140, 212
16:12–13	27, 38, 173, 202
16:12–15	208, **214–16**
16:13	7, 17, 27, 29, 31, 32, 36, 39, 42, 84, 101, 104, 138, 140, 141, 142, 168, 172, 194, 203, 214–15
16:13–14	8, 14, 213, 218
16:13–15	215
16:14	24, 141, 142, 143, 203
16:14–15	140
16:16	138, 144
16:16–17	141
16:17	96, 133, 138
16:20–22	126
16:21	212
16:22	28
16:23	89, 138
16:23–24	18
16:25	141, 192, 214, 215
16:26	138
16:27	138

16:28	133, 138, 141
16:32	115, 192
16:33	126
17:1	81, 132, 141, 191
17:1–2	80
17:2	78
17:3	107, 108, 166, 200, 202
17:4	80, 81, 83, 108, 134, 140, 141, 202
17:5	112
17:6	106, 109, 202
17:8	108, 109, 200, 202
17:11	172
17:12	109
17:14	108, 202, 203
17:15	35, 144
17:17	202
17:17–19	121
17:18	89, 120, 140, 199, 200, 202, 203, 204
17:19	185, 202
17:21	60, 108, 172, 199, 200, 202
17:21–23	201
17:23	60, 89, 108, 200, 202
17:25	108, 200, 202
17:26	172
18:2–6	182
18:9	109
18:11	135
18:14	185
18:18	107
18:19	141
18:21	107
18:23	107
18:24	200
18:25	107
18:32	109
18:37	37, 112, 141, 194
19:7	109
19:11	168
19:14	191
19:17	145
19:23	168
19:24	109
19:27	191
19:28	135
19:28–30	134
19:30	45, **133–35,** 134, 168, 169
19:34	45, 88, 90, **93– 95,** 96, **133–35,** 152, 154, **155,** 156, 165, 166, 169, 210
19:35–37	95
19:36	96, 109, 196
20:1	73, 122
20:8	212

20:9	212
20:10	119
20:17	122, 124, 137
20:17–18	**136–37,** 146
20:17–19	119
20:18	136
20:19	118, 122, 124, 125, 126, 127, 139
20:19–23	124, 134, 137
20:20	118, 120, 126
20:21	107, 118, 119, 120, 126, 127, **199–204,** 200, 202, 204
20:21–22	84, 203
20:21–23	124, 131
20:22	21, 42, 44, 88, 90, 95, **114–49,** 116, 117, 118, 119, 121, 122, 123, 124, 125, 126, 131, 134, 135, 136, 140, 142, 143, 147, 148, 149, 156, 158, 169, 186, 199, 204, 212
20:23	118, 119, 120, 126, 127, 199
20:24	120
20:24–25	119
20:26	122, 124, 126
20:27	124
20:28	116
20:28–29	119
20:29	124
20:30	78, 79
20:30–31	75
20:31	25, 205
21:8–9	83
21:12	151
21:18	153
21:19	132
21:21	144
21:22	146
21:23	35
21:24	27, 34, 210

Acts

1:2	127
1:3–4	136
1:4	151
1:6–11	118
1:8	118, 126, 127, 199
1:9	124, 127, 131, 136, 148
1:13	127
1:14	51, 127
2	28, 117, 121, 122, 123, **125–31, 148–49**
2:1	127
2:1–4	51
2:2	124, 130
2:4	126, 130
2:5	127

Acts (cont'd)

2:17	32, 51
2:19	78
2:22	66, 67
2:32	127
2:32–33	136
2:33	49, 130, 132
2:38	90, 97, 126, 127
2:40	9
3:22	70
4:23–24	51
4:27	85, 175
5:8	199
5:30–31	132, 136
5:32	199
6:10	8
7:37	70
7:42	89
7:49–50	196
8:7	126
8:15	51, 118, 126
8:17	126
8:18–19	126
8:20	90, 97
9:31	9
10:38	51, 63, 66, 85, 175
10:40–41	151
10:45	90, 97
10:47	126
11:16	212
11:17	97
13:15	9
15:26	134
16:7	49, 99
17:25	130
19:1–7	165
19:2	126
20:23	199
24:47	118
27:35	179

Romans

1:17	89
4:11	84
5:5	126
8:9	49, 131
8:13	181
8:15	118, 126
8:16	20
8:34	14, 18, 136
12:8	9
15:28	84

1 Corinthians

2:12	118, 126
2:13	28
5:1–11	120
9:1	131
9:2	84

10–11	156, 189
10:1–4	180
10:4	91
10:16–17	188
11:24	178
12:3	38
12:10	66
12:11	20
12:13	165
12:28	66
12:29–30	215
13:3	134
15:5–8	131, 136
15:6	130, 131
15:24–28	49
15:45	49, 99, 131
15:51	144

2 Corinthians

1:7	28
1:21	85
1:21–22	175
1:22	84, 126
2:5–10	120
3:17	38, 99
5:1	91
11:4	126
12:12	66

Galatians

1:8	19, 21
2:20	134
3:2	126
3:5	66
3:6	89
3:14	126
3:19	21
4:6	49, 131

Ephesians

1:13	84
1:17–18	28
1:20	136
4:8	133
4:30	84

Philippians

1:19	49, 131
2:6–7	112
2:8–9	136
2:10	19
2:12–13	170
4:1	179

Colossians

1:15–17	112
1:27	36
2:18	19, 21

1 Thessalonians

3:2	9
4:15	144
4:16–17	145

1 Timothy

1:3	40
3:16	19

2 Timothy

2:19	84

Titus

1:9	40
3:5	162

Hebrews

1:1	84
1:4	19
1:4–5	21
1:7	130
1:9	85, 175
2:4	66
3:1	201
6:4	97
7:25	6, 14
9:24	6
13:22	9

James

1:18	176
3:12	189

1 Peter

1:23	162, 176
3:18–21	57
3:21–22	136
4:10	126
4:14	55

2 Peter

1:13–14	91
1:15	26
3:3–10	34
3:4	144

1 John

1:1	219
1:1–3	210
1:1–5	219
1:5	172, 192, 215
1:6	194, 195
1:7	94, 172
1:8	172
1:10	172, 219
1:18	218
2:1	6, 7, 8, 14, 18, 141, 143
2:4	172
2:5	172, 219

2:6	172	4:3	172, 218	2:16	177
2:7	219	4:6	173, 194	2:17	177
2:8	172	4:7	171, 173, 197	2:25	177
2:9–11	172	4:8	192	2:29	177
2:13	219	4:9	200	3:3	177
2:14	172, 219	4:10	200	3:6	177
2:15	172	4:12	147	3:11	177
2:17	54	4:12–13	149, 172	3:13	177
2:19	172	4:13	40, 97, 126, 150,	3:19–20	176–77
2:19–21	174		171, **173–74**	3:20	149, 177
2:20	85, 150, 172, **174–**	4:13–14	9, 204	3:22	177
	75, 177, 189, 197, 221	4:14	200	5:1–2	84
2:21	40	4:15	54	5:5	84
2:24	126, 172, 219	4:15–16	172	5:9	84
2:26	172	4:17	174	6:1	84
2:26–27	173, 219, 221	4:17–18	172	6:3	84
2:27	40, 85, 104, 126,	5:1	171	6:5	84
	150, 172, **174–75,** 177,	5:1–5	173	6:7	84
	197, **218,** 220	5:4	171	6:9	84
2:28	146, 172	5:6	142, 155	6:12	84
2:29	171, 175, 197	5:6–8	94, **95–96**	7:1	130
3:1	35	5:6–10	150	7:2	84
3:1–2	61	5:7	194	7:3–5	84
3:2	139, 146	5:7–8	171	7:8	84
3:5	172	5:8	155	7:16–17	91
3:6	172	5:10–11	172	7:17	28, 97
3:8	219	5:16–17	120	8:1	84
3:9	161, 171, 172, **175–**	5:18	171	9:4	84
	76, 219	5:19	18	10:4	84
3:10	176			11:11	130
3:11	215, 219	**2 John**		12:7	16, 20, 22
3:14	176	5	219	12:9	18
3:14–15	172	6	219	14:18	189
3:15–17	139	8	219	14:19	189
3:17	172	10	120	16:15	218
3:18	219	12	204, 219	19:11	86
3:23–24	139			19:11–20:10	18
3:24	40, 54, 150, 171,	**Revelation**		20:3	84
	172, **173–74,** 175	1:1–2	39	21:4	28
3:24–25	27	1:1–3	218	21:6	91, 97
4:1	39, 40, 42, 218	1:7	143	21:14	120
4:1–2	173	1:10	218	22:1–2	90, 91
4:1–6	40, 171, 195	2:5	177	22:7	90
4:2	95, 173, 182, 185	2:7	177	22:10	84
4:2–3	216	2:11	177	22:17	91, 97, 176

Printed in the United States
3111